*It was a quaint and curious pastime, wandering
through this old silent city of the dead – lounging
through utterly deserted streets where thousands and
thousands of human beings once bought and sold,
and walked and rode, and made the place resound
with the noise and confusion of traffic and pleasure.*

Mark Twain, *The Innocents Abroad*, 1869

JOANNE BERRY

The Complete
Pompeii

with 318 illustrations, 275 in colour

Thames & Hudson

Contents

Half-title Portrait of a young man reading a scroll, from Herculaneum.
Title-page Narcissus gazing at his reflection, wall-painting from the House of Loreius Tiburtinus (II.2.2).
This page Landscape painting from the House of the Ceii (I.6.15).

First published in the United Kingdom in 2007 by
Thames & Hudson Ltd,
181A High Holborn,
London WC1V 7QX

First paperback edition 2013
Reprinted 2014

The Complete Pompeii © 2007
Thames & Hudson Ltd, London

British Library Cataloguing-in-Publication Data
A catalogue record for this book is available from the British Library

ISBN 978-0-500-29092-7

Printed and bound in Singapore
by Craft Print International Ltd

To find out about all our publications, please visit
www.thamesandhudson.com. There you can subscribe to our e-newsletter, browse or download our current catalogue, and buy any titles that are in print.

Introduction:
The Geographical and Cultural Context

(Opposite) Pompeii is just 10 km (6 miles) from Vesuvius. To date, 42 hectares (104 acres) of this ancient town have been freed from the volcanic debris that buried it in AD 79.

POMPEII CAN JUSTIFIABLY BE DESCRIBED AS THE MOST famous archaeological site in the world. It was here that the modern discipline of 'archaeology' began over 250 years ago, and the extent of excavations and the remarkable finds they have yielded mean that over two and a half million people visit the ancient town every year. The size of the town – 66 hectares – often causes great surprise to new visitors and means that those returning on subsequent visits inevitably see something new each time they pass through the town's gates.

In antiquity, Pompeii's importance was less pronounced. It was a small provincial Roman town in its last period of life, one of many in the shadow of Vesuvius and in the wider region of Campania. It was Campania, not Pompeii, that was famous in this period. The borders of modern Campania have changed, but broadly speaking ancient Campania was bounded in the north by the mountains of the Aurunci, in the east by the Apennines and in the south by the mountain spur that ends in the Sorrentine peninsula. Thus it consisted of an extensive, fertile plain surrounded by mountains and the sea and cut by the important River Volturnus. Several smaller rivers, the Clanius, the Sarno, the Sebethus and the Savo, also fed the plain. The beauty and fertility of the region were renowned, and capable of producing three or four crops in a year. Spelt, wheat and millet are mentioned as particularly good crops by the ancient writers, as well as fruit and vegetables. Olives grew especially well on the slopes of Vesuvius and the surrounding mountains, and certain types of Campanian wine were famous throughout the Roman world, as was the perfume made from roses. As a result, the region was heavily populated and farmed. Thus Pompeii was part of a network of towns and cities with outlying farms and estates that were connected by an extensive road system.

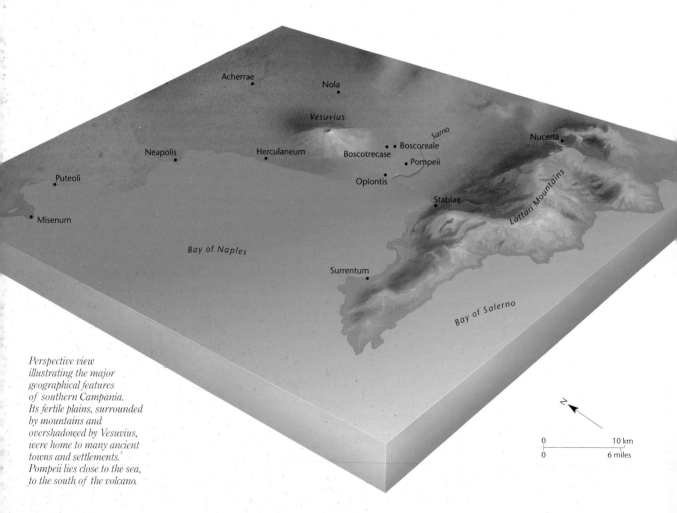

Perspective view illustrating the major geographical features of southern Campania. Its fertile plains, surrounded by mountains and overshadowed by Vesuvius, were home to many ancient towns and settlements. Pompeii lies close to the sea, to the south of the volcano.

Plan of Pompeii

Roman towns were divided into wards, known as *vici* (or *vicus* in the singular). When Pompeii became a Roman colony, vici – each with their own magistrates – appear to have been set up, modelled on the system already in use at Rome.

Unfortunately the names of only a few of the vici at Pompeii are known. Six electoral notices have been found that refer to the 'Forenses', 'Campanienses', 'Salinienses' and 'Urbulanenses'. It has been suggested that the Campanienses were the inhabitants of the district of the Campana Gate

(that is, the Nola Gate), the Salinienses lived around the Saliniensis Gate (that is, the Herculaneum Gate) and the Urbulanenses around the Urbulana Gate (the Sarno Gate). The Forenses have not been located, but based on the other examples it has been suggested that some districts were organized around the gates to the town. It is likely that there were many more districts in Pompeii, but their names and geographical extent remain unknown. Attempts have been made to identify districts on the basis of the location of street shrines and

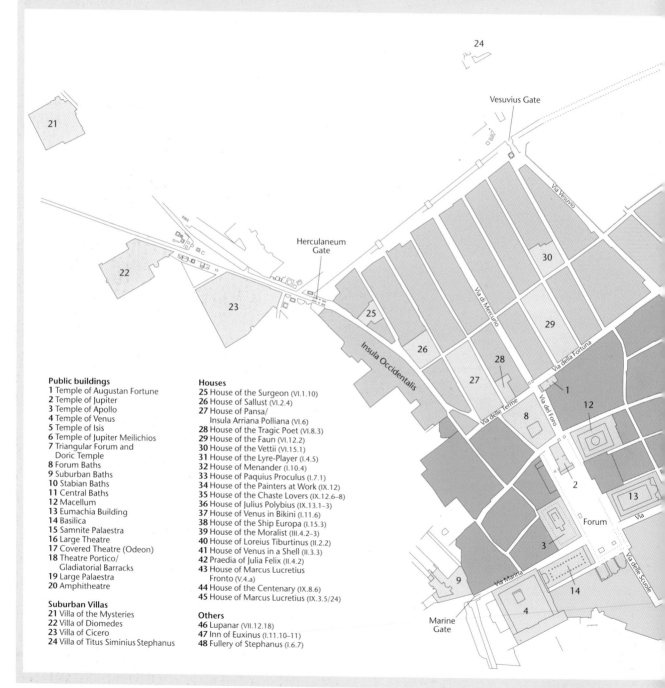

Public buildings
1 Temple of Augustan Fortune
2 Temple of Jupiter
3 Temple of Apollo
4 Temple of Venus
5 Temple of Isis
6 Temple of Jupiter Meilichios
7 Triangular Forum and Doric Temple
8 Forum Baths
9 Suburban Baths
10 Stabian Baths
11 Central Baths
12 Macellum
13 Eumachia Building
14 Basilica
15 Samnite Palaestra
16 Large Theatre
17 Covered Theatre (Odeon)
18 Theatre Portico/ Gladiatorial Barracks
19 Large Palaestra
20 Amphitheatre

Suburban Villas
21 Villa of the Mysteries
22 Villa of Diomedes
23 Villa of Cicero
24 Villa of Titus Siminius Stephanus

Houses
25 House of the Surgeon (VI.1.10)
26 House of Sallust (VI.2.4)
27 House of Pansa/ Insula Arriana Polliana (VI.6)
28 House of the Tragic Poet (VI.8.3)
29 House of the Faun (VI.12.2)
30 House of the Vettii (VI.15.1)
31 House of the Lyre-Player (I.4.5)
32 House of Menander (I.10.4)
33 House of Paquius Proculus (I.7.1)
34 House of the Painters at Work (IX.12)
35 House of the Chaste Lovers (IX.12.6–8)
36 House of Julius Polybius (IX.13.1–3)
37 House of Venus in Bikini (I.11.6)
38 House of the Ship Europa (I.15.3)
39 House of the Moralist (III.4.2–3)
40 House of Loreius Tiburtinus (II.2.2)
41 House of Venus in a Shell (II.3.3)
42 Praedia of Julia Felix (II.4.2)
43 House of Marcus Lucretius Fronto (V.4.a)
44 House of the Centenary (IX.8.6)
45 House of Marcus Lucretius (IX.3.5/24)

Others
46 Lupanar (VII.12.18)
47 Inn of Euxinus (I.11.10–11)
48 Fullery of Stephanus (I.6.7)

fountains (working on the assumption that there would be one shrine or one fountain per district), but it is impossible to confirm these results.

How to read the plan
Modern conventions were applied to the plan of Pompeii from the late 19th century to make it easier to locate particular buildings or houses within the plan. Pompeii was divided into nine regions. Within each region each separate block of buildings, known as an 'insula', was given a number, and each doorway within an insula was also numbered. Thus, VIII.4.5 is the address of a house or shop located in Region 8, Insula 4, doorway 5.

Later a similar system was applied to Herculaneum, although the much smaller size of the excavations there meant that there was no need to divide the town into Regions. All modern scholarship follows these conventions.

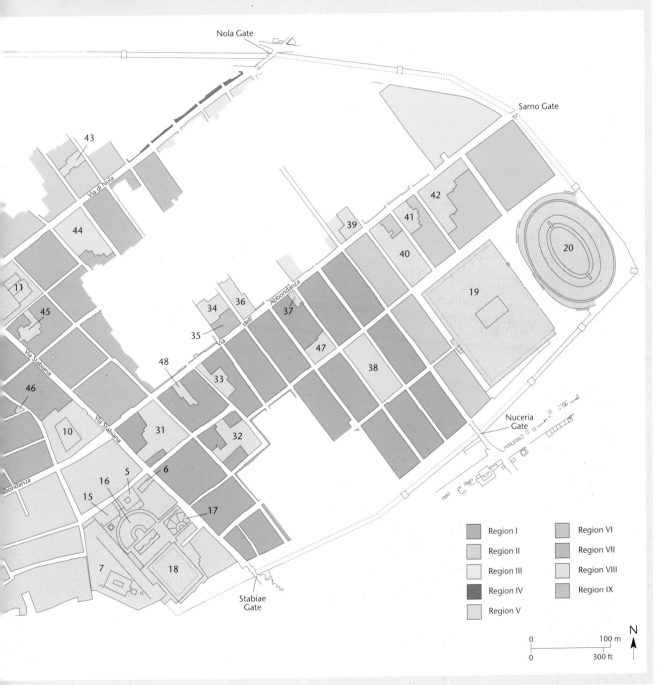

Region I		Region VI
Region II		Region VII
Region III		Region VIII
Region IV		Region IX
Region V		

*A reconstruction of what
ancient Pompeii may have
looked like before its sudden
and violent demise in AD 79.*

This harbour scene – found in one of the villas of Stabiae – gives a good idea of what any of the harbours in the region might have looked like. The harbour is heavily built up, its jetties adorned with statues. A number of ships are anchored within the harbour basin, and fishing boats can be seen in the foreground.

Pompeii

Pompeii lies in southern Campania, between Naples (ancient Neapolis) and Sorrento (ancient Surrentum), and near to the sea. It sits on a prehistoric lava flow that stretched all the way to the sea, and overlooked the River Sarno, once broad and navigable. This can be hard for the visitor to the site to visualize today because the eruption of AD 79 irrevocably altered the geography of the area. The Sarno now runs further to the south and cannot be seen from Pompeii's walls. The coastline, too, is now approximately 1 km (3,250 ft) further from the town than it was in antiquity. Thus ancient Pompeii was essentially a harbour town with a good strategic position. This location, on the River Sarno in the fertile plains of Campania, meant that Pompeii enjoyed considerable economic prosperity and it is likely to have exercised some

The development of Pompeii

10th–8th centuries BC
There may have been a small prehistoric settlement at Pompeii.

8th–6th centuries BC
Greek and Etruscan settlements founded in Campania.

6th century BC
The entire present circuit of Pompeii is fortified and the street grid laid out. There are two major cult sanctuaries, the Temple of Apollo and the Doric Temple.

5th century BC
The Samnites take control of many Greek and Etruscan towns in Campania, including Pompeii.

4th century BC
Pompeii is probably part of a loose confederation of Samnite settlements headed by Nuceria and including Herculaneum and the villages of the Sarno Valley.

Late 4th/early 3rd centuries BC
Rome conquers the Bay of Naples, and Pompeii comes under Roman control as an 'allied' town. In this period, Pompeii is still a largely agricultural settlement.

218–210 BC
The Second Punic War. In the wake of the Roman victory over Hannibal, Pompeii experiences an economic boom. By the beginning of the 2nd century BC the town has been completely built up.

90 BC
Pompeii, along with many other allied cities in Italy, demands full citizenship and rebels against Rome in the Social War.

89 BC
The Roman dictator, Sulla, conquers Pompeii.

80 BC
Pompeii resettled as a Roman 'colony', the 'Colonia Cornelia Veneria Pompeianorum'.

AD 59
There is a riot in the Amphitheatre between the peoples of Pompeii and Nuceria. Gladiatorial games are banned for ten years.

AD 63
A serious earthquake in the region causes extensive damage to Pompeii.

AD 79
Pompeii is destroyed, and buried, by an eruption of Vesuvius.

control over the import and export of goods in the area of the Sarno Valley. Indeed, the Greek geographer, Strabo, claimed that Pompeii served as a port for Nola, Nuceria, and Acherrae.

It is no surprise that a settlement should have been established in this spot from at least the 6th century BC, or that various cultural groups – the Greeks, Etruscans, Samnites and Romans – should have taken an interest in its urban development over the centuries until its destruction in AD 79. A circuit of walls surrounded it from early in its history, and served to protect both the settlement and its farmland. Seven fortified gates permitted entry to the town. Over the centuries the farmland within the walls was built over with houses and public buildings, which followed the gradient of the prehistoric lava spur and sloped noticeably from north to south. Major temples were located on the edges of the spur, where they would have been easily visible from both the river and the sea, their dominant positions designed to emphasize the power of Pompeii's patron deities. By the time of its

A defensive wall surrounded Pompeii from the 6th century BC onwards. The Nuceria Gate, to the south of the town, was one of seven fortified gates in the wall. Outside the walls, the main roads to the town were lined with the tombs of its inhabitants.

destruction, Pompeii had a full complement of public buildings, such as temples, theatres, baths, administrative buildings and an amphitheatre, as well as houses, shops and craft premises. It is this extensive range of building and the different aspects of life that it represents that have held the fascination of antiquarians, scholars and tourists since the town's discovery in 1748.

Herculaneum: the poor relation

Herculaneum stood at the foot of Vesuvius, 16 km (10 miles) from Pompeii. It was located between two small streams on a lava plateau overlooking the sea, and the ancient writers inform us that its harbour was safe and its climate made it a pleasant place to live. As a result, it appears to have become a fashionable holiday resort in the Roman period. During the 1st century BC, many luxury villas were built by the Romans close to the town, one reportedly owned by the emperor Caligula, attracted by its climate and good road connections. Large houses with spectacular views were built over the sea wall, and there were elaborate bath complexes and public buildings, some of which were donated by important Romans who patronized the town.

So much attention has focused on Pompeii that it is easy to forget that excavations took place at Herculaneum before they began at Pompeii. Herculaneum was discovered first (in 1738) and tunnelled extensively for ancient statues and valuable artifacts. But such mining was difficult and dangerous and it was this that led to attention being shifted to Pompeii. Vesuvius had buried the two towns in different ways. Pompeii was closer to the surface and the material that buried it was easier to excavate. More was exposed to the air, making it more

(Below right) View of the excavated remains of Herculaneum, which lies directly beneath Vesuvius and was buried by over 20 m (65 ft) of volcanic material in AD 79. The modern town of Ercolano can be seen in the background. Parts of Ercolano had to be demolished in the early 20th century to permit the open-air excavation of this small section of Herculaneum.

The development of Herculaneum

Nothing is known of Herculaneum's foundation; it is claimed in ancient literature that the town was founded by Hercules on his return from Iberia.

4th century BC
Herculaneum (like Pompeii) is a member of the Nucerian League.

89 BC
Herculaneum is occupied by Italic rebels during the Social War against Rome.

1st century BC – AD 79
The area around Herculaneum becomes fashionable as a holiday resort. A great deal of construction and renovation within the town dates to this period.

attractive to excavators, tourists and students. In contrast, Herculaneum was buried by 20 m (65 ft) of volcanic material. This means that only a small part of this town – 4.5 hectares (11 acres) of an estimated 20 hectares (50 acres) – has been completely uncovered, and it is poorly studied, published and visited. This is a shame since Herculaneum has great charm and in many respects is very different from Pompeii. In particular, wood and organic materials have been

Other dates of importance in the Roman world

343–341 BC, 327–304 BC and 298–290 BC
The Samnite Wars between Rome and the Samnites. By the end of this period, Rome controls Campania.

218–210 BC
The Second Punic War between Rome and Carthage. Hannibal crosses the Alps to invade Italy.

44 BC
Assassination of Julius Caesar.

31 BC
Octavian defeats Mark Antony and becomes Rome's first 'emperor', taking the name 'Augustus' in 27 BC.

27 BC – AD 14
Reign of Augustus.

AD 14–37
Reign of Tiberius.

AD 37–41
Reign of Caligula.

AD 41–54
Reign of Claudius.

AD 54–68
Reign of Nero.

AD 68–69
Year of the four emperors.

AD 69–79
Reign of Vespasian.

AD 79–81
Reign of Titus.

Theatre

Villa of the Papyri

Palaestra

Harbour

preserved to a far greater degree than at Pompeii, and the upper storeys of many houses (including evidence for separate apartments within housing blocks) can still be seen today.

The way in which Pompeii and Herculaneum were buried by Vesuvius in AD 79 means that today it is possible to traverse their streets in the footsteps of their ancient inhabitants. This does not mean that the archaeological record is perfect – the frequent claim that Pompeii is a 'time capsule' or was 'frozen in time' by the eruption of Vesuvius is simply not true and will be discussed at length during the course of this book. However, the preservation of Pompeii is so much better than at other archaeological sites that it is no wonder scholarly and popular interest in it is still alive more than 250 years after its discovery.

(Above) Herculaneum was located on a lava plateau overlooking the sea. This reconstruction reveals the extent of the town, known from the tunnelling and excavations since 1738, and the proximity of the famous Villa of the Papyri.

I
DISASTER IN THE SHADOW OF VESUVIUS

*Today Vesuvius erupted. It was the most majestic and
terrible sight I have ever seen, or ever expect to see.
The smoke from the crater slowly built up into a great
bulging shape having all the appearance of solidity.
It swelled and expanded so slowly that there was no sign
of movement in the cloud which, by evening, must have
risen thirty or forty thousand feet into the sky,
and measured many miles across.*

Norman Lewis, *Naples '44*, 19 March, 1944

In AD 79, Vesuvius erupted for the first time in 700
years with devastating impact, destroying all the
towns and villas to the southeast of the volcano and
leaving a remarkable heritage to posterity – a Roman
town preserved in a single moment of its history.
But the eruption did not merely preserve, it also
destroyed. Comparison with volcanic eruptions in the
modern era, such as Mount St Helens in 1980 and
Pinatubo in 1992, reveal the devastation caused by
such events, and give an idea of their far-reaching
consequences. The violent eruption of Vesuvius
caught the people living in its shadow by surprise;
those who survived found their lives changed forever.

*The destruction of Pompeii by Vesuvius in AD 79 has appealed
to the imaginations of generations. This scene, painted
by Pierre-Henri de Valenciennes, depicts the death of Pliny the
Elder on the beach at Stabiae. De Valenciennes had witnessed
an eruption of Vesuvius in August 1779 and used his experience
to capture the violence of the earlier eruption, and the terror of
those caught up in it.*

The Volcano

VESUVIUS IS ONE OF A CHAIN OF VOLCANOES THAT stretch from north of Rome into southern Italy. Most people have heard of Etna and Stromboli since these volcanoes are still active; other Italian volcanoes, such as the 'crater-lakes' of Lake Nemi and Lake Albano, are extinct. The last eruption of Vesuvius took place in 1944 and today it is classified as dormant. It lies to the south and east of a large collapsed caldera, 13 km (8 miles) in diameter, known as the Phlegraean Fields, now consisting of around 30 craters that still emit sulphurous gases. The last eruption in the Phlegraean Fields took place in 1538. It has also suggested that the Bay of Naples itself, which is an almost perfect semicircle in shape, was formed from the crater of a huge ancient volcano. Whether or not this is true, the area around Naples has long been subjected to the effects of volcanic activity, and, to this day, areas to the north of the city near the Phlegraean Fields (particularly Pozzuoli) suffer from slow movements of the earth known as 'bradyseism'.

Vesuvius itself stands about 1,200 m (almost 4,000 ft) high and today has two craters. Monte Somma is the older and partially surrounds the younger Monte Vesuvio. It is unclear whether in AD 79 both craters already existed or whether Monte Somma collapsed and Monte Vesuvio rose up due to the force of that eruption. It is often thought that prior to AD 79 Vesuvius was a single coned volcano, although it has been suggested that, as today, the volcano took on different aspects, of one or two cones, when seen from different directions. What is clear is that the volcano has always dominated the landscape of the Bay of Naples.

We have no idea whether the people who lived in the Bay of Naples in the 1st century AD knew that Mount Vesuvius was a volcano. The ancient evidence is contradictory. Some ancient discussions of volcanoes, such as those by Seneca and Pliny the Elder, completely omit Vesuvius, leading one to think that they did not know that it was a volcano. But there are some ancient writers who demonstrate an awareness of the volcanic character of Vesuvius. The geographer Strabo described the summit of Vesuvius as burnt and infertile and suggested that there had been 'craters of fire' there in earlier times:

> Mount Vesuvius is situated above these places and people live all around on very beautiful farms, except at the summit. This is flat for the main part, but completely unfruitful, like ashes to look at, and it displays porous hollows of rocks blackened on the surface, as if devoured by fire. As a result, one would deduce that this area was previously on fire and held craters of fire, and that it was extinguished when the fuel failed. Perhaps this is also the reason for the fruitfulness of the surrounding area, just as at Catana they say that the part covered by ash carried up by the fire of Etna made the country suited to vine-growing.
>
> Strabo, *Geography* V.4.8

Vitruvius and Diodorus Siculus, writing in the early 1st century AD, also show awareness of the true nature of Vesuvius. However, it is unlikely that many people living in the region would have read these treatises.

Modern volcanologists believe that Vesuvius had not erupted for approximately 700 years before the deadly events of AD 79. Even if they had been aware of the threat, given the fertility of the region it would have been easy for the people living in the shadow of Vesuvius to ignore it (just as the inhabitants of the Naples area today ignore the potential danger).

The slopes of Vesuvius, covered in vines, are depicted in a wall-painting found in a shrine in the House of the Centenary (IX.8.6). The figure of Bacchus, god of wine and fertility stands alongside the mountain, and perhaps can be interpreted as evidence that some Pompeians at least understood that the richness of their lands was due to Vesuvius.

The Eruption of Vesuvius in AD 79

IN AD 79, VESUVIUS ERUPTED WITH DEVASTATING violence. Its destructive power was documented in the earliest surviving eye-witness account of a large-scale natural disaster.

At the time of the eruption, Pliny the Younger was a young man staying with his uncle, Pliny the Elder. The elder Pliny was commander of the Roman fleet, based at Misenum, the main naval station of the fleet from *c.* 31 BC, located to the west of Naples. He was also a scientist and scholar, and author of the *Natural History*, a compendium of geography, botany, zoology, astrology and many other subjects. The combination of his desire to study the eruption and his responsibility, as commander of the fleet, to help evacuate the towns under threat led to his death in AD 79. Years later, the younger Pliny was asked by his friend, the historian Tacitus, to describe how his uncle died. Tacitus' account of the eruption is lost, but Pliny himself later published these letters. His detailed observations have formed the basis of our understanding of the eruption, and have been supplemented by more recent studies of the volcanic deposits that buried the settlements in the shadow of Vesuvius. Thus we have a remarkably accurate account of the different stages of the eruption of Vesuvius in AD 79 (the traditional versions of Pliny's letters to Tacitus – which date the eruption to August – have been followed here).

Pliny's account of the eruption

'Gaius Pliny sends greetings to his friend Tacitus.

'You ask me to write about my uncle's death, so you can provide posterity with as accurate a version as possible. I'm grateful for this; for I'm sure that if you write an account of his death, it will become widely known, to his everlasting fame. His memory will live on forever, in some sense at least, just like the names of peoples and cities that perish in some memorable catastrophe, because he died in a disaster that affected some of the finest lands on earth. Furthermore he himself wrote many books that will survive. Nevertheless the lasting nature of your writing will contribute a great deal to keeping his memory alive. The gods allow some lucky men to do great deeds that deserve to be recorded. Other lucky men are granted the gift of being able to write about things that people should read about. The gods grant to the luckiest men of all both the opportunity to do great things, and also to write about important things, and my uncle will be one of them, because he wrote his own books and because you will include an account of his deeds in your book. I'll do what you ask all the more willingly because it's something I'd choose to do myself.

The exact date of the eruption

Traditionally, the eruption of Vesuvius in AD 79 has been dated to 24 August. But there has been some debate amongst scholars about this. Could the eruption have taken place in the autumn instead? The answer hinges on the problem of textual transmission. It has been claimed that Pliny's original text was 'corrected' by medieval scribes. There are more than 12 different versions of the date of the eruption given in the existing manuscripts, such as: IX Kal. Septembris (that is, nine days counting backwards from the Kalends (1st) of September = 24 August); IX Kal. Decembris (that is, nine days counting backwards from the Kalends of December = 23 November); Kal. Novembris (that is, the Kalends of November = 1 November); and III Kal. Novembris (that is three days counting backwards from the Kalends of November = 30 October). But which of these dates is correct?

In support of an autumn date, various pieces of archaeological evidence have been put forward. For example, some bodies found at Pompeii appear to be wearing heavy clothing inappropriate for a hot summer month, and fruits such as pomegranates, which normally ripen in late autumn, have been found during the excavations. But those who argue for an August date point to, among other things, the leaves of deciduous trees found at Herculaneum (these trees would have been bare of leaves in autumn), herbs that would have finished flowering by autumn found at Villa A in Oplontis, and broad beans mixed with oats found in a stable in the House of the Chaste Lovers (IX.12.6) at Pompeii (broad beans ripen in late summer and once picked do not stay fresh for long). It has also been suggested that the pomegranates and other late-ripening fruits had been picked before they had ripened and preserved since there is some ancient literary evidence to support this practice. And heavy clothing may have been donned by the victims of the eruption to give protection from the heavy rain of pumice that afflicted Pompeii in the first stage of the eruption.

The debate has recently resurfaced: study of a hoard of coins found in the House of the Golden Bracelet (VI.17.42) in 1974 revealed a silver denarius with a portrait of the emperor Titus and the legend 'IMP TITUS CAES VESPASIAN AUG PM' ('Imperator Titus Caesar Vespasian Augustus Pontifex Maximus'). On the coin reverse are a capricorn and the rest of the emperor's titles, 'TR P VIIII IMP XV COS VII PP' ('with tribunician power for the 9th time, acclaimed Imperator for the 15th time, consul for the 7th time, father of his country'). The fact that Titus is consul for the 7th time securely dates this coin to AD 79; in addition, he assumed tribunician power for the 9th time in July that year, so the coin was definitely minted later than that. Finally, epigraphic evidence suggests that Titus could not have been acclaimed Imperator for the 15th time earlier than September AD 79. This means that the eruption of Vesuvius in AD 79 may not have taken place in August that year, and should be dated to the autumn.

'He was at Misenum, where he was in command of the fleet. On 24 August, at about the seventh hour [early afternoon], my mother pointed out to him a cloud that had just appeared. This cloud was unusual in appearance and exceptionally large. My uncle had spent some time in the sun, then had taken a cold dip, eaten lunch reclining and was now doing some work; he called for someone to bring his shoes, and climbed up to a location from which he could see that amazing sight as clearly as possible. The cloud was rising from a mountain, although to people watching from such a distance it wasn't clear which one. Later they realised that it had been Vesuvius. The general appearance and shape of the cloud were like those of an umbrella pine. For it was borne up into the sky by, so to speak, its tall trunk, and then it dissipated into a number of branches. I believe this was because it had been thrown up by the fresh blast, but as the latter diminished with the passing of time, the cloud was no longer supported by it and was overcome by its own weight, and so spread sideways. Sometimes it was white, at others it was dirty and blotchy, depending on the amount of dirt or ash caught up in it.

'My uncle, a man of great intellectual curiosity, decided that this was a phenomenon of great importance, which had to be investigated at closer quarters. He gave orders for a small ship to be made ready; he offered me the opportunity to go with him if I wanted to; I replied that I preferred to continue my studies, and as it happened he himself had provided me with a writing exercise. My uncle was leaving the house when he received a note from Rectina, wife of Tascus. She was terrified by the danger that literally hung over her, as her country house lay right below the mountain, and there was no escape except by ship. She begged him to rescue her from this terrible danger. My uncle changed his plan, and approached in a spirit of bravery the mission that originally he had undertaken in a spirit of inquiry. He took some warships out to sea, taking his place on board to help not just Rectina but as many other people as possible – for the beauty of the coast there meant it was densely inhabited. He rushed towards what others were fleeing, and steered a direct course towards the danger. He was so fearless that he was able to dictate and record every aspect of the development and appearance of the disaster as he saw it.

'Soon ash was falling on the ships, hotter and thicker as they drew nearer; soon there were lumps of pumice and rock scorched and shattered by fire; then they soon reached shallow water and the shoreline that was blocked by debris from the mountain. My

In this 18th-century painting by Angelica Kauffmann, Pliny the Younger refuses to leave his studies, despite the chaos around him, the terror of his mother and the pleas of his uncle's friend.

uncle wondered briefly whether he should turn back, but when the helmsman advised him to do so, he replied 'No! Fortune favours the bold. Head towards Pomponianus'. For Pomponianus was at Stabiae, cut off by the inner part of the bay (for the sea there takes the form of a curved inlet); while the danger there was not immediate, it was clearly visible and was drawing closer as the situation developed. Pomponianus had put his possessions on board some ships, intending to flee if the unfavourable wind subsided. This very same wind effectively carried my uncle to the shore, and so he was able to greet his terrified friend, and console and encourage him. My uncle asked to be taken to the bath suite, in order to sooth Pomponianus' fears by his own composure. When he had bathed, he reclined and ate dinner, either because he was genuinely cheerful or (equally bravely) feigning cheerfulness.

'Meanwhile fires erupted from different points all over Mount Vesuvius, and the towering flames gave off a light whose brightness and clarity contrasted with the shadows of the night. My uncle kept asserting that these were just fires that had been left when the country-dwellers had fled in fear, and abandoned villas burning without anyone to prevent them. This was his way of diminishing his companions' fears. Then he gave in to his tiredness and relaxed into a deep sleep. His snoring, loud and deep because of his stoutness, was audible to people coming and going by the doorway. But the antechamber of his room soon began to fill up with a mix of ash and pumice, to the extent that staying in his bedroom any longer would have made it impossible to get out. When he was woken up, he left the bedroom and went back to Pomponianus and the others, who had stayed awake. They argued among themselves as to whether they should stay inside the house or go out into the open. For the buildings were being shaken by frequent and strong tremors, and they seemed to move to and fro as if they had been shifted from their foundations. Outdoors, on the other hand, they feared the falling pumice, even though it was light and porous. Nevertheless, they chose this as the lesser of the two dangers. For my uncle, it was a case of one rational choice outweighing another; for his companions, one fear overcame another. They tied cushions on their heads with pieces of sheet; this was their protection against falling debris.

'Soon it was day elsewhere, but for my uncle and his companions it was still night, and a night blacker and darker than any other. However, they had plenty of torches and lights of other kinds that diminished the darkness. They decided to go down to the shore and see at first hand whether they could escape by sea now – but it was still rough and hostile. My uncle lay down there on a cloth that had been spread on the ground, and he asked for and drained several drinks of cold water. Then the flames and the smell of sulphur that preceded them made the others decide to flee and woke up my uncle. Leaning on two slaves, he got up, and straight away he collapsed. I believe this was because his breathing had been choked by the denser fumes and his windpipe had been blocked. It had always been weak and narrow, and often was inflamed.

'When the light of day returned (the third day after the last he had seen), his body was found, untouched, apparently unharmed and still dressed the way he had been. His body looked more like that of a man asleep than one who had died.

'Meanwhile my mother and I were at Misenum, but that's not relevant to your history and you only wanted to know about my uncle's death, so I'll bring this to a conclusion. I'll add just one thing. I've set down everything I experienced myself or heard soon afterwards, when memories are still accurate. You can pick out the things that you think are most important for your work. For there is a big difference between a letter and a work of history; one is written for a friend, while the other is intended for everyone to read.

'Farewell.'

'Gaius Pliny sends greetings to his friend Tacitus.

'You say that the letter I wrote at your request about the death of my uncle makes you want to know about the fears and dangers that I had to face when I was left behind at Misenum. For I broke off at the start of that part of the story. As Virgil wrote, "Though my mind shrinks from remembering…. I will begin".

'After my uncle left, I spent the rest of my time studying, for that was why I had stayed behind. Then I took a bath, ate dinner and had a restless and short sleep. An earthquake preceded these events over several days, but these things don't cause much concern in Campania because they are common there. That night the earthquake grew so strong that it seemed as if everything was not just being shaken but even turned upside down. My mother burst into my bedroom just as I was getting up to wake her, on the off-chance she was still asleep. We sat down in the entrance court of the house, which lay in the narrow space between the building itself and the sea. I don't know whether I should call my behaviour brave or foolish (for I was in my eighteenth year), but I called for my book of Livy and read it as if I had nothing to do, and even went on with writing the excerpts I had begun. Then a friend of my uncle, who had recently come from Spain to visit him, saw me and my mother sitting there, and me reading, and he told us off, me for my lack of concern, and my mother for putting up with it. But I continued to concentrate on my book with no less attention.

'By now it was the first hour of daylight, but the light was still dim and feeble. The buildings around us were shaking, and although we were in an open space, it was surrounded by buildings, and we were very scared that they would collapse. So eventually it seemed best to leave the town. A frantic mob followed

Inspired by the eruption of Vesuvius in 1828, Karl Briullov painted 'The Last Days of Pompeii' (1833), which was one of the most acclaimed paintings of its day in Europe. It can now be seen in the Russian Museum in St Petersburg.

Plaster cast of a victim of the eruption, made in November 1874. This watch-dog, with studded collar, had been chained to a post in the entrance of the House of Vesonius Primus (VI.14.20) and was unable to flee. The bodies of many of those who died have been found on the rooftops and in the streets. They died because they left it too late to escape the doomed town.

us, preferring to let someone else make the decision, a response that passes for wisdom when one is afraid. They pushed us on as we escaped and we were driven forward by the weight of the crowd. When we had got away from the buildings, we stopped. There we experienced many amazing and terrifying things. For the carts that we had ordered to be brought with us were being carried off in different directions, even though the ground was level, and they didn't stay in the same place even when they had been wedged with stones. Also we saw the sea dragged back into itself and then apparently driven back by the shaking of the earth. Indeed, the shoreline had retreated, and many sea creatures were stranded on the dry sand. In the other direction a terrible black cloud, split by jagged and quivering bursts of fiery air, gaped open to reveal tall columns of flame. They were like lightning bolts, but even bigger.

'Then my uncle's friend from Spain suddenly and insistently spoke up. 'If your brother, your uncle is alive, he wants you to be safe; if he is dead, he wants you to survive. So why are you delaying your escape now? We responded that we would not even agree to consider our own safety while my uncle's was uncertain. Without delaying any longer, he rushed off and took himself away from the danger in rapid flight. Soon afterwards, the cloud came down and cloaked the ground and covered the sea. It enveloped Capri and concealed it, and hid from view the part of Misenum that sticks out into the sea. Then my mother begged, pleaded and ordered me to escape in any way I could. She said that a young man could escape, while she was hindered by her age and infirmity, but she would die in peace so long as she wasn't the cause of my death too. I replied that I would not save myself unless she came with me; then, seizing her hand I forced her to move faster.

She did what I asked, but reluctantly, and blamed herself for slowing me down.

'Soon ash was coming down, but the fall wasn't heavy yet. I looked back. A dense dark cloud was just behind us, flooding over the earth like a torrent. "Let's go in a different direction, while we can still see," I said, "or we'll be trampled in the darkness by the crowds on the road." We had only just sat down to rest when it became dark, not the darkness of a moonless or cloudy night, but the darkness of a closed room when the light has gone out. You could hear women shrieking, children crying and men shouting. Some called out for their parents, their children or their wives, trying to find them by the sound of their voices. Some were bemoaning their own fates, others those of their relatives. Some prayed for death because they were afraid of dying. Many of them raised their hands to the gods in supplication, but even more took this disaster as a sign that the gods were no more and the world had been overtaken by an endless night. There were some people who exaggerated the real dangers by inventing and imagining other horrors. Some people said that part of Misenum had collapsed, or part of the town was on fire, which was untrue, but some believed them.

'It got a little lighter, but it seemed to us that the light wasn't daylight but just an indication of the flames that were coming upon us. But the fire remained at a distance, and there was darkness again, and the ash fell again, in quantity, heavily. Getting up time and time again we shook off this ash; otherwise we would have been buried by it or even crushed under its weight. I could boast that I didn't utter any complaint or cry of fear except that I believed that the whole world was perishing as wretchedly as me and this was a great consolation to me in my mortality.

'Eventually the dark cloud diminished and dispersed like smoke or fog. Soon real daylight returned and the sun even shone, but it shone a ghastly pale light like when it is eclipsed. Before our terrified eyes everything appeared changed, and was covered by a deep layer of ash, like snow. We returned to Misenum and, having taken care of our bodies' demands, we passed a restless night caught between hope and fear. It was fear that prevailed, for the earthquake continued, and several panic-stricken people made their own and others' predicament seem trivial compared to the doom that they predicted. Even then we had no intention of leaving until there was news of my uncle, despite the danger we had endured and the danger we still awaited.

'Thus you can read about these things that happened to me, although you won't write about them as they aren't worthy of a work of History. You may even think them unworthy of a letter, but you have only yourself to blame as you were the one who asked me to describe them to you.

'Farewell.'

A modern reconstruction of the eruption

The eruption began between 11 and 12 noon with a minor explosion of steam that caused a fine ash fall to the east of the volcano. The evidence for this explosion comes from modern studies of the stratigraphy of the eruption and is not described by Pliny. It is likely that this first stirring of Vesuvius was not noticed in Misenum, which is 30 km (18 miles) away, although it is likely to have caused alarm in the towns and villas closer to the volcano.

The main eruption began at around noon when a column of pumice exploded from the volcano, climbing to a height of *c.* 15–30 km (*c.* 10–20 miles), then spreading out to form what Pliny described as an 'umbrella pine' (giving rise to the modern terminology which describes this phase of an eruption as the 'Plinian phase'). The settlements under this cloud would have been plunged into darkness, undoubtedly causing panic. Gradually pumice (known as 'lapilli') and rock fragments began to fall from the cloud and were carried along by the prevailing winds to the southeast. For the next 18–20 hours, this area (including Pompeii, Oplontis and Stabiae) was showered with lapilli at a rate of about 15 cm (6 in) an hour. This deposit slowly accumulated until, in places, it reached a depth of up to 2.8 m (9 ft). There is evidence that roofs collapsed under the cumulative weight of the lapilli, and it would have been progressively more difficult for people to move through the streets.

Areas to the east and west of the volcano suffered less; in Herculaneum the deposit of lapilli was less than 20 cm (8 inches). However, the proximity of Herculaneum to the volcano meant that its inhabitants would have been forcefully aware of the noise and sheer violence of the eruption, and were probably affected by earthquakes and lightning. Many sought to escape by fleeing to the harbour area and taking shelter in what were probably boat houses.

The second phase of the eruption (the Peléan phase, named after the famous eruption of Mount Pelée on Martinique in 1902) began on the following morning. The column of hot gas and pumice was unable to maintain its buoyancy and began to collapse, causing a series of *nuées ardentes*, flows

Timeline of the eruption of Vesuvius in AD 79

Day 1, 11–12 pm	Minor explosion of steam.	Fine ash fell to the east of Vesuvius.
Day 1, 12pm	Column of hot gas and pumice exploded from the volcano, climbing to a height of *c.* 15–30 km (*c.* 10–20 miles) then spreading out to form what Pliny described as an 'umbrella pine'.	The settlements beneath this umbrella pine were plunged into darkness.
Day 1, 12pm – Day 2, 4–6am	Pumice and rock fragments began to fall from the cloud and were carried along by the prevailing winds to the southeast. Pompeii, Oplontis and Stabiae were showered with pumice, at a rate of *c.* 15 cm (*c.* 6 in) an hour.	At Pompeii, roofs began to collapse under the cumulative weight of the lapilli. It would have been progressively more difficult for people to move through the streets. Areas to the east and west of the volcano suffered less. Less than 20 cm (8 in) of pumice fell on Herculaneum. However, Herculaneum was probably affected by earthquakes and lightning, and its inhabitants would have been shaken by the sheer noise and violence of the eruption.
Day 2, 4–6 am	The column of hot gas and pumice was unable to maintain its buoyancy and began to collapse, causing a series of flows and surges of hot ash and gases travelling at enormous speed that swept down the volcano to the south and west.	
Day 2, 4–6 am	First surge.	Herculaneum was overwhelmed by 3 m (10 ft) of hot ash.
Day 2, 5–7 am	Second surge.	A further 1.5 m (5 ft) of ash was deposited on Herculaneum.
Day 2, *c.* 6.30 am	Third surge.	This surge reached the Herculaneum Gate of Pompeii but may not have penetrated into the town itself.
Day 2, 7.30–8 am	Three more surges in quick succession.	The fourth surge, reaching temperatures of 100–400 °C (212–750 °F) overwhelmed the interior of the town. The next two surges then swept over the town, burying the town up to a depth of 60 cm (2 ft) to the south of the town and 1.8 m (6 ft) to the north. The sixth and final surge reached Misenum.
For several more days, possibly weeks	Volcanic activity probably continued.	

On 18 May 1980, after a series of steam explosions and small earthquakes, Mount St Helens, in Washington state, erupted in an explosion several times stronger than the Hiroshima bomb. The eruption lasted for 9 hours and destroyed everything within a 16 km (10 mile) radius, including 600 sq. km (230 sq. miles) of forest. Only 57 people were killed, but thousands of deer, elk, bear and other animals perished. Losses to property and crops were estimated at more than $1.8 billion.

and surges of hot ash and gases travelling at enormous speed, that swept down the volcano to the south and west and devastated the region. In total there were six major *nuees ardentes* that devastated the environs of Vesuvius, destroying Herculaneum, Pompeii and Stabia and other nearby settlements. The sixth and final surge was so powerful that it swept across the Bay of Naples to the island of Capri in the south and to Misenum in the west, both 30 km (18 miles) from the volcano, causing the panic and fear described by Pliny the Younger in his second letter to Tacitus. Luckily for Pliny, this surge had lost its heat and power by the time it reached Misenum and caused only a dense deposit of ash.

Herculaneum, only 7 km (4 miles) to the west of Vesuvius, was destroyed well before Pompeii. The first *nuée ardente* reached Herculaneum two to five minutes after the eruption column started to collapse, and deposited 3 m (10 ft) of hot ash over the town. An hour later another surge, documented by the layers of material containing large amounts of tiles, parts of walls and columns, and charcoal fragments, was even more violent and deposited a further 1.5 m (5 ft) of ash. Four further *nuées ardentes* buried the town to a maximum depth of 23 m (75 ft) and extended the coastline by around 400 m (1,300 ft).

Pompeii was further from Vesuvius and the first two *nuées ardentes* that buried Herculaneum did not reach it. The third reached the Herculaneum Gate of Pompeii but may not have penetrated into the town itself, although the powerful heat of the cloud would have been felt by those still inside. It was the fourth surge that overwhelmed the interior of the town. It is estimated that this surge reached temperatures of 100–400 °C (212–750 °F) and may have carried toxic gases. A further two surges then swept over the town causing major damage to any structures protruding from the pumice-fall deposit. In the northern parts of the town, approximately 1.8 m (6 ft) of ash was deposited on top of the deep layer of lapilli that already smothered the town. The

southern parts were further from the volcano and the ash deposits here were approximately 60 cm (2 ft). It is possible that, in the south at least, some structures were still partially visible after the eruption had finished.

Volcanic activity probably continued for several days after Pompeii, Herculaneum and the other settlements of the Bay of Naples were destroyed.

(Above) The phases of the eruption can be seen clearly in the stratigraphy of the street to the west of the House of the Chaste Lovers (IX.12.6). White and grey lapilli are covered by several different deposits of ash and volcanic debris.

This view shows the distribution of the six major surge deposits of the AD 79 eruption. Lapilli from the earlier phases of the eruption fell on settlements almost 100 km (60 miles) from Vesuvius, in the neighbouring Bay of Salerno.

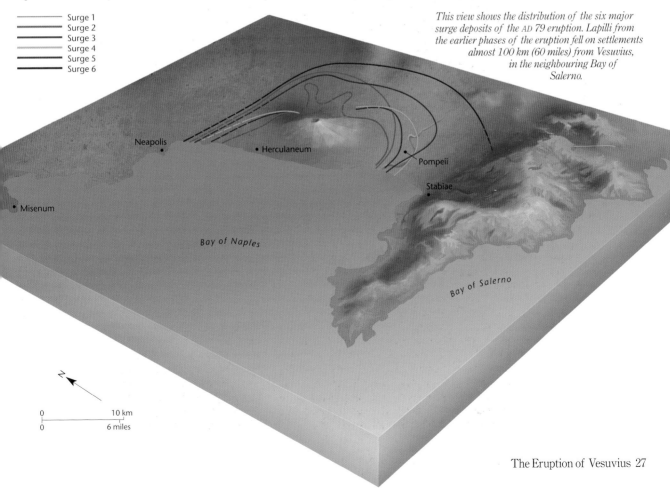

————	Surge 1
————	Surge 2
————	Surge 3
————	Surge 4
————	Surge 5
————	Surge 6

Neapolis
Herculaneum
Pompeii
Stabiae
Misenum
Bay of Naples
Bay of Salerno

N

0   10 km
0   6 miles

The Eruption of Vesuvius 27

Aftermath of the Eruption

UNTIL RECENTLY IT WAS COMMONLY THOUGHT THAT the majority of the population of Herculaneum succeeded in escaping the town, since very few bodies had been found during the excavations. Then, in 1982, over 300 victims of the eruption were discovered during excavations at the waterfront, where they had fled in their efforts to escape. Some were found on the beach in front of the town; the majority were crammed into the vaulted chambers (probably boat houses) that served as the foundations of the Sacred Area of Herculaneum. Each chamber contained between 15 and 40 bodies, mostly curled up and huddled together. These people were killed by the first surge to hit the town, by a combination of asphyxiation and severe burns. This surge was hot enough to carbonize wood but not human flesh. The second surge was much hotter. The bodies found in the chambers illustrate the difference between the two surges. Any limbs sticking up out of the deposit left by the first surge were carbonized by the even more extreme heat of the second.

Generally it has been thought that most of the inhabitants of Pompeii left the town as the pumice became dense and that there were few fatalities during this part of the eruption. However, recent research suggests that more people than first thought were killed by collapsing buildings during the pumice-fall. A good example is the body discovered beneath collapsed columns in the Triangular Forum. The majority of people who died in this phase of the eruption were found inside buildings, where they had been taking shelter.

Those inhabitants of Pompeii who did not flee or die during the pumice-fall phase were killed in the fourth surge, the first to envelop the town. Many were found at roof-level, where they had climbed to escape the dense pumice that clogged the streets. Most were killed by asphyxiation, although there are some examples of death by thermal shock – revealed by the mummification of limbs and desiccation of internal organs – and other injuries. During the excavations of the House of the Chaste Lovers, several skeletons were discovered of people whose bodies appear to have been broken by the force of the eruption. Many of the bodies excavated at Pompeii were found in groups, often thought to represent families. Almost equal numbers of bodies were found inside buildings and on the streets.

Although the majority of the population of Pompeii managed to escape from the town, it is likely that many still perished in the surrounding countryside. We have some evidence to support this notion, such as the body of a man found in a tree outside the Nola Gate, and the discovery of a group of 48 bodies near the River Sarno, found at the end of the 19th century. Unfortunately, the density of habitation today in the area around ancient Pompeii means that much evidence relating to the town's hinterland has been destroyed forever.

The relief effort

The Roman writers Suetonius (*Titus* 8) and Dio Cassius (*Roman History* 66.24) record the aftermath of the eruption. Titus, who had been emperor for only a month, rushed to Campania to organize the relief effort. The property of those who had died without making a will was donated to a relief fund, and a group of senators was appointed to look into the possibility of rebuilding the towns. Survivors of the disaster fled to Nola, Naples, Sorrento and Capua, and these towns were given privileges and benefits as a reward. One district in Naples even became known as the Regio Herculanensis after AD 79.

It is unclear whether those inhabitants of Pompeii who survived were able to return to the town to salvage goods and building materials. None would have been able to return to Herculaneum, which was buried too deeply. The volcanic deposit over Pompeii varies greatly in depth, and it is possible that at least some structures were still partially visible immediately after the eruption. Certainly there is much evidence of post-eruption disturbance of the site, but usually we have no way of telling when this disturbance took place. Some may relate to post-eruption salvage, but the majority can probably be explained by treasure-hunting in later periods.

Victims of the eruption found in the excavations of the boat sheds at Herculaneum in 1982.

Vesuvius since AD 79

Eruptions of varying severity were reported in 203, 472, 512, 787, 968, 991, 1007, 1036 and 1139. The eruption in 203 was heard 30 km (18 miles) away in the town of Capua. Those of 472 and 512 were large Plinian eruptions, although not of the same magnitude as the eruption of AD 79. However, that of 472 was reported to have spread ashes all over Europe as far as Constantinople and the eruption of 512 was so severe that Theodoric the Goth released the people living on Vesuvius from payment of taxes.

Following the eruption of 1139, there was a period of quiescence. During this time, vegetation covered the volcano and it was farmed intensively. Then, in 1631, there was a series of earthquakes over a period of six months that gradually increased in violence and culminated in a large Plinian eruption at the end of the year. Many of the villages on and around Vesuvius were destroyed and about 30 cm (12 in) of ash fell on Naples. The village of Massa, 5 km (3 miles) away, was hit by a 24-ton rock. Approximately 3,000 people and 6,000 animals were killed.

Since the eruption of 1631, Vesuvius has been more active and in the period until 1944 erupted 21 times. In 1903, 300,000 tons of volcanic debris fell on Naples, causing hundreds of deaths. In 1944, the Allied fleet evacuated 5,000 inhabitants from Naples and had to use bulldozers to clear roads. Falling rocks damaged 60 Allied aircraft. Since 1944, Vesuvius has been classified as dormant. It has been estimated that 3 million people could be affected if Vesuvius awakens once more.

The eruption of Vesuvius on 13 March 1944 was a surprise. The Observatory on the volcano had been occupied in large part by Allied troops, hindering the ability of its staff to monitor volcanic activity. Nobody died in this event, but the village of San Sebastiano was destroyed by lava flows.

The Preservation of Pompeii and Herculaneum

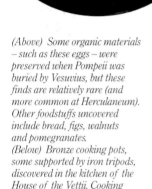

(Above) Some organic materials – such as these eggs – were preserved when Pompeii was buried by Vesuvius, but these finds are relatively rare (and more common at Herculaneum). Other foodstuffs uncovered include bread, figs, walnuts and pomegranates.

(Below) Bronze cooking pots, some supported by iron tripods, discovered in the kitchen of the House of the Vettii. Cooking took place on top of the masonry range, with wood stored beneath.

POMPEII AND HERCULANEUM HAVE OFTEN BEEN described as towns that were frozen in time, giving a perfect picture of everyday life in the Roman period. Even the Romans believed this, if the writings of the historian Dio Cassius, writing in the 3rd century AD, can be taken as representative of general opinion. In a description of the eruption, he writes, 'Furthermore, it buried two entire cities, Herculaneum and Pompeii, the latter place while its populace was seated in the theatre' (Dio Cassius, *Roman History* 66.21–23). There are many examples of evidence from Pompeii to support this image of a frozen town, since many details of ordinary life have been preserved. The most famous and most commonly cited include the meal of eggs and fish found on a table in the Temple of Isis; the 81 loaves of bread discovered in the oven of the Bakery of Modestus (VII.1.36); the bronze pots containing animal bones uncovered in the kitchen of the House of the Vettii (VI.15.1); and the fruit on display in glass containers in the Macellum (market) in the Forum.

These examples are, however, the exception rather than the norm. Due both to the process of the eruption and to the way the towns have been excavated since the 18th century, the evidence from Pompeii and Herculaneum is far from the perfect time-capsule of popular belief.

Firstly, the initial phase (pumice-fall) of the eruption lasted about 18 hours, which means that many inhabitants had time to escape from Pompeii before the devastating *nuées ardentes* of the second phase. Only *c.* 1,150 bodies have been found in Pompeii (394 in the pumice level, 653 in ash; plus *c.* 100 documented bodies without precise details of find-spots or condition), and around 300 in Herculaneum (the majority in the harbour area). A significant proportion of these had with them money or jewelry, and it makes sense that people attempted to escape with their valuables. There are some evocative examples of this. For example, near the 'gladiatorial barracks' (theatre portico) at Pompeii a body was found with a horse that had been loaded up with cloth, clothing and valuables.

Secondly, the eruption caused considerable damage to the towns. Columns and colonnades collapsed, mosaics buckled, walls were knocked from their foundations. There is evidence of an enormous degree of random destruction in both Pompeii and Herculaneum that has had a major impact on their state of preservation.

Thirdly, most organic materials have perished. Either they burnt and were destroyed during the eruption, or they slowly decomposed through the centuries after the eruption. At Pompeii, evidence for wooden furniture, basketry, foodstuffs, curtains, clothes, and so on usually consists of mere carbonized scraps of material or fragments of wood, or metal nails and studs that once belonged to wooden furniture; more complete examples are extremely rare. At Herculaneum, the evidence is better, since the extreme heat of the pyroclastic surges carbonized wood and other organic materials and caused them to be preserved within the deposited ash. But the evidence has not always been preserved after excavation.

The fourth factor disrupting this picture of daily life is the wide evidence of post-eruption disturbance. Artifacts and building materials have been salvaged. There has been extensive and undocumented treasure-hunting throughout Pompeii and Herculaneum. This phenomenon was noted even during excavations dating back to the 18th century. For example, pre-existing tunnels were noted during the excavation of the Villa of the Papyri near Herculaneum from 1750–62, and a contemporary observer of this excavation believed that these tunnels were ancient and dug by people who knew where to look for valuable finds. Today there is some debate over whether such tunnelling in Herculaneum and Pompeii dates back to the immediate aftermath of the eruption or to later periods. Either way, it is rare to find a house or building that has not been disturbed in some way. Even today, wall-paintings and other objects are sometimes stolen from the site. A famous example is the theft of a marble

relief thought to depict an earthquake scene from the House of Caecilius Jucundus (VI.1.26) on 14 July 1975. In the 1990s, a man attempted to leave Pompeii with a small wall-painting concealed under his t-shirt – luckily he was caught.

Finally, excavations at Pompeii and Herculaneum have often been of poor quality and poorly recorded. When the towns were first rediscovered, wall-paintings and statues were taken to adorn the palaces of the king of Naples or given as gifts to visiting monarchs and dignitaries. Such objects were sometimes damaged during their excavation. Edward Falkener wrote an interesting description (or rather, criticism) of the excavation of the House of Marcus Lucretius Fronto (IX.3.5) in 1847:

> In front of the garden are two other hermal statues of the same height, and each representing the Indian Bacchus and Ariadne. These were discovered perfect at the time of excavation; but happening to be found when nobody of consequence was present, they were immediately covered up again, and the remainder of the day occupied in heaping ashes over them. The works were then discontinued till some illustrious foreigner should arrive at Naples, when an excavation was ordered to be made in his honour. At length the opportunity offered. Some much longed-for person visited Pompeii; the excavation commenced; and, after two or three ineffectual endeavours in other places, where they knew they would obtain nothing, the workmen were ordered, as if by accident, to try in the peristylium. The pick-axes are struck vigorously in, as if to break the ground; the shovels cast aside the ashes for the second time; and after some few minutes, these works of art are brought to light, to the great satisfaction of the beholders. But as the workmen were aiming blows at random, one of them unfortunately chipped off a piece of Bacchus' nose with a stroke of his pick-axe. The spectators thought nothing of the blow, believing it to be an accident; the only other persons conscious of the outrage, being Bacchus and the manes [deceased ancestors] of the departed owner. But though these held their peace, I could not refrain my indignation at witnessing the evil effects arising from this ridiculous and long-continued custom of the authorities at Pompeii.

Edward Falkener,
'Report on a house at Pompeii excavated
under personal superintendence in 1847'

At least Falkener knew where the statues came from; for many such artifacts there are no records at all and we have no idea of their original provenance. Other objects, such as some types of pottery, were regarded as unimportant during the earliest excavations and simply thrown away. In general, the records of the earliest excavations are extremely poor, although it is only fair to say that the documentation has improved gradually over the centuries so that today the quality of the evidence varies considerably according to when excavations took place.

Pompeii, Herculaneum and other settlements buried by Vesuvius are not perfect time-capsules of ancient life, and there are problems with the evidence that will be considered during the course of this book; but these sites are remarkable all the same. Their value lies in the breadth of evidence they provide for public life and politics, for entertainment, for art, for domestic and everyday life. At these sites archaeologists and historians have architecture, wall decoration and mosaics, gardens, inscriptions and graffiti, artifacts of everyday use, sacred objects, evidence of commerce and craft. The sheer quantity and quality of the evidence is breathtaking, and it is this fact that makes Pompeii and Herculaneum so unique.

(Above) Three birds perch on a branch. This lovely bronze sculpture was found during the excavations of the House of Fabius Rufus (VII. Ins. Occ. 16–19) in 1967.

Amphorae in House of the Lyre-Player (I.4.5). These Roman storage vessels were probably stacked together during the excavation of the house from 1853 to 1869, but their different shapes reveal that the inhabitants of the house were consuming imported as well as Italian wine.

Other Sites Buried by Vesuvius in AD 79

MORE THAN 140 VILLAS HAVE BEEN DISCOVERED IN THE area around Pompeii, many in the modern districts of Boscoreale and Boscotrecase. Some are small working farms, but others are big enough to have both working and luxury areas. One example is the Villa of Publius Fannius Synistor, discovered at the end of the 19th century. Now demolished, wall-paintings from the villa can be seen in museums around the world (particularly in the Metropolitan Museum in New York). Another example is the Villa Pisanella, also demolished after excavation. More recently, a working farm in this area – known as the Villa Regina – has been excavated and published to modern standards (see p.212).

Murecine

Located *c.* 600 m (*c.* 2,000 ft) from Pompeii, between modern Scafati and Castellammare di Stabia. Three villas were excavated in this area at the end of the 18th century, although their locations are now unknown. In 1959, a building with a series of triclinia (dining-rooms, identified from masonry couches) arranged around a portico was discovered here during the construction of a new highway. It was found to contain an archive of wax tablets belonging to the Sulpicii family of financiers (all freedmen) and relating to their business activities in Puteoli. More recent excavations in this area found a large house with elaborate wall decorations and bath suite. Another building was discovered *c.* 100 m (*c.* 300 ft) to the west of the complex, consisting of several shops, within which were found skeletons.

Oplontis

Located *c.* 5 km (*c.* 3 miles) from Pompeii, in modern Torre Annunziata. Two villas (A and B) were excavated here between 1964 and 1984. The first is a luxury villa, often thought to have been owned by Poppaea, the second wife of Nero. The second was an agricultural villa thought to specialize in the production of wine. Baths were also found at nearby Punta Oncina in 1834. On the basis of these discoveries, Oplontis is thought to have been a small town on the outskirts of Pompeii.

(Below and opposite above) Elaborate wall-paintings from Villa A at Oplontis. Discovered in the 18th century, it was systematically excavated and restored from 1964. Parts of it remain buried beneath the modern town of Torre Annunziata.

Stabiae

Stabiae was originally an older settlement than Pompeii, located on the coast further to the south. Its precise location is unknown, however, because it was completely destroyed by the Roman general Sulla during the Social War (89 BC). In AD 79, Stabiae was the location of a series of luxury villas – famous examples are the Villa San Marco and Villa Arianna, which overlooked the Bay of Naples. A small part of the Villa Arianna was excavated in the 1950s. Sixteen working farms were also excavated in this area between 1759 and 1782.

(Below) The Villa Arianna at Stabiae was tunnelled extensively between 1753 and 1762 and found to contain fine frescos and mosaics – such this wall-painting of a Nereid.

II
REDISCOVERING POMPEII'S BURIED PAST

On Sunday we were in Pompeii.
So many disasters have happened in the world,
but none that have given so much pleasure to posterity.
I can think of nothing more interesting.

Goethe, *Italian Journey*, 13 March 1787

The area laid waste by Vesuvius in AD 79 was abandoned. Eventually the fertile earth covering Pompeii would be farmed and vineyards would climb the slopes of Vesuvius, and a new town called Resina would grow up over ancient Herculaneum. The existence of the ancient towns was largely forgotten, except by local people who often made chance discoveries of ancient artifacts when digging wells. It was only during the Renaissance when allusions to the buried cities were found in ancient literature – above all in the letters of Pliny that describe the eruption – that interest in the fate of these towns was renewed. For the first excavators of Herculaneum and Pompeii, however, the principal value of these sites lay in the riches they might yield.

The Via dell' Abbondanza. The excavations of this main street cut through cultivated fields in an attempt to unite the Amphitheatre with the other excavated parts of the town.

The Earliest Excavations

COLORED PIECES OF MARBLE WERE UNCOVERED DURING the deepening of a well on an estate in Resina in 1709. Hearing of the discoveries, the Austrian Prince d'Elbeuf purchased the property because he wanted to acquire marbles to decorate a villa he was building. He excavated the spot using local labourers and believed he had found the ruins of an ancient temple. In fact, the well shaft had been sunk into the theatre of Herculaneum. Over the next few years, the theatre was plundered of its marble and bronze statues. Some of these statues were surrendered to the king, but others were smuggled to Prince Eugene of Savoy in Austria and possibly to France.

In 1734, Charles, son of Philip V of Spain, wrested southern Italy from Austrian control and established an autonomous monarchy there. He was crowned Charles VII in Palermo in 1735 but made Naples his capital. There, Charles sought to gain status and regard for his fledgling kingdom by encouraging

Was the location of the cities destroyed by Vesuvius forgotten?

Although the formal rediscovery of Pompeii, Herculaneum and the other sites destroyed by Vesuvius took place in the 18th century, there is evidence to suggest that the location of these places had not been completely forgotten. Ancient writers continued alluding to the eruption for centuries after it occurred, and antique maps give the locations (not always correctly) of Pompeii and Herculaneum. There is also evidence that Pompeii had been explored by treasure hunters. Late antique lamps and pottery dating from the 6th to the 16th centuries were discovered in the Suburban Baths, the Praedia of Julia Felix (II.4), and the House of Fabius Rufus (VII. Ins. Occ. 16–19), and from the 16th century there are plenty of reports of local people discovering inscriptions, coins, wall-paintings, mosaics and columns on their property. The start of formal excavations in 1738 at Herculaneum was the culmination of these activities, rather than a new beginning.

12th century AD	The locations of Pompeii, Herculaneum, Stabiae and Oplontis appear correctly marked on the Peutinger Table, a map of the main roads and cities. However, this map is heavily reliant on earlier Antique maps and may not represent the actual topographic knowledge of the 12th century.
1503	The cartographer Ambrogio Leone made a map of Campania and marked the location of Herculaneum close to its actual site.
1592	The Roman architect Domenico Fontana excavated a canal from the River Sarno through raised fields known as 'La Città' to a munitions factory in Torre Annunziata. Ancient ruins at 'La Città' were discovered but reburied.
1637	Based on Fontana's discoveries, the antiquarian Lucas Holstenius proposed that 'La Città' was the location of ancient Pompeii.
1689	An inscription with the word 'POMPEI' was discovered during well-digging in the area of 'La Città'. This was believed to refer to the Roman general Pompey the Great and so ignored.
1699	Giuseppe Macrini stated in his 'De Vesuvio' that Pompeii lay beneath 'La Città'.

The Peutinger Table is a medieval copy of a Roman road map dating to the 4th century BC. The map is not geographically correct, but it shows Roman places and roads connecting them and indicates distances between them. Pompeii and Herculaneum are shown on the plan, even though they had been destroyed centuries before the map was drawn up.

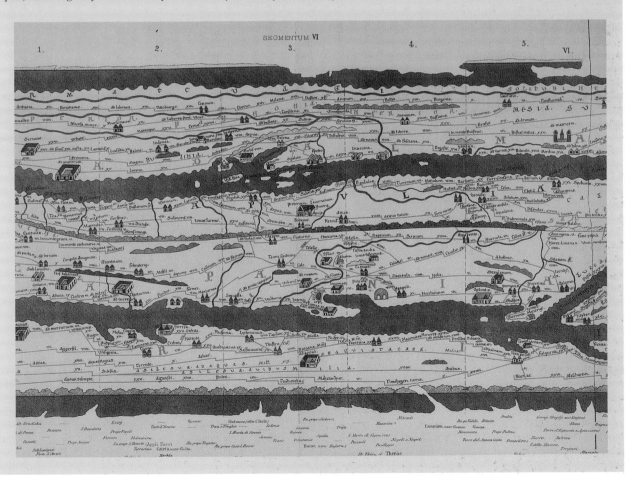

(Opposite) Theseus victorious
over the Minotaur, from the
basilica of Herculaneum, one
of the earliest wall-paintings
to be discovered. The
Athenian children who would
have been sacrificed to the
beast surround Theseus.

(Below) This anonymous
lithograph of visitors to the
tunnels that criss-cross the
theatre of Herculaneum
probably dates to the 18th
century. The visitors see by
the light of burning torches.

cultural and artistic pursuits. Opera, art and archaeology all benefited from Charles' attentions.

Charles married in 1738 and began the construction of a new royal villa at Portici. This villa was on the same estate where the Prince d'Elbeuf had made his finds from 1709 to 1716, and the king decided to continue the excavations begun by the Austrian prince. Both Charles and his wife, Maria Amalia, had been intrigued by the previous discoveries, and were generous patrons of the excavations. The king put in charge of the work Rocque Joaquin de Alcubierre, a military engineer trained in mining techniques and tunnelling. Existing well shafts were used to access the remains and Alcubierre used miners, soldiers and prisoners to dig tunnels along the lines of ancient walls. The tunnels were narrow and dangerous, damp with poor air circulation and there was a constant threat of collapse. Initially some of the excavated fill was

used to landscape the gardens of the new palace, but later tunnels were backfilled once artifacts and wall-paintings had been removed. There is no accurate plan of the network of tunnels that the excavators used to crisscross Herculaneum in this period, but we know that the theatre, a building identified as a basilica, the Villa of the Papyri, part of the Palaestra, and shops and houses in the northeast part of the town were all explored. Some of the most important finds include bronze statues of Nero and Germanicus (members of the imperial royal family), equestrian statues of Marcus Nonius Balbus and his son of the same name, and a wall-painting depicting Theseus victorious over the Minotaur. Many statues were excavated, particularly from the basilica and theatre, only some of which can be identified today.

One of the earliest accounts of the excavations at Herculaneum is to be found in a letter by Horace Walpole, dated 14 June 1740:

'One hates writing descriptions that are to be found in every book of travels; but we have seen something today that I am sure you never read of, and perhaps never heard of. Have you ever heard of the subterraneous town? a whole Roman town with all its edifices remaining under ground? Don't fancy the inhabitants buried it there to save it from the Goths: they were buried with it themselves; which is a caution we are not told they ever took. You remember in Titus's time there were several cities destroyed by an eruption of Vesuvius, attended with an earthquake. Well, this was one of them, not very considerable, and then called Herculaneum. Above it has since been built Portici, about three miles from Naples, where the king has a villa. This under-ground city is perhaps one of the noblest curiosities that ever has been discovered. It was found out by chance about a year and a half ago. They began digging, they found statues; they dug farther, they found more. Since that they have made a very considerable progress, and find continually. You may walk the compass of a mile; but by the misfortune of the modern town being overhead, they are obliged to proceed with great caution, lest they destroy both one and t'other. By this occasion the path is very narrow, just wide enough and high enough for one man to walk upright. They have hollowed as they found it easiest to work, and have carried their streets not exactly where were the ancient ones, but sometimes before houses, sometimes through them. You would imagine that all the fabrics were crushed together; on the contrary, except some columns, they have found all the edifices standing upright in their proper situation. There is one inside of a temple quite perfect, with the middle arch, two columns, and two pilasters. It is built of brick plastered over, and painted with architecture: Almost all the insides of the houses are in the same

This drawing from the Voyage pittoresque ou description des Royaumes de Naples et de Sicilie *by the Abbé de Saint-Non (1781–86) illustrates the transportation of antiquities from the royal museum at Portici to the Palazzo degli Studi in Naples. Crowds lined the streets to see the procession of statues, ornaments and other objects from Herculaneum and Pompeii.*

manner; and what is very particular, the general ground of all the painting is red. Besides this temple, they make out very plainly an amphitheatre: the stairs, of white marble, and the seats are very perfect; the inside was painted in the same colour with the private houses, and great part cased with white marble. They have found among other things some fine statues, some human bones, some rice, medals, and a few paintings extremely fine. These latter are preferred to all the ancient paintings that have ever been discovered. We have not seen them yet, as they are kept in the King's apartment, whither all these curiosities are transplanted; and 'tis difficult to see them – but we shall. I forgot to tell you, that in several places the beams of the houses remain, but burnt to charcoal; so little damaged that they retain visibly the grain of the wood, but upon touching crumble to ashes. What is remarkable, there are no other marks or appearance of fire, but what are visible on these beams.

'There might certainly be collected great light from this reservoir of antiquities, if a man of learning had the inspection of it; if he directed the working, and would make a journal of the discoveries. But I believe there is no judicious choice made of directors. There is nothing of the kind known in the world; I mean a Roman city entire of that age, and that has not been corrupted with modern repairs. Besides scrutinizing this very carefully, I should be inclined to search for the remains of the other towns

that were partners with this in the general ruin. 'Tis certainly an advantage to the learned world, that this has been laid up so long. Most of the discoveries in Rome were made in a barbarous age, where they only ransacked the ruins in quest of treasure, and had no regard to the form and being of the building; or to any circumstances that might give light into its use and history….'

The discovery of Pompeii

Within a few years of the discovery of Herculaneum, a search for other ancient sites in the region began since the tunnelling at Herculaneum proved difficult and dangerous and would be completely abandoned by 1780. Local inhabitants had been finding artifacts in fields near Torre Annunziata, so Alcubierre made trial excavations in this area in April 1748. At this time the excavators did not know that this was the site of Pompeii; the locals called it 'La Cività', while Alcubierre himself believed it to be ancient Stabiae. Excavations moved to the area now known to be the Amphitheatre in October 1748 – its sunken outline was identifiable in the landscape – in the hope of finding a major public building with its associated sculpture. This hope was not fulfilled, and excavations moved to another part of the town. By 1750 the lack of significant finds led the work to be abandoned. At Herculaneum, in contrast, exciting finds had been made in June 1750 in what would become known as the Villa of the Papyri.

Brief history of the excavations of Pompeii

1748
The first formal excavations of Pompeii.

1763
Discovery of an inscription firmly identifies the ruins as the ancient town of Pompeii.

1806–1815
The French occupation of Naples. Excavations intensify at Pompeii. The Forum and Basilica are uncovered.

1816
Restoration of the Bourbon monarchy. Intensity of excavations fluctuates due to various financial crises. Important discoveries include the House of the Tragic Poet, the House of the Faun, and the Forum Baths.

1860
Unification of Italy. Pompeii becomes a showpiece of the new kingdom.

1910–1923
Excavations along the Via dell' Abbondanza.

1924–1939
The Fascist era: The Villa of the Mysteries and large parts of Region I are uncovered.

1939
World War II stops most work at Pompeii.

1943
Pompeii bombed by the Allies.

1945
Excavations start again in Regions I and II as part of a campaign of public works to revitalize southern Italy and bring in tourists.

1962
Excavations are restricted to certain areas and houses in an effort to preserve the site from further ruin.

1980
A major earthquake causes enormous damage to the ruins of Pompeii. Many parts of the town have been closed to the public since this date.

1997
A Special Law gives the Soprintendenza di Pompei unprecedented financial autonomy. All money taken at the gates now goes towards conservation and providing facilities for tourists.

Plan of Pompeii highlighting the areas uncovered in particular chronological periods during the long history of the excavations.

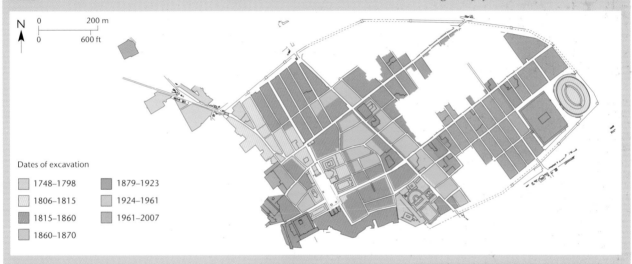

N
0 — 200 m
0 — 600 ft

Dates of excavation

- 1748–1798
- 1806–1815
- 1815–1860
- 1860–1870
- 1879–1923
- 1924–1961
- 1961–2007

Brief history of the excavations of Herculaneum

1709–10
The theatre is discovered during work to sink a well-shaft. Lots of statues are removed, firstly to a nearby villa, later to France and Savoy.

1738
The King of Naples orders the site to be tunnelled. Valuable finds are transported to the Royal Palace at Portici.

1750
The Villa of the Papyri is discovered and tunnelled.

1780
Excavations are suspended in favour of work at Pompeii.

1828–35
The first open-air excavations take place. Parts of two insulae are uncovered, but valuable finds are scarce.

1850–55, 1869–77
Brief periods of excavation.

1869–75
Under Fiorelli's direction, parts of two more insulae are uncovered. Excavation is eventually abandoned in the face of opposition from landowners.

1927–1942
The Fascist period. The majority of what can be seen today is uncovered.

Since World War II
Excavations have been on a smaller scale: the Palaestra, Suburban Baths, along the Decumanus Maximus, and in various houses and shops.

1981–98
Excavations on the beach in front of Herculaneum and in the Villa of the Papyri.

Karl Weber and the Villa of the Papyri

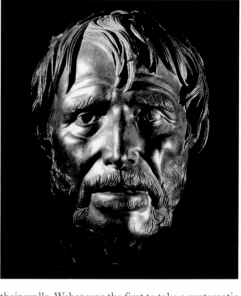

(Right) This bronze bust, found in the main peristyle of the villa, was once identified as Seneca, but is now thought to be a famous poet: suggestions include Hesiod, Callimachus and Apollonius of Rhodes.

KARL WEBER WAS A SWISS MILITARY ENGINEER OF THE Royal Guard, a battalion of Swiss troops contracted to serve Charles VII. In 1749, Weber became Alcubierre's assistant and was entrusted with the task of overseeing the daily operation of the excavations at Herculaneum and Pompeii. In particular his duties included compiling weekly summaries of all finds and producing detailed plans of the excavations. By excavating tunnels that respected the lines of streets and walls and entering houses through their front doors rather than through holes knocked in their walls, Weber was the first to take a systematic approach to the excavations. Weber's plans and sketches form a major part of the documentation of the excavations in this early period; without these, very little would be known now about the excavation of some important discoveries. One such is the Villa of the Papyri, excavated from 1750–62.

In similar circumstances to the ancient theatre of Herculaneum, the Villa of the Papyri was discovered when a landowner drilling a well turned up coloured fragments of marble. A circular pavilion lay 30 m (100 ft) below the modern surface, and was later revealed to have been connected by means of a footpath to a large suburban villa, *c*. 100 m (*c*. 320 ft) to the west of the theatre, so only just outside the town's limits. Weber's tunnelling revealed a villa descending towards the sea. There was a bath complex and library and several large garden areas with pools surrounded by fountains and statues. These include the now-famous 'Mercury in repose', and the 'Drunken faun'. These statues became the centrepiece of Charles' collection in the Portici museum. The floors of the villa were of coloured marble or mosaic, and it was actually the different patterns of mosaic in the various rooms that helped Weber to navigate his tunnels through the villa. During these excavations the workmen discovered other, older tunnels – perhaps evidence of salvage immediately after the eruption or later treasure-hunting by locals living in the area. Many important finds were made during Weber's excavation of this villa, yet the evidence of the older tunnels makes it clear that they do not represent the sum of its contents in AD 79. Weber made detailed notes, sketches and illustrations of the discoveries during the excavations, and also a plan of the villa that has recently been shown (with a few exceptions) to be remarkably accurate in its details. These documents form the basis of our knowledge of the villa, and the plan in particular was used in the 1970s as a template for the construction of the Getty Villa in Malibu, which recreated the large peristyle garden of the villa. Unfortunately the excavation was never completed. Originally it was believed that the villa lay on a single level, but it is clear from subsequent excavations in the 1990s that the villa is in fact terraced over four levels down to the sea.

The villa would be notable for its location, size, decoration and statuary alone, but its fame was guaranteed by the discovery of a collection of over 1,800 carbonized papyri. Resembling lumps of charcoal, initially many of the papyri were discarded. It was only when characters were identified on one of them that the excavators realized their significance. Unfortunately the first technique used to open a scroll (by cutting it in half) served to

destroy all but a small part of the text. In 1753, Father Antonio Piaggio, a Jesuit priest, was brought to Naples to unroll and decipher the scrolls. He had been recommended by the Vatican Library for his skill in transcribing texts. In 1756, he succeeded in inventing a machine to slowly unroll the papyri, which were then cut into sections.

The majority of the papyri were found in a room along with four inscribed busts of the philosophers Epicurus, Hermarchus and Zeno, and the orator Demosthenes. These statues echo the theme of the library. Although many scholars had hoped the papyri would prove a valuable repository of ancient Greek and Roman literature previously thought lost (such as the missing books of Livy's *History of Rome*), it is now clear that three-quarters of all those opened so far are works of Philodemus of Gadara, a minor Epicurean philosopher of the 1st century BC. The discovery of these scrolls represents the only library known to have survived from the ancient world and for this reason remains important to scholars. To date only half of the papyri have actually been read since the other half are too blackened to be legible. Recently there has been some progress in reading these damaged scrolls using a multi-spectral imaging technology first developed by NASA.

We know from ancient literary sources that libraries were often organized into two separate sections, representing Greek and Latin texts. Interestingly, only a few fragments of Latin (including a poem about the battle of Actium) have been found in the Villa

(Above) The Getty Villa in Malibu, California, is based on the Villa of the Papyri. It features gardens, reflecting pools, and replicas of statues and fountains. In 2006, the Villa reopened after undergoing extensive renovations, and now houses the J. Paul Getty Museum's permanent antiquities collection.

These 'dancing maidens' (opposite) belong to a group of five bronze statues identified as the Danaids (who were condemned to draw water for eternity) found in the inner peristyle of the villa. The bronze statue of an athlete (left) was one of two identical statues from the main peristyle. All have glass paste eyes; traces of red paint were also found on the lips of the athlete. Eighty statues were found during the excavations of this luxury villa.

(Opposite) A fragment of a wall-painting from the Villa of the Papyri. Four ducks have been hung above two antelope. The antelopes are still alive, and their hooves have been tied. Such scenes related to hunting are common in the wall-paintings of Herculaneum and Pompeii.

(Below) A small part of the Villa of the Papyri was finally opened to the light during excavations in the 1990s.

of the Papyri, which has led some scholars to believe that only half of the library was excavated, leaving the other half yet to be discovered. In the 1990s this belief gave impetus to the new excavations that uncovered a total surface area of 3 hectares (7.5 acres) to the north of the existing excavations, and eventually around one-tenth of the villa. The atrium and 16 other rooms were exposed to the air for the first time since AD 79. On the second level of the villa huge wooden doors were found, which the excavators suggest mark the entrance to an important part of the house. Many scholars hope that this is the entrance to the second part of the villa's library. Unfortunately, the excavations ran out of funds before further investigations could take place and there is no immediate plan to resume them. As at Pompeii, the exposure of the ancient ruins has created grave problems of conservation. In particular, the excavations had been conducted 4 m (13 ft) below the water table and exposed the villa to the threat of flood. The current authorities have decided to give

precedence to conservation of the exposed parts of the villa over further excavation. This decision is hotly debated. However, the success of recent conservation work means that it is now possible, for the first time ever, for tourists to visit limited parts of the villa.

The Villa of the Papyri is one of the most important discoveries to have been made during the history of the excavations of Herculaneum and Pompeii. Villas of such size have been found only rarely in the Roman empire, and represent a world of luxury inaccessible for the vast majority of the inhabitants of the Roman world. Certainly the scale and opulence of the villa have led scholars to believe that its owner was extremely rich and powerful. It has been suggested – but not on the basis of any firm evidence – that the villa was once the property of Lucius Calpurnius Piso, whose daughter married Julius Caesar. Piso was a student of Philodemus, and later became his patron, which might explain the presence of so many of Philodemus' works at the villa.

Work Returns to Pompeii

IN 1755, A FARMER FOUND A MARBLE PILLAR AT 'LA Città', immediately to the north of the site of the earlier excavations. This led to excavations in a large house and garden later identified as the 'Praedia' (estate) of Julia Felix (II.4.2). It was the first building from either Herculaneum or Pompeii to be explored in its entirety and a large number of wall-paintings, mosaics, statues and inscriptions was uncovered and removed to the king's museum. Excavations then took place in the Large Theatre, Covered Theatre (Odeon), Triangular Forum, and the Villa of Diomedes. The nature of the excavations was very different from those at Herculaneum, and much easier since the work was conducted in the open air. The aim of this initial work was to uncover significant structures and valuable artifacts rather than to expose parts of the town permanently. The excavations resembled a quarry, the excavators digging here and there without any coherent plan or strategy in their search for treasure. Wall-paintings were ripped from walls, inscriptions and 'worthless'

The Society of Dilettanti was a London club founded in 1734 by noblemen and gentlemen who had been on the Grand Tour. This painting by Sir Joshua Reynolds – himself a member – depicts members of the Society. From left to right: Sir Watkin Williams Wynn, Sir J. Taylor, Mr. Payne Galway, Sir William Hamilton, Mr. Richard Thompson, Mr. Stanhope, and Mr. Smith of Heath.

objects such as pottery destroyed, statues and objects of interest carried off to the Royal Museum and excavated areas backfilled to prevent others from carrying off those things not taken by the excavators. There are reports from this period of the practice of destroying wall-paintings not considered good enough for the museum at Portici. A stop was put to this only in 1763.

Reactions in Europe to the discovery of Herculaneum and Pompeii

Under Charles's orders, the first excavations were conducted in great secrecy, but it proved impossible to hide such an important discovery from the wider world. In 1739, just one year after the excavations began, the French scholar and magistrate Charles de Brosses sent a report on the discovery of Herculaneum to the French Academy. There was great excitement throughout Europe at the news, since it coincided with a growing belief that classical antiquity should form an essential part of the education of Europe's gentlemen. In this period societies such as the Society of Dilettanti in England had been formed to promote discussion of antiquities. Wealthy young men were encouraged to complete their education by undertaking the Grand Tour, a journey through Europe. The primary destination was Italy, whose classical remains were much admired. Naples, Vesuvius (which had entered one of the most active periods in its history), and the archaeological sites of Herculaneum and later Pompeii, would become popular attractions. But visitors to the excavations were greatly disappointed. Many letters of the period criticize the progress and method of excavation, and lament the destruction caused by the excavators and their lack of interest in historical questions. Alcubierre was singled out in much of the criticism. One of his most famous detractors was Johann Joachim Winckelmann:

> The management of the works has been entrusted to a Spanish engineer by the name of Rocque Joachim de Alcubierre, who has come as part of the king's retinue: he is currently a colonel and head of the corps of engineers of Naples. The incompetence of this man, who had as much to do with antiquity as the moon with prawns, as the Italian proverb has it, has caused the loss of many beautiful things….

> *Sendschreiben von den herculanischen Entdeckungen*, Rome 1762

Yet Alcubierre's brief initially was to locate and excavate valuable artifacts for his king; it was not his concern to document the ruins beyond providing lists of finds, or to engage in scholarly enquiry. Charles himself and his court at Naples were interested in collecting antiquities rather than in ancient architecture for its own sake, and Alcubierre was expected to increase the king's collection. Despite the criticisms of outsiders, Alcubierre did his job well.

Unfortunately, the situation was not helped by Charles's possessive control of the excavations. He considered the archaeological finds to be his personal possessions, an attitude that was shared by his son and heir, Ferdinand, and which is illustrated by an anonymous letter of 1749 reporting the discovery of a four-page bronze book: 'it has not yet been read by scholars, since the King keeps it for himself'. Much to the disgust of European collectors, and in contrast to the situation in Rome, a law was passed explicitly forbidding export of antiquities in 1755, and was confirmed by Ferdinand in 1766 and 1769 (this law does not appear to have been completely effective; certainly Sir William Hamilton not only exported antiquities himself but acted as agent for other collectors while he was British ambassador in Naples). To make matters worse, even after news of the excavations had spread through Europe, Charles instructed that the excavations be conducted in secrecy. Indeed, Winckelmann complained about the difficulty of access to the remains during his first visit in 1758, while Sir John Soane told students of the Royal Academy in London that his sketches of the Temple of Isis at Pompeii in 1779 were made 'by stealth, by moonlight'. Visitors needed invitations to view the excavations, and even then were not allowed to take notes or make sketches. The thirst for knowledge of the excavations throughout Europe led visitors to make illustrations or write descriptions from memory of the antiquities they saw. One such example is the *Observations sur les antiquités d'Herculaneum* ('Observations on the antiquities of Herculaneum') published in 1754 by Charles Nicolas Cochin and Jérôme Charles Belicard. Partly in reaction to the publication and distribution of unauthorized and inaccurate reproductions of wall-paintings and other artifacts, Charles set up the Regia Accademia Ercolanese (Royal Herculaneum Society) in 1755 to record the finds from Herculaneum. Roman and Neapolitan artists were commissioned to illustrate the excavated paintings, statues, bronzes and furnishings, and their work was published between 1757 and 1792 in eight volumes of *Le antichità di Ercolano esposte* ('The antiquities of Herculaneum displayed'). Initially the king presented these volumes to fellow monarchs and to scholars throughout Europe, and thus their distribution was restricted. However, in 1770, in reaction to an unauthorized English translation of *Le antichità*, Charles's son and heir, Ferdinand, allowed the original Italian version to be purchased. These volumes were extremely expensive, and have been criticized for the artistic licence taken in the depiction of the ancient artifacts. Despite this, they became the basis for other publications on the excavations in this period and also for the pattern books commonly used in the decorative arts of the 18th and 19th centuries. Herculaneum had a profound influence on ornamentation, furniture and domestic decoration as it became fashionable to illustrate certain motifs seen in art from the site, such as dancing figures, on the household objects and wallpaper of the day.

The Villa of Diomedes was excavated between 1771 and 1774 and is located among the tombs of the Via dei Sepolcri, outside the Herculaneum Gate. This large and luxurious villa, built over two levels with a private bath suite and sea views, is often thought to have been the property of Marcus Arrius Diomedes, whose tomb lies directly in front of the entrance to the villa. Twenty bodies, including women and children, were found in the villa by the excavators.

(Right) A fine example of Pompeian-style decoration can be seen in the 'Small Dining Room' of the Winter Palace, St Petersburg, which was originally designed by Karl Briullov (but later altered) and completed between 1830 and 1840.

(Below) Pompeian decoration illustrated in the highly influential Grammar of Ornament *(1856) by Victorian architect and artist Owen Jones was intended to introduce designers to the decorative arts of other cultures.*

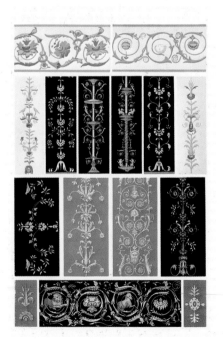

Excavations during the reign of Ferdinand

Charles VII left Naples to become Charles III of Spain in 1759. His eight-year-old son, Ferdinand (known as Ferdinand IV in Naples and Ferdinand III in Sicily) inherited the kingdoms of Naples and Sicily. As he grew up, Ferdinand showed little interest in cultural issues, preferring to hunt, but his wife, Maria Carolina, maintained the Bourbon interest in architecture, music and antiquities. Unfortunately, problems during Ferdinand's reign, such as a devastating famine in 1764, meant that the work at Pompeii was sporadic and poorly funded. Yet there were gradual improvements in the quality of the excavations. This change is often ascribed to the discovery in August 1763 of an inscription that definitively identified the site as Pompeii. From this date, the backfilling of the excavations was forbidden and the ruins were left exposed. For the first time the question of the conservation and the presentation of the ruins to visitors was considered, and in the 1760s and 1770s it became somewhat easier to visit the site. Indeed, this new concern for public opinion directly influenced the progress of the excavations. In 1764, the excavations shifted from the area around the Herculaneum Gate to the theatre district, since this was more easily reached from the Royal Road that passed the excavations to the south. The Temple of Isis became the focus of visitor attention, and the excavators left curiosities in place – such as bones and ash from a sacrifice found on one of the temple's altars – for the benefit of visitors. Paintings were still removed to the museum, but from 1765 they were drawn first. Then, in 1769, Emperor Joseph II of Austria visited Pompeii and commented on the abandonment of the ruins around the Herculaneum Gate: the excavations were promptly transferred back to this area and would remain there for the next 20 years. The Villa of Diomedes became the new visitor attraction, and for the first time there are records of efforts made to repair the ancient ruins. From 1780 the first attempts were made to preserve wall-paintings in situ by providing some houses and buildings with roofs. Some of the excavated areas were left as they had been found with their decorations and furnishings intact, and some objects that had been taken to the museum were even returned to the site, such as marbles from the Covered Theatre.

(Opposite) The excavation of the Temple of Isis, drawn by Pietro Fabris for Sir William Hamilton's Campi Phlegraei *(1776). The temple slowly emerges from the lapilli as aristocratic visitors – possibly including Hamilton himself – look on. Hamilton was a frequent visitor to the excavations in this period.*

(Below) This view of the Large Theatre was painted by the German landscape artist Jacob Philipp Hackert in 1793, one of a series of paintings he made of the excavations.

A Period of Political Turmoil

THE LAST DECADE OF THE 18TH AND THE EARLY YEARS of the 19th centuries were ones of political turmoil throughout Europe. These were the years of the Napoleonic Wars, and Ferdinand was forced to flee to Sicily on two occasions, first when liberal Neapolitans (with the aid of the French) declared a republic in Naples in 1799 (lasting a mere six months), and later during the French conquest of Naples in 1806. Surprisingly, the political upheavals of this period served to aid the progress of the excavations.

The French occupation

In 1808 Napoleon's sister, Caroline, and her husband, Joachim Murat, became monarchs of Naples. Caroline in particular was an enthusiastic supporter of the excavations and frequently visited the site. The work at Pompeii intensified. The first real scholarly studies of the excavations can be dated to this period, such as François Mazois' *Les ruines de Pompéi* ('The ruins of Pompeii'), published from 1812 onwards. Mazois was the first to present the town as a whole, rather than as a collection of monuments. He intended to publish Pompeii in its entirety, with the aim of giving life to the town. This was an aim shared by the French excavators who desired to create a vision of the town as it had

been in antiquity as opposed to the series of quarries that had been left by the Bourbons. To achieve this, excavations focused on the town walls (by soldiers), the Amphitheatre and the major public buildings of the Forum (by civilian workmen). The excavation of the town gates revealed for the first time the main roads that crossed the town. Land over the buried cities was purchased to facilitate excavation, the number of workers on site was gradually increased to 624 by 1813. By the time that Ferdinand was restored to the throne in 1815 the excavations of Pompeii had been radically altered.

The restoration of Ferdinand

The period after Ferdinand's restoration in 1815 was one of deep political unrest at Naples, and the progress of the excavations at Pompeii fluctuated as a consequence. There was also some backlash against the activities of the French – land expropriated for the excavations was resold into private hands, for example. Excavations took place in Region VI, and despite the chronic lack of funds, a series of important discoveries was made, including the Forum Baths, the House of the Tragic Poet (VI.8.5) and the House of the Faun (VI.12.2). By the middle of the century, the greater part of Regions VI and VII had been uncovered and excavations were taking place in Via di Nola and Via Stabiana. It also became easier to visit Pompeii – from 1840 the site could be reached by train from Naples and a new entrance at the Marine Gate was created for the benefit of tourists. Indeed, the period after the French defeat in 1815 saw the revival of the Grand

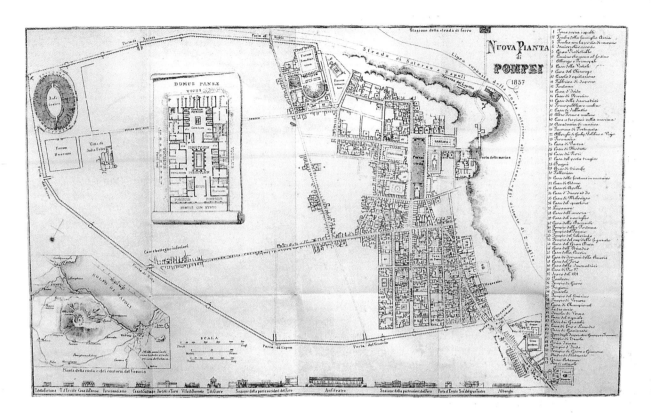

Tour. Visitors may have been impressed by what they saw, but this was also a period of serious corruption and malpractice at Pompeii, and in Naples in general. In 1848, proposals were drawn up to transform the administration of the excavations radically, with the aim of putting an end to theft and bribery by regularizing practices and establishing codes of conduct. But nothing would come of these proposals until Giuseppe Fiorelli gained charge of the site in 1863.

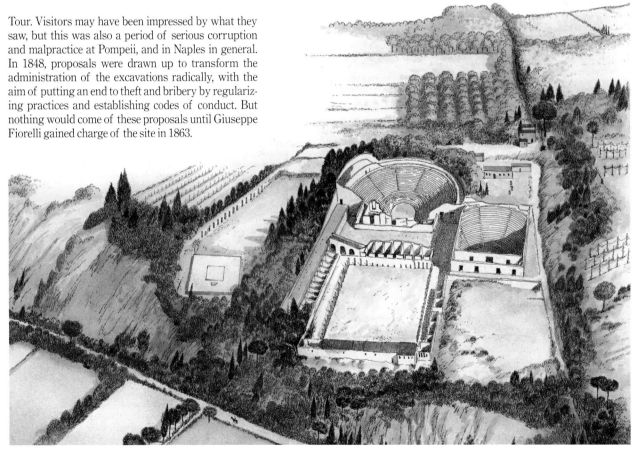

The Unification of Italy and the Impact of Giuseppe Fiorelli

This painting by Edouard Alexandre Sain in 1865 shows women working in the excavations. Now in the Musée d'Orsay in Paris, the painting was originally part of the private collection of Napoleon III.

THE CONQUEST OF SOUTHERN ITALY BY GARIBALDI in 1859 and its incorporation into the unified Kingdom of Italy in 1860 had a dramatic impact on the excavations at Pompeii, not least due to the energy and vision of Giuseppe Fiorelli (1823–96). By this time, more than 22 hectares (55 acres), or one-third, of the site had been uncovered. Fiorelli's intention was to finish its excavation. Pompeii was to become a show-case of the new kingdom.

Fiorelli had been born locally and trained as a lawyer and numismatist. On completion of his studies in 1844 he worked in the coin room of the Naples Museum, but, after an argument with the director of the museum, was transferred to Pompeii as an inspector of the excavations in 1847. Here he quickly came into conflict with Carlo Bonucci, the director of the excavations, accusing him of bribery and corruption. In a period of deepening political unrest that eventually would lead to the demise of the Bourbon dynasty, Bonucci's revenge was to accuse Fiorelli of political crimes, an accusation that led Fiorelli to be imprisoned for ten months. We do not know whether there was any basis in these claims or the extent of Fiorelli's involvement in the political events of the day, but once released from prison he was barred from any public position until Garibaldi's conquest of Naples enabled him to further his career at Pompeii.

Initially, Garibaldi appointed Alexandre Dumas (French author of *The Three Musketeers* and *The Man in the Iron Mask*), to the position of honorary director of the Naples Museum and of the excavations at Pompeii. Dumas had held a personal vendetta against the Bourbon dynasty and had provided Garibaldi's army with muskets and rifles. His new position was reward for his support. His plan was to write an illustrated history of Pompeii, and he wanted to intensify the excavations to generate more material for his study. Unfortunately for Dumas, the people of Naples were outraged at the appointment of this outsider and demonstrated in the streets. Dumas was forced to resign.

In 1860, Giuseppe Fiorelli became once more an inspector of the excavations; by 1863 he was Director of Pompeii and the Naples Museum and began to transform local archaeological methods. He was deeply influenced by the liberal thinking of his day, and the idea that archaeological remains should be more than simply entertainment for visitors.

Liberals sought to use archaeology as a tool to illustrate that unification of Italy was a natural and inevitable process, a restoration of former greatness rather than the creation of a new state. Perhaps the most important thing that Fiorelli did at Pompeii was to allow, for the first time, anyone to visit the excavations by instituting an entrance fee which paid for custodians and guides. Previously only nobles and notables had been able to obtain permission to see the antiquities; now they became part of the cultural heritage of the Italian people for the education and enjoyment of all.

In general under Fiorelli, the excavations became more systematic. Work focused on the area around the Stabian Baths and around the Via di Nola. At the same time, the areas left between the old excavations were cleared and old spoil heaps were removed to improve the appearance of the site. Excavators sought to penetrate buildings from above for the first time, layer by layer, rather than tunnelling in from the streets as had been the previous practice. This helped to prevent buildings from collapsing, until then a common problem during the excavations.

In order to put an end to amateur excavation, Fiorelli established an archaeological school in 1866 to train future excavators. To make it easier to locate particular houses and buildings within the excavations, and to put an end to the practice of

The remains of the Herculaneum Gate in 1890. This area of the town was one of the first to have been excavated after the discovery of the site in the 18th century.

naming buildings after random visitors or events, Fiorelli subdivided the town into Regions, *Insulae* (blocks of buildings) and doorways. This system, somewhat modified, is still in operation today. The address of the House of Menander, for example, is I.10.4, that is – Region I, Insula 10, entrance 4 (see also pp.8–9).

The excavation of Pompeii

Directors of the excavations
The titles and specific responsibilities of official members of Pompeii's administration have changed in different periods. The following is a brief chronology of those in charge of the excavations.

1748–1780	Rocque de Alcubiere (with Karl Weber from 1750–64, and Francesco La Vega from 1764–80)
1780–1804	Francesco La Vega
1807–1838	Michele Arditi
1808–1814	Pietro La Vega
1814–1825	Antonio Bonucci
1825–1828	Nicola D'Apuzzo
1839–1850	Francesco Maria Avellino
1850–1863	Sangiorgio Spinelli
1863–1875	Giuseppe Fiorelli
1875–1893	Michele Ruggiero
1893–1901	Giulio De Petra
1901–1905	Ettore Pais
1906–1910	Giulio De Petra and Antonio Sogliano
1911–1923	Vittorio Spinazzola
1924–1961	Amedeo Maiuri
1961–1976	Alfonso De Franciscis
1977–1981	Fausto Zevi
1981–1984	Giuseppina Cerulli Irelli
1984–1995	Baldassare Conticello
1995–	Pietro Giovanni Guzzo

Excavation dates of selected buildings

Public buildings
Amphitheatre 1748, 1813–16
Temple of Isis 1764–66
Large Theatre 1764–65, 1767–69, 1773, 1789, 1791–94
'Gladiatorial barracks' (theatre portico) 1766–69, 1771, 1792–95
Triangular Forum 1765, 1767–68, 1773, 1796–97, 1813
Covered Theatre (Odeon) 1769, 1792–95
Basilica 1813
Forum and all surrounding buildings 1816–21
Central Baths 1877–78
Temple of Venus 1897–98
Large Palaestra 1937–41

Houses
Praedia of Julia Felix (II.4.2) 1755–57
Villa of Cicero 1763
House of the Surgeon (VI.1.10) 1770–71, 1777
Villa of Diomedes 1771–74
House of Sallust (VI.2.4) 1805–9
House of the Tragic Poet (VI.8.5) 1824–25
House of the Dioscuri (VI.9.6) 1828–29

House of Meleagro (VI.9.2) 1829–30
House of the Faun (VI.12.2) 1830–32
House of the Labyrinth (VI.11.10) 1834–35
House of Apollo (VI.7.23) 1838
House of the Lyre-Player (I.4.25) 1853–72
House of Caecilius Jucundus (VI.1.26) 1875–76
House of the Centenary (IX.8.6) 1879–80
House of the Silver Wedding (V.2.i) 1891
House of the Vettii (VI.15.1) 1894–95
House of Marcus Lucretius Fronto (V.4.a) 1895
Villa of the Mysteries: room with the 'mysteries' paintings 1909–10; remainder of villa 1929–30
Fullery of Stephanus (I.6.7) 1911
House of Paquius Proculus (I.7.1) 1912–23
House of Menander (I.10.4) 1930–31
House of Fabius Rufus (VII. Ins. Occ. 16–19) 1960–79
House of Julius Polybius (IX.13.1–3) 1964–77
House of the Chaste Lovers (IX.12.6) 1987–

Fiorelli is possibly best known for creating plastercasts of victims of the eruption of AD 79. His training as a numismatist before coming to Pompeii had accustomed him to making casts of coins. The excavators of the site had been aware for some time that volcanic ash hardened around organic materials and preserved their shape even after soft tissue had decayed. In 1771, during the excavation of the Villa of Diomedes, the skeleton of a young girl had been uncovered. The shape of her bosom had been perfectly preserved when ash from the second phase of the eruption had hardened around her. Even before Fiorelli's arrival, the technique of using plaster of Paris to fill such cavities in the ash had been used to make plastercasts of wooden furniture. But Fiorelli was the first to apply the technique to the victims of the eruption and his results were remarkable, revealing details such as clothing and facial expression. Many bodies have since been found in rigid poses, due to the so-called 'pugilistic effect' – the extremely high temperatures during the eruption caused powerful muscle spasms and contractions that caused the contorted positions of many of the bodies. Since then, the technique has also been used to make casts of root cavities, which allows excavators to identify which plants and crops were grown in different gardens through the town.

Fiorelli's hand can also be seen in the new

An eye-witness account of the early plastercasts
The Times, *17 June 1893*

POMPEII. – A recent visitor writes as follows:-
There are now boulevards around Pompeii, and a road is being made for the carts which convey the rubbish in the direction of the Amphitheatre. From the top of those boulevards the visitor has a view of the whole city, and can form a tolerably correct idea of the interior of the houses uncovered. Excavations are now going on in two eminences near the Temple of Isis, and the house called Abondonza. Our inspection was chiefly confined to the former site, where, in a house situated in a narrow street recently opened, we saw several bodies, or rather forms of bodies, which now attract universal attention. The unfortunate inhabitants of this house fell, not on the bare ground, but on heaps of pumice stones, and were covered to a great depth by torrents of ashes and scoria, under which they have lain for nearly 2,000 years.

One day, inside a house, amid fallen roofs and ashes, the outline of a human body was perceived, and M. Fiorelli, the chief of the works for excavation, soon ascertained that there was a hollow under the surface. He accordingly made a small hole through its covering, and filled it up with liquid plaster of Paris, as if it were a mould. The result was that he obtained a complete plaster statue of a Roman lady of the first century of the Christian era. Close by were found the remains of a man, another woman, and a girl, with 91 pieces of silver money; four earrings and a finger-ring, all gold; two iron keys, and evident remains of a linen bag or purse. The whole of those bodies have been carefully moulded in plaster. The first body discovered was a woman lying on her right side, with her limbs contracted, as if she had died in convulsions. The form of the head-dress and the hair are quite distinct. On the bone of the little finger were two silver rings, and with this body were the remains of the purse above mentioned with the money and keys. The girl was found in an adjoining room, and the plaster mould taken of the cavity clearly shows the tissue of her dress. By her side lay an elderly woman, who had an iron ring on her little finger. The last personage I shall describe was a tall, well-made man, lying full length. The plaster distinctly shows his form, the folds of his garment, his torn sandals, his beard and hair. I contemplated these human forms with an interest which defies expression. It is evidence that all these unfortunates had made great efforts to escape destruction. The man appears to have perished in a vain attempt to rescue the terrified women, who thought they could be nowhere so safe as in their own home, and hoped that the fiery tempest would soon cease. From the money and the keys found with the body of the first woman, she was probably the mistress of the house and the mother of the girl. The slender bones of her arms and legs and the richness of her head-dress seem to indicate a woman of noble race. From the manner in which her hands were clenched she evidently died in great pain. The girl does not appear to have suffered much. From the appearance of the plaster mould it would seem that she fell from terror, as she was running with her skirts pulled over her head. The other woman, from the largeness of her ear, which is well shown by the plaster, and the iron ring on her finger, evidently belonged to a lower class, and was probably a servant of the family. The man appears to have been struck by lightning, for his straightened limbs show no signs of a death struggle. It is impossible to imagine a more affecting scene than the one suggested by these silent figures; nor have I ever heard of a drama so heartrending as the story of this family of the last days of Pompeii.

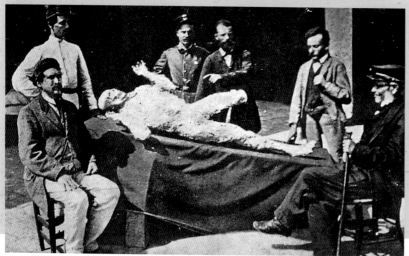

This photo from the late 19th century records one of the earliest plaster casts to have been made (in 1868).

Two of the first casts made by Fiorelli in 1863, illustrated by K. Grob, and (far right) an illustration of how plastercasts are made. The ash of the second phase of the eruption settled around the bodies of those who died in the disaster; as the bodies decomposed they left voids in the hardened ash which archaeologists have been able to fill with plaster.

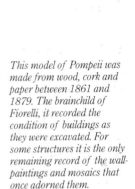

methods of documentation adopted. These included the first accurate plan of Pompeii and a cork model of the excavated remains was made, on a scale of 1:100, that accurately recorded the condition of the standing remains at that time. In addition, Fiorelli was responsible for the first real collation and publication of the excavation reports from the Bourbon period (*Pompeianarum Antiquitatum Historia*, 1860–64) and began publication of his own excavations (*Giornale degli Scavi di Pompei,* 1861–72). A guide to the town was also completed (*Descrizione di Pompei,* 1875), and, for the first time, foreign scholars were actively encouraged to publish their work on the remains.

Fiorelli's impact on Pompeii cannot be overestimated. Fundamentally he was motivated by an intense respect for the site and he defended it robustly. Ironically, these attitudes would lead to serious problems in succeeding years. Firstly, Fiorelli's over-respect for the monuments meant that he was against any form of restoration because he was anxious not to change anything. Secondly, under his tutelage it became almost impossible to export antiquities from Pompeii and Fiorelli ensured that the excavated finds remained in the possession of the Italian state, either on site or in the Naples Museum. This was a positive development, but unfortunately his influence could not extend to the territory surrounding Pompeii. Museums and private collectors could no longer obtain objects and wall-paintings from Pompeii itself, but they could still buy antiquities plundered from villa sites outside the town walls. The problem of unauthorized and unsupervised excavations on private land would eventually become a serious one.

This model of Pompeii was made from wood, cork and paper between 1861 and 1879. The brainchild of Fiorelli, it recorded the condition of buildings as they were excavated. For some structures it is the only remaining record of the wall-paintings and mosaics that once adorned them.

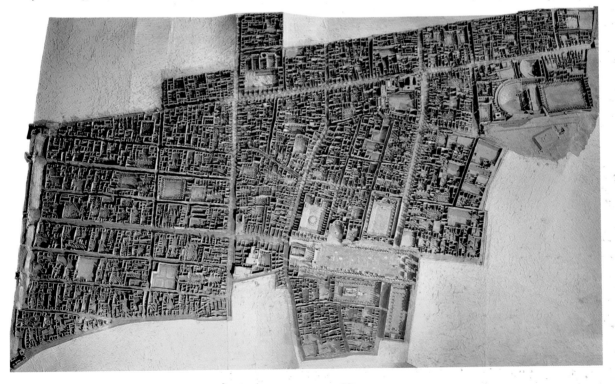

Developments at the Turn of the 20th Century

FIORELLI LEFT POMPEII FOR A NEW POSITION IN ROME IN 1874 but his work at Pompeii was continued by his successors. Old spoil heaps continued to be removed and excavations concentrated in the area of the Via di Nola. There was one vital difference, a new emphasis on the preservation and restoration of the ruins. It was during this time that serious attempts were made to preserve wall-paintings in situ, in response to the influential work on wall-painting published in 1882 by the German scholar, August Mau. Small roofs were constructed over some paintings to protect them from the elements and wax-coats were applied over others for the same reason. During this period only 50 out of 700 wall-paintings found during the excavations were removed to the museum. Perhaps the greatest act of restoration, however, was the reconstruction of parts of the House of the Silver Wedding (VI.2.1), which took place to honour the wedding anniversary of the king of Italy in 1893. This was the first

large-scale reconstruction to take place in Pompeii, and served as a model for future such work. In 1894 the House of the Vettii (VI.15.1) was completely excavated and restored. All the garden sculpture and many of the household objects were preserved in situ in the house, with the aim of recreating an image of daily life in the ancient town. Consequently the House of the Vettii became the most lauded and most visited house in the whole of Pompeii.

The problem of clandestine excavations

It was around this time that the problem of private and clandestine excavations outside the town limits came to a head. These excavations were largely unsupervised by the authorities and artifacts were commonly removed and sold. In 1895 the authorities were unable to stop the export of large numbers of silver vessels, gold coins and jewelry discovered in a villa at Boscoreale to the Louvre in Paris (see box overleaf).

The excavation of the Via dell' Abbondanza

It was not until 16 July 1910 that excavations within the walls of Pompeii intensified once more, when a new director, Vittorio Spinazzola, initiated a new campaign of work. In his publication of these excavations (1953), he describes how, during an earlier study of wall-paintings, he had noticed that ancient houses were often represented as having

upper floors with windows, balconies and terraces. Previous excavators had generally removed the more fragmentary evidence for upper floors (usually damaged in the eruption) in order to reach the more complete and more interesting ground floor of a house or shop. Therefore Spinazzola's new excavations were designed to reconstruct systematically, and as fully as possible, the facades of the Pompeian houses along with their windows, balconies and roofs. In order to achieve this aim, the excavations were conducted along almost the whole length of the Via dell' Abbondanza with the aim of reaching the Sarno Gate. Excavations proceeded horizontally, level by level, in order to record carefully the remains of the house facades, which were restored as they were excavated. In total, Spinazzola's campaign uncovered 600 m (2,000 ft) of the Via dell' Abbondanza, and revealed one of the most important thoroughfares of the ancient town. On occasion, Spinazzola also excavated further into some of the more interesting looking houses along this street, such as the House of the Cryptoporticus (I.6.2), House of the Moralist (III.4.2–3), House of Loreius Tiburtinus (II.2.2), and the House of Paquius Proculus (I.7.1). Unfortunately, he was unable to finish his work at Pompeii – the advent of World War I brought an abrupt end to his work. After the war, his opposition to the new Fascist regime meant that he was forced to step down as director at Pompeii.

Excavations of the Via dell' Abbondanza from 1910 onwards revealed the vibrancy of this arterial street in antiquity – the painted facades of its shops and houses, the street shrines and paintings of the gods, and the electoral posters – together with previously undiscovered upper storeys and balconies.

The Boscoreale Silver

In 1876, several rooms of a Roman villa were discovered on the property of Luigi Modestino Pulzella in Boscoreale. The excavation of these rooms was halted when it became clear that the ancient remains crossed into the property of Pulzella's neighbour, Angelo Andrea de Prisco. De Prisco himself was not interested in the excavations, but his son, Vincenzo, asked permission from the authorities to continue them in 1894. Vincenzo discovered a large country villa, with richly decorated rooms and a bathhouse, and areas for the pressing and storage of wine and olive oil. Although impressive, it was the fabulous finds made here that gave the villa its fame – 108 silver vessels and 1,037 gold coins dating to the Augustan age.

The events surrounding the discovery of the Boscoreale treasure remain obscure. Vincenzo had already made a few finds of bronze and silver during his excavations, and had offered to sell them to the Italian State at a very high price. The Director of the Naples Museum, Giulio De Petra, had asked the government for funds to purchase these objects but had been refused. So Vincenzo sold them to the highest bidder. This caused outrage amongst the authorities and Vincenzo's permit to excavate was revoked. Despite this, he widened his excavations and some time over Easter 1895 made a sensational discovery. At a time when most of the workmen were absent, either due to the Easter holiday or because of bad weather, a few men were finishing the excavation of two cisterns that led into the wine cellar. A workman called Michele complained that there were poisonous fumes in one of the cisterns. None of the workmen wanted to carry on digging, so they left. Michele himself went to Vincenzo and told him that he had seen a dead body in the midst of silver vessels, earrings, rings, bracelets and a bag full of gold coins. As soon as night fell, the two men returned to the cistern and recovered the treasure. Its discovery was kept secret from the start.

De Petra was aware that excavations had continued on Vincenzo's land, but the ambiguity of Italian law made him unsure what to do. On the one hand, Bourbon decrees that forbade private

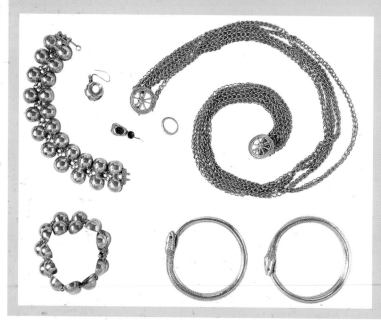

(Above and left) The silver service and gold jewelry found in a cistern of the Villa Pisanella. Their illegal sale to the Louvre caused outcry in Italy and eventually led to the clarification of the laws concerning the export of Italian antiquities. Few equivalent hoards have ever been found at Pompeii.

excavations had been adopted by the new Italian State; on the other, these laws were incompatible with the new and inviolable right of private landowners in unified Italy to do as they pleased on their own property. Vincenzo was not the only landowner to flout the ancient laws. De Petra hesitated, and asked for clarification from the government – should he suspend the excavations straight away or wait until objects were found? Before the issue could be resolved, news came of Vincenzo's spectacular discovery and almost immediately afterwards of its sale and clandestine export. Vincenzo had approached the Louvre in Paris, offering to sell the entire collection for half a million francs. The Louvre was prepared to pay only half of the requested price, but it still gained the treasure: it was bought by Baron Edmond de Rothschild who kept a few pieces for his own collection and donated the remaining silver vessels and all of the gold coins to the Louvre. Less than a month had passed from the initial discovery of the treasure.

De Petra was accused of incompetence and was suspended from his position at the museum. Investigations into the affair continued for several years, and eventually new laws were passed to prevent the sale and export of such important artifacts. However, another scandal had occurred in the meantime – the famous wall-paintings from the Villa of Publius Fannius Synistor near Boscoreale were sold to the Metropolitan Museum in New York. This villa had been discovered on private property in 1900 and the paintings were removed, framed and auctioned off.

'Room M' from the Villa of Fannius Synistor at Boscoreale, now in the Metropolitan Museum, New York. The frescos of this bedroom depict landscapes and townscapes within architectural frameworks and date to the 1st century BC. The bed is a modern addition and has been reconstructed wrongly – it should have only one headrest.

Amedeo Maiuri and the 'Nuovi Scavi'

AMEDEO MAIURI OFFICIALLY SUCCEEDED SPINAZZOLA as Superintendent of Naples and Campania on 1 September 1924, and held this post for a period of 38 years, until 1962. Initially, his task was to finish the excavations begun by Spinazzola along the Via dell' Abbondanza, and he focused on clearing particular houses, including the House of the Ephebe (I.7.11), the House of Fabius Amandus (I.7.3) and the House of the Cryptoporticus. But Maiuri had grander plans and the political climate of the time enabled him to pursue them.

With an attitude similar to that held by politicians in Fiorelli's day, Mussolini and his Fascist party saw the archaeological remains of Italy as evidence of Italy's greatness in the past and the inevitability of her future greatness. Maiuri benefited from enormous funding and was able to

Amedeo Maiuri during the excavations of the House of Venus in a Shell (II.3.3). Unveiling the now-famous wall-painting of Venus to scholars and journalists in October 1952, Maiuri described her as 'the prototype of a Neapolitan beauty – florid, fleshy, luscious. In short, what you Anglo-Saxons would call a girl with sex appeal.'

Bomb damage to Pompeii
The Times, *9 November, 1943*

DAMAGE AT POMPEII.
BRITISH OFFICER'S ACCOUNT
'We have received from a British officer, who recently visited Pompeii, an account of the damage done to the place during September, when the Germans were encamped on the site and allied aircraft were obliged to treat it as a military objective. The following is a summary of the damage observed:

'There is one crater in the arena of the Amphitheatre, and several near misses. The wall of the Gladiator's Training School was hit in three places. There is a crater in the eastern end of the Via dell' Abbondanza, to which incomplete excavation had prevented further damage. The houses of Rex Tiburtinus and of Trebius Valens were hit. The Cenacoli and house of Epidius Rufus were destroyed. The houses used for restorations north of the Via degli Augustali and the adjoining house were destroyed. The Temple of Jupiter on the western side of the Forum was hit. The Temple of Apollo and the House of Triptolemus north of the Via Marina were badly damaged. The Museum is now in ruins, but how much of the contents perished remains to be disclosed. The director of the excavations at Pompeii, Professor Maiuri, whose contributions to The Times will be remembered, was last heard of in a hospital at Torre del Greco with a leg injury received in an air raid.

'The officer was told that two bombs had fallen on the Temple of Hercules in Region 8, and that the Houses of Sallust and Pansa in Region 6 had also received direct hits.'

Plan of Pompeii showing some of the houses and buildings damaged in the Allied bombing of 1943.

conduct his excavations on an extremely large scale. One of the major results of this was the revival of excavations at Herculaneum in 1927. By 1942, only 15 years later, almost the whole area of the town visible to visitors today had been uncovered. Excavations at Pompeii also gained new impetus from the available funds and were intensified. A large part of Region I was excavated, and work was continued along the Via dell' Abbondanza to reach the Large Palaestra and the Amphitheatre. The period leading up to World War II included his two greatest discoveries, the Villa of the Mysteries outside the Herculaneum Gate and the House of Menander (I.10.4). Maiuri produced elaborate publications of both these 'prize' excavations, which were immediately restored and opened to the public. Moreover, for the first time in Pompeii's history, restoration of nearly all the excavated buildings took place, not just of those deemed exceptional or interesting. Maiuri was also interested in the history and development of Pompeii as a town and conducted excavations beneath the subsoil in various parts of the town, including the Forum, Triangular Forum, and the House of the Surgeon (VI.1.10).

World War II stopped all work at Pompeii. On 24 August and from 13–26 September 1943, in the belief that German soldiers were hiding in the ruins, the Allies bombed Pompeii. In fact, there were Germans stationed in hotels outside the Marine Gate, but none in the excavations. At least 150 bombs were dropped. Maiuri himself was shot in the foot while attempting to escape to Naples during the bombardment. As the Germans later retreated, there were some reports of looting in the excavations.

The 3rd Algerian Regiment of the French army held a feast in the Amphitheatre of Pompeii on 22 April 1944. Seen here are the Commander of the US 2nd Corps, Major General Geoffrey Keyes, the British General Officer Commanding Naples District, Major General J. L. Collier and the Commander of the French Expeditionary Corps, General Juin.

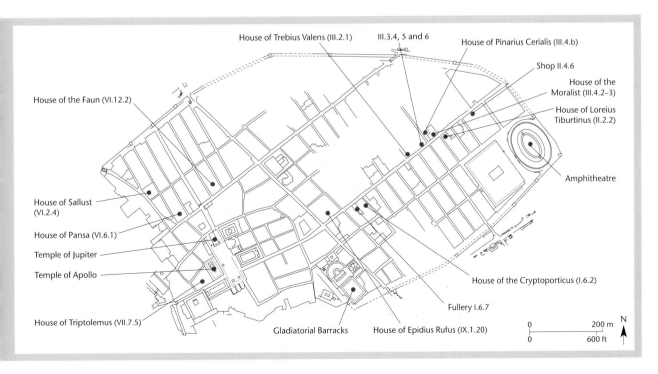

House of Trebius Valens (III.2.1)
III.3.4, 5 and 6
House of Pinarius Cerialis (III.4.b)
Shop II.4.6
House of the Faun (VI.12.2)
House of the Moralist (III.4.2–3)
House of Loreius Tiburtinus (II.2.2)
Amphitheatre
House of Sallust (VI.2.4)
House of Pansa (VI.6.1)
Temple of Jupiter
Temple of Apollo
House of the Cryptoporticus (I.6.2)
House of Triptolemus (VII.7.5)
Fullery I.6.7
Gladiatorial Barracks
House of Epidius Rufus (IX.1.20)

0   200 m
0   600 ft

N

Post-War Developments and Changes

AFTER THE WAR THE EXCAVATIONS WERE STARTED again as part of a five-year plan of public works designed to provide employment in the region, particularly by opening up centres of interest to tourists. The enormous old spoil heaps from past excavations of Pompeii that had built up next to the southern town walls were removed. This material was rich in humus and was used as fertilizer on land neighbouring the site. Excavations also continued in Region I at an incredible speed, sometimes with up to a hundred workmen in one house. The volcanic fill that was removed from these excavations was used in the construction of the motorway from Naples to Salerno. The excavation of the remaining parts of Region I and of Region II was completed within the space of ten years. There are no publications at all of this work, and in general the surviving excavation reports are of extremely poor quality. This is hardly surprising given the speed of the excavations, but it means that there is little available information about a large part of Region I.

Excavations since the 1960s

Since Maiuri's retirement in 1962, excavations at Pompeii have been restricted to certain areas and houses in an effort to preserve the site from further ruin. With such large areas of the town open to the elements, conservation has become a major issue. Thus only a few new houses have been excavated: the House of Fabius Rufus (VII. Ins. Occ. 16–19), the House of Julius Polybius (IX.13.1–3) and the House of the Chaste Lovers (IX.12.6) and the neighbouring House of the Painters at Work. Excavation has proceeded hand in hand with restoration, and there is detailed documentation for all these houses. In the last ten years or so there have also been a growing number of projects designed to investigate beneath the AD 79 level of the town, to understand its history and development.

Today the major concern of Pompeii's superintendent is conservation, and rightly so. There are over 15,000 buildings to maintain on the site, and 20,000 sq. m (215,000 sq. ft) of wall-paintings to conserve – an almost impossible task. Conservation is painstaking and extremely expensive, and only slows down

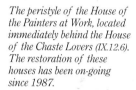

The peristyle of the House of the Painters at Work, located immediately behind the House of the Chaste Lovers (IX.12.6). The restoration of these houses has been on-going since 1987.

(Left) This room in the House of the Painters at Work was being redecorated in AD 79. The central panel of this wall contains only a traced outline of a scene that has not yet been painted. Paint-pots and the remains of brushes and other tools had been abandoned here, presumably as the artists sought to flee the eruption.

(Below) Conservation of the wall-paintings of Villa A at Oplontis in November 2006. The preservation of the excavated sites is a major concern today, and a hugely expensive one.

the inevitable decay. The situation has been made much worse by the growth of mass tourism. In January 2007 alone there were over 50,000 visitors to the site, and each year there are more than 2 million visitors in total – and they are having a dramatic impact. Many buildings are now structurally unsound and have been shut to the public. In other houses, such as the House of Menander (I.10.4) and the House of Julius Polybius (IX.13.1–3), efforts have been made to restrict the number of visitors by requiring tourists to book guided tours. The result is that visitors can now wander freely in only 30 per cent of the site; the rest is closed off or restricted. The situation is similar at Herculaneum where there is now a major project aiming to slow down the rate of decay.

The experience of the visitor to Pompeii and Herculaneum today is deeply influenced by the history of the excavations of these two sites. Work has been going on at Pompeii for over 250 years. Aims and methods have changed according to political circumstances and the agendas and beliefs of the men in charge of the excavations, and this in turn has affected what can be learnt about these sites today. Large parts of Regions VII and VIII appear ruinous today in marked contrast to the recently restored parts of Region I, simply because of the different periods in which they were excavated and the different attitudes held by their excavators. Archaeological techniques have changed dramatically from period to period and have only become what might be described as modern and scientific in the last 20 years.

III
BIRTH AND GROWTH OF A ROMAN TOWN

Every where, you see things that make you wonder how old these old houses were before the night of destruction came….

Mark Twain, *The Innocents Abroad*, 1869

It did not occur to the first excavators of Pompeii that they should do anything other than clear the volcanic debris and remove the treasures that had been buried by it – they had no interest in digging beneath the surface of the town to find out how it had developed. As later scholars have become interested in the origins of Pompeii, its remarkable preservation has actively hindered their investigations. To dig beneath the level of AD 79 in many parts of the town would require the destruction of floors and decorative pavements. Understandably, the authorities have been reluctant to allow this to happen, which means that such excavation can only take place in areas where there is little or nothing to destroy, such as rooms with no permanent flooring or gardens.

In recent years, despite these problems, there has been an upsurge of interest in the history of Pompeii before AD 79, and a corresponding increase in the number of stratigraphic excavations in different parts of the town. The results of these excavations, together with descriptions by ancient writers of events in the 1st millennium BC, have begun to generate a clearer picture of Pompeii's origins and development, even if there are many questions yet to be answered in full.

View of Pompeii's Forum – the heart of the town – looking north towards Vesuvius. It was formally laid out in the 2nd century BC, although there is some evidence of activity on the site before this.

The Traditional Account of Pompeii's Origins and Development

IN THE EARLY 1ST CENTURY AD, THE GREEK GEOGRAPHER Strabo wrote a description of the Bay of Naples, and commented on the history of some of its settlements:

> Near to Naples is the hill-fort of Herculaneum whose highest point juts out into the sea, catching the sea-breeze so wonderfully as to make it a healthy place to live. The Oscans used to occupy both Herculaneum and Pompeii next to it, past which the River Sarno flows. Then the Etruscans and the Pelasgians, and after that, the Samnites; these peoples were also thrown out of these places.
>
> Strabo, Geography V.4.8

Debate about the origins and urban development of Pompeii (Herculaneum has been largely ignored) has hinged on this passage, and another similar to it by Pliny the Elder (*Natural History* 3.60–2), for the past hundred years and more. Traditionally, it has been thought that Pompeii was inhabited first by local Oscan people, then taken over in succession by the Greeks, Etruscans and Samnites before falling under Roman control around 290 BC. The problem with the traditional picture of Pompeii's development is that little of it is based on archaeological evidence. But with the growing number of stratigraphic excavations at Pompeii it is possible to give a more detailed account of Pompeii's early history.

Stratigraphic excavations at Pompeii

What follows is a very brief account of some of the major archaeological work that has taken place.

The first to draw attention to Strabo's account was Giuseppe Fiorelli, in 1873. He related the physical development of Pompeii to changes in its population and proposed that the Greeks, Etruscans, Samnites and Romans used different building materials in their structures. Almost immediately, in 1877, Heinrich Nissen claimed that Fiorelli's chronological framework was too rigid, but he was largely ignored. Within a few years, August Mau had revised Fiorelli's chronology and added a further chronology of wall decoration. Again based on a literary account (this time by the Roman architect, Vitruvius, who wrote in the Augustan period), Mau divided wall-painting into four 'styles', each relating to a different chronological period (see Chapter VI).

The next major contribution to study of Pompeii's prehistory came in 1913 when the renowned British historian Francis Haverfield hypothesized an original nucleus or 'Altstadt' ('old city') in the southwest corner of the town (the area surrounding the Forum and Triangular Forum), around which the rest of the town grew up over time. This remains a controversial and much debated idea.

When Amedeo Maiuri became Superintendent of Pompeii in 1926 he set out, amongst his many other

This plan indicates where archaic (8th–6th century BC) structures and objects have been found in Pompeii, and demonstrates that they are not restricted to the 'Altstadt' but are found all over the site.

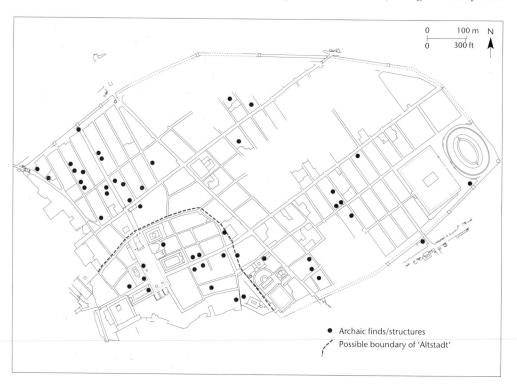

● Archaic finds/structures
╌╌ Possible boundary of 'Altstadt'

labours, to test the by now established chronology of Pompeii's foundation and development. Between 1926 and 1942, Maiuri undertook stratigraphic excavations in a series of houses, and in the Forum, Basilica, Stabian Baths, Large Theatre, Doric Temple and Temple of Apollo. His most famous excavation was in the House of the Surgeon (VI.1.10), thought by many scholars to be the oldest house in Pompeii on the basis of its facade of huge tuff blocks (a technique known as opus quadratum). Instead, the discovery of black-glaze Campanian pottery led Maiuri to date its construction to the 3rd century BC. However, the foundations of older houses were found frequently beneath the houses in which he excavated, and his excavations of the Doric Temple and the Temple of Apollo uncovered 6th-century BC Etruscan and Greek pottery.

Interest in Pompeii's foundation and development revived in 1970 when the German archaeologist Hans Eschebach revisited the question of the 'Altstadt' and proposed that it grew up in two distinct phases. Other research projects quickly followed. Between 1976 and 1979, Cristina Chiaramonte Treré and Maria Bonghi Jovino of the University of Milan conducted excavations in Insula VI.5, and particularly in the House of the Etruscan Column (VI.5.17). The standing structures of this house could only be dated to the 2nd century BC, and the excavators later concluded that it was likely that the majority of Pompeii's houses dated to the 3rd or 2nd centuries BC, and not to the 4th century as previously believed.

In 1980–81, during work to supply the modern offices on the site with new electric cables, Paul Arthur supervised stratigraphic excavations in and around the Forum. The excavations were expected to uncover the perimeter of the 'Altstadt', but failed to do this. Although some deposits of pottery could be dated to the 6th and 4th centuries BC, in general it was concluded that the monumentalization of the Forum had not begun before the 2nd century BC.

The fortifications were next area to be investigated. In 1985 Stefano De Caro excavated the walls at the Nuceria Gate and uncovered an archaic pappamonte (soft volcanic tuff) wall beneath the later wall and pottery of the 6th century BC. He concluded that the walls had been built at the same time that the town plan was laid out. Then in 1989, with Antonio D'Ambrosio, De Caro published the results of excavations in the House of the Clay Moulds (VII.4.62). Once again, the standing structures could only be dated to the 2nd century BC. Beneath these, traces of a 4th/3rd BC century structure were uncovered.

Major work took place between 1987 and 1995 in Regions I and II. Antonio De Simone and Salvatore Nappo excavated a series of 'row houses', and on the basis of ceramic finds suggested that the original layout of Region I should be dated to the late 3rd century BC or early 2nd century BC. Further excavations along the facades of houses on major thoroughfares of the town revealed little or no building activity earlier than the 3rd century BC. The excavators suggested that there was a rapid expansion of the town and simultaneous development of many insulae at the end of the 3rd century BC or beginning of the 2nd century BC.

Since the mid-1990s there have been many stratigraphic excavations in different parts of Pompeii. From 1995 to 1999, the British School at Rome and the University of Reading (led by Andrew Wallace-Hadrill and Michael Fulford) excavated in Houses 11 and 12 in Insula I.9 (known collectively as the House of Amarantus). The house itself was dated to the 2nd century BC, but archaic structures were found beneath it on the same alignment as the later house. The excavators concluded that Pompeii's road layout, and thus probably its entire wall circuit, gates and towers, dated to the 6th century BC. In the same period, from 1995 to 2000, the the University of Rome 'La Sapienza' (directed by Andrea Carandini and Paolo Carafa) conducted excavations in various parts of the proposed 'Altstadt'. There was some evidence of archaic structures in this area, but no evidence of major building activity prior to the 2nd century BC. And from 1995 to 2005 the University of Bradford (directed by Rick Jones and Damian Robinson) excavated in Insula VI.1, including the House of the Vestals and the House of the Surgeon. The earliest evidence of occupation on this site dates to the 4th century BC.

Understanding of Pompeii's origins and development is increasing every year.

This terracotta bust, along with other votives and offerings such as miniature vases and loom weights, was found in 1995 during stratigraphic excavations of the portico of the Triangular Forum. The objects were discovered in a series of rooms that had been constructed along the north side of the Triangular Forum in the 2nd century BC, and later demolished to make room for the portico.

Traditional chronology of construction techniques

Strabo's chronology of Pompeii had profound influence on how the origins and development of Pompeii have been studied. Primarily, attempts have been made to associate particular parts of the town, different construction techniques and materials, and different decorative styles with the different peoples he described. Thus particular construction techniques have been attributed to discrete chronological periods.

c. 650 BC onwards	**Opus Quadratum.** Large squared blocks of local tuff, erected without mortar.
500 BC onwards	**Opus Africanum.** Grids of large blocks of Sarno limestone filled with rubble, bonded with clay.
c. 200 BC onwards	**Opus Incertum.** A concrete core, combining limestone and tuff rubble, sand and lime mortar, faced on both sides with small irregular stones.
60 BC onwards	**Opus Reticulatum.** Concrete-faced with pyramid-shaped blocks forming a regular pattern and **Opus Latericium**, the same but using fired brick instead of stone for the facing.
late 1st century BC onwards	**Opus Craticum.** Thin wall of lightweight Opus Incertum enclosed within a wooden frame, used mainly for partition walls and in the construction of upper storeys.
AD 35 onwards	**Opus Vittatum Mixtum.** Concrete core faced with alternating rows of rectangular blocks and courses of brick or tile.

(Below) The opus quadratum walls of the House of the Surgeon (VI.1.10).

Opus Quadratum

Opus Africanum

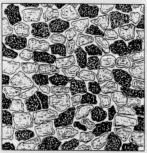

Opus Incertum

Opus Reticulatum

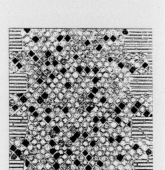

Opus Latericium

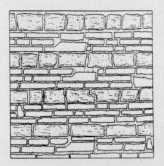

Opus Vittatum Mixtum

(Left) The six main construction techniques in evidence at Pompeii.

House III.13–15 at Herculaneum, one of the best examples of a timber framework filled with rubble and lime known as Opus Craticum. This light-weight technique was used mainly in the construction of upper storeys and partition walls.

Campania before the Foundation of Pompeii: The Cultural Context

CAMPANIA IS A REGION OF FLAT PLAINS AND GOOD natural harbours, encircled by mountains on three sides, and it is hardly surprising that there is evidence of settlement dating back to the Neolithic and Bronze Ages throughout its confines. Most recently, in 2001, the remains of an early Bronze Age village that had been destroyed in an eruption of Vesuvius in the 4th millennium BC were discovered on the outskirts of the modern town of Nola.

By the Iron Age, relatively large numbers of small farming settlements were already exploiting the fertility of these plains. Many of these settlements also became important trading-posts due to Campania's central location within Italy and the ease of communications by river and coastal waters. Metal objects and armour found in tombs reveal that by the 9th century BC there had already been contact between the native peoples of Campania and the Villanovan peoples to their north. Trade in metals also brought the Greeks to Campania in the course of the 8th century BC.

At the beginning of the 8th century BC, a trading-post was established at Pithecusae (the island of Ischia) by Greeks who came from Euboea. Excavation at the site of this emporium revealed evidence of smelting and demonstrates clearly the purpose of the Greek settlement on the island. The Greeks must have been encouraged by their success and unthreatened by the local population for, by 775 BC, they had established a proper colony on the mainland, at Cumae. This settlement, the first 'city' in Campania, came to dominate northern Campania over the next three centuries. Not only did it control a large territory, it had political control other Greek colonies later established at Misenum, Dicaearchia (Puteoli) and Neapolis (Naples). By the second half of the 6th century BC, the western parts of the Bay of Naples were securely in Greek hands, under the control of Cumae. To the south, Greek political influence is not explicitly attested, but it is likely that at least some of the southern settlements were Greek in origin – Herculaneum, whose layout owes much to Greek ideas of town-planning, is one possibility. Greek influence was also felt in the smaller coastal settlements and villages of the interior. Nothing is known of the political organisation of these villages – such as Aequanum (Vico Equense) and Surrentum (Sorrento) on the coast and Striano and San Valentino Torio in the Sarno Valley – but archaeological finds from their cemeteries include Greek pottery and (in the 6th century) inscriptions that use a Greek alphabet. This reveals a high degree of contact between the newly-arrived Greeks and the local peoples of Campania.

Other common archaeological finds in the region (and in the region to the north of Campania) dating from the 8th century BC are Etruscan. The Etruscans are thought to have been an indigenous Italian people. Their culture was at its height during the 6th century BC. They were great traders, and their metalwork was highly valued by others. The arrival of the Greeks in Campania appears to have stimulated trade with the Etruscans, and

Attic black figure vases – such as this amphora which depicts Dionysus with two Maenads – have been found in many different sites on the Bay of Naples, and attest to the presence of Greek traders and settlers in the region from the 8th century BC.

(Right) This Etruscan bronze warrior, a votive offering found in Campania, dates from the 5th century BC, when Etruscan influence in the region was beginning to wane.

Etruscan pottery (known as bucchero), architectural terracottas and metal artifacts were widespread in the region in this period. It appears that relationships between the Greeks and Etruscans were initially friendly. One of the oldest Etruscan inscriptions in the region (dating to the end of the 8th century BC) comes from the Greek town of Cumae and records a gift made by an Etruscan to a Greek inhabitant of Cumae. The complexity of ethnic relationships in Campania in this period are further highlighted by the discovery in the Etruscan town of Nola of an Attic black-glazed bowl, on which had been scratched in the Oscan language, but using Etruscan letters, 'I am of Lucius Nevius'.

For a time, the Etruscans were content merely to trade with the peoples of Campania, but in the mid-7th century BC they began to settle in Campania themselves. This was a period of Etruscan expansion in Italy documented by our ancient literary sources. The Etruscans settled first at Cales and Capua, then in Nola, Nuceria and in the towns of the Sarno Valley. Archaeologically, this is seen in the large amounts of Etruscan metalwork and pottery found at Capua and Nola from c. 650 BC. We have no idea how the Etruscans gained control of these settlements, which had already been established by native Campanians, but under the Etruscans they were quickly built up. Nor do we have a clear picture of the political organization of these towns. The Etruscans may have formed an aristocratic class over the native inhabitants, they may have formed political alliances with the local peoples, or they may simply have exerted cultural and economic influence over the native Campanians. The evidence of ceramics and inscriptions demonstrates that Stabiae, for example, was a strongly Etruscophone trading-post from the 7th century BC, but its inhabitants also maintained their own cultural identity by using a local Nucerian, rather than Etruscan, alphabet that developed in the 6th century BC.

By the mid-6th century both the Greeks and the Etruscans had established stable power-bases in Campania, located on the coast and in the interior respectively, and the first signs of conflict between them started to appear.

(Above) This drawing made by Christoph Heinrich Kniep in 1790 depicts Sir William and Emma Hamilton standing beside an open tomb in the forest of Nola, examining newly discovered Greek painted vases.

(Right) Model of a tomb at Nola, based on Kniep's illustration, and one of several made by Domenico Padaglione. Both the drawing and the model depict 'un tombeau ordinaire', an ordinary tomb, and illustrate the context in which Greek vases were normally discovered.

The Foundation of Pompeii

(Opposite) Wall-painting of Hercules discovering his son, Telephus, from the basilica in Herculaneum. Images of Hercules are common at Pompeii and Herculaneum.

This architectural terracotta, which would probably have adorned the roof of the Doric Temple, depicts the goddess Minerva. It was found during the 18th-century excavations of the Triangular Forum and Doric Temple.

THE ANCIENT WRITERS BELIEVED THAT POMPEII AND Herculaneum were founded before the Trojan War, at the time of Hercules' travels. Modern historians, however, have been reluctant to accept the possibility of a permanent settlement on the site of Pompeii before the 6th century BC. The reason for this is the lack of evidence for a nearby cemetery or of remains of physical structures before this date – the oldest structures in Pompeii, the Temple of Apollo, the so-called Doric Temple and the town walls, were all initially constructed in the period *c.* 600–550 BC.

Despite this, there is some evidence of prehistoric activity on the site, dating back to the Neolithic period (namely a stone axe discovered outside the Nuceria Gate and material beneath the street next to the House of the Chaste Lovers (IX.12.6)). From the Bronze Age, pottery fragments dating to the first half of the 2nd millennium BC were found during stratigraphic excavations in the House of Marcus Lucretius Fronto (V.4.a) and near the Temple of Venus. Pottery and bronzes dating to the 9th and 8th centuries BC have been found in the Temple of Apollo, the so-called Doric Temple, the Temple of Isis, and again in the House of Marcus Lucretius Fronto. There is now also evidence for Iron Age cemeteries in the area around Pompeii, such as the recently discovered burials at Striano.

Should these signs of activity be interpreted as evidence of settlement on the site before the 6th century BC? As the number of stratigraphic excavations at Pompeii has increased over the last few years, so too has evidence for occupation that dates to at least the 8th or 7th centuries BC – small pits, post-holes and a very few potsherds in the House of Amarantus (I.9.11/12), deposits of Etrusco-indigenous pottery (although not related to structures) under the House of the Etruscan Column (VI.5.17), post-holes under the House of Joseph II (VIII.2.38–39), possible evidence of wooden huts in the area of the Triangular Forum and ceramic fragments under a shop (VII.2.16–17). Further excavations are likely to turn up even more evidence. It seems probable, then, that there was a small rural settlement or settlements here before the foundation of the town proper, which most likely occurred during the 6th century BC.

The nature of Pompeii's foundation in the 6th century is another contentious issue. Given the extensive influence of both Greeks and Etruscans in Campania, the question is whether either group was directly responsible for establishing this new settlement, or whether it evolved from a native rural settlement already on the site. Certainly the enlargement from small rural settlement to small town implies an increase in population that probably came from outside. There is no clear answer to this question since the evidence itself is ambiguous. Given the strategic importance of Pompeii's location, overlooking the mouth of the Sarno, it is likely that both Greeks and Etruscans were interested in its development, and we find archaeological evidence for the presence of both groups at Pompeii in the 6th century BC.

The so-called Doric Temple is Greek in plan and ornament, suggesting at the very least that Greek workmen, if not Greek settlers, were employed in its construction. Indeed, there are parallels with other Greek cities: the architectural terracottas that decorated the Doric Temple are very similar to ones found at Cumae, and on the basis of these terracottas it has been suggested that the Doric Temple was dedicated to the deities Minerva and Hercules. However, both Greek and Etruscan pottery has been found at this site. The evidence of the existence of the Temple of Apollo in this period is shakier, since the only structural evidence for it is a stone block of Greek-style architectural moulding. But ceramic evidence on this site, again consisting of both Greek and Etruscan pottery fragments, some of them with dedicatory inscriptions in Etruscan, has been dated to the 6th century BC, so it is not unreasonable to hypothesize a temple here. There is no evidence to confirm that this temple was

actually dedicated to Apollo in its earliest phase, but cults of Apollo are known from the Greek cities of Cumae and Neapolis in this period so Pompeii may well have had such a cult as well. The mix of Greek and Etruscan archaeological material found at these two temple sites forms a pattern found elsewhere at Pompeii. In the House of Amarantus and the House of Bacchus (VII.4.10), for example, both Attic pottery and Etruscan bucchero were uncovered in the same 6th-century contexts.

It may be that Pompeii was a Greek settlement that traded with Etruscans, although it is interesting that the ancient historians themselves considered the territory around Pompeii either to be Etruscan or settled by peoples allied to the Etruscans. In addition, it is important to ask why this small community felt the need for the fortifications that were constructed at the time of its foundation. Did a Greek settlement fear Etruscan attack, or vice versa? Did a native population seek to protect itself from both Greek and Etruscan domination? Or did the walls function merely to mark out and defend agricultural land from other potential settlers? As yet, we have no clear answers to these questions.

Another traditional debate concerns the hypothetical existence of an original urban nucleus, described by German scholars as the 'Altstadt' ('old city'). Since 1913, scholars have pointed to the irregular layout of streets and housing blocks in the southwest corner of the town and suggested that this was the first part of the town to be settled. Other areas of the town, with their more regular grid layouts are thought to have developed gradually over the following centuries as deliberate acts of town planning. The entire question of the 'Altstadt' remains controversial, particularly since recent stratigraphic excavations have begun to increase our knowledge of Pompeii in its earliest phases. There may have been a concentration of settlement in the area of the so-called 'Altstadt', but there were certainly also scattered structures throughout the walled extent of Pompeii. Thus, for example, we now know that there were archaic buildings under the Basilica and under the municipal buildings at the south end of the Forum, an H-shaped building under the House of Amarantus, and pappamonte (soft local tuff) foundations under the House of the Wedding of Hercules (VII.9.47). What is interesting is that these fragmentary remains of Pompeii's first structures often have the same alignment and orientation as the houses of later periods. This suggests that the town was planned and laid out at the time of its foundation.

The street grid appears to be much older than the existing standing structures. In this early period, the number of inhabitants presumably was still small and the community was mainly agricultural in character, similar to other known settlements in the region, such as nearby Stabiae. It is likely that much of the land within the walls that would later be built over was farmed.

This picture of archaic Pompeii may seem very incomplete, and it is hard to visualize what Pompeii would have looked like in the first years after its foundation. Later building has obliterated the original archaic structures and despite the increasing numbers of stratigraphic excavations, there are no complete plans of any buildings that date back to the 6th century BC, only fragments. Yet, archaeologically, we know more about Pompeii in the 6th century BC than we do about Pompeii in the 5th or 4th centuries BC. The 5th century in particular was a tumultuous period in Campanian history, recorded in detail by the ancient historians, and it may well be that the inhabitants of Pompeii suffered as a result. It was in this period that the Greeks and Etruscans first came into conflict, and the Samnites began to exert influence in the region.

The Samnites

The Samnites were an Oscan-speaking indigenous people living in the mountains of central and southern Italy. They appear to have been loosely organized into a tribal federation. There is some evidence to suggest that small numbers of Samnites began moving down from the hills into the Campanian plains during the 6th century BC, in a search for fertile land to farm. They soon became entangled in the growing conflict between the Greeks and Etruscans.

In 525 BC, the Etruscans of Capua attacked the Greek city of Cumae, using a mercenary force of Samnite tribes. The Greeks successfully repelled this attack, and 50 years later managed to defeat the Etruscan fleet and definitively destroyed the Etruscan power-base in Campania. They did not, however, have long to enjoy their success, for by this time increasing numbers of Samnites were moving into Campania and coming into conflict with those already settled there. Eventually there may have been some sort of political recognition or arrangement between the existing inhabitants and the newly arrived Samnite tribes. The Sicilian historian Diodorus Siculus claimed that in 438/7 BC 'the Campanian people were formed', and from this time the Samnites took the name 'Campani'. But the Samnites were not content with this arrangement, whatever it might have been, for long. In 423 BC, groups of Samnites were employed to work in the fields around Capua. Under cover of night they crept into the city and slaughtered its population. By 420 BC they had also captured Cumae, whose Greek inhabitants fled to Neapolis. Both Capua and Cumae appear to have been resettled by Samnites. On the basis of the evidence from surviving inscriptions from this period, Oscan took the place of Greek as the main language, and in general

The Greek-style Doric Temple, which dates to the 6th century BC. Some scholars have suggested that the temple had fallen out of use in the 1st century BC, but it may have been robbed of its marble by the treasure-hunters in the 18th and 19th centuries.

Greek influence declined throughout the region. By the end of the 5th century BC, it is likely that the settlements of the Sarno Valley and the coastal villages to the south of Neapolis, including Pompeii and Herculaneum, had all come under Samnite control.

Pompeii in the 5th and 4th centuries BC

In general, there is little archaeological evidence in Pompeii datable to the period between the end of the 6th century and the end of the 4th century BC, which suggests that this was a period of stagnation or recession for the town. Thus, for example, on the site of the House of Amarantus there is no secure evidence of occupation throughout the entire 5th century. During this period, votive deposits in the Temple of Apollo also appear to have ceased. It may

be that the on-going conflicts in the region led to a decline in population. Certainly trade and agriculture must have suffered profoundly, and it is easy to speculate that some inhabitants decided to abandon Pompeii.

The Samnites may have occupied Pompeii by the end of the 5th century BC. From at least the 4th century BC, Pompeii is thought to have been part of a loose confederation of Samnite settlements headed by Nuceria and also including Herculaneum, Stabiae and the villages of the Sarno Valley. Pompeii's status within this confederation is unknown, although it appears to have had a recognizable territory. It is thought likely that the new Samnite masters of Pompeii continued to use the existing political institutions, rather than create their own. They had not been an urbanized people

Excavations in the 'Altstadt'

The irregular layout of the town around the Forum and Triangular Forum led Francis Haverfield to propose the existence of an 'Altstadt' ('old city'). During the period from 1994 to 2000, the University of Rome 'La Sapienza' conducted stratigraphic excavations in the area of the sanctuary of the Triangular Forum, including the House of

Joseph II (VIII.2.38–9) and on the edge of the Forum in the House of the Wedding of Hercules (VII.9.47) – that is, on the presumed edge of the so-called 'Altstadt'.

The House of Joseph II

Post-holes were found, indicating that there had been a wooden hut with a rectangular plan and rounded

If it indeed existed, the 'Altstadt' had a strategically important position, dominating the river-mouth of the Sarno and visible from the sea.

before they conquered the towns of Campania and had no appropriate political system of their own to introduce.

There are no buildings visible today that were built during the era of Samnite power at Pompeii, but there is growing evidence of structures beneath later houses and public buildings dating to the 4th century BC. Good examples are the foundations discovered beneath the Sanctuary of the Public Lares in the Forum, the House of the Clay Moulds (VII.4.62), the House of the Faun (VI.12.1), and the House of Amarantus. Mostly these are the remains of simple houses, consisting of two or three rooms only and poorly constructed. As well as these domestic structures, in 2004 archaeologists discovered under the later Roman Temple of Venus a pre-Roman wall and clay offerings to the Samnite goddess of love. It is thought that this was a temple and sanctuary dedicated to the Samnite goddess Mephitis and overlooking the harbour and mouth of the River Sarno. Simple non-monumental Samnite tombs that date from the 4th century BC have been found outside the Stabian and Herculaneum Gates. Those outside the Stabian Gate are part of what appears to be the burial-ground of a single family, the Epidii, members of which still lived in Pompeii in AD 79. But it is hard to characterize the settlement as a town at this point of its history. It is more likely that Pompeii was a large village of scattered buildings and farms.

There was little political stability within the region of Campania from the middle of the 4th century BC. Within the space of a hundred years the Samnites would lose their conquests.

corners here. Its construction was dated to between the 9th and 7th centuries BC by the excavators. In the period between the middle of the 4th century BC to the end of the 3rd century BC, this hut was replaced by a small walled building of unknown plan and use. The House of Joseph II was built in the second half of the 2nd century BC (probably after 130 BC), employing a range of building materials and techniques at the same time. It was now a large 'atrium' house with terraced lower floors and a small bath complex.

The portico of the Triangular Forum
Post-holes were discovered under the portico of the Triangular Forum, probably relating to wooden structures, possibly huts, in the area of the sanctuary, and have been tentatively dated to 600/500 BC. In the second half of the 2nd century BC, modest buildings of unknown function were constructed here. Their proximity to the so-called Doric Temple and the discovery of votive deposits of terracottas, statuettes and ceramics in the levels associated with the later destruction of these buildings suggests that they may have been related to sanctuary activities. A portico was later built on this site, after these buildings had been demolished. Traditionally, the portico has been dated to the 2nd century BC; instead, the excavations demonstrated that the structure was built in the 1st century AD.

House of the Wedding of Hercules
Fragmentary foundations in pappamonte (lava blocks) were discovered beneath this house, revealing that there had been an earlier building on the site, possibly dating to the end of the 6th century BC. These foundations indicate that the building had been on the same alignment as the later house, but the excavators were unable to reconstruct its plan or give a more precise date for its construction. By the late 4th century or early 3rd century BC the same area was occupied by two or three small buildings, again on the same alignment as the later House of the Wedding of Hercules. These were built close to one another, separated by a road made from beaten earth and pebbles. They had limestone foundations and walls of wood and clay. The House of the Wedding of Hercules itself was built in the second half of the 2nd century BC (probably after 130 BC).

The House of the Wedding of Hercules was named after a wall-painting found during the original excavations in 1820. The painting itself has been lost, but is reproduced in this 19th-century watercolour. It depicts the wedding of Hercules before the Temple of Venus. To either side of the temple priestesses lead a procession of young men and women holding sacred objects. There was evidence that wooden brackets had been inserted into the walls on either side of the painting, possibly for garlands to be hung from, leading one scholar to suggest that this had been the house of a priest.

The Romans in the Bay of Naples

BY THE MID-4TH CENTURY BC, HORDES OF SAMNITES WERE moving into Campania, leading to conflict with both native and existing Samnite ('Campanian') inhabitants. In 343 BC the people of Capua appealed to the Romans for help against the new Samnite incursions. The Romans were happy to oblige, and by the end of the ensuing war (known as the 'First Samnite War'), they had defeated the Samnites and gained control of much of northern Campania, including Capua itself. But the conflict did not end there. The Romans accused the Greek inhabitants of Neapolis of committing crimes against new Roman settlers in Campania. In 327 BC the Samnites helped to garrison the Greek city of Neapolis against the Romans, and war broke out once more (the 'Second Samnite War'). Initially the Romans suffered setbacks, but between 311 and 304 BC Rome won a series of victories against the Samnites. The Greek inhabitants of Neapolis finally surrendered to Rome, accusing the Samnites of atrocities against their women and children. By the end of this conflict the Romans controlled the whole of Campania. All the cities of Campania now became 'allies' of Rome with varying degrees of independence.

Peace was slow to follow. In 218 BC Hannibal invaded Italy at the head of an army of 40,000 Carthaginians. In 216 BC he swept into Campania, plundering as he went. Many Italian cities joined with Hannibal in his war against the Romans, including Capua. Pompeii remained loyal to Rome, but undoubtedly suffered from the conflicts taking place around it – Neapolis, Nuceria and Nola were all attacked by Hannibal, and communications, trade and agriculture must have been deeply affected. Eventually, in 194 BC, Rome founded a series of military colonies in Campania, at Salernum, Volturnum, Liternum and Puteoli with the aim of securing the coast from future invasion.

Pompeii as an allied Roman town

Pompeii and the other towns of Campania were absorbed into the Roman empire at the beginning of the 3rd century BC. These towns retained power over local affairs, but Rome took control over wider issues of war and foreign policy. The allies were obliged to contribute troops and arms to Rome's conquering armies.

At this time, Pompeii was still a small farming community. Recent excavations along the facades of many houses found little evidence of building activity prior to the 3rd century BC. A number of wells have been excavated that pre-date the nearby standing structures, which is consistent with a primarily agricultural use of the land. In essence, Pompeii may have been a network of urban farms located within large open spaces (all within fortified walls), and, based on the very few archaeological finds apart from pottery, was poor. Analysis of faunal remains

Excavations in the House of Amarantus

Archaeologists from the University of Reading and the British School at Rome undertook stratigraphic excavations in two houses (I.9.11 and 12, collectively known now as the House of Amarantus) in 1995–99. These houses were partly built using the opus quadratum and opus africanum construction techniques, traditionally dated to the 4th or 3rd century BC. One of the aims of the excavation was to examine whether this dating of the walls was correct. Excavations took place in the atrium and adjoining rooms of House 12 and the garden of House 11.

Evidence of the earliest occupation of the site was provided by post-holes and small pits containing a few potsherds, datable to the 8th or 7th century BC. There was no evidence of a clear house plan associated with this phase, but some time during the 6th century BC, a substantial H-shaped structure was built where later the atrium of House 12 would stand. This structure has been dated from the small quantities of Attic black-glazed and Etruscan bucchero pottery present in the foundation trenches of its walls. More importantly, it appears to have been built on the same alignment as the later House 12, leading the excavators to suggest that the street-grid that divides Pompeii into regular blocks of housing was already in existence in this part of the town in the 6th century. Below the neighbouring House 10, there were also traces of early structures. Ceramic finds such as bucchero, impasto and Corinthian ware indicated activity here in the 5th or even 6th century BC, when traditionally the town was thought to be undeveloped.

There appears to have been a break in occupation in the 5th century BC. The next structures on the site probably date to the 4th and 3rd centuries; the heavily disturbed evidence consists of fragments of unmortared walls, lines of post-holes, lots of pits and post-holes, so it is difficult to identify any pattern in the remains, beyond the fact that they were built on the same alignment as the later House of Amarantus. In general there were few finds related to this period, which may indicate that the inhabitants were poor. There was very little evidence of latrine waste, which also suggests that the population was sparse.

Houses 11 and 12, as they stand today, were constructed in the 2nd century BC. Fine and coarse pottery and amphorae have been excavated that relate to this period, suggesting that the inhabitants relating to this period give some idea of what life was like for the inhabitants of the town. Excavated bones from the House of Amarantus reveal that pork, lamb and beef were all eaten, as were different types of fish. In general there was very little latrine waste, which implies a small population and large open spaces, probably used for the cultivation of cereals and vegetables. A similar picture can be seen from the excavations on the site of the House of the Vestals (VI.1.6–8, 24–26). The earliest deposits contain cereal chaff and fish bones and heads, evidence that cereals were processed nearby and fish were processed for cooking inside the house. It is clear that farm animals were kept there, too.

were more affluent than in earlier periods. There was little structural change in House 12 over the next 200 years. The house was relatively simple in design with no evidence for a roof over the atrium courtyard or of cisterns or drains. House 11 underwent more extensive changes. The level of the peristyle garden was raised several times, and there is some evidence of the deposition in pits of cremated votive offerings in the intervals between the changes of level. In AD 79 large numbers of amphorae were being stored in both houses.

(Above) This photograph taken in the 1950s when the house was excavated reveals rows of upright (and presumably full) Cretan wine-amphorae stacked in the corner of the atrium. The impluvium instead contains empty amphorae.

(Left) The stratigraphic excavations of 1995–99 focused on the garden of House 11 and the atrium of House 12.

House 12   House 11

The next two centuries saw many changes at Pompeii, undoubtedly due to the new political stability created by Roman hegemony in Italy. Most importantly, there appears to have been a marked growth in building activity, particularly from the end of the 3rd century BC. From this period Pompeii can be considered a proper town. But it is not clear how the town developed. Was its growth planned or spontaneous? We have already seen that in broad terms Pompeii's town plan was laid out in the 6th century BC since archaic buildings share their alignment with later ones. This would mean that the founders of the settlement foresaw and planned its development into a larger urban centre. This appears to have occurred during the 3rd century BC. Outside the Nuceria Gate and the Vesuvius Gate pebbled roads dating to the late 3rd century have

been excavated beneath the later road surfaces. These suggest that the road layout in different parts of the town was established at the same time. The next step would be the formal subdivision of space within the town. It has been suggested that an influx of refugees from other towns necessitated such a step, and it is possible that refugees fled to Pompeii during the Hannibalic War. For example, both Capua and Nuceria were destroyed during the war; inscriptions bearing Latin gentilician names associated with these towns have been found at Pompeii, supporting the possibility that at least some of their inhabitants sought refuge there. In order to accommodate large numbers of new settlers, a planned response would have been necessary to ensure that all received a fair and regular plot of land – the 'row' houses of Region I

View of the House of the Faun (VI.12), painted by Teodoro Duclère in the late 19th century. This was the largest of Pompeii's houses, adorned with many elaborate mosaics and imposing First Style wall decoration. It was constructed in the 2nd century BC.

may be an example of such planning at the end of the 3rd century or beginning of the 2nd century BC. Initially these plots would have been used for farming, but gradually they began to be built up.

The very end of the 3rd century BC saw the beginning of great prosperity for Pompeii. Most of the existing standing structures of the town date to either the 2nd or 1st century BC, and it is clear that in this period Pompeii began to take on its final form. An increasing number of high-status houses were built, including the House of the Etruscan Column, the House of the Clay Moulds, the House of Pansa (VI.6.1), the House of the Faun and the House of the Centenary (IX.8.6). These houses are characterized by 'atrium' courtyards and replaced the simple and poorly constructed houses of the 4th and 3rd centuries BC. At times, this redevelopment seems brutal, such as in the wholesale replanning of Insula VI.1 when the House of the Vestals doubled in size and swallowed up two earlier houses. Private building such as this represents the growing personal wealth of particular individuals or families, who undoubtedly began to exert political influence in the town as well.

As a whole the population of Pompeii benefited from the new prosperity of the 2nd century BC, as can be seen in the construction of new public buildings and the renovation of existing ones. Particularly affected was the Forum, an area for which there is little evidence of buildings before this date. The Macellum (market), Basilica and Temple of Jupiter were constructed, the floor of the Forum was paved, and a colonnade was added.

The evidence for prosperity in this period is not limited simply to private and public architecture. Stratigraphic excavations demonstrate that there was a greater range of imported pottery, including new types of finewares, coarsewares and amphorae from the 2nd century BC. For example, there are large numbers of amphorae that were imported from Tunisia and Rhodes and other types of vessel that came from the Greek island of Kos and from southern Italy. Coins have been found that came from Egypt. The names of some inhabitants of Pompeii appear across the Mediterranean, demonstrating that they were exploiting the new possibilities for trade and profit. In addition, the diet of Pompeii's inhabitants appears to have become more varied at this time. For example, evidence that domestic fowl and olives were consumed appears for the first time in the House of Amarantus. The analysis of rubbish deposits from the House of the Vestals suggests that food was no longer processed within the house. Later deposits

This temple, which dominates the northern end of the Forum, was probably dedicated to Jupiter from the time of its construction in the 2nd century BC. An inscription reveals that it was later transformed into a capitolium *(a temple dedicated to the Roman triad of Jupiter, Juno and Minerva). A colossal bust of Jupiter was found in the temple when it was excavated at the beginning of the 19th century.*

Excavations have been conducted in Insula VI.1 since 1995. The earliest evidence of occupation on the site comes from successive surfaces of compacted earth, with some post-holes cut into them, dated to the late 4th century BC. The distribution of the post-holes may represent fence-lines – a marking out of the landscape. The first traces of buildings on the site come from earth and rubble remains set directly on top of this compacted earth. These are roughly aligned with the Via Consolare, which suggests that this street, which leads from the Herculaneum Gate to the Forum, already existed in 4th century BC.

From the 3rd century BC there is evidence of stone-built architecture on the site of the insula. Two small buildings (later to become the House of the Surgeon and the House of the Vestals) have been identified, although their initial ground-plans were obscured by later building on the site. The remainder of Insula VI.1 was still open land in this period.

In the early part of the 2nd century BC, a large building was constructed in the northern part of the insula; this fronted onto the Vicolo di Narciso and indicates that the street network was in place by this time. In the following years, a range of small courtyard houses and commercial properties was built over the previously open ground surrounding the House of the Surgeon and the House of the Vestals, suggesting that there was a planned division of space

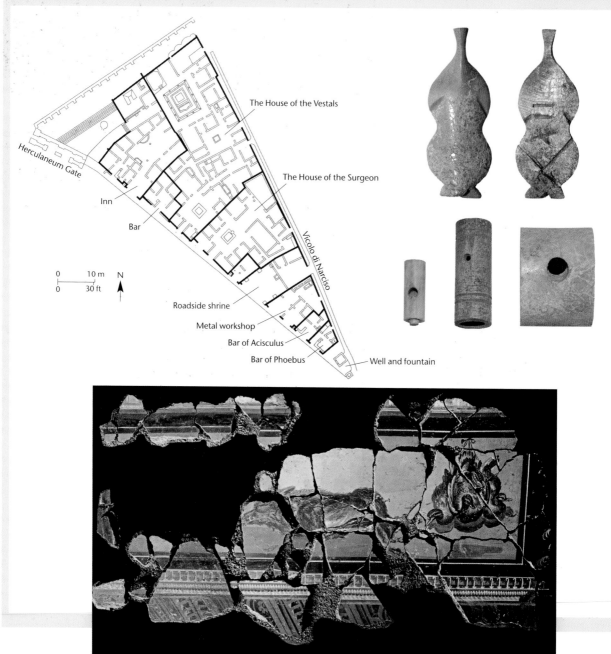

The House of the Vestals

Herculaneum Gate

Inn

Bar

The House of the Surgeon

Vicolo di Narciso

0   10 m
0   30 ft
N

Roadside shrine

Metal workshop

Bar of Acisculus

Bar of Phoebus

Well and fountain

within the insula. However, this division was not regular. The House of the Vestals more than doubled in size in this period and became the most important building in the insula. At the northern end of the Insula, a series of workshops along the Via Consolare was linked to the House of the Vestals, and the expansion of the house coincided with the first real evidence for the development of commercial activities in the insula. The southern part of the insula was also built in a single phase of construction during this period. There is a series of tanks lined with waterproof plaster in these properties, and it is thought that in this period they were used for fish-processing activities. Later, in the 1st century BC, the function of these workshops appears to have changed. There is evidence for metal-working in the form of slag and other by-products of smithing, and also of the construction of a bar.

The next major changes in the development of the insula occurred in the wake of the Roman general Sulla's siege of Pompeii in 89 BC. During the bombardment of the town, there was widespread destruction of the buildings in the northern part of Insula VI.1, which flanks the town wall. The owners of the House of the Vestals appear to have used these events as an opportunity to expand their property to cover the entire northern end of the insula.

By the late 1st century BC, the House of the Vestals was elaborately redecorated. In addition, the owners of the house had taken advantage of the new availability of piped water in the town to construct a series of fountains, a swimming-pool and a new bath-suite.

Dramatic structural changes took place after a major earthquake, most likely that of AD 63. Water was no longer piped to private houses in the area immediately surrounding Insula VI.1, so the owners of the House of the Vestals built an above-ground cistern to provide water for a gravity-fed fountain in part of the swimming-pool (the rest of it was filled in). The other fountains in the house were turned into static water-features and the bath-suite was taken out of use. An extensive upper storey was constructed to provide both reception rooms and service rooms as well as to house part of the new cistern. There was also extensive redecoration. At the time of the eruption in AD 79 some of the building work was still in progress. Changes also took place in the commercial properties in the south of the insula. A bar was constructed here and an upper floor extending over all four properties was built, possibly as a rental apartment.

Plan of Insula VI.1 and objects found during the excavations conducted by the Anglo-American project, including bone tokens or gaming pieces and hinges from the House of the Vestals, and fragments of a wall-painting from the House of the Surgeon.

The 'tholos' set up by Numerius Trebius on the east side of the Triangular Forum. It was constructed of seven Doric columns and may have had a conical roof. This photograph was taken between 1920 and 1930.

contain no chaff and fish remains are predominantly scales and vertebrae, which means that crop-processing had moved away from the house and its inhabitants now were buying ready-processed fish. In both the House of the Vestals and the much smaller adjacent house there is also a greater range of spices and fruits, including chickpeas, olives, walnuts, pine nuts and dates. The excavators suggest that the only visible difference in diet between these two houses was the age of the meat consumed – the presumably better-off inhabitants of the larger House of the Vestals ate younger meat, lamb as opposed to mutton. However, such analysis of waste material has been limited at Pompeii, so it is not clear whether these results should be taken as evidence that diet at Pompeii was improved for all its inhabitants.

In terms of political life, things appear to have carried on as before. There are quite a few surviving inscriptions in Oscan, and the earliest examples of political propaganda on the walls of Pompeii are all Oscan. For the first time we can identify the names of some of the politically active men at Pompeii in this period. A good example is the Oscan inscription on the 'tholos' (a circular Doric colonnade with a well at the centre) in the Triangular Forum, which records that it had been constructed by a Samnite magistrate called Numerius Trebius.

By the end of the 2nd century BC, Pompeii was a proper urban community. Yet despite the improved living conditions, prosperity and increased population, discontent with the existing political situation, the burden of heavy taxes and the dominance of the Romans remained. In 91 BC, Pompeii joined a widespread rebellion by the allied cities of Italy against Roman control, an act that had drastic consequences for the town.

The 1st Century BC

The Social War

Rome's Italian allies were obliged to provide troops and fight for Rome in its wars of conquest. In 91 BC, the allies rose up in rebellion, with the aim of setting up an independent Italian Federation. Initially, they enjoyed success in their fight against Rome, but there was soon stalemate. In 90 BC the Romans passed a law granting citizenship to the allies who had remained loyal to Rome and those who laid down their arms immediately. The allies were divided by this act and the rebellion collapsed. The Romans then spent the next two years defeating those cities that remained in arms. Herculaneum was stormed and conquered. Stabiae was completely destroyed and ceased to exist as a town. Pompeii was forced to capitulate in 89 BC.

The Colonia Cornelia Veneria Pompeianorum

In 89 BC Pompeii was besieged and bombarded by the Roman general, Sulla. The northern part of Insula VI.1 was damaged during this assault. Stone ballista balls have been found in this area, and the town walls around the Herculaneum Gate still bear the scars of

Ballista balls found during the excavations of the Anglo-American project; the marks of such projectiles are clearly visible on Pompeii's walls, particularly near the Herculaneum Gate.

the conflict. Opposition to Sulla within the town appears to have been well organized. A series of inscriptions in Oscan were painted on street corners and these are thought to refer to mustering points in case of emergency. These efforts were in vain. Pompeii surrendered to the greater Roman forces but, unlike Herculaneum and Stabiae, was not pillaged.

It was, however, punished. In 80 BC land was confiscated from the inhabitants of Pompeii and given to military veterans from Sulla's army. The town was refounded as a Roman colony, and renamed the 'Colonia Cornelia Veneria Pompeianorum'. This name was derived from the *gens* (family) name of Lucius Cornelius Sulla and from the goddess Venus whom he claimed as his patron. The leader of the new colony was Publius Cornelius Sulla, probably Sulla's nephew. Along with the new settlers and new name, the town received a new Roman constitution, new magistrates, and a new patron deity (Venus). Latin became the official written language of the town. The colonists formed a new political elite at Pompeii, and it is possible that the original inhabitants were excluded from political life, at least in the earliest years of the colony. We can only imagine how the existing inhabitants of Pompeii felt about giving up large parts of their land to new, Roman, settlers and the changes they represented. There must have been resentment, at least initially, and there is tantalizing evidence in a speech by Cicero about a dispute between the old and the new Pompeians. Unfortunately the details are vague, and we are left to speculate on the precise nature of the disagreement.

The impact of the Roman colony on Pompeii can hardly be underestimated, and can be seen most clearly in the radical physical changes that took place within the town. A range of new public buildings was constructed to suit Roman needs and fashions. Houses in the southeast corner of the town were demolished to make way for an Amphitheatre. A Covered Theatre was constructed, possibly to house concerts and poetry recitals. Administrative buildings were constructed in the Forum. A new altar was dedicated in the existing Temple of Apollo. New bath buildings were constructed just off the Forum, and the existing Stabian Baths were enlarged. A temple was constructed at the edge of the Forum near the Marine Gate and may have been dedicated to Venus, the town's new patron (a fact suggested by the discovery of a fragment of a statue of the goddess). Significantly, this temple appears to have been built over an earlier Samnite temple and sanctuary dedicated to Mephitis, and may well have functioned to emphasize Roman superiority to the old inhabitants.

Significant developments can be seen in domestic architecture, too. It is clear that many houses were either constructed or received their final form during the 1st century BC. A good example is the House of the Vestals, which grew in size to accommodate a variety of decorated reception areas and gardens.

The civil wars of the 1st century BC

Although Pompeii prospered, civil wars dominated the Roman world during the 1st century BC. Roman generals – such as Pompey, Julius Caesar, Mark Antony and Octavian – vied for power and dragged Italy into civil war. Ultimately, Octavian was victorious. Taking the title 'Augustus', he became the first Roman emperor. Augustus' control of the Roman empire was based on his power over Rome's armies, but he also sought to win the hearts and minds of the Romans by emphasizing his restoration of 'traditional' Roman values and religion.

Prosperity in the early imperial period

There is no evidence that Pompeii was particularly affected by the civil wars of the 1st century BC, but its prosperity continued and increased from the age of Augustus. The reaction of local towns to the new political climate and new ideology promoted by their first emperor can perhaps be seen in a number of building projects that honour Augustus and his family. At Pompeii the Temple of Augustan Fortune and the Eumachia Building (which was dedicated to Augustan Concord and Piety) were constructed as part of a wider monumentalization of the Forum area which also included the construction of the Sanctuary of the Public Lares and the remodelling of the Macellum (meat and fish market). In addition, the Temple of Apollo appears to have been enlarged (Apollo was Augustus' patron deity) and given a new colonnade. The Large

Theatre was converted and a new system of hierarchical seating, according to social status, was established. The Palaestra, an exercise ground for the youth of the town, also probably dates to the Augustan period. By the end of the 1st century BC an aqueduct was carrying water to different parts of the town. A series of public fountains were set up and water was also piped into the public baths and into some of the largest houses.

The developments in Pompeii's public architecture also reflect its economic vitality in this period. Rome was master of a global empire, and Italy benefited from its conquests in the form of new consumer goods. Excavations at Pompeii have revealed that wine was imported from Greece, Turkey, Sicily, Palestine and central Italy, olive oil came from Libya and Spain, and fine pottery came from France, Cyprus and northern Italy. Pompeii's location by the mouth of the Sarno gave it an important role as a market town. Not only did its inhabitants import goods from all over the empire, but they exported products too. We know, for example, that Pompeii was well-known for its fish sauce (called garum).

The majority of today's Pompeii dates to the Roman period; there is very little visible evidence of the town before the late 3rd century BC. However, from the existing archaeological and literary evidence, it is possible to trace the slow development of a small agricultural settlement into a large urban community over a period of at least 600 years. As yet, many of the details of this process are not known or understood, but it is clear that the settlement was deeply affected by outside influences and events occurring in Campania and Italy as a whole. It was only with the peace and prosperity of the Roman period that Pompeii was able to become a fully-fledged urban centre.

The Temple of Augustan Fortune, constructed in the Augustan period at private expense and on his own land by the prominent magistrate Marcus Tullius. There was a statue of Tullius within the temple.

IV
THE PEOPLE OF POMPEII

…ramble on, and see, at every turn, the familiar little tokens of human habitation and everyday pursuits; the chafing of the bucket-rope in the stone rim of the exhausted well; the track of carriagewheels in the pavement of the street; the marks of drinking-vessels on the stone counter of the wine-shop; the amphorae in private cellars, stored away so many hundred years ago, and undisturbed to this hour – all rendering the solitude and deadly lonesomeness of the place, ten thousand times more solemn, than if the volcano, in its fury had swept the city from the earth, and sunk it in the bottom of the sea.

Charles Dickens, *Pictures from Italy*, 1844–45

The names of hundreds of people who lived and died at Pompeii and Herculaneum are known. They are identified on public buildings and tombs, painted electoral graffiti and shop signs, scratched graffiti on walls, and wax tablets documenting business agreements. Sometimes we know only that a particular person was responsible for constructing a particular building or was running for a certain political office. But in other cases we have very detailed knowledge of their activities, their families, or events in their lives. We even know what a few looked like, from statues and busts. We can also reconstruct the lives of the population in more general terms – what it was like, for example, to be a member of the elite or a woman in the town. And we have a good idea of how many wanted to be remembered after death, and the aspects of their lives that their families were proud of.

Banqueting scene from the House of the Chaste Lovers (IX.12.6). A slave-girl looks on as two semi-naked couples enjoy their dinner-party.

The Population of Pompeii

POMPEII WAS SUBJECT TO OUTSIDE INFLUENCES FROM the time of its foundation and throughout its development until its destruction in AD 79. This fact, and its important role as a river port at the mouth of the River Sarno, has led to the general assumption that the inhabitants of Pompeii were of mixed ethnicity. It has been possible for scholars to find evidence for the presence of several different ethnic groups in the final decades of the town's existence. This evidence is mostly based on surviving written material in the town. The majority of inscriptions are in Latin, as would be expected in a Roman colony; but a limited number of inscriptions in the Oscan language suggest the continued presence of indigenous people; there are also inscriptions in Greek and Greek names in financial accounts may relate to a Greek presence, and rare examples of Hebrew or of Jewish names such as Martha. Some of the evidence cited is less convincing, however: wall-paintings such as the 'Judgment of Solomon' have been interpreted as evidence that Jews lived in Pompeii. Unfortunately, we have no way of knowing for sure what the racial background of Pompeii's population was, either in origin or in later periods. The most recent analysis of some of the skeletal remains from Pompeii suggests that its inhabitants in AD 79 may not have been as racially diverse as assumed, but the results are not conclusive.

It is also impossible to give a precise figure for the size of the population of Pompeii. Various estimates have been made, varying from 6,400 to 30,000 people, based on evidence such as the estimated seating capacity of the Amphitheatre or the

The famous wall-painting thought to depict 'The Judgement of Solomon' from the House of the Physician (VIII.5.24), in which Jews are depicted as pygmies. In the past, some scholars suggested that the fresco was a caricature representing anti-Semitic feeling, and thus that there was a community of Jews living in the town.

One of the most detailed reconstructions of events in an individual's life derives from the discovery of wax tablets during the excavation of a house in Herculaneum in 1938. These tablets document a lawsuit brought by Calatoria Themis against a young woman called Iusta.

Sometime in the early AD 60s a baby girl named Iusta was born in the house belonging to Gaius Petronius Stephanus (known to us today as the House of the Bicentenary). The father of this child is not identified, but her mother, Vitalia, had been a slave in the household. Vitalia had been freed or had managed to buy her freedom, but continued to live with her former owners. Iusta was brought up in Petronius' home. The situation changed ten years later when Petronius' wife, Calatoria Themis, had children of her own. Vitalia decided to leave the household and set up her own home, but Petronius and Calatoria refused to allow Iusta to go with her. Vitalia sued her former owner, and won. Iusta went to live with her mother. At this point, tragedy stuck. Both Vitalia and Petronius died within a short time of each other, and Iusta inherited her mother's property. But Calatoria then brought a lawsuit of her own. She claimed that when Iusta had been born Vitalia had still been a slave. This meant that both Iusta and all the property she had inherited belonged to Calatoria.

Unfortunately for both parties, there was no formal record of the date of Vitalia's freedom. Neither Calatoria nor Iusta could prove their side of the story. The local magistrates at Herculaneum referred the case to magistrates in Rome in AD 75. These magistrates declared that they needed time to consider the matter. There is no evidence that a decision had been made by the time of the eruption in AD 79.

Wall-painting from the House of Terentius Neo (VII.2.6), often thought to represent Neo and his wife. The man holds a papyrus, the woman a stylus and wax tablet, to highlight their intellectual aspirations.

number of excavated rooms in the town. Most scholars accept a population of between 8,000 and 12,000 people. At Herculaneum the seating capacity of the theatre has also been also used to estimate a population of 4,000. However, these figures are not definitive and can be used only as a guide. The population of both towns may have been fairly fluid. Pompeii was a harbour town, so foreign traders were probably common. Herculaneum was a popular holiday resort for Romans from the 1st century BC onwards, so it may have had greater numbers of residents at particular times of the year. One notable Roman reported to have had a villa in the vicinity of Herculaneum was the emperor Caligula, and the remains of many luxurious villas have been uncovered along Herculaneum's coast.

The Social Composition of the Town

THE INHABITANTS OF THE ANCIENT ROMAN TOWN consisted of the freeborn, the freed and the slaves. Perhaps the most important distinction between these groups was the ability to participate in politics. Only freeborn male Roman citizens had full legal rights, and could hold high political office. A freedman – a slave who had been freed by his master – could vote in elections, own a business and wield significant resources and power that he might use to benefit the community as a whole (or not, as the case may be). He could participate in certain religious cults or become a priest of the cult of the emperor. But he would always be barred from formal political office at the highest levels. Slaves had no rights, political or otherwise. Both free and freed women were equally barred from formal participation in politics, but might have had some independence in matters of business and an important role in public religion.

Pompeii's elite

The freeborn male citizens and their families made up the political and social elite of Pompeii. Their names appear in the monumental inscriptions on statues, buildings and tombs. These families might be either of local Oscan descent with a long history at Pompeii, or the descendants of the Roman colonists of 80 BC. A speech by Cicero suggests that there may have been some initial tension between these two groups in the years after the foundation of the colony, when the new Roman settlers took land from local Pompeians and probably came to dominate the town politically. According to Cicero this tension lasted for some decades after the foundation of the colony, but eventually the two groups formed a unified elite. Later, the descendants of some wealthy freedmen succeeded in entering the ranks of the elite.

Pompeii's elite was made up of wealthy landowners who lived in or near the town. Although Rome's aristocracy publicly disdained direct involvement in trade and commercial activities, there is plenty of evidence that Pompeii's elite supplemented their agricultural wealth with business transactions in town. More importantly, Pompeii's council was formed from the male members of the elite. The elite thus controlled the public purse, public spaces and official public religion. Their position was further emphasized by the privileged seats they received in the theatre and Amphitheatre, particularly from the Augustan period, the honorific statues set up to them, and their prominent burial sites.

A good example of a member of this elite is Marcus Tullius. He had a distinguished political career in the Augustan period, holding all the chief magistracies, and was responsible for building the Temple of Augustan Fortune at the north end of the Forum. This was constructed on his own land and at his own expense. When he died, the council set up an elaborate tomb to him outside the Stabian Gate.

Freedmen

Freedmen were, of course, slaves who had been freed by their masters. Once freed, they might continue to live with and work for their former masters, or they could strike off on their own to start a business and build up their own extended family (including slaves), although they retained certain obligations to their ex-masters. It is clear that many freedmen (and women) were extremely successful and became wealthy and influential members of society. But any political ambitions they might have were strictly controlled. The most important formal office that they could hold was priest of the cult of the emperor (known as an *Augustalis*) or of certain other religious cults (particularly that of Mercury and Maia and the district and suburban cults of the Lares).

Being an Augustalis appears to have been particularly important, to judge from the epitaphs set up on the tombs of wealthy freedmen. Both free citizens and freedmen could join the 'college' of priests involved in emperor worship, but freedmen, denied other public offices, appear particularly to have coveted the honour. Augustales were appointed by the town councillors and were obliged to pay a fee to the public purse. As a priest of the cult of the emperor, these men had the opportunity to demonstrate their loyalty to Rome and to the emperor, while at the same time increasing their own social status within the local community. Indeed, they could be honoured by the town – some, for example, Gaius Calventius Quietus and Gaius Munatius Faustus, received honorific seats (*bisellia*) for use on public occasions such as performances in the theatre. The meeting place of the college of Augustales at Pompeii has not been discovered (either it was located in one of the unexcavated parts of the town or it has simply not been identified). At Herculaneum, a building near the Forum was identified as the Hall of the Augustales in the 1960s, but this identification has since been challenged.

Citizenship depended upon the status of the mother – a child born to a freedwoman was free, but a child born to a slave girl (even if the father was free or freed) was a slave. The male child of a freedwoman was able to hold the highest public offices. There are some examples of freedmen using their freeborn children to acquire the political influence otherwise denied to them. The six-year-old son of the freedman Numerius Popidius Ampliatus was admitted to the town council when his father rebuilt

Mural of slaves at a banquet. Slaves might be owned by private individuals or by the town itself, and they were essential to all sorts of economic and domestic activities. They might clean and maintain public buildings or private houses, or work in publicly or privately owned craftshops and businesses. Once they had earned their freedom, it was common for freed slaves to continue to live with or work for their former owners.

the Temple of Isis after AD 63. Presumably it would have been the father who benefited from the honour and status given to his son.

Numerius Popidius Ampliatus appears to have been the freedman of a prominent and old Pompeian family, known to us from several different sources, including monumental inscriptions, electoral *programmata* (painted slogans) and graffiti. Members of this family held high office at different times – for example, a Vibius Popidius was responsible for building the Nola Gate. He is referred to as *meddix tuticus*, the Oscan title of the chief magistrate of Pompeii before the foundation of the Roman colony in 80 BC. The same man built a portico, the location of which is unknown. Another Vibius Popidius, who held the office of *quaestor* (dating to the interim government of the town before the formal foundation of the Roman colony), also constructed a portico, possibly in the Forum, in the late 80s BC. In AD 79, another member of the family, Lucius Popidius Secundus, was a candidate for the junior magisterial office of aedile. It may be that Numerius Popidius Ampliatus dreamt of being as influential as the members of this other, freeborn, branch of his family.

Evidence for slavery at Pompeii

Slavery was a fundamental part of Roman life. Although we know that slavery must have been widespread in Pompeii and Herculaneum, it is very difficult to find tangible evidence of slaves in the surviving archaeological record. There are few inscriptions or other types of writing that can be securely related to them, and few houses had distinct areas that can be identified as slave quarters (examples of houses that do appear to have had separate slave quarters are the House of Menander (I.10.4) and the House of the Centenary (IX.8.3), two of the largest houses in Pompeii). Slaves must have slept either in their owners' quarters or in whatever corner of the house they could find (it is often thought that slave quarters were located in the upper storeys of houses, but there is no evidence to support or contradict this). We are not even sure where slaves were buried. It is extremely rare to find a tombstone recording that the deceased was a slave. Often it is thought that when the deceased has only one name he or she was probably a slave, particularly if the person has a foreign name. There is evidence to suggest that some slaves at least were buried in the family tombs of their masters. A good example is the Tomb of Munatius Faustus outside the Nuceria Gate. This enclosure contained a number of headstones marking the burial of freed and slave members of his household. But we do not know what happened to the bodies of the majority of slaves when they died. Most probably lie in unmarked graves.

(Opposite) This fine male portrait (top) was found in the House of the Gilded Cupids (VI.16.7). Another head of the same man was found in Herculaneum, leading one scholar to suggest that he was a member of the famous Poppaei family, important landowners in Pompeii and the wider region. In contrast, the second portrait (below) is of a freedman, and was one of many busts that adorned the Tomb of the Flavii outside the Nuceria Gate, a multi-occupancy tomb.

Death and Burial

ALTHOUGH THERE IS LITTLE INFORMATION ABOUT THE death and burial of slaves (and children), the cemeteries of Pompeii are an important source of information about the social composition, status and aspirations of its inhabitants. No cemeteries have yet been found at Herculaneum.

As at other Roman towns and cities, anyone entering Pompeii could not fail to notice the tombs that crowded the sides of the roads leading to all the gates of the town. The tombs were designed to be seen. Those of the rich elite clustered in prominent positions immediately in front of the gates; those of the poor and less socially privileged were squeezed in around them or further down the roads that led into the countryside. Some of these tombs have benches where travellers could rest. The inscriptions on others call out to passers-by to stop and consider the life of the person buried there. At most of the gates only a few tombs are now visible because the excavations never went much beyond the town walls. This means that we can't say with certainty how far these streets of tombs stretched, but it may have been for several miles. There have been occasional discoveries of groups of tombs in Pompeii's hinterland, such as the Tomb of the Lucretii Valentes discovered in the nearby modern town of Scafati, which must have been located on roads leading into Pompeii.

The largest numbers of tombs are to be found outside the Herculaneum and Nuceria Gates. The tombs of the Herculaneum Gate are particularly famous. These were excavated from 1763 to 1838, and consist of some of the largest tombs at Pompeii. It would seem that this was the most prestigious place to be buried, and the tombs of many members of Pompeii's social and political elite are located here. More recently, in 1953–56, excavations took place outside the Nuceria Gate, to the south of the town, and uncovered tombs for a distance of 275 m (900 ft).

In the Roman world, tombs were not simple commemorations of the deceased. They had significance for both the living and the dead. The Romans did not believe in an afterlife as we understand it, but they believed that the spirits of the dead could do harm to the living unless appeased. This explains why the dead were buried outside the boundaries of towns, and why families performed regular ceremonies at their household tombs. But tombs were also used to construct a particular image of the deceased person, his or her achievements or particular events in their life. This might be an image chosen by the deceased (we know from ancient literary sources that some people planned their funerals and tombs before their death, and inscriptions demonstrate that they might build them while alive too) or by his or her family. An imposing tomb of an important member of the elite added to the prestige of his living descendants. For freedmen and women, an elaborate tomb emphasized the change in their status and their success in life. It proved that their descendants were free, too – an important fact in a society where slavery was so important. Tombs could have as much to do with the living as the dead.

This is emphasized, too, by the facilities provided at some tombs. Benches were probably used by

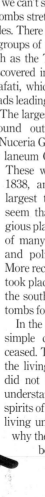

Only a few cameo-glass vessels have been found in Pompeii and the other sites buried by Vesuvius. The 'Blue Vase', found in 1834 in a tomb outside the Herculaneum Gate, is the most famous. Cupids harvesting wine decorate one side of the vase; on the other cupids play music. Vines sprout from a Dionysiac mask and extend across the surface of the vase.

passers-by to rest, but they were also designed to accommodate family members who visited the tombs of their families regularly to celebrate the various rituals and ceremonies associated with the dead, starting with the funeral banquet and then, for example, on subsequent anniversaries of the death or on official state festivals. Some tombs even had pipes that led into the buried cinerary urns. These allowed family members to pour libations onto the ashes of the deceased.

The majority of Pompeii's tombs mark the burials of members of the elite and their families or of wealthy freedmen and family, but small individual tombs and multi-occupancy tombs can be found among the larger and most prestigious tombs. With the exception of slaves, the tombs represent a fair cross-section of Pompeian society, the rich and the poor, male and female, and they tell us about the lives, and more importantly, about the aspirations of many of them. We can see, too, how burials change over the years.

The majority of the tombs at Pompeii date to the period from the mid-1st century BC to the mid-1st century AD, and can contain either single or multiple (family) burials. There are, however, a few examples of earlier tombs. The best examples come from the Fondo Azzolini necropolis, which was discovered in 1911, about 500 m (1,600 ft) from the Stabian Gate. It is thought that the site was the burial ground of one particular extended family, the Epidii. There were 44 inhumation burials dating to the 4th – 2nd centuries BC, that is, to before the Roman period. These burials were simple and often contained grave-goods such as coins and jewelry. There appears to have been a change of practice in the Roman period. The later Roman burials on this site – 119 in total – are all

A lantern slide of the Via dei Sepolcri taken before 1905. The Herculaneum Gate can be seen at the far end of the street. Tombs lined the main roads to all Roman towns.

cremations. This serves to emphasize the changes that occurred in all areas of life – not just in politics and public building – after the Romans founded their colony at Pompeii. Old, local families, such as the Epidii, came to adopt Roman funerary practices rather than hold on to their own traditions.

Elite tombs

The elaborate tombs of the Roman period were clearly used to honour important citizens and their families. But it is interesting to see the different degrees of honour that could be bestowed, depending on the location, type and payment for the tomb. The town council controlled the land immediately outside the gates for a distance of *c*. 30 m (*c*. 100 ft), and permission was required before a tomb could be set up there. The highest honour that could be bestowed was for the council both to give the land on which the tomb was built and to use public funds to pay for the tomb itself and the funeral. In other cases, the council might give the land and a contribution towards the funeral expenses, or just the land.

Generally speaking, the most important tombs are the monumental 'exedra tombs'. These are semi-circular structures with benches, often with columns or altars. There are eight examples at Pompeii, and they

are found only in the immediate vicinity of the town gates. Good examples are the tombs of Aulus Veius outside the Herculaneum Gate and Marcus Tullius outside the Stabian Gate. But this level of honour was not just reserved for prominent male members of the council – it could also be given to women. In most cases, the aim was probably to flatter a prominent family rather than to acknowledge any particular deed or service. For example, the council gave the land for Arellia Tertulla's tomb outside the Vesuvius Gate and her funeral was paid for by public expense. She was probably the wife of Marcus Stlaborius Veius Fronto, a prominent magistrate. Such tombs honoured the family as much as the individual and enhanced their collective social status.

There are other less prestigious types of tomb that were used to honour less prominent members of the elite or their families. Once again, the town council would give the land and perhaps a contribution towards the funeral. A good example is the enclosure Tomb of Gaius Vestorius Priscus outside the Vesuvius Gate. This simple, unroofed enclosure surrounded an elaborately decorated altar. Inside the enclosure are wall-paintings of gladiators and of a service of silver vessels. The images of gladiators may represent games that this young magistrate (he

This 1793 watercolour by Philipp Hackert shows the exedra tombs of Aulus Veius (left) and Mamia (right) to either side of the altar Tomb of Marcus Porcius. Some 18th-century visitors to the site rest on the benches of Veius' tomb, just as ancient passers-by would have done.

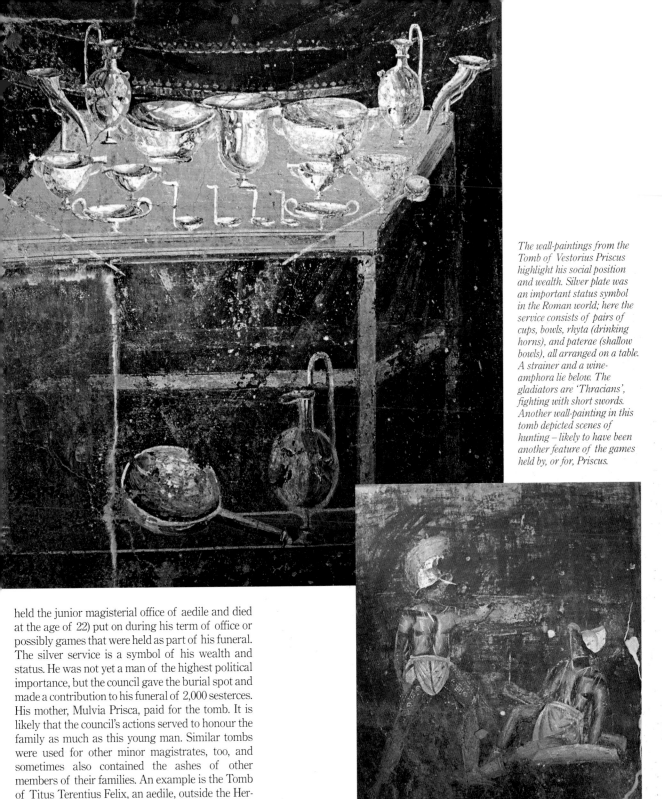

The wall-paintings from the Tomb of Vestorius Priscus highlight his social position and wealth. Silver plate was an important status symbol in the Roman world; here the service consists of pairs of cups, bowls, rhyta (drinking horns), and paterae (shallow bowls), all arranged on a table. A strainer and a wine-amphora lie below. The gladiators are 'Thracians', fighting with short swords. Another wall-painting in this tomb depicted scenes of hunting – likely to have been another feature of the games held by, or for, Priscus.

held the junior magisterial office of aedile and died at the age of 22) put on during his term of office or possibly games that were held as part of his funeral. The silver service is a symbol of his wealth and status. He was not yet a man of the highest political importance, but the council gave the burial spot and made a contribution to his funeral of 2,000 sesterces. His mother, Mulvia Prisca, paid for the tomb. It is likely that the council's actions served to honour the family as much as this young man. Similar tombs were used for other minor magistrates, too, and sometimes also contained the ashes of other members of their families. An example is the Tomb of Titus Terentius Felix, an aedile, outside the Herculaneum Gate. His burial place was given by the town council along with 2,000 sesterces for his funeral. His ashes may have been put in a glass urn beneath a small altar within the tomb; nearby were the urns of other family members.

The tombs of freedmen

The tombs of the social and political elite are particularly visible in the archaeological record, but funerary architecture of freedmen is equally represented. This is interesting because it reveals the importance that tombs had in Roman society. The ability to pay for and construct a family tomb was a sign of free status and success. Freedmen and women were clearly concerned to show off their new status and other achievements or honours earned after their emancipations. Gaius Cuspius Cyrus and Gaius Cuspius Salvius are thought to have been freedmen of an important and wealthy elite family, the Cuspii Pansae. They share a tomb at the Nuceria Gate necropolis along with Cyrus' wife, Vesuvia Iucunda.

The Tomb of Publius Vesonius Phileros

This is one of the few examples where the inscription on the tomb gives an insight into the life of the deceased. The tomb was built by a freedman, Publius Vesonius Phileros, for himself, his family and a friend, while he was still alive. Like the tombs of other freedmen, the inscription records his freed status and that he had achieved the position of Augustalis (priest of the cult of the emperor). Interestingly, the word 'Augustalis' was inserted into the text after it had been inscribed. It appears that this freedman had built his tomb before he gained this office. He was sufficiently proud of his new achievement that he had it added to his tomb, despite spoiling the appearance of the inscription:

> Publius Vesonius Phileros, freedman of a woman, Augustalis, built this monument for himself and his family while they were still alive, and for his patron, Vesonia, daughter of Publius, and for his friend, Marcus Orfellius Faustus. (*AE*, 1986, 166a)

The tomb would be important for that fact alone, since it illustrates the importance of displaying public status on these monuments. But there is another reason why the tomb is interesting. A second inscription was added to the tomb later, and records some sort of legal dispute between Publius Vesonius Phileros and his friend Marcus Orfellius Faustus. It appears that Marcus had accused Vesonius of some felony, but Vesonius had been found innocent of the charges. The details of the dispute are unknown, but the inscription conveys Vesonius' outrage at his friend's behaviour.

> Stranger, if it's not too much trouble, delay for a while and you'll discover what you should avoid. This man whom I thought was my friend produced informers against me, and a lawsuit was begun. I thank the gods and my innocence that I am free from all that trouble. I hope that neither the household gods nor the gods of the underworld receive the man who lied about our dealings. (*AE*, 1964, 160)

This tomb is unique. Here we have a glimpse into the world of the living, a world of human passions and conflicts that are normally ignored in the commemoration of the dead.

Three statues are displayed in the Tomb of Publius Vesonius Phileros – probably Phileros himself and a female member of his family, and perhaps his erstwhile friend Marcus Orfellius Faustus. The altered inscription can be seen beneath the statues.

The inscription on this tomb records their freed status and also that both men achieved the position of *magister* of the Pagus Augustus Felix (the suburban district of Pompeii, which probably encompassed all of Pompeii's surrounding territory).

The tombs of other freedmen reveal that they, like members of the elite, could be honoured by the town. For example, the inscription on the Tomb of the Augustalis Gaius Calventius Quietus outside the Herculaneum Gate, records that he was honoured with a bisellium by decree of the town councillors and with the consent of the people of Pompeii. Nearby, the tomb of another Augustalis, Marcus Cerrinius Restitutus, was erected immediately outside the gate with the permission of the town council. The position of this tomb and its form (a low arch with benches on either side), along with the discovery there of a victim of the eruption and a helmet, led the excavators of the 18th century to believe that this tomb was a sentry box. The myth of the sentry who remained at his post while Pompeii was destroyed was later immortalized by Sir Edward Bulwer Lytton in his novel *The Last Days of Pompeii*, and in a painting by Sir Edward Poynter.

(Below) Tomb or cenotaph to an unknown person outside the Herculaneum Gate (Tomb 9), similar to the Tomb of Marcus Cerrinius Restitutus. The latter's low arch, benches and position by the Herculaneum Gate led early excavators to think it was a sentry box, and (left) inspired Sir Edward Poynter to paint Faithful unto Death *(1865). The sentry stands at his post despite the chaos behind him as Pompeii is destroyed.*

Multi-occupancy tombs

Many tombs commemorate entire families rather than a single prominent individual. This is true of the Tomb of the Flavii, which dates from 50 to 30 BC. It appears to have belonged to the freedmen of Publius Flavius (thought to be one of the original colonists after 80 BC). This tomb is unusual in form, consisting of a wide facade with a series of niches that contained herms (small stone heads supported by pillars, sometimes identifiable as male or female by the hairstyle carved into the rear of the herm), and some epitaphs, of the deceased who lay within the tomb.

From the 1st century AD a new type of tomb became popular. This is the 'house tomb', a multi-occupancy tomb that can be seen particularly outside the Nuceria Gate. These tombs were built to look like houses. They have roofs, doors and windows. Some have mosaic floors and painted walls. The inscriptions on this type of tomb are generally brief and do not always give the relationship between those buried inside, although they were probably family groups or members of a burial college. The cremations were placed directly into the ground inside the chambers – there are no altars or niches. Some of the larger house tombs contain individual stelae, usually identical in shape and size and without any inscription or identification of sex or status. Finally, some burials are marked simply by stelae. These can be found amongst the tombs –

The Tomb of the Flavii, a family tomb outside the Nuceria Gate. The stelae representing individual family members can be seen in the niches in the facade of the tomb.

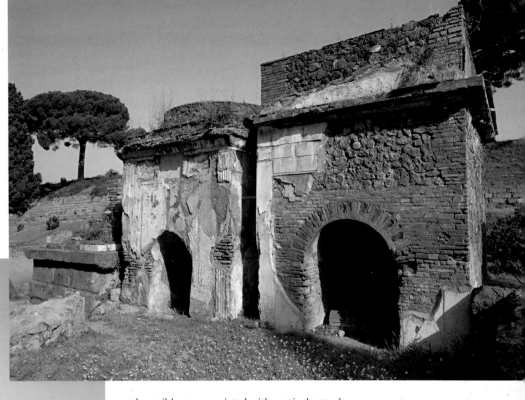

House tombs outside the Nuceria Gate, a popular form of multi-occupancy tomb in the 1st century AD. Their external walls were decorated with painted stucco, although little survives of this today.

and possibly are associated with particular tombs – or in groups in more remote spots. Some appear to relate to painted inscriptions found on the town's walls. For example, a series of names, including ' Fausta Iulia' (*CIL* X 8353) and 'Gaius Cosidius' (*CIL* X 8350), were inscribed on the walls between the Nola and Sarno Gates. These may mark the burials of some of Pompeii's poorer inhabitants.

There is an extremely diverse range of memorials to the dead at Pompeii, many of which were decorated with reliefs or wall-paintings, and most of which had inscriptions identifying the deceased. The majority of Pompeii's tombs – with the exception of the most important tombs of the elite – were designed to contain more than one burial. Within a communal tomb, however, there was often one main occupant, and the tomb was used to illustrate the status of this person. The others buried in the tomb would be members of the extended family, and often their names were not recorded. In general, the inscriptions found on the tombs of Pompeii (and elsewhere in the Roman world) are brief and formulaic. They record the name and achievements of the deceased, such as public offices held. There is little personal information. The emphasis is on status – the status of the dead person and thus the status reflected on the living members of his or her family.

An alabaster funerary urn from one of the tombs outside the Nuceria Gate. The ashes of the deceased were placed in such urns, which could also be made from clay or glass, and placed inside the tomb.

The Herculaneum Gate tombs

The Herculaneum Gate was the place to be buried if you were a member of Pompeii's elite. Many of the largest and most ornamental tombs were located here, the resting-places of many of the town's most important magistrates. The inscriptions on the tombs reveal the public and religious offices they held and whether the town council gave their burial spot and paid for their funeral. The tombs of a few freedmen – presumably wealthy ones – are spotted between those of the social elite. A line of shops can also be seen behind the tombs on the left of the street, and several large villas were located on either side of it. The tombs, shops and villas were excavated between 1763 and 1838.

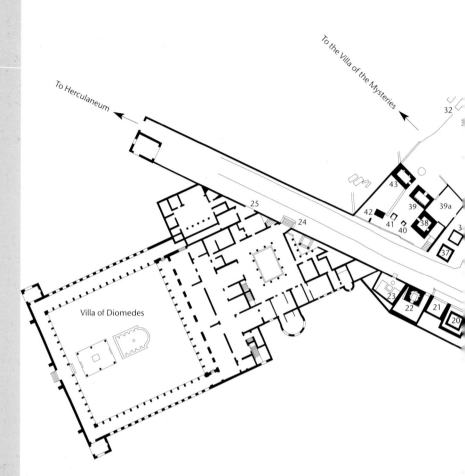

South of the road

1 'Marcus Cerrinius Restitutus, *Augustalis*, a burial place was given by decree of the town council' (*CIL* X 994)

2 'For Aulus Veius, son of Marcus, duumvir with judicial power, quinquennial duumvir for the second time, military tribune by popular demand, by decree of the town council' (*CIL* X 996)

3 'For Marcus Porcius, son of Marcus, by decree of the town council, funeral plot 25 feet wide, 25 feet deep' (*CIL* X 997)

4 'For Mamia, daughter of Publius, public priestess, this burial place was given by decree of the town council' (*CIL* X 998)

4a Inscriptions include: 'Istacidia Rufilla, daughter of Numerius, public priestess' and 'For Numerius Istacidius Campanus...' (*CIL* X 999 and *CIL* X 1005)

5 Street shrine

6 Villa of Cicero entrance

7–15 Shops

16 'For A. Umbricius Scaurus, son of Aulus, of the Menenian tribe, duumvir with judicial power, the decurions decreed the place for his monument and 2,000 sesterces towards the cost of his funeral and an equestrian statue to be placed in the Forum. Scaurus, the father, to his son' (*CIL* X 1024)

17 The main inscription is fragmentary, but another on the famous relief depicting gladiators reads: 'At the games of [Numerius Fes]tius Ampliatus on the last day' (*CIL* IV 1182)

18 'Marcia Aucta, his wife, made this tomb for Gaius Fabius Secundus and for herself and for Fabia Gratina, daughter of Gaius, her daughter' (*CIL* X 1003)

19 Unidentified tomb

20 'For Gaius Calventius Quietus, *Augustalis*. To him, on account of his generosity, the honour of a *bisellium* was given by decree of the town council and by popular consent' (*CIL* X 1026)

21 'To Numerius Istacidius Helenus, inhabitant of the Pagus Augustus Felix Suburbanus, to Numerius Istacidius Ianuarius, to Mesonia Satulla. 15 feet deep, 15 feet wide' (*CIL* X 1027)

22 'Naevoleia Tyche, freedwoman of Lucius, set this up for herself and for Gaius Munatius Faustus, *Augustalis* and country dweller, to whom on account of his merits the town council with the approval of the people decreed a *bisellium* (honorific chair). Naevoleia Tyche built this monument for her freedmen and freedwomen and for those of Gaius Munatius Faustus during her lifetime' (*CIL* X 1030)

23 'To Gnaeus Vibrius Saturninus, son of Quintus, of the tribe Falerna, his freedman Callistus set it up' (*CIL* X 1033)

24–25 Villa of Diomedes entrances

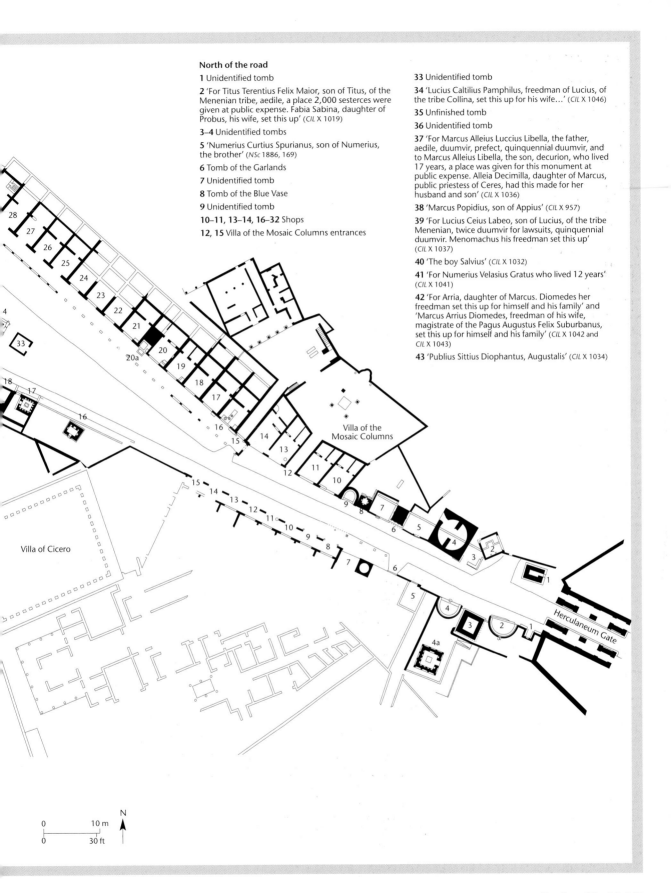

North of the road

1 Unidentified tomb

2 'For Titus Terentius Felix Maior, son of Titus, of the Menenian tribe, aedile, a place 2,000 sesterces were given at public expense. Fabia Sabina, daughter of Probus, his wife, set this up' (*CIL* X 1019)

3–4 Unidentified tombs

5 'Numerius Curtius Spurianus, son of Numerius, the brother' (*NSc* 1886, 169)

6 Tomb of the Garlands

7 Unidentified tomb

8 Tomb of the Blue Vase

9 Unidentified tomb

10–11, 13–14, 16–32 Shops

12, 15 Villa of the Mosaic Columns entrances

33 Unidentified tomb

34 'Lucius Caltilius Pamphilus, freedman of Lucius, of the tribe Collina, set this up for his wife…' (*CIL* X 1046)

35 Unfinished tomb

36 Unidentified tomb

37 'For Marcus Alleius Luccius Libella, the father, aedile, duumvir, prefect, quinquennial duumvir, and to Marcus Alleius Libella, the son, decurion, who lived 17 years, a place was given for this monument at public expense. Alleia Decimilla, daughter of Marcus, public priestess of Ceres, had this made for her husband and son' (*CIL* X 1036)

38 'Marcus Popidius, son of Appius' (*CIL* X 957)

39 'For Lucius Ceius Labeo, son of Lucius, of the tribe Menenian, twice duumvir for lawsuits, quinquennial duumvir. Menomachus his freedman set this up' (*CIL* X 1037)

40 'The boy Salvius' (*CIL* X 1032)

41 'For Numerius Velasius Gratus who lived 12 years' (*CIL* X 1041)

42 'For Arria, daughter of Marcus. Diomedes her freedman set this up for himself and his family' and 'Marcus Arrius Diomedes, freedman of his wife, magistrate of the Pagus Augustus Felix Suburbanus, set this up for himself and his family' (*CIL* X 1042 and *CIL* X 1043)

43 'Publius Sittius Diophantus, Augustalis' (*CIL* X 1034)

Villa of the Mosaic Columns

Villa of Cicero

Herculaneum Gate

0 — 10 m
0 — 30 ft

N

The Evidence of Graffiti and Other Writings

(Right) Figurative graffiti are common at Pompeii. This head of an old man (accompanied by the graffito 'Rufus est' or 'This is Rufus') was found in the Villa of the Mysteries. The figure of Mercury is from the Bar of Asellina (IX.11.12), and the hunt scene is from the House of Obellius Firmus (IX.14.2/4).

(Opposite) A young girl in profile, who appears to be gazing at something in her hands, possibly a scroll. Her intensity of expression has led some scholars to suggest that she was a figure drawn from life. Although from Pompeii, the exact provenance of this wall-painting is now unknown.

ANOTHER WINDOW INTO THE EVERYDAY LIFE OF SOME OF the people of Pompeii is provided by graffiti. Many of the most famous examples are vulgar or erotic or are lines from the poems of Virgil or Ovid or other Roman writers. The following examples were all found in Pompeii's Basilica in the Forum:

> Samius to Cornelius: go hang yourself. (*CIL* IV 1864)
>
> Phileros is a eunuch. (*CIL* IV 1826)
>
> Virgula to her bloke Tertius: you're a dirty old man. (*CIL* IV 1881)
>
> Chios, I hope your piles irritate you so they burn like they've never burned before! (*CIL* IV 1820)

But the vast majority of graffiti are banal. These also were found in the Basilica:

> Gaius Pumidius Dipilus was here on 3 October in the year when Marcus Lepidus and Quintus Catulus were consuls [88 BC]. (*CIL* IV 1842)
>
> Auge loves Allotenus. (*CIL* IV 1808)
>
> Gaius Aufidius. (*CIL* IV 1793)
>
> Lucilla was making money from her body. (*CIL* IV 1948)

Many examples are simply names or illegible scratches on a wall. Occasionally they have a specific purpose – to record a business transaction or advertise something lost or found, as in this fragmentary advertisement painted on the Via dei Teatri:

> A brass pot disappeared from this shop. If anyone brings it back, he'll be rewarded with 65 sesterces. If he hands over the thief…. (*CIL* IV 64)

Sometimes graffiti give advice or instructions:

> I hate poor people. Anyone who asks for anything free is a fool; he should hand over his money and take the goods. (*CIL* IV. 9839) (I.12.1)
>
> Gaius Sabinus Statio greets you. Traveller, you eat bread at Pompeii, but you drink at Nuceria. (*CIL* IV 8903) (III.5)
>
> If you want to waste time, scatter millet and collect it up. (*CIL* IV 2069)
>
> At Nuceria, look for Novellia Primigenia near the Roman gate in the prostitute's district. (*CIL* IV 8356) (I.10.4)

Sometimes the graffiti relate to particular groups of people or occasions. The following were all found in what is thought to have been an inn (VII.12.35), probably the scratchings of visitors to Pompeii:

Gaius Valerius Venustus, soldier of the first cohort
(*CIL* IV 2145)

Good fortune to the colonia Claudia Neronensis of
Puteoli! Gaius Julius Speratus wrote this. (*CIL* IV 2152)

Vibius Restitutus slept here alone and all the time
longed for his Urbana. (*CIL* IV 2146)

Lucifer and Primigenius came this way. (*CIL* IV 2156)

Lucceius Albanus of Abellinum, with.... (*CIL* IV 2159)

Marcus Clodius Primio was here. (*CIL* IV IV 2147)

In general, graffiti represent spontaneous emotions
or thoughts, or reactions to commonplace events.
Their topics include love, disappointment, malice
and joy, and it is for this reason that they seem so
familiar to the modern observer.

Crescens is master of the girls. (*CIL* IV 8916) (III.6)

Coelius, with Rufus and Eburiolus and Faustus are
like brothers. Eburiolus greets Marina and Valeria.
Eburiolus greets his friend Faustus and Coelius and
the Faustiani. (*CIL* IV 8227) (I.10)

Nucerinus is a fine man.
(*CIL* IV 8966) (IX.14.4)

Marcellus loves Praestina and is not loved in return.
(*CIL* IV 7679)

Only Marcus Terentius Eudoxsis always supports
his friends – he keeps them and protects them and
supports them in every way.
(*CIL* 4456) (VI.13.5–7)

Paris was here. (*CIL* IV 1305) (VI.9.5)

Atimetus got me pregnant. (*CIL* IV 3117) (VII.2.18)

It took 640 paces to walk back and forth between
here and there ten times. (*CIL* IV 1714) (VII.1.40)

Who could read and write at Pompeii?

There are over 11,000 examples of the written word
at Pompeii, in the form of inscriptions, painted
notices, graffiti and wax tablets. From the sheer
extent of this material, it is easy to assume that the
majority of the inhabitants could read and write.
This is, however, a controversial issue and there is
much disagreement over the extent of literacy. The
problem is that a piece of writing does not necessarily reflect an individual's ability to read and write.
For example, a 'to do' list serves as an aide memoire
to the person who wrote it, but reveals little about
that person's knowledge of grammar and spelling
or ability to express their thoughts clearly in
writing. This means that it is important to consider
the function of a piece of writing. The inscriptions
on the tombs of Pompeii are mostly brief and formulaic, with the aim of commemorating a
particular person and their family. Graffiti were
more personal, but generally equally brief. Painted
notices aimed to impart particular information,
wax tablets to record important events or agreements. None of these types of information tell us
whether the majority of Pompeii's inhabitants
could read and write fluently without difficulty, or
whether they had learned to recognize and read particularly common types of writing.

An important question is whether the people of
Pompeii needed to be able to read and write to
function fully in their society. Was there any real
motivation to learn these skills? Did everyone have
the same motivation or need for a high level of literacy? There were undoubtedly people in Pompeii
with a high level of literacy – such as members of
the upper classes and particular types of trader or
craftsmen. But the ability to read Virgil or spell
correctly was unnecessary for the majority of
people. There must have been a large number of
people who today would be considered semi-liter-
ate: people who picked up the skills of reading and
writing only to the extent that they were useful to
them in their daily lives and occupations. Some

people would simply have relied on family members or friends to read for them when the need arose. There is an example of a wall-painting from the Praedia (estate) of Julia Felix (II.4.2) that appears to show this happening in the Forum: a banner is hung between two statues and a man appears to be reading the notice to other people.

Finally, how did people learn to read and write? There was no compulsory or free school system as in the modern west. The ancient authors tell us that schools existed in the Roman world, but they are hard to pinpoint in the archaeological record, at Pompeii and elsewhere. For example, at Pompeii a graffito was found on a column in the Large Palaestra that may relate to a school:

> May anyone who has paid me for teaching get what he asks for from the gods. (*CIL* IV 8562)

Another graffito on the same column appears to relate to the payment of school fees:

Albanus	1 as
Albanus	2 asses
Agathemerus	2 asses
Acathemerus	1 as
Acanthus wrote this.	
(*CIL* IV 8565)	

There is also another a wall-painting from the Praedia of Julia Felix that has been interpreted as a school scene: a row of boys sit in the Forum with wax tablets on their knees while another boy is flogged. From these examples, it is possible to conclude that schools may well have existed at Pompeii, but that they did not have permanent locations. But this still does not tell us how many people received formal schooling. The majority of those who could read and write to any degree probably would have learnt in the home from other members of their family.

(Above) This wall-painting from the Praedia of Julia Felix (II.4.2) depicts writing materials – ink-pot and stylus, papyrus roll and wax tablets. On the shelf above them are two piles of coins on either side of a bag.

(Opposite) One of a series of frescos depicting scenes in the Forum, from the Praedia of Julia Felix. A banner has been strung across three statue bases: one man appears to be reading the banner to two others.

(Below) Examples of writing implements – ink-pots and a stylus – found during the excavations.

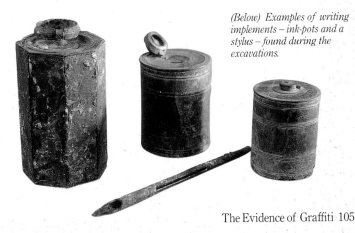

Erotic Pompeii

ONE OF THE FEATURES OF POMPEII THAT OFTEN SURPRISES modern visitors is the frequency of erotic images. Erotic art, in the form of wall-paintings, graffiti and artifacts, is found all over the town, in private houses, public buildings and on the street facades. It so shocked the sensibilities of the earliest excavators that erotic art and objects were removed from the excavations by order of King Charles III and kept under lock and key. Later, in 1817 a 'Secret Cabinet' was created in which these items were displayed – but only to important male visitors with express permission.

There was no attempt to hide away explicit scenes at Pompeii, although it is fair to say that there are different categories of erotic art that are displayed in different contexts. Firstly, a particularly common find at Pompeii are phalluses and images of Priapus. These, however, were not intended as erotic symbols but as charms to ward off the 'evil eye' and ensure prosperity. It is for this reason that a large wall-painting of Priapus, with enormous phallus, is found at the entrance to the House of the Vettii (VI.15.1). Another famous example is the phallus carved into terracotta outside the bakery at VI.6.1 (on the Via delle Terme), with the following slogan above and below it:

Good fortune dwells here. (*CIL* IV 1454)

Other categories are more overtly sexual in nature. There are abundant mythological scenes, displayed

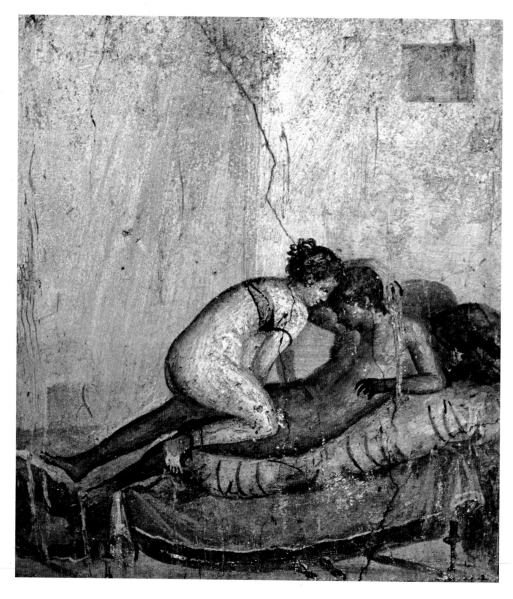

Erotic wall-painting from the so-called 'hidden chamber' in the House of the Centenary (IX.8.6), a room tucked away to one side of the house's private bath suite. A 'peephole' allowed activities in the room to be observed. On the basis of this and other erotic paintings, and a few explicit graffiti, this house is sometimes identified as a high-class brothel.

Priapus, the god of fertility, weighs his penis against a bag of coins over a basket overflowing with fruits. This wall-painting, from the fauces (entrance) of the House of the Vettii (VI.15.1), would have been considered a symbol of good luck and prosperity. Images of Priapus are found all over Pompeii.

The famous wall-painting of Venus and Mars, watched by Eros, from the House of Marcus Lucretius Fronto (V.4.a). Mythological scenes with sexual allusions are common at Pompeii.

openly in different rooms of private houses. Common scenes include Venus and Mars, and Pan with a nymph. These scenes are suggestive rather than explicit. Another common category found openly in houses comprises scenes of banquets, with ordinary people whose inhibitions have been loosened by wine, but, again, the scenes are mostly suggestive. Then there are sexually explicit, realistic, scenes, most commonly found in bedrooms, back rooms or brothels. These were not generally open to public view like the previous categories. An exception to this rule can be seen in the Suburban Baths. The apodyterium (changing room) of these baths had once been decorated with erotic scenes, displayed in numbered boxes. Two of the scenes were of group sex, with three or four people. There has been much debate over their function. Did they represent a sex manual, were they advertisements for a brothel in the baths, or were they merely designed to entertain and titillate those visiting the baths? Whatever the case, by AD 79 these scenes had been covered over with new, non-erotic, decoration.

There is plenty of evidence for prostitution at Pompeii, such as the following recommendation, scratched on the wall just outside the Marine Gate:

Anyone who sits here should read this first.
Anyone who wants to fuck should ask for Attice
for 16 asses. (*CIL* IV 1751)

Prostitutes were tolerated in Roman law although they formed the lowest category of citizen, held in direct contrast to 'respectable' matrons. Attempts were made to regulate prostitution, and prostitutes were taxed; but they also had certain rights, such as the right to keep their fee. In theory, all Romans – male or female – could prostitute themselves, or they could sell the sexual services of their slaves. In practice, most prostitutes were probably members of the poorer classes or slaves.

There is disagreement over the number of brothels in Pompeii because the identification of such properties is not easy or straightforward.

Traditionally they have been identified on the basis of explicit graffiti or wall-paintings, or located in the small cell-like rooms (*cellae*) with masonry beds that are found on some of Pompeii's streets, for example at VII.11.12 and IX.6.2. It is possible that some brothels were located in private houses and that some prostitutes worked out of baths, but it is unlikely that prostitution was the primary function of these buildings. As we have seen, erotic art was extremely common in the Roman world; in addition, it has been pointed out that explicit graffiti need not relate to sex for money or mark the precise location of a brothel, and the *cellae* could have had other possible uses, such as for storage or for guards and watchmen. It is also apparent from the ancient literary sources that prostitution was common in bars and inns, which means that many innkeepers may have supplemented their income by providing 'company' for their customers.

Only one premises, known as the Lupanar (VII.12.18), appears to have been purpose-built as a brothel. It consisted of two floors. The five rooms of the upper floor were accessed by a separate entrance. The lower floors had five small rooms with masonry beds off a hallway with a latrine at the opposite end to the entrance. The hallway was decorated with explicit wall-paintings (now mostly faded). There was also a large painting of Priapus with two phalluses near the latrine. The walls of the rooms were simply decorated and covered with over 100 graffiti, variously documenting the names of prostitutes and customers, dates, sexual acts and prices. The following are examples:

(Below and right) The apodyterium (changing room) of the Suburban Baths was decorated with erotic scenes in numbered panels. Often taken as evidence for the presence of a brothel in the rooms above the baths, the scenes had been painted over in AD 79.

I fucked many girls here. (*CIL* IV 2175)

Felix, you fuck well. (*CIL* IV 2176)

Phoebus the perfumer fucks the best. (*CIL* IV 2184)

Scordopordonicus had a good fuck with whoever he wanted here. (*CIL* IV 2188)

Arphocras had a good fuck here with Drauca (for a) denarius. (*CIL* IV 2193)

I was fucked here. (*CIL* IV 2217)

Here Victoria is unconquered. (*CIL* IV 2226)

Victor fucked with Attine here. (*CIL* IV 2258)

Most of the graffiti are in Latin, but a few are written in Greek. Women's names include Fortunata, Drauca, Murtis, Nice and Attine (presumably prostitutes); male names include Hermeros, Phoebus, Hyginus, Victor, Arphocras and Felix (either customers or prostitutes). It is likely that many different prostitutes, both female and male, worked in the Lupanar. But we do not know how it worked, whether particular prostitutes worked for the owner of the Lupanar or whether independent prostitutes could bring clients there.

(Right) One of the explicit wall-paintings found in the hallway of the Lupanar (VII.12.18). These were perhaps advertisements for the types of sexual service offered in the establishment. The whitewashed walls of its individual chambers were covered in graffiti.

Women in Pompeii

THE ACTIVITIES OF WOMEN WERE RESTRICTED IN ROMAN law. Originally, they were subject to the legal control of their fathers, husbands or nearest male relative. They had no voice in politics and no resources of their own. Their political situation did not change, but by the Augustan period some women were allowed to own property in their own right and to manage their affairs (although officially they had to have a male financial guardian to authorize actions

(Above) Wall-painting of a young woman wearing a laurel wreath and gold earrings, from Herculaneum. This fragmentary painting is thought to have been part of a mythological scene (the arrival of Jason at the court of Pelias), but its precise provenance is now unknown.

(Right) In this unprovenanced wall-painting from Herculaneum, two women (left) watch another having her hair styled. The women wear flowing tunics, jewelry and sandals, and one wears a veil.

(Opposite above) Portrait of a girl wearing a golden hairnet and holding a stylus and wax tablet, from a house in the Insula Occidentale (Region VI). Although unlikely to have been the portrait of a real girl, the writing implements she holds, and other paintings in the house that have the themes of music and theatre, suggest that the commissioner of the painting was interested in the world of learning and culture. Some scholars have identified the portrait as the Greek poet, Sappho.

(Opposite below) This elaborate silver hand mirror was found in the House of Menander (I.10.4), along with a large collection of silver vessels. It is decorated with an emblema of a female head in profile. The glass perfume bottles were found in various houses, and illustrate the different types of glass and vessel used for unguents. The blue bottle in the form of a bunch of grapes is the less common type; it was found in a wooden cupboard in the atrium of I.13.2 along with 44 other perfume bottles of differing types.

such as borrowing money). Evidence from Pompeii and Herculaneum reveals that many women conducted business, owned property, constructed buildings and tombs, held priesthoods and gave support to electoral candidates, and that some women were honoured for the services they performed. However, whereas for many of the male inhabitants of the town we can reconstruct careers and business activities in some detail, we usually only have brief impressions of the lives of women. The women of Pompeii were not a homogeneous group – they had different statuses and wealth, and the variety of the available evidence reflects these factors. Some are recorded in honorific inscriptions, others in wall-scratchings.

Inscription on the Eumachia Building in the Forum, and the statue of Eumachia found inside the building (right). The priestess Eumachia was an important patroness of the town and paid for one of its largest public buildings.

Possibly the most famous woman in Pompeii is Eumachia, a public priestess (possibly of Ceres), who clearly had great influence in the town. She came from a wealthy family; amphorae discovered all over the Mediterranean suggest that her father exported Pompeian wine. She married into another prominent Pompeian family. Her husband was Marcus Numistrius Fronto. Either he or his son of the same name held the office of duumvir in AD 3. Eumachia's activities are described in several marble inscriptions. Over the two entrances to the building she constructed in the Forum, known to us as the Eumachia Building, two inscriptions identical in wording, although not appearance, were placed:

> Eumachia, daughter of Lucius, public priestess, in her own name and that of her son, Marcus Numistrius Fronto, built at her own expense the chalcidicum (porch), crypta (covered passage), and porticus, and dedicated them to Augustan Concord and Piety. (*CIL* X 810 and 811)

This inscription is revealing for a number of reasons. Foremostly it emphasizes Eumachia's wealth. She was able to build the largest building in Pompeii's Forum from her own funds. The fact that a woman was allowed to build such a prominent building in this location attests to her influence among the local elite. By dedicating her building jointly, she was permanently associating the name of her husband or her son with this major benefaction, which would have enhanced his status within the community (and in the case of the son may have helped his election campaign). Finally, she emphasized her loyalty to Rome and to Augustus by dedicating the building to Augustan Concord and Piety. These were virtues that were central to Augustan ideology and commonly associated with Augustan buildings in Rome and copied by provincial towns all over Italy and the Mediterranean.

Eumachia's influence is further highlighted by another inscription in the Eumachia Building, associated with a statue of her set up by Pompeii's guild of fullers:

To Eumachia, daughter of Lucius, public priestess, from the fullers. (*CIL* X 813)

We do not know why the fullers chose to honour Eumachia in this way, but it further emphasizes her influence within the town. Eumachia is portrayed in the statue with her head veiled, in her guise as priestess, which represents her piety and womanly virtue. Despite her obvious political influence, she is depicted as a woman of traditional values. Frequent comparisons have been made between this statue and statues of Livia, the emperor Augustus' wife, in a similar pose. We do not know whether this similarity was deliberate, and, if so, an attempt to draw a comparison between Eumachia and the most powerful woman in the Roman empire.

The final piece of evidence for Eumachia is her tomb, located just outside the Nuceria Gate. Its inscription records that she built the tomb for herself and her family at her own expense. This is rather surprising, since the tombs of Pompeii's prominent inhabitants were often paid for by public money or built on donated public land. Other women were honoured in this way, and it seems strange that Eumachia was not, given her status as public priestess and her construction of the Eumachia Building. Despite this, the tomb was the largest in Pompeii, measuring almost 14 sq. m (150 sq. ft). It consists of a terrace, a seating area and an enclosure that contained the burials. A decorative frieze depicted Amazons fighting, and there were herms displayed of the deceased members of her household. This imposing tomb dominates the others at the Nuceria Gate. Eumachia may not have had the honour of a publicly funded burial, but her tomb visibly announced her status and wealth to all who passed by.

The priestess Mamia was a Pompeian woman who did something important enough to warrant being buried on public land donated by order of the town council. A damaged and difficult-to-read inscription found somewhere in the Forum (its exact provenance is unknown) suggests that she was responsible for the construction at her own expense of a temple to the *genius* ('divine spirit') of someone or something, but the location of this temple is uncertain. One hypothesis is that it was located on the west side of the Forum, next to the Eumachia Building, and has been wrongly labelled as the Temple of Vespasian. Mamia seems to have been a member of a very old Samnite family. Her tomb was a prestigious 'exedra tomb', with a prominent location, just outside the Herculaneum Gate, alongside the tombs of some of Pompeii's most important inhabitants. The inscription on the tomb reads:

To Mamia, daughter of Publius, public priestess, a burial place was given by decree of the town councillors. (*CIL* X 998)

Photograph dating to c. 1920–30 of the 'exedra' Tomb of Aesquillia Polla, outside the Nola Gate. Her ashes are located in the urn on top of the column. The tomb provided a circular bench for passers-by to rest, an opportunity for them to read the tomb's inscription.

There are other examples of women who were honoured at their death by the town, but little more is known about them. The Tomb of Septumia was set up by her daughter, Antistia Prima, on public land outside the Vesuvius Gate, by decree of the town council. Public money was also given towards the cost of her funeral. But there is no surviving evidence to indicate what she might have done to receive this honour. Similarly, the exedra Tomb of Aesquillia Polla outside the Nola Gate was set up by her husband on public land. The inscription reads:

Numerius Herennius Celsus, son of Numerius, of the Menenian tribe, duumvir with judicial power for the second time, *praefectus fabrum*, dedicates this to his wife Aesquillia Polla, daughter of Gaius. She lived 22 years. The burial place was given publicly by decree of the town councillors. (*AE*, 1911, 71)

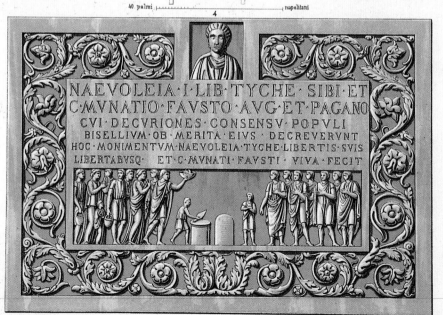

NAEVOLEIA · I · LIB · TYCHE · SIBI · ET
C · MVNATIO · FAVSTO · AVG · ET · PAGANO
CVI · DECVRIONES · CONSENSV · POPVLI
BISELLIVM · OB · MERITA · EIVS · DECREVERVNT
HOC · MONIMENTVM · NAEVOLEIA · TYCHE · LIBERTIS · SVIS
LIBERTABVSQ · ET · C · MVNATI · FAVSTI · VIVA · FECIT

It is the status and achievements of Aesquilla's husband that are recorded. Nothing is known about her, other than her age and her father's name. This tomb is designed to mark her family's status rather than to commemorate her in her own right.

Some women, like Eumachia, were responsible for building their own funerary monuments, although in contrast to Eumachia we have no supplementary evidence of their activities in the town apart from the tomb itself. A good example is Naevoleia Tyche. She was a freedwoman married to Gaius Munatius Faustus, a freedman who had achieved the position of Augustalis. He had built a fairly simple tomb for himself, his wife and his family outside the Nuceria Gate. When he died, he was buried there, along with other members of his extended family. Naevoleia Tyche seems to have inherited his property and business concerns after his death, and promptly built another tomb, this time outside the Herculaneum Gate. She was obviously more concerned than her husband had been to emphasize their status and wealth. The new tomb was an 'altar tomb', a raised altar within a low enclosure. It was decorated with relief sculpture depicting a ship on one side and a bisellium on the other – probably representing Gaius' source of wealth (shipping) and an honour given to him during his lifetime (a magisterial bench at games or performances). There is also a depiction of some sort of public ceremony, and a portrait of Naevoleia Tyche. Inside the tomb were a number of glass cremation urns, each accompanied by a lamp. The inscription on the tomb reads:

> Naevoleia Tyche, freedwoman of Lucius, set this up for herself and for Gaius Munatius Faustus, Augustalis and country dweller, to whom on account of his merits the town council with the approval of the people decreed a bisellium (honorific chair). Naevoleia Tyche built this monument for her freedmen and freedwomen and for those of Gaius Munatius Faustus during her lifetime. (*CIL* X 1030)

(Opposite) This 19th-century drawing illustrates the different components of the Tomb of Naevoleia Tyche – the enclosure and altar, and the location of the glass cremation urns found inside the tomb. A portrait of Naevoleia Tyche herself overlooks the inscription and the depiction of a public ceremony beneath it.

(Right) This gold and pearl ornament would have formed the centrepiece of an elaborate hairstyle. The cluster earrings – gold and emerald, and gold and pearl – were found in the House of Menander (I.10.4). Bracelets and rings in the form of snakes were a common form of jewelry in the Roman world. This gold armband, with its finely incised scales and snake's head with eyes of green vitreous paste, is one of a pair, probably found in Pompeii but now in the Naples Museum.

Wall-painting of a female painter, excavated in 1771 from the House of the Surgeon (VI.1.10). She dips her paintbrush into a box of colours and paints a herm of Priapus.

Clearly Naevoleia Tyche wanted her husband's achievements to be recorded more fully and was prepared to pay for this to happen. But the inscription on the tomb underlines her own role in its construction, and draws attention to her wealth and status. Husband and wife are equally recorded in this inscription on the new tomb. Ironically, despite what the inscription says, her husband's ashes remained in his original tomb outside the Nuceria Gate.

What all these tombs reveal are the resources available to certain Pompeian women of elite families. In some cases they also shed some light on the ambitions that these women held and the aspects of their lives that they felt most proud of, such as being a priestess. Eumachia, Mamia, Arellia Tertulla and Aesquillia Polla were all members of prominent and wealthy Pompeian families. Eumachia, Mamia and Arellia Tertulla were also public priestesses. There are five priestesses of Venus known from the Julio-Claudian period, such as Alleia, daughter of Gnaeus Alleius Nigidius

Maius (one of Pompeii's most prominent men, see p.140), who was priestess of Venus and Ceres during the reign of Nero. The cults of Venus and Ceres were the only ones that allowed women to participate in public life at this level.

Although women couldn't vote, they were certainly interested in the outcome of the elections. There are at least 52 electoral posters on the walls of Pompeii by women asking for certain men to be elected. Sometimes the names of women appear jointly with those of men, but there are also examples of women acting independently.

For example:

> Statia and Petronia ask you to make M. Casellius and L. Albucius aediles. May there always be such fine citizens in the colony. *(ILS 6414)*

Unfortunately, we have no way of knowing how seriously their opinions were taken.

Some women also had wide-ranging commercial and business interests. Some were obviously wealthy property-owners. A painted notice dating to AD 64–79 advertised a large property for rent:

> For rent from the Ides of August until the Ides of August five years hence: a charming bath suitable for the best people, shops and the rooms above them, and upper storey apartments, on the estate of Julia Felix, daughter of Spurius. (*CIL* IV 1136)

Other women are seen entering into formal business agreements with men: there are 14 women named in the archive of the banker Lucius Caecilius Jucundus (see p.220). For example, in AD 56 Jucundus sold goods at auction on behalf of Umbricia Januaria, and received a commission from her for his service. This is also evidence that women transacted business amongst themselves, without the involvement of men. A graffito in a tavern reveals that a woman named Faustilla loaned two denarii to someone and charged a fee of one as. Earrings were left with her as security. On another occasion she lent 15 denarii to a woman called Vettia and charged eight asses in interest. Wax tablets found in the Sarno Baths (VIII.2.17) record that Poppaea Note, a freedwoman, borrowed money from Dicidia Margaris in AD 61 and left two slaves with her as security. These tablets were found with a collection of silver plate, including sets of trays, goblets and cups, along with a silver statue of Jupiter on a bronze pedestal and three pairs of earrings. It is easy to speculate that these valuables – the wax tablets as well as the silver – were gathered up during the eruption as the people of Pompeii began to realize their need

to escape. But these collected items may also be evidence of the wealth that Dicidia Margaris had accrued through her business dealings.

Women clearly had an important role to play in economic, religious and even political life at Pompeii. But the scale of their economic activity varies drastically and no doubt reflects the differing social status and resources of the women involved. Julia Felix had a whole estate to rent, Faustilla's dealings involved small amounts of money. Other women are known for their jobs rather than for their business dealings, and little is known about them apart from their names. For example, the names of 11 female spinners are listed in a graffito from the House of Marcus Terentius Eudoxus (VI.13.6), but no other details. We also know the names of women who worked in taverns and as prostitutes. However, unless women were wealthy and either were honoured by the town council or put up an inscription to record their deeds, we know virtually nothing about their lives. It is difficult to give a clear picture even for women like Eumachia who have left behind several different types of evidence. Some women appear to have had influence in the community, others may have controlled business enterprises. But it is hard to know the real extent of their activities, and it is difficult to generalize about the lives of women in Pompeii on the basis of such limited evidence. Ultimately this was a male-dominated society, and thus it is the men of Pompeii's elite that we have far more evidence about.

The garden of the Praedia of Julia Felix (II.4.2), around which were located rental apartments and a private bath suite. This is one of only two securely known examples of rental accommodation at Pompeii.

V
LIFE IN THE PUBLIC EYE

All, then, united, nothing could exceed in variety the costumes, the ranks, the manners, the occupations of the crowd; – nothing could exceed the bustle, the gaiety, the animation, the flow and flush of life all around. You saw there all the myriad signs of a heated and feverish civilisation, – where pleasure and commerce, idleness and labour, avarice and ambition, mingled in one gulf their motley rushing, yet harmonious, streams.

Sir Edward Bulwer Lytton, *The Last Days of Pompeii* ('The Forum of the Pompeians'), 1834

The Roman empire consisted of countless towns and their territories. The town was the focus of Roman administration, justice and religion in the empire, and, despite some regional diversities, Roman towns shared many common features. Monumental baths, amphitheatres, basilicas and temples all characterize the Roman town and became symbols of empire – indeed, there was an expectation that a town be architecturally worthy of its civic status within the empire. Many of these buildings were constructed at the expense of local elites, who competed to supply facilities within their towns and who were sometimes rewarded with political office and social prestige.

The dynamics of urban life can be studied in detail at Pompeii. Not only is the political set-up apparent, there is plenty of evidence for election campaigns and the ways in which candidates for public office sought to enhance their reputations and status. A common means of achieving this was by the provision of public buildings and entertainments. Public buildings also reflect social, political and cultural changes that occur at Pompeii over its long history and illustrate the ways in which its inhabitants could underline their loyalty to Rome and to Roman ideals.

Mosaic from the Villa of Titus Siminius Stephanus, discovered in 1897 outside the Vesuvius Gate, thought to represent Plato's Academy in Athens. Plato, third from the left, leans against a tree, which symbolizes wisdom and knowledge.

The Political Structure of Pompeii

OSCAN INSCRIPTIONS SURVIVE THAT DOCUMENT THE POLITical structure of Pompeii before 80 BC. There was a senior magistrate, or *meddix*, and one or more junior magistrates known as *aidilis* and *kvaisstur* who were responsible for roads and public finances respectively. There was also an elected Senate and a popular assembly. The titles aidilis and kvaisstur are similar to those in use at Rome – *aedile* and *quaestor* – and demonstrate the influence that Rome was already having in the towns of Italy in this period. When Pompeii became a Roman ally at the beginning of the 3rd century BC, Rome took control of wider issues of war and foreign policy, but Pompeii's political structure remained the same.

At its foundation in *c.* 80 BC, the Colonia Cornelia Veneria Pompeianorum was given a *lex* (or charter) that set out the political and administrative structure still in use at the time of the eruption in AD 79. This lex would have been inscribed in bronze and set up in a public place, but has never been discovered during excavations of the site. Despite this, it is possible to reconstruct Pompeii's political structure from other inscriptions and electoral notices and also from comparison with other Roman towns in Italy.

There were three political institutions at Pompeii: the *comitium*, the *ordo decurionum* and the magistracy.

Political offices known at Pompeii in the Roman Period

Aedile	Junior magistrate in charge of public temples, buildings and markets, and with responsibility for games.
Decurion	Local town councillor.
Duumvir (or duovir)	The senior magistrate.
Military tribune	An honorific title awarded by popular demand to notable citizens.
Patron	A man selected by the town council to protect the community's interests at Rome.
Prefect	A magistrate appointed in special circumstances.
Quaestor	A junior magistrate in charge of public finance (only found at Pompeii before *c.* 80 BC).
Quinquennial duumvir	A magistrate elected every five years to carry out the census of the population.

The comitium or 'people's assembly'

The comitium was made up of all adult male citizens of the town, including freedmen. By the 1st century AD it functioned solely to elect magistrates and to vote honours.

The ordo decurionum

This was the legislative body of Pompeii, able to make decisions on any matter that concerned the colony as a whole. Decisions of the ordo were implemented by its magistrates. Its members were called 'decurions', most of whom had served previously as junior magistrates, although sometimes members were admitted who did not fulfil this qualification (for example, there are rare examples of children being admitted to the ordo). New members were admitted into the ordo every five years, and it is likely that most remained until their deaths. Traditionally it has been thought that the ordo consisted of 100 members; however, it has been pointed out recently that the size of the ordo varied in different towns. Although entries to the ordo were fairly constant (the junior magistrates each year became members), vacancies (due to death) were unpredictable. Thus the size of the ordo would have varied at different times.

The magistracy

The comitium elected two senior magistrates (known as duumvirs or duovirs) and two junior magistrates (aediles) who were responsible for the judicial system, administration, public works and buildings, municipal cults and games-giving. The magistrates presided over proceedings in the ordo and elections in the comitium. Every five years the duumvirs held a census to revise the list of ordo members and were given the title quinquennial duumvirs. In order to hold office, a candidate for a magistracy had to be male, free-born, over 25 (unless exempted), have a fortune above a certain level and be of unblemished reputation. To become duumvir, a candidate first had to be elected aedile.

Occasionally the Roman emperor or his heir was nominated duumvir. Inscriptions record that Gaius Caligula was duumvir at Pompeii twice, in AD 33 while he was Tiberius' heir and in AD 40 after he had become emperor. These were, of course, honorary positions and special magistrates – known as prefects – were appointed to fulfil the role of duumvir in Caligula's place. Prefects could also be appointed in special circumstances, such as after the riot in the Amphitheatre in AD 59 (discussed below) and after the earthquake of AD 63 (see Chapter IX).

Other honours

The most prestigious honour to be bestowed on a citizen was that of 'patron' of the town. A patron was formally selected by the town council to represent and protect the interests of the community

A 19th-century reconstruction by G. Cel of the imposing interior of Pompeii's Basilica, as seen from the Forum entrance. The Basilica was at the heart of Roman public life, a centre for justice, politics and business.

at Rome. The names of only a few patrons are known at Pompeii – it seems to have been a very rare honour, given only to the most important and powerful citizens, or to members of the imperial family. Publius Cornelius Sulla, the man responsible for founding the colony was also its patron, as were leading citizen Marcus Holconius Rufus and Marcellus, Augustus' nephew, son-in-law and heir. Another rare, purely honorific, title was that of 'military tribune'. This was awarded to a citizen by popular demand, presumably in return for services to the community as a whole. It has been suggested that this title was bestowed only in the Augustan period on local political leaders who had helped to organize the oath of allegiance sworn to Augustus after the civil wars that ended in 31 BC. Examples include Aulus Clodius Flaccus, Marcus Holconius Rufus, Marcus Tullius and Aulus Veius, all indeed prominent in the Augustan period.

Herculaneum

The political set-up at Herculaneum was similar, although unlike Pompeii Herculaneum did not suffer the imposition of a colony after the Social War of 91–87 BC. Surviving inscriptions demonstrate that Herculaneum was run by two annually-elected duumvirs. Aediles, also attested, would have supervised the markets, roads and public buildings. The town's finances may have been overseen by a third official, a quaestor, who is mentioned in a single inscription.

The Politics of Public Building

for rubbing down after exercise] and for the refurbishment of the portico and palaestra, in accordance with a decree of the town councillors, using the money that the law requires them to spend for games or public works. The same officials oversaw the construction and approved it. (*CIL* X 829)

Rich officials might donate entire buildings; the less well-off might provide smaller facilities within a building. Thus, the priestess Eumachia built the largest building in the Forum, while Marcus Nigidius Vaccula donated three benches to the Forum Baths and gave a brazier to the Stabian Baths. Both types of donation were commemorated by inscriptions, which acted as permanent reminders of the generosity of the donors. By spending money in this way, these men (and occasionally women) gained popularity and status within the local community. For junior magistrates, this might secure their election to higher political office in the future; for senior magistrates,

HOLDING PUBLIC OFFICE BROUGHT WITH IT OBLIGATIONS. It was required by law that magistrates and Augustales spend a certain amount of money for the good of the people as a whole by donating public buildings or providing facilities, or by putting on public entertainments. A marble inscription dating to the mid-1st century BC found in the Stabian Baths illustrates the point:

> Gaius Uulius, son of Gaius, and Publius Aninius, son of Gaius, duumvirs, awarded the contracts for the *laconicum* [sweat-baths] and *destrictarium* [room

The Covered Theatre

A dedicatory inscription reveals that the Covered Theatre (or Odeon) was built by Gaius Quinctius Valgus and Marcus Porcius soon after the establishment of the Roman colony in *c.* 80 BC:

> Gaius Quinctius Valgus, son of Gaius, and Marcus Porcius, son of Marcus, duumvirs, by decree of the town council contracted for the construction of the Covered Theatre and approved it. (*CIL* X 844)

A square frame of outer walls supported the roof and contained the semicircular *cavea* (seating area). Magistrates would have sat on chairs (*bisellia*) on the lowest four steps (the *ima cavea*) and were separated from the seating above (*media cavea*) by a balustrade. There were also boxes (*tribunalia*) over the side passages for honoured guests. Performances took place from a stage building (*scaenae frons*), in front of which was a semicircular orchestra. In the Augustan period, a magistrate named Marcus Oculatius Verus paid for the orchestra to be paved in coloured marble and for marble veneer to be applied to the front wall of the scaenae frons. Around 1,000 people could have been seated in this theatre, which was much smaller and more intimate than the large open theatre adjoining it.

The roof of the theatre would have improved the acoustics, making it suitable for readings of poetry and rhetoric, or both. In form, however, it is similar to a Greek *bouleuterion* (council chamber) and it has been suggested that it may also have been intended for the political meetings of the new colonists.

The Covered Theatre, constructed after the foundation of the Roman colony. Unlike the Large Theatre, which is situated on a natural slope, an artificial substructure had to be built to support the cavea of the Covered Theatre. Two kneeling telamones (one shown here) add a touch of elegance to the steps of the theatre. Actors would have worn masks, probably relating in origin to the cult of Dionysus. Two painted Dionysiac masks from the House of Fabius Rufus (VII. Ins. Occ. 16–19) are illustrated here.

it cemented their social standing within the community and could lead to all sorts of civic honours. Public munificence was the passport to political success and could also have an impact on the prestige of a family in later years.

There are also cases where officials appear to have been instructed by the town council to commission the construction of a building – probably at public rather than private expense. Possible examples are the Covered Theatre (or Odeon) and the Amphitheatre, overseen by Gaius Quinctius Valgus and Marcus Porcius. These men were Pompeii's first quinquennial duumvirs, responsible for the first census of the population after the foundation of the Roman colony in 80 BC and clearly two of the most important men in the colony at this period. But regardless of who paid for the construction, a series of monumental inscriptions forever associated the names of Valgus and Porcius with these two buildings.

The brazier donated by Marcus Nigidius Vaccula to the Stabian Baths, drawn by Giuseppe Abbate in the 19th century. A relief of a cow replaces the word 'Vaccula' (meaning 'little cow') in the inscription.

Civic Buildings in the Forum

THE FORUM STOOD AT THE HEART OF PUBLIC LIFE IN THE Roman world. All Roman towns were provided with a forum and related public buildings where politics, religion and business activities took place.

There is evidence of activity on the site of the Forum that dates to the 5th or 6th century BC, but its current form is the result of developments from the 2nd century BC, namely the construction of the Temple of Jupiter, the Basilica, the Macellum, and the paving of the Forum. Other public buildings were added later, and statues on monumental bases stood between columns of the portico and within the Forum square itself.

The Basilica

The Basilica was the venue for legal proceedings and business transactions. Pompeii's Basilica is located at the southwest end of the Forum. It was first excavated in 1813–16, and, on the basis of tile stamps, is thought to have been constructed around 100 BC, making it the oldest surviving basilica in Italy. Stratigraphic excavations conducted by Amedeo Maiuri revealed traces of an earlier building beneath the later Basilica and on the same alignment, but its function is unknown.

The Basilica covers an area of almost 5,000 sq. m (16,000 sq. ft). The main entrance to the Basilica had five large doors fitted with wooden shutters. Steps led up to a large nave or hall, framed by colossal columns. These are now reduced to stumps. No fragments of capitals belonging to these columns were reported by the excavators, but capitals survive from the engaged Ionic columns of the second storey of the building. The lower walls are covered in the remains of First Style wall-painting, imitating marble veneer. At the far (west) end of the

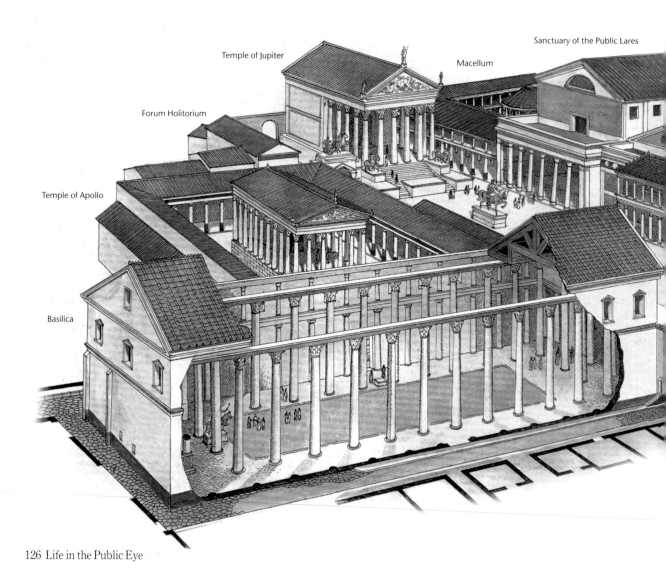

Temple of Jupiter

Sanctuary of the Public Lares

Macellum

Forum Holitorium

Temple of Apollo

Basilica

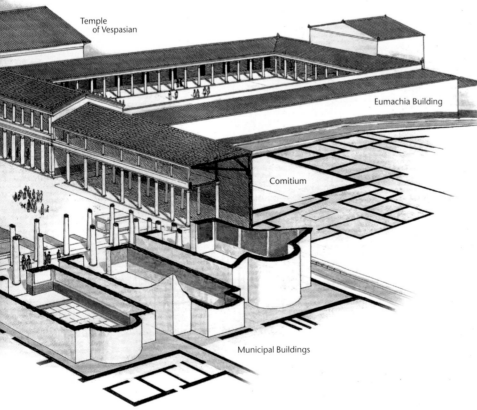

Temple of Vespasian

Eumachia Building

Comitium

Municipal Buildings

All the most important public buildings and temples were located around the Forum, which was dominated at its northern end by the Temple of Jupiter. Excavated in the 19th century, the Forum is ruinous in comparison to how it would have looked in the 1st century AD. At the time of the eruption in AD 79 the Forum appears to have been undergoing fairly extensive restorations, which would have made it all the more architecturally imposing. Although hypothetical, the reconstruction presented here gives a good idea of the grandeur of the Forum, with its double portico and the scale of its various buildings.

building is a raised platform (tribunal), possibly for auctions or trials (although the view to the platform is obscured by a large statue base). Beneath the platform is a vaulted cellar of uncertain function. It has sometimes been suggested that this was a lockup for prisoners awaiting trial, but it is more likely to have been a storage space of some sort.

'Municipal buildings'

The specific functions of these three buildings at the south end of the Forum are unknown, although they are commonly identified as the meeting places of the magistrates and the town councillors, and the location of the town archive. Similar buildings – rectangular halls with curved apsidal ends – have been found in many other Italian cities, generally erected by wealthy families either to celebrate their ancestors or to honour the imperial family. It is possible that the ones at Pompeii served similar purposes.

The Comitium

This building is often thought to have been the venue for municipal elections, although more recently it has been claimed that the entire Forum would have been used during elections. Possibly constructed in the 2nd century BC, its dating is uncertain. It was unroofed and at one time had five entrances from the Forum and four from the Via dell' Abbondanza. Some of these later were closed off, presumably after the earthquake of AD 63. There was a raised platform inside and many statue niches. The floor was paved with marble and the walls were decorated with stucco and marble.

The Basilica. A recent view towards the Tribunal, and a photograph from the beginning of the 20th century looking towards the Forum entrance. The colossal columns are broken stumps, probably damaged during the eruption and later taken by salvagers, evidence of whose activities are recorded in the excavation reports of 1814.

The Eumachia Building

The Eumachia Building (see also pp.114–5) was excavated from 1821–22, and its purpose has been debated ever since. Its modern name derives from that of the priestess Eumachia who constructed it and dedicated it in her name and that of either her husband or, more probably, her son to the cult of Concordia Augusta and Pietas (Augustan Concord and Piety). It is the largest building in the Forum, consisting of three parts: a *chalcidicum*, or deep porch, at the front of the building, making up part of the portico that runs along the east side of the Forum; a *porticus*, a four-sided colonnade surrounding a large rectangular court; and a *crypta*, a semi-subterranean corridor behind the colonnade on the north, east and south sides of the building. It could be entered either by the main entrance off the Forum or via a side-entrance on the Via dell' Abbondanza. Two statues of women were found during the excavation, a large headless statue (possibly representing either Augustan Concord or the Empress Livia, wife of Augustus, although these identifications are disputed) which may have been located in the large central apse on the rear wall of the building opposite the main entrance, and a smaller statue of Eumachia herself found in a niche at the centre of the back corridor and dedicated to her by the town's fullers.

It has been argued that the Eumachia Building had deliberate similarities of design and decoration to other buildings in Rome, such as the porticus built by Augustus in the name of the Empress Livia. The marble doorframe of the main entrance has also been thought to copy motifs such as acanthus leaves that were common on buildings in Rome in the Augustan period (in recent years, however, it has been pointed out that the doorframe does not actually fit the entrance very well; it probably never belonged to the Eumachia Building in antiquity, but was placed there by the excavators). In line with the dedication of the building to Augustan Concord and Piety, these similarities could possibly be interpreted as a means for Eumachia and her family to illustrate their allegiance to Rome and to Augustus. Interestingly, there are similarities between the Eumachia Building, the so-called 'basilica' at Herculaneum and other porticoed structures in Italy. This may reflect a new fashion for porticoes in Italy in the Augustan period, based on new buildings in Rome. It has been suggested that such buildings became indicators of the importance of the towns in which they were built, and conferred status on their local benefactors.

The Eumachia Building is the largest building in the Forum and must have played an important part in civic life. Despite this, its function remains obscure. One major study proposed that the building was the headquarters of the fullers' guild, a place for guild meetings and even auctions of wool and cloth. The evidence cited includes the dedicatory

The entrance to the Eumachia Building is framed by an elaborate marble frieze of acanthus leaves, although this may not have belonged to the building in antiquity. The Eumachia Building is the largest building in the Forum, an indication of its importance – even though its precise function is unknown.

inscription and statue to Eumachia set up by the fullers, and the fact that some of the earliest descriptions of the building report that the excavators uncovered the remains of cistern mouths, several vats, basins and stone tables (none of which can be seen today). Some scholars have even argued that the building was a fully functioning fullery. Others think that the vats and basins could relate to building work taking place at the time of the eruption or repair of damage caused in the earthquake of AD 63. Alternatively the building could have been an additional market-place, or – most plausibly – it may have had more than one use. Most recently it was suggested, again on the basis of similarities with the so-called 'basilica' of Herculaneum, which may have been connected to the College of the Augustales in that town, that the Augustales of Pompeii may have used the Eumachia Building for their meetings and feasts. Ultimately, however, there is not enough evidence to attribute a precise function to the Eumachia Building.

The Macellum

First constructed in the 2nd century BC, this building was remodelled and embellished in the 1st century AD, and consisted of a rectangular courtyard with a central 'tholos' (circular building). Much of it was redecorated with Fourth Style wall-paintings after the earthquake of AD 63. Once thought to be a Temple to Hercules, the Macellum was identified as the meat and fish market when a large

A 19th-century painting of the Fourth Style wall-painting from the Macellum, excavated 1821–22, and the same painting in its present, much deteriorated, condition. (Below) The remains of the tholos of the Macellum; once thought to be a pantheon (temple of all the gods), fish bones found in the drains beneath it revealed it to be the fish and meat market of the town.

number of fish bones were found in the drains beneath the tholos. There were porticoes to the west and north sides where market stalls may have been set up, and shops along the south side. There was a suite of three halls directly opposite the entrance. The central hall housed portrait statues, apparently members of the (unknown) family who paid for the building, and possibly members of the imperial family. The hall to the right may have been intended for public banquets; it has been suggested that that to the left may have been associated with the Imperial Cult. The Macellum was entered from the Forum through a two-storey portico; honorary statues were located between its columns.

Mensa Ponderaria

This was the table of official weights and measures, located near the Forum Holitorium (market for cereals and pulses). It consists of a bench with nine cavities of different sizes, relating to different measured amounts. The amounts were originally inscribed in Oscan; they were later adapted for Roman measures and the Oscan letters were erased.

Forum Holitorium

This may have been the warehouse market for cereals and pulses. However, it does not appear to have been in use in AD 79, since there was no roof and the walls had not been plastered.

Politics and Propaganda

THERE ARE TWO PARTICULARLY IMPORTANT TYPES OF evidence for political life in Pompeii and Herculaneum, the 'programmata' and monumental inscriptions on stone and bronze.

Programmata

Programmata are unique to Pompeii. They are painted posters, usually red or black on a white background, that support particular candidates for political office. It is thought that it was often the candidates themselves who commissioned them. As such they may not have been serious attempts to influence the election process but rather advertisements of support. They have been found on the facades of houses throughout Pompeii, particularly on major thoroughfares where they would have attracted the attention of large numbers of passers-by.

The majority of the programmata are unlikely to have been more than ten years old in AD 79, and there are examples of new programmata painted over old ones. A significant proportion cannot be attributed to particular candidates or even dated with accuracy. However, it has been possible to identify 131 candidates, 90 per cent of them dating to election campaigns after AD 62. Based on the number of programmata and their 'freshness' at time of excavation, the candidates for the aedileship in AD 79 are thought to have been Gaius Cuspius Pansa, Lucius Popidius Secundus, Marcus Samellius Modestus and Gnaeus Helvius Sabinus. The candidates for the office of duumvir in AD 79 were probably Gaius Gavius Rufus and Marcus Holconius Priscus.

Wall-painting and electoral programma on the facade of the workshop of Verecundus (IX.7.5). Mercury, holding his caduceus and a bag of money, can be seen leaving a small temple. The programma above him reads HOLCONIUM PRISCUM IIVIR(UM) I(URE) D(ICENDO) D(IGNUM) R(EI) P(UBLICAE) O(RO) V(OS) F(ACIATIS) ('I ask you to elect as duumvir Holconius Priscus, worthy of public office').

Programmata on the facade of Insula II.5.2–4 (House of Loreius Tiburtinus)

The following are some of the programmata found on a single insula facade:

Athictus calls for…. (*CIL* IV 7523)

Tiburtinus calls for Lucius Popidius Secundus as aedile. (*CIL* IV 7524)

I call on you to elect Helvius Sabinus aedile. Astylus wants this. (*CIL* IV 7525)

I ask you to elect as aedile for taking care of sacred and public buildings Lucius Popidius Ampliatus, a fine young man worthy of public office. (*CIL* IV 7526)

I ask you to elect Publius Sittius aedile. (*CIL* IV 7529)

Tiburtinus calls for Lucius Popidius Secundus as aedile, a man worthy of public office. (*CIL* IV 7530)

Client of Loreius, elect the man you esteem. (*CIL* IV 7531)

I ask you to elect Lucius Secundus aedile. Papilus wrote this. (*CIL* IV 7536)

I ask you to elect Gavius aedile. (*CIL* IV 7537)

I ask you to elect Gaius Gavius Rufus as duumvir for lawsuits. (*CIL* IV 7538)

Loreius (Secundus) asks that you elect Lucius Ceius Secundus duumvir, and he will elect you. (*CIL* IV 7539)

I ask you to elect Capella duumvir. (*CIL* IV 7540)

Messius calls for Aulus Suettius Verus as aedile. (*CIL* IV 7541)

Athictus, make…. (*CIL* IV 7545)

Here are some examples of programmata relating to these final elections:

> Fabius Ululitremulus with Sula asks you to elect Gaius Cuspius Pansa and Lucius Popidius Secundus, son of Lucius, aediles. (*CIL* IV 7963)
>
> I ask that you elect Gnaeus Helvius Sabinus and Marcus Samellius Modestus aediles, men worthy of public office. (*CIL* IV 6616)
>
> Phoebus and his customers call for Marcus Holconius Priscus and Gaius Gavius Rufus as duumvirs. (*CIL* IV 103)
>
> All the fruit-sellers with Helvius Vestalis call for Marcus Holconius Priscus as duumvir for lawsuits. (*CIL* IV 202)

The election campaign of Gnaeus Helvius Sabinus is particularly well documented. Programmata relating to his attempt to become aedile in AD 79 have been found on major thoroughfares, such as the Via dell' Abbondanza, the main road to the Forum. Sabinus' campaign was highly visible and his candidature was widely publicized. The following are some examples of the programmata:

> Helvius Sabinus, a young man of good character, for aedile! (*CIL* IV 1145, Via dell' Abbondanza)
>
> I ask you to elect as aedile Gnaeus Helvius Sabinus, a young man worthy of every reward, worthy of public office. (*CIL* IV 706, behind wall of Basilica)
>
> Members of the Poppaeus family call for Helvius Sabinus to be made aedile. (*CIL* IV 357, Via di Nola)

It appears from the programmata that a wide selection of Pompeian society supported Sabinus, including chicken-keepers, millers and dice-throwers. There are endorsements from well-known elite families – such as the Popidii and the Poppaei – but also calls for support from women (who didn't have the vote) and men with obviously foreign names (their status is unclear). Several of the supporters claim to be his neighbours, leading some scholars to hypothesize that Sabinus lived somewhere on the Via Stabiana. It would appear that there was lively interest in the outcome of the election, even amongst those who did not have the vote themselves, and that Sabinus had support across the community.

Monumental inscriptions

Monumental inscriptions on stone and bronze are found at both Pompeii and Herculaneum. Marble is more common, but bronze was used for the most important inscriptions (bronze inscriptions rarely survive today since bronze was more valuable and thus more likely to be reused). Unlike programmata, monumental inscriptions were usually permanent. There are only a few surviving Oscan inscriptions, mostly relating to earlier periods of Pompeii's history. The names of Oscan magistrates are mostly unknown because the inscriptions recording them have rarely survived, unless, for example, the marble they were inscribed upon was used in another monument. Some Oscan inscriptions were erased or torn down by later inhabitants of the town. Those that survive tend to relate to building work, regulation of roads or minor works, and they are often very difficult to date. The following is a typical example:

> Maras Atinius, son of Maras, quaestor, with the money raised from fines, by decree of the assembly, saw to this being set up. (Vetter (1953) no. 12)

This inscription relates to a sundial set up in the

Known Pompeian magistrates

Date	Office held	Name of magistrate	Date	Office held	Name of magistrate
14 BC	Duumvir	Marcus Melsonius	AD 31	Aedile	Lucius Eumachius Fuscus
14 BC	Duumvir	Publius Rogius Varus	AD 31	Aedile	Numerius Herennius Verus
14 BC	Aedile	Marcus Ninnius Pollio	AD 33	Prefect	Marcus Lucretius Epidius Flaccus
14 BC	Aedile	Numerius Paccius Chilo	AD 33	Duumvir	Marcus Vesonius Marcellus
2 BC	Duumvir	Marcus Holconius Rufus	AD 33	Aedile	Lucius Albucius Celsus
2 BC	Duumvir	Aulus Clodius Flaccus	AD 33	Aedile	Decimus Lucretius Satrius Valens
2 BC	Aedile	Publius Caesetius Postumus	AD 40	Prefect	Marcus Holconius Macer
2 BC	Aedile	Numerius Tintirius Rufus	AD 40	Quinq. duumvir	Marcus Lucretius Epidius Flaccus
AD 1	Duumvir	Marcus Pomponius Marcellus	AD 40	Aedile	Gaius Adius
AD 1	Duumvir	Lucius Valerius Flaccus	AD 40	Aedile	Lucius Licinius
AD 1	Aedile	Lucius Obellius Lucretianus	AD 50	Duumvir	Publius Gavius Pastor
AD 1	Aedile	Aulus Perennius Merulinus	AD 52	Duumvir	Quintus Coelius Caltilius Iustus
AD 2	Duumvir	Marcus Numistrius Fronto	AD 52	Duumvir	Lucius Helvius Blaesius Proculus
AD 2	Duumvir	Quintus Cotrius	AD 55	Quinq. duumvir	Gnaeus Alleius Nigidius Maius
AD 2	Aedile	Decimus Alfidius Hypsaeus	AD 55	Quinq. duumvir	Helgius
AD 3	Duumvir	Gnaeus Melissaeus Aper	AD 56	Duumvir	Gaius Vibius Secundus
AD 3	Duumvir	Marcus Staius Rufus	AD 56	Duumvir	Quintus Postumius Modestus
AD 3	Aedile	Gaius Annius Marulus	AD 56	Aedile	Quintus Bruttius Balbus
AD 13	Aedile	Seius Flaccus	AD 56	Aedile	Gaius Memmius Iunianus
AD 15	Quinq. duumvir	Marcus Holconius Celer	AD 57	Duumvir	Gaius Cornelius Macer
AD 22	Duumvir	Marcus Holconius Gellius	AD 58	Duumvir	Lucius Veranius Hypsaeus
AD 22	Aedile	Gaius Vergilius Salinator	AD 58	Duumvir	Lucius Albucius Iustas
AD 23	Duumvir	Lucius Aelius Tubero	AD 59	Duumvir	Gnaeus Pompeius Grosphus
AD 25	Quinq. duumvir	Marcus Alleius Luccius Libella	AD 59	Duumvir	Gnaeus Pompeius Grosphus Gavianus
AD 25	Quinq. duumvir	Marcus Stlaborius Veius Fronto	AD 59	Duumvir	Numerius Sandelius Messius Balbus
AD 25	Aedile	Marcus Fulvinius Silvanus	AD 60	Duumvir	Publius Vedius Siricus
AD 25	Aedile	Quintus Pompeius Macula	AD 60	Prefect	Sextus Pompeius Proculus
AD 31	Duumvir	Lucius Albienus Staius	AD 61	Duumvir	Tiberius Claudius Verus
AD 31	Duumvir	Marcus Lucretius Manlianus			

Stabian Baths, probably in the 2nd century BC. It is interesting that, unlike in the Roman period, there appears to have been no tradition of setting up honorific statues and commemorations. Thus the vast majority of monumental inscriptions date to after the foundation of the Roman colony and particularly from the Augustan period onwards. The inscriptions fall into the categories of official declarations, honorific inscriptions and dedications.

Official declarations record public pronouncements or decisions. Examples are the boundary markers set up outside the gates of Pompeii by Titus Suedius Clemens, an official sent by the emperor Vespasian to resolve a dispute over the use of public land. The markers record his judgment on the dispute (see pp.242–3 for further discussion).

Honorific inscriptions record honours voted by the comitium to particular individuals who had their statues set up in public places. Some prominent individuals had their statues set up at public expense, but others were simply given permission to set up their statue at their own expense. In the Forum 41 bases for standing statues along the porticoed sides of the Forum and 16 equestrian bases can still be seen (although the statues they once held were never found). The equestrian statues in the Forum were the most visually prominent and could be viewed from all sides. One was set up at the south end of the Forum to Quintus Sallustius, who had held all the major magistracies at Pompeii, and had also been chosen as patron of the town. Aulus Umbricius Scaurus and Decimus Lucretius Valens were similarly honoured with equestrian statues. Standing statues were set up to Gaius Cuspius Pansa and his son of the same name, and to Marcus Lucretius Decidianus Rufus, who had a particularly distinguished career. The inscription on his statue base reads:

To Marcus Lucretius Decidianus Rufus, three times duumvir, [once as] quinquennial duumvir, priest, military tribune by popular decree, military aide-de-camp, in accordance with a decree of the decurions after his death. (CIL X 789)

From this inscription we know that he began his career in the army, as an aide-de-camp, and later returned to Pompeii to hold public office. So far, six inscriptions have been found in the town that record bequests left at his death.

Dedications are found on public buildings (or objects within buildings) and record who or what the building is dedicated to and who paid for it. They commemorate buildings or facilities constructed by private individuals for the benefit of the community, and were set up in prominent locations for all to see.

Honorifics and dedications often overlap. This can be seen in the theatres of Herculaneum and Pompeii.

The Theatres of Herculaneum and Pompeii

The theatre of Herculaneum

The excavations of Herculaneum began in its theatre in 1738 and it remains the only public building in the town to have been completely excavated, by means of an extensive network of tunnels – the theatre remains buried. It is the most complete Roman theatre surviving today. Unlike the Large Theatre at Pompeii, which was constructed against a hillside, Herculaneum's theatre was free-standing. It could seat approximately 2,000 spectators, half the capacity of Pompeii's theatre.

Several inscriptions found during the tunnelling record that the theatre was designed in the early Augustan period by the architect Publius Numisius, and financed by the quinquennial duumvir Lucius Annius Mammianus Rufus. A financial contribution to the cost of the building by Appius Claudius Pulcher (Roman Senator and Consul in 38 BC) is also recorded.

Many other inscriptions and pieces of sculpture were found during the tunnelling of the theatre. For example, there are inscriptions commemorating another prominent Roman, Marcus Nonius Balbus (Roman Senator in the Augustan period and Proconsul of Crete and Cyrene). These may have been set up on statue bases since at least two statues of Nonius Balbus were found just outside the theatre, but, as for the majority of the inscriptions and statues uncovered, their find-spots were not recorded by the excavators. Some attempts have been made to reconstruct the provenances of statues found within the theatre. Marble statues of Hercules, Bacchus and possibly the Muses appear to have been positioned around the scaenae frons. Hercules was, of course, the mythical founder of the town, Bacchus an important god in the region as a whole, and the Muses were the goddesses who presided over the arts. Bronze statues of imperial and municipal dignitaries were positioned at the rear of the *summa cavea* (the uppermost seating area), some on horseback, others standing. These

The marble equestrian statue of Marcus Nonius Balbus, now displayed in the central hall of the Naples Museum, was found in the portico behind the stage-building of the theatre at Herculaneum. In the same area were found fragments of a bronze equestrian statue, also of Nonius Balbus, another marble equestrian statue, of his son, and two colossal marble statues. A heroic nude statue of Nonius Balbus was also found inside the theatre.

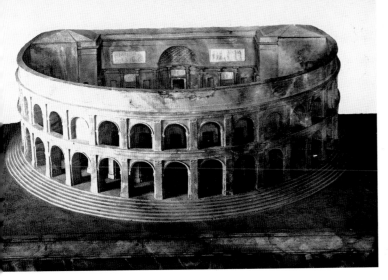

(Left) Model of the theatre of Herculaneum, made by Domenico Padaglione in 1808. The theatre is still buried but can be visited via the network of tunnels dug by its excavators in the 18th century.

(Below) This mosaic – one of two signed by Dioskourides of Samos and found in the Villa of Cicero outside the Herculaneum Gate – depicts musicians with flute, castanets and tambourine. It is thought to depict a scene taken from a play by Menander (Theophorumene, or 'The Possessed').

overlooked the entire area of the theatre and would have been highly visible. Six have been tentatively identified: the empress Livia and her son the emperor Tiberius, and four local magistrates, Lucius Annius Mammianus Rufus, Marcus Calatorius Rufus, Lucius Mammius Maximus and Marcus Calatorius Quartio. The other statues were presumably of important locals. The statue of the main benefactor of the theatre, Lucius Annius Mammianus Rufus, was positioned next to Tiberius and Livia, highlighting his particular importance and status.

Inscriptions were also found on steps to either side of the cavea (opposite each other), marking the locations of honorary bisellia. One was dedicated posthumously to Nonius Balbus, another to Appius Claudius Pulcher. The inscription on

Marble statue of Marcus Holconius Rufus, originally set up at the crossroads outside the Stabian Baths. His military garb highlighted his position as 'military tribune of the people', and the inscription on the base of the statue listed the political offices that he had held in Pompeii.

Nonius Balbus' cenotaph outside the Suburban Baths of Herculaneum records that the town council had decreed that his bisellium should be placed in the theatre during games held there. Thus important town benefactors could be honoured and their influence and prestige remembered even after their deaths.

Marcus Holconius Rufus and the Large Theatre of Pompeii

One of the best examples of the relationship between public beneficence and personal advertisement can be seen in the inscriptions recording the gifts of Marcus Holconius Rufus. Pompeii's Large Theatre had originally been built some time during the 2nd century BC. It has a classic Hellenistic design, with tiered seating on a natural slope that faces a free-standing stage. Some modifications were made

in the early 1st century BC, and the scaenae frons was rebuilt in the Augustan period, possibly under the direction of the architect Artorius Primus who is recorded in an inscription, but paid for by a now anonymous donor. The changes commissioned by Marcus Holconius Rufus and his brother Marcus Holconius Celer also took place in the Augustan period, and consisted of an extensive refurbishment of the theatre. The seating area of the theatre was increased, and alterations were made to allow spectators to be separated from each other according to their social status and in line with new Augustan legislation. The wealthy (male) elite sat in spacious, marble-clad lower rows of seating or in newly constructed 'boxes' over the side passages; behind them sat the free citizens; then came freedmen, slaves and women. The Large Theatre had an estimated capacity of 4,000 people.

Two identical inscriptions recording this work, both over 6 m (20 ft) in length, were found in the area of the stage (but had probably been located over the main entrances to the theatre):

> Marcus Holconius Rufus and Marcus Holconius Celer at their own expense built the vaulted corridor, the boxes and the auditorium. (*CIL* X 833 and 834)

A third similar inscription was located at the entrance to the theatre from the Triangular Forum. It is hard to imagine more prominent positions to draw the attention of spectators to the names of the men who had substantially increased the capacity of the theatre. All three inscriptions emphasize the particular elements of the theatre that were changed – this was not a simple renovation or embellishment but a major structural alteration.

The Large Theatre is still occasionally used for performances today. Able to seat c. 4,000 people, the theatre was closely associated with the Holconii, one of the most prominent families of Pompeii.

Bronze letters set into the stone seating of the cavea recorded Marcus Holconius' distinguished career and may well have marked the spot reserved for his bisellium.

An inscription incised on coloured marble (very rare) was set up in Rufus' honour by decree of the decurions, and was probably located in the area of the stage where it would have been visible to all. This recorded his career:

> To Marcus Holconius Rufus, duumvir for lawsuits four times, quinquennalis, elected military tribune by the people, priest of Augustus, by decree of the town councillors. (*CIL* X 837)

An honorific inscription to Augustus was found in the same area:

> To Imperator Caesar Augustus, father of his country, hailed imperator 14 times, consul 13 times, high priest, holding tribunician power for the 22nd time. (*CIL* 842)

This may well have been a deliberate juxtaposition, aimed to highlight Rufus' priesthood and his connection to the emperor. An inscription of a later date, in bronze letters set into the marble platform of the cavea, reveals additional honours given to Rufus:

> To Marcus Holconius Rufus, son of Marcus, duumvir for lawsuits five times, quinquennalis twice, elected military tribune by the people, priest of Augustus, patron of the colony, by decree of the town councillors. (*CIL* X 838)

It is likely that this inscription also marked the spot where an honorary bisellium was set up for Rufus, possibly as a posthumous honour, as was the case for Marcus Nonius Balbus in the theatre of Herculaneum.

In these ways the Large Theatre was permanently and repeatedly associated with Marcus Holconius Rufus from the Augustan period down to the destruction of the town in AD 79.

There was also one inscription recording the career of Marcus Holconius Celer:

> To Marcus Holconius Celer, duumvir for lawsuits, quinquennalis designate, priest of Augustus. (*CIL* X 840)

Celer was clearly the junior member of the Holconii partnership, but his career may have benefited from his association with Rufus. In AD 15 he became a quinquennial duumvir.

Rufus' civic prominence was also highlighted by another inscription, reiterating his public offices, on a large statue base at the crossroads outside the Stabian Baths on the Via dell' Abbondanza, thus fairly close to the theatre. This base held a statue of Holconius Rufus, in military dress to highlight his position as military tribune. The statue had originally been painted – the paint was still visible when the statue was excavated in 1853; the cloak was red, the shoes black and the tunic white. An arch was associated with the statue and is thought to have honoured other members of the Holconii family, including a Holconia, probably his daughter and a public priestess of Pompeii.

Not all magistrates who paid for public buildings and facilities went on to have distinguished careers, but the cases of Marcus Holconius Rufus and others demonstrates the incentive that existed for magistrates to spend money for the public good during their term of office. Public buildings and facilities were not their only option, however. There was another important means of gaining popularity and support, and thus high political office – the provision of entertainment.

The politics of entertainment

Some public officials chose to put on public entertainments rather than to donate buildings or facilities. Although not permanent, painted advertisements of games and entertainments – like programmata – might be left on walls long after the event had taken place, forming a semi-permanent memorial of the event. There are even programmata that remind people of games paid for by individuals. Lucius Munatius Caeserninus was a candidate for the office of quinquennial duumvir at Nuceria; an electoral notice at Pompeii relating to this campaign points out that the people have already benefited from his generosity (*CIL* IV 9939). Clearly he was hoping that he would now reap the benefits. Alternatively, permanent inscribed records of entertainment could be placed on tombs, to commemorate the generosity of the deceased and also to bring prestige to his living family. The Tomb of Vestorius Priscus (see pp.94–5), for example, contains elaborate paintings of gladiatorial games, to commemorate either games held by this young man when he had been aedile or games held as part of his funerary rites.

Similarly, an elaborate relief (now lost) was discovered on a tomb outside the Herculaneum Gate that depicted different types of gladiators fighting, presumably commemorating games paid for by the deceased. The putting on of gladiatorial games appears to have been a particularly popular means of fulfilling the magisterial obligation to the people.

Theatrical entertainment

Mosaic of actors, rehearsing for a Satyr play or preparing for its performance, originally the centrepiece of the tablinum of the House of the Tragic Poet (VI.8.5). The chorus-master (the seated, bearded figure) looks on as actors in loincloths dance to music played by the robed flautist. Behind the chorus-master, another actor is being helped into his costume.

An afternoon or evening's entertainment in one of Pompeii's theatres might include a mixture of different types of entertainment. One of the most popular was pantomime, introduced into Rome during the age of Augustus from the eastern Mediterranean. This was not at all similar to modern pantomimes, but was a traditional story told by means of wordless gesture and thought to be similar to a ballet. A single 'player' was supported by a chorus and a group of musicians. At Pompeii, pantomimes are listed among the events of the Games of Apollo from the end of the 1st century BC and beginning of the 1st century AD, and could be held in the Forum as well as in the theatre.

Other forms of performance had local roots. Atellan farce was a local Oscan form of entertainment that focused on bawdy jokes and low-life characters. Mime was a popular Campanian entertainment that involved improvisation. Greek drama was another type of performance. Actors could become very famous, and the names of touring groups of actors are known from inscriptions and graffiti. For example, the touring group of Actius Anicetus is known from inscriptions in Pompeii, Herculaneum and Puteoli, such as:

Gaius Cominius Pyrrichus, Lucius Novius Priscus and Lucius Campius Primigenius, three fans, intimates(?) of the dining couch, were here with their companion Martialis. Genuine fans of Actius Anicetus. Good luck to our companion Salvius. (*CIL* IV 2155) (VII.12.35)

Famous theatrical touring troupes are known from literature and also from inscriptions found in Pompeii and elsewhere. Particularly famous actors were Paris and Pylades, who are known to have also performed at Rome. A funerary inscription records that Pylades was brought to Pompeii by Aulus Clodius Flaccus. The actor Norbanus Sorex is thought to have been a Pompeian. Although he was only an actor 'of second parts' (a supporting actor) he is honoured with two herms in Pompeii, one in the Temple of Isis, the other in the Eumachia Building.

Gladiatorial Games

GLADIATORIAL GAMES RELATED TO FUNERARY RITES had a long history in Campania. In origin, these games did not take place in purpose-built structures, but in any public space. Even once amphitheatres began to be built (from the 1st century BC), games could still take place in other public areas. This was the case at Pompeii where there is evidence that games dedicated to Apollo, particularly bull fights and boxing, took place in the Forum even after the Amphitheatre had been built (bull-fighting may have formed part of a religious rite specific to the Forum and Temple of Apollo, since bulls were traditional sacrifices to the town gods). However, the construction of a dedicated building for games obviously satisfied a local desire or need, and demonstrates both the popularity that games had and the growing frequency with which they were being held. In addition, games in other towns in the region, such as Herculaneum, Nola, Nuceria, Puteoli, Capua, and Cumae, were advertised on the walls of Pompeii:

> 49 pairs of gladiators from the Capinian troupe will fight in the games of the Augusti at Puteoli on the 4th day before the ides of May, the day before the ides of May and the 17th and 15th days before the kalends of June (i.e. 12, 14, 16 and 18 May). There will be awnings. Magnus wrote this. (*CIL* IV 7994, III.4.1–2)

Games could be put on for a variety of reasons. Originally they were designed to commemorate a deceased person, but by the 1st century BC epigraphic evidence reveals that they could be organized as part of the inauguration of a new monument, in response to a military victory, in honour of the emperor, or, most commonly, in fulfilment of a magisterial obligation. Regardless of motive, the permission of either the local civic authorities or the emperor was required before games could take place. The games would then be organized by a specialized agent, known as a 'lanista', but paid for by a wealthy member of the elite. The names of many men who paid for spectacles are recorded in the epigraphic evidence from Pompeii. Marcus Tullius paid for a wild beast hunt and 20 pairs of gladiators (*CIL* IV 9979–81). Tiberius Claudius Verus held games in honour of Nero in AD 62 (*CIL* IV 7989a). Marcus Casellius Marcellus was praised for his organization of games (*CIL* IV 4999). Graffiti wish good fortune to Lucretius Satrius Valens on account of the games that he had paid for (*CIL* IV 2993x).

Typically, games would be advertised in advance by means of adverts painted on walls (known as 'edicta munerum') along main thoroughfares and roads. Many have been found painted on tombs

This helmet of a Thracian (a type of gladiator) was one of several found in the gladiatorial barracks located behind the Large Theatre.

Gnaeus Alleius Nigidius Maius

Gnaeus Alleius Nigidius Maius was born into the Nigidius family (of which little is known), but adopted into the powerful Alleius family. Other distinguished Alleii of this family include Marcus Alleius Luccius Libella (quinquennial duumvir and prefect in place of Caligula in AD 25) and Marcus Alleius Minius (duumvir in the Augustan period). His adoptive mother was Pomponia Decharis, who was buried in the Tomb of Eumachia (who was related to the Alleii in some way) outside the Nuceria Gate. His daughter, Alleia, was a priestess of Venus and Ceres and was buried at public expense in a tomb outside the Herculaneum Gate.

The wax tablets of Lucius Caecilius Jucundus (see Chapter VIII) reveal that Alleius Nigidius Maius served as quinquennial duumvir in AD 55–6. Before this date, he must have been aedile and duumvir, but the dates that he held these offices are unknown.

Alleius' public activities are recorded in several painted notices. Two reveal that during his quinquennial year he presented games in the Amphitheatre at his own expense. One reads:

> 20 pairs of gladiators of Gnaeus Alleius Nigidius, quinquennalis, and their attendants will fight at Pompeii without cost to the state.
> (*CIL* IV 7991, Via dell' Abbondanza)

So lavish were his games that a poster on the facade of the house at II.7.7 nicknamed him the 'chief of games' (*CIL* IV 7990).

Another acclaimed him 'leader of the colony' (*CIL* IV 1177). Another poster records that after AD 62 – and during the 10-year ban on games at Pompeii – he was responsible for providing a series of paintings of gladiators and hunting scenes to decorate the Amphitheatre. These were dedicated on an unknown date at a show in the Amphitheatre featuring 'athletes' (in place of the banned gladiators), a parade and a hunt.

Alleius remained prominent until the last years of Pompeii's life. He became a priest of the emperor (probably Vespasian) and gave more games to honour Vespasian and to celebrate the dedication of an altar to him. This altar has often been identified as the marble altar in the Temple of Vespasian in the Forum.

outside the gates of the town – more than 15 were found on the tombs of the Nuceria Gate, for example (although several of these advertised games at Nuceria, rather than Pompeii). Games may also have been advertised by the sale of 'pamphlets' ('libelli munerari') that listed the order of events and could be consulted during the spectacle itself. Roman literary sources reveal that an average spectacle would begin with a parade, which might include musicians; then there might be an animal hunt before the main gladiatorial combat. Edicta munerum are unique to Pompeii because of the way it was preserved by the eruption of AD 79, although they would have been common in other towns of the Roman empire. They were painted by professional scribes at the behest of the local magistrate who was responsible for organizing the games. Typically they reveal the reason for the games, name of the man paying for them, the time and place that they would take place, and the number of gladiators who would compete. It is clear from these painted adverts that games took place all year round, although the period from mid-March to mid-June appears to have been particularly popular.

There are no surviving examples of libelli munerari at Pompeii, but there is a graffito dating to the Neronian period that reproduces one. The graffito, which is poorly preserved in parts, records the name of the lanista – Marcus Mesonius – and the date of the spectacle, which took place on several consecutive days in May. It lists the gladiators who fought and their affiliations; the outcomes of their bouts appear to have been added later by a different hand. The following are examples of the results recorded in this graffito:

	Thracian vs. Murmillo
Won.	Pugnax, Neronian, fought 3.
Killed.	Murranus, Neronian, fought 3.
	Thracian vs Murmillo
Killed.	Lucius Fabius, fought 9.
Won.	Astus, Julian, fought 14.

(*CIL* IV 2508)

Epigraphic evidence from Pompeii demonstrates that the Amphitheatre and the games it offered

People from all over the region would have been attracted to Pompeii by the games held in its Amphitheatre. This famous wall-painting from the house at I.3.23 depicts a riot in the Amphitheatre in AD 59 that is also recorded by the historian Tacitus, between people from Pompeii and the neighbouring town of Nuceria.

attracted people from all over the local region, at times leading to conflict between the inhabitants of different towns. The historian Tacitus reports how in AD 59, during the reign of Nero, a riot broke out between people of Pompeii and Nuceria during gladiatorial games in Pompeii's Amphitheatre.

> At about this time there was a serious fight between the inhabitants of two Roman settlements, Nuceria and Pompeii. It arose out of a trifling incident at a gladiatorial show given by Livineius Regulus, whose expulsion from the Senate I have mentioned elsewhere. During an exchange of taunts – characteristic of these disorderly country towns – abuse led to stone-throwing, and then swords were drawn. The people of Pompeii, where the show was held, came off best. Many wounded and mutilated Nucerians were taken to the capital. Many bereavements, too, were suffered by parents and children. The emperor himself instructed the Senate to investigate the affair. The Senate passed it to the consuls. When they reported back, the Senate debarred Pompeii from holding any similar gathering for ten years. Illegal associations in the town were dissolved; and the sponsor of the show and his fellow-instigators of the disorders were exiled.
>
> Tacitus, *Annals* 14.17

A wall-painting from the House of Actius Anicetus (I.3.23) documents this riot, and a graffito may relate to it:

> Campanians, by this victory you've been destroyed with the Nucerians. (*CIL* IV 1293, Via di Mercurio)

During the ten-year ban, games were held that featured only 'athletes' standing in for actual gladiators until the emperor Nero lifted the ban, probably in AD 64.

Other graffiti, unrelated to the events of AD 59, reflect the passions that the games invoked:

> Bad luck to the people of Nuceria!
> (*CIL* IV 1329, Via di Mercurio)
> Good luck to all the people of Puteoli, good fortunes to the people of Nuceria, and the hook to the people of Pompeii. (*CIL* IV 2183, Vico del Lupanare)

Regardless of the vehement competition, the influx of neighbouring peoples into Pompeii to watch the games must have had a significant impact on both her economy and status in the region. Painted inscriptions found beneath the external arches of the Amphitheatre (no longer surviving) reveal that stalls were set up here for the sale of food and drink. For example:

> Gnaeus Aninius Fortunatus occupies this spot with the permission of the aediles. (*CIL* IV 1096)

These stalls can also be seen in the wall-painting of the riot, described above. There were also lots of shops and bars in the vicinity of the Amphitheatre. Many shop-owners must have profited when games took place at Pompeii.

The results of gladiatorial contests were frequently recorded in graffiti. In the House of the Labyrinth (VI.11.10) a scene of combat was etched into the plaster of a wall and underneath was written:

> Faustus, (slave) of Ithacus, a Neronian, at the Amphitheatre; Priscus, a Neronian, fought 6, won; Herennius, freedman, fought 18, killed. (*CIL* IV 1421)

Another example was found on a tomb outside the Nuceria Gate, which refers to games in the nearby town of Nola:

> There will be four days of games at Nola given by Marcus Cominius Heres.
> 'The Chief', a Neronian, fought 13, won 10, victorious. Hilarus, a Neronian, fought 14, won 12, victorious. Creunus, fought 7, won 5, spared. (*CIL* IV 10237)

There are even some scratchings on walls that seem to have been written by gladiators themselves:

> Five days before the Kalends of August [i.e. 28 July], Florus won at Nuceria; 18 days before the Kalends of September [i.e. 15 August], won at Herculaneum.
> (*CIL* IV 4299)
> Celadus, belonging to Octavus (?), fought 3, won 3.
> (*CIL* IV 4297)
> Girls' heart-throb, Thracian gladiator Celadus, belonging to Octavus (?) fought 3, won 3. (*CIL* IV 4342)
> Celadus the Thracian, fancied by all the girls.
> (*CIL* IV 4345)
> Samus the Murmillo and Eques lives here. (*CIL* IV 4420)

These final examples were found in a house now known as the House of the Gladiators (V.5.3), along

Terracotta figurines of gladiators (unprovenanced). (Left) A Thracian, wearing greaves and an unvisored helmet and armed with a short sword. (Right) Probably a Hoplomachus, wearing a single greave and visored helmet and carrying a rectangular shield and short sword. Several of these figurines have been found in Pompeii, some retaining traces of colour.

with many other such graffiti (*c.* 120) which record the types of gladiators, their weapons, their battles and victories. On the basis of these scratchings, along with wall-paintings depicting animal hunts in the peristyle, this house is usually identified as a gladiatorial barracks. It has been estimated that 15 to 20 gladiators could have lived and trained here, although there are no cells in this building for the gladiators. Paleographic analysis of the graffiti suggests that they date from the Augustan period to the time of the major earthquake of AD 63. The house was damaged in this earthquake, and the

Types of gladiator attested at Pompeii

From the ancient literary sources, we know that there were different types of gladiator, and the discoveries from Pompeii serve to highlight this fact. Armour relating to different types of gladiators has been discovered, and the various types of gladiator are also depicted in the frescos painted on the podium of the Amphitheatre, and in other wall-paintings and graffiti.

The Thracian was the most popular type of gladiator. He fought with a short, curved, sword (*sica*). He carried a small square shield (*parmula*) and wore an arm-guard (*manica*) on his right arm and two high leg-guards, which could be highly decorated. His helmet (see pp.140 and 145 for Pompeian examples) was also highly decorated, featuring a tall crest ending in a griffin's head. The Thracian usually fought the Hoplomachus, but could also fight the Murmillo or another Thracian.

The *Hoplomachus* fought with a straight sword, but otherwise wore armour – high leg-guards and helmet – similar (but less ornate) to that of the Thracian. He carried a small shield. The Hoplomachus fought either the Murmillo or the Thracian.

The *Retiarius* fought with a net and trident or short sword (an example of which is illustrated on p.145). He wore an arm-guard (*manica*) on his left arm. A rectangular bronze plate (*galerus*) (*c.* 12 cm (5 in) in height) was also tied to his left shoulder to help protect his head. Decorated examples of the galerus were found in the Theatre Portico. The Retiarius fought the Murmillo or the Secutor.

The *Secutor* fought with a short sword and a long rectangular shield. He wore metal greave (*ocrea*) and an enclosed and plain helmet. The Secutor fought the Retiarius.

The *Murmillo* fought with a short sword (*gladius*) and carried a 1-m (3-ft) high wooden rectangular shield that was covered in leather. His helmet had a visor and squared crest. He wore an arm-guard (*manica*) on his right arm and possibly a leg-guard on his left leg (an example of Murmillo leg armour is known from Pompeii). The Murmillo fought the Thracian, the Hoplomachus or the Retiarius.

The *Eques* fought on horseback with a lance and small round shield (*parma equestris*). His helmet had a visor and he wore a short tunic and guards on his thighs and right arm. The Eques only fought other Equites.

The *Essedarius* fought from a cart or chariot.

'Neronians' were gladiators who had been trained at the imperial training school at Capua (the *Ludus Neronianus*).

A selection of graffiti with images of gladiators, many found on the external wall of the Large Theatre, the House of the Dioscuri (VI.9.6–7) and the House of the Labyrinth (VI.11.10). Number 8 is a depiction of the riot between the Pompeians and Nucerians in AD 59 with the caption 'Campanians, by this victory you've been destroyed with the Nucerians'.

gladiators may have been forced to find other accommodation. Alternatively the building may have ceased to function as a barracks after the riot of AD 59 when gladiatorial games were banned in Pompeii. Whichever was the case, after the earthquake of AD 63 the portico attached to the Large Theatre appears to have been converted into barracks. There were a series of 30–40 cells over two levels, possibly with straw mattresses (no evidence of beds was discovered), and some common rooms including a kitchen. Gladiatorial armour and weapons were found here, and all exits apart from the main door had been closed off. One part of the area was clearly a prison, and shackles were found here. However, it seems that most of the gladiators were free to come and go. One of the rooms on the south side of the portico, an exedra, was decorated with elaborate Fourth Style wall-paintings that depicted trophies with gladiatorial arms, and Mars and Venus. A large number of skeletons were found in this building, including the skeleton of an infant in one of the cells and also the skeleton of a woman, heavily adorned with jewelry in another. It has often been speculated that this was an upper-class woman who was having an affair with a gladiator at the time of the eruption.

Some gladiators were condemned prisoners, hence the prison area in the barracks; others were slaves trained to fight in the arena, with the hope of one day winning their freedom; and some were free-born with the aim of winning fame and glory. They were organized into schools of private or public ownership, some of which can be identified from advertisements painted on the walls of Pompeii. An advert in the Via dell' Abbondanza, on the external wall of the Eumachia Building near the Forum, reads:

The gladiatorial troupe of Aulus Suettius Certus, aedile, will fight at Pompeii on the day before the kalends of June [i.e. 31 May]. There will be a hunt and awnings. Good fortune to all the games of the Neronians. (CIL IV 1189)

The portico of the Large Theatre was converted into gladiatorial barracks, probably after the earthquake of AD 63 – demonstrated vividly by the gladiatorial armour and weapons found in the cells and communal rooms that were arranged around the portico.

Aulus Suettius Certus was a public official; his ownership of gladiators no doubt made him popular and helped in his election campaign.

Some games were particularly elaborate, with the benefactor providing awnings for the spectators' comfort and additional entertainments to keep them amused, as seen in this inscription from the Tomb of the Clodii family (*CIL* X 1074d, now lost), dating to the Augustan period:

Aulus Clodius Flaccus, son of Aulus, of the Menenian tribe, duumvir for lawsuits three times, quinquennalis, elected military tribune by the people. In his first duumvirate, at the Games of Apollo in the Forum, he presented a procession, bulls, bull-fighters and goaders, three pairs of platform fighters, a company of boxers and some Greek-style boxers, and games with all the usual acts and pantomimes and Pylades, and spent 10,000 sesterces for the common good for his duumvirate. In his second quinquennial term as duumvir at the Games of Apollo in the Forum he presented a procession, bulls, bull-fighters and goaders, a company of boxers; on the following day in the Amphitheatre he presented by himself 30 pairs of athletes and five pairs of gladiators, and with his colleague he presented 35 pairs of gladiators and a hunt with bulls, bull-fighters, wild boars and bears and in another hunt he presented various animals.

In his third duumvirate, he put on with his colleague games by a top-notch company of performers along with their supporting acts.

This inscription records Aulus Clodius' political achievements and the offices he had held, as well as detailing at length the games that he paid for during his terms in office. It gives the impression that his provision of entertainment was more elaborate and expensive than that usually put on by magistrates, and this was probably its deliberate intention. It serves to highlight Clodius' wealth and beneficence to the community. It also leaves out the names of his fellow magistrates who were probably also involved in the organization of these games. The inscription is also interesting because it details the types of entertainments that could take place, and also one of the occasions on which they were put on. In this case, the occasion was the Games of Apollo, an annual celebration that started beside the god's temple on the Forum and carried on in the Amphitheatre. This tomb inscription demonstrates how games could take place in the Forum and Amphitheatre as part of the same festival, and also reveals how politicians sought to outdo each other.

Examples of the armour and weapons found in the gladiatorial barracks in the portico behind the Large Theatre. The bronze shield has a silver medallion of Medusa at its centre; olive leaves and branches picked out in silver complete the decoration. The helmet belonged to a Thracian. Its elaborate relief decoration depicts scenes from the sack of Troy. The iron sword has a bone handle, and was the weapon of a Retiarius.

The Amphitheatre

> Gaius Quinctius Valgus, son of Gaius, and Marcus Porcius, son of Marcus, quinquennial duumvirs, for the honour of the colony, saw to the construction of this *spectacula* at their own expense and gave the land in perpetuity to the colonists. (*CIL* X, 852)

(Opposite) One of two identical dedicatory inscriptions recording that the Amphitheatre was built at private expense, and dedicated in perpetuity to the colonists of Pompeii.

THE AMPHITHEATRE AT POMPEII IS THE OLDEST KNOWN permanent amphitheatre in Italy, having been constructed shortly after the foundation of the Roman colony at Pompeii. Thus it was closely associated with the new colonists, and a symbol of the new political order. It was built at private expense by Gaius Quinctius Valgus and Marcus Porcius. These men, who were also responsible for building the Covered Theatre, were the quinquennial duumvirs at the time of the dedication of the Amphitheatre and the games that they organized and financed to mark the event may have functioned also to confirm the new political hierarchy. Two identical inscriptions, located over the main entrances to the Amphitheatre, record that it was dedicated in perpetuity to the colonists of Pompeii:

Legally, the term 'colonists' refers to all the inhabitants of Pompeii, old and new, but the repeated reference to the colony in the inscription may have been an intentional means of emphasizing the dominance of the new Roman elite over the local population.

Houses were demolished to make room for the new Amphitheatre, which was built in the southeast part of the town, and was made up of two parts, the 'cavea' (spectator seating) and the 'arena' where the games actually took place.

The structure of the cavea was partly supported by the embankment of the town walls and partly by another artificial embankment that was built up using earth excavated to create the arena. It has been suggested that in the years immediately after the construction of the Amphitheatre, spectators

The Palaestra

In the Augustan period houses were demolished to make way for a Large Palaestra (training ground), built at public expense, next to the Amphitheatre. The Palaestra measured 141 x 107 m (460 x 350 ft). It was surrounded by a portico on three sides, the end walls of which were decorated in Third Style wall-painting. There was a swimming pool at the centre of the Palaestra, supplied with continuously flowing water by the public aqueduct. A large altar was located in a nave off the western portico, possibly connected with religious rites to Augustus or for prize-giving ceremonies. Large numbers of graffiti were found in the porticoes, suggesting that it was open to the public.

This was not Pompeii's first palaestra. Another, the 'Samnite Palaestra' (VIII.7.29), was located near to the Doric Temple. An Oscan inscription records its construction:

> Vibius Atranus, son of Vibius, granted money in his will to the people of Pompeii; with this money, the Pompeian quaestor, Vibius Vinicius, son of Maras, by decree of the assembly, issued a contract for this to be built, and he himself approved it. (Vetter (1953) no. 11)

Originally the Samnite Palaestra appears to have been connected to the 'Republican Baths' (VIII.5) and possibly to a gymnasium (VIII.6). All three were large buildings constructed in the 2nd century BC at the same time as the grand entrance porch and colonnaded portico of 100 columns framing the adjacent Doric Temple. It is thought that they were related to the Pompeian *Vereia*, a club formed of the

(Right) The Samnite Palaestra, constructed in the 2nd century BC, was possibly used for meetings and banquets connected to the Vereia. In contrast, the large Palaestra (opposite) near the Amphitheatre was a proper exercise ground, with swimming pool, that appears to have been open to the general public.

were separated from each other according to military rank. Later, in response to Augustan policies relating to maintaining strict social hierarchies, some public officials paid for permanent sections of seating that formalized the seating divisions according to social status. Inscriptions on the balustrades that separate the different sections record the names of magistrates who paid for the constructions of sections of the seating. These are some examples:

> The magistrates of the Pagus Augustus Felix Suburbanus, in place of games, by decree of the town council. (*CIL* X 853)

> Titus Atullius Celer, son of Gaius, duumvir, built a section of seating in place of games and lights, by decree of the town councillors. (*CIL* X 854)

> Lucius Saginus, duumvir for lawsuits, [built] a section of seating in place of games and lights, by decree of the town councillors. (*CIL* X 855)

> Marcus Cantrius Marcellus, son of Marcus, duumvir, built three seating sections in place of games and lights, by decree of the town councillors. (*CIL* X 567d)

local aristocratic and military elite (similar clubs existed in other towns of southern Italy in the 4th and 3rd centuries BC). The Samnite Palaestra is rather small to be a proper exercise ground, and may well have been used as a meeting place for banquets, ceremonies and martial displays. It was later restored in the Augustan period, at the same time as the construction of the Large Palaestra. But before the end of the 1st century BC the baths had been demolished to make way for houses and the gymnasium had become a garden. Only the Samnite Palaestra was still standing in AD 79, and this had been reduced in size when the Temple of Isis was rebuilt and extended in AD 63.

Thus, the cavea consisted of 35 rows of seating which were divided horizontally into three separate sections that were separated from each other by balustrades. In total, 10,000–15,000 spectators could be accommodated, far more than the male citizen body of Pompeii and so deliberately intended to hold large numbers of visitors from other settlements in the region.

The lowest section of seating was known as the 'ima cavea' and consisted of four flat terraces on which wooden seats for members of Pompeii's elite would have been set up. The other two sections, the 'media cavea' and the 'summa cavea' were larger and would have seated many more spectators. Seats in these sections were either stone or wood and were divided into wedges by flights of steps. Women may have been allocated seating in 'boxes' at the very top of the cavea.

The arena measures 66.8 x 34.5 m (219 x 113 ft) and is bordered by a parapet that is 2.18 m (7 ft 2 in) high. The level of the arena is around 4.5 m (15 ft) lower than the level of the ground outside the Amphitheatre. It could be accessed directly through two steep tunnels that were paved with basalt blocks – presumably so that carts carrying equipment for the games could enter easily. Four spaces at the end of each tunnel, immediately before the entrance to the arena, appear to have been reserved for the gladiators and wild animals. A smaller

tunnel led from the outside directly to the best seating area, the ima cavea, and may have been intended to allow elite spectators to gain their seats without mixing at all with people of lowest status. A passageway or 'crypta' ran beneath the media cavea. This could be accessed from the main entrance passages and permitted spectators to enter the media cavea at many different points, obviously designed as a means of ensuring that seats were taken in an orderly fashion. Finally, there were two double stairways and two single stairways on the external walls of the Amphitheatre that led to the upper passageway and the seating in the summa cavea. Not only were spectators of different social status separated from each other during events in the Amphitheatre, potential intermingling was limited too.

One aspect of the Amphitheatre that is no longer visible today is its decoration. During the excavations of 1815 a series of thematic frescos on the podium wall were exposed. By 1816 they had been destroyed by frost. Fortunately, drawings had been made of them before they were lost. The frescos consisted of large panels depicting wild beast hunts (such as a bear fighting a bull) and combat between different types of gladiator. Winged victories and shields of various shapes could be seen in many smaller panels, and much of the podium was painted to imitate coloured marble slabs.

Aerial view of the Amphitheatre; the arena was dug out and the excavated earth used to create an artificial embankment that – along with the town wall – supported the seating (cavea).

Baths and Bathing

FOR THE ROMANS, THE BATHS HAD AN IMPORTANT social and cultural function. They were a means to clean the body, but also a source of entertainment and a centre for social, political and economic activity. The literary sources reveal that it was usual for Roman citizens to go to the baths in the afternoon, and to spend a significant amount of time there. Communal bathing was one of the fundamental parts of everyday life, and purpose-built public baths with distinctive technological features – namely under-floor hypocaust heating – are a distinctive Roman phenomenon.

Despite this, 'Roman-style' baths first developed in Campania, not Rome, and one of the best places to trace their development is Pompeii. The early development of baths in Campania was influenced by Greek practices, and the earliest evidence for them comes from Pompeii. Stratigraphic excavations beneath the Stabian Baths revealed a large palaestra and associated row of small chambers that contained Greek-style hip-baths supplied with water by a well. These were dated to the 5th or 4th century BC. By the 3rd century BC, these hip-baths had been replaced by immersion baths, and during the second half of this century the bath building had been extended and a portico added to the Palaestra. Further enlargements to provide separate facilities for men and women took place in the 2nd century BC, but the most important development came during the 1st century BC (c. 90–80 BC) with the introduction of the hypocaust (prior to the invention of the hypocaust, baths had been heated by charcoal braziers). This is the earliest known hypocaust, and was made possible by the development of concrete, also a Campanian invention.

By AD 79, there were three functioning public bath buildings at Pompeii, one that had fallen out of use, and another that was still under construction at the time of the eruption.

The Stabian Baths

Shortly after, or contemporary with, the installation of the hypocaust, the Stabian Baths (VII.1.8) were refurbished by Gaius Uulius and Publius Aninius (see p.124 for the commemorative inscription), with the addition of a *laconicum* and *destrictarium*. However, the baths only achieved their final form in the Augustan period, when water began to be supplied by the town's new aqueduct. An entire new wing was added, the palaestra was extended and a swimming pool added to the complex. Elaborate stucco decoration and Fourth Style wall-paintings adorned walls and ceilings of many of the rooms of the baths.

(Opposite) A photograph taken before 1905 of the apodyterium of the Stabian Baths, which has elaborate stucco decoration on its ceiling.

(Below) This reconstruction of the Stabian Baths illustrates the different sections of the building, including the men's bath (the larger rooms to the left) and the women's bath (the much smaller suite, accessed from the side road to the north). The palaestra and swimming pool were for men only. The main entrance onto the Via dell' Abbondanza was flanked by a series of shops.

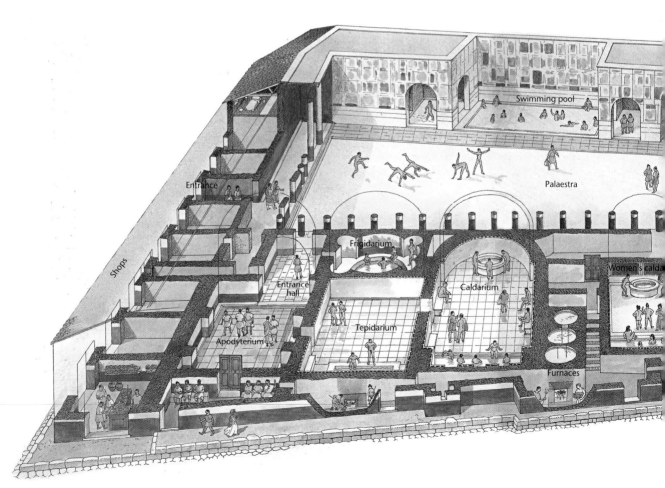

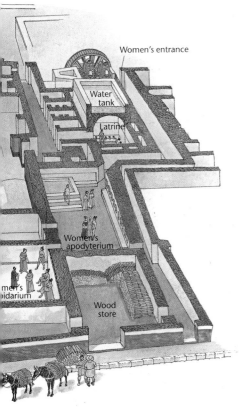

Women's entrance

Water tank

Latrine

Women's apodyterium

Wood store

Men's apodyterium

The Roman baths

Some of the individual elements of the Roman baths are as follows:

Apodyterium. Changing-room with benches and shelves or niches for clothes.

Frigidarium. A vaulted chamber for cold baths, containing one or more cold-water pools. Normally visited after the heated rooms.

Tepidarium. A vaulted chamber designed to acclimatize visitors passing from the apodyterium to the caldarium, with benches where people could sit to get used to the heat and/or wash themselves.

Caldarium. The principal bath chamber for a hot-water or steam bath, containing a communal pool and a basin (*labrum*, which contained cold water).

Laconicum. A small round room used as a sweat-bath, usually with dry heat. The room was heated either by a fireplace, hot stones or a brazier placed at the centre of the room.

Destrictarium. Scraping-room, where oil and sweat were removed from the body with strigils.

Strigils could be made of bone, bronze, iron or silver, and were used after exercise or bathing to clean off perspiration. This example was found in I.18.14.

The Forum Baths

The Forum Baths (VII.5) were built soon after the foundation of the colony in 80 BC at the political and economic heart of the town. This, and the fact that the baths were paid for with public money, underlines the importance of the baths and bathing to the Romans. The facilities provided by the Stabian Baths were not sufficient for the new Roman colonists.

An inscription records the construction of the baths:

> Lucius Caesius, son of Gaius, duumvir for lawsuits, Gaius Occius, son of Marcus, and Lucius Niraemius, son of Aulus, duumvirs, undertook the construction at public expense in accordance with the wishes of the town councillors, and approved it. (*CIL* X 819)

Bronze letters inlaid in this large marble labrum in the caldarium of the Forum Baths recorded that it had been set up by the duumvirs Gaius Melissaeus Aper and Marcus Statius Rufus.

In AD 3–4, a marble *labrum* (basin) was added to the caldarium. Inlaid bronze lettering around its rim recorded its donors and, interestingly, how much it cost:

> Gnaeus Melissaeus Aper, son of Gnaeus, and Marcus Statius Rufus, son of Marcus, duumvirs for lawsuits for the second time, had this labrum made at public expense by decree of the town councillors. It cost 5,250 sesterces. (*CIL* X 817)

A bronze brazier was added to the men's tepidarium in the mid-1st century BC:

> Marcus Nigidius Vaccula at his own expense. (*CIL* X 818)

The same man also donated three bronze benches. 'Vaccula' means 'little cow' and both brazier and benches were decorated with cow motifs – a deliberate pun drawing extra attention to his gifts.

During the Augustan period a second, smaller suite of rooms was installed in the northwest corner for women to bathe separately (the men's section was the more elaborate). In their final form, the Forum Baths included a small palaestra and a public latrine. There were surrounded by shops and bars.

The Suburban Baths

The Suburban Baths were located immediately outside the Marine Gate, close to the large terraced houses built over the town walls in that part of the town, and were excavated very recently, from 1985 to 1987. The bath building was constructed over two levels, connected by an internal staircase: the upper level consisted of rooms with panoramic views to the sea; the lower level contained the bath complex. The upper level could also be reached by a separate door from the Via Marina. The bath suite consisted of ten rooms, including an apodyterium, frigidarium, tepidarium, laconicum and caldarium. It was built in the first decades of the 1st century AD and later enlarged (possibly after AD 63). In the period immediately before the eruption it appears that some restoration work was under way, including a new decorative scheme. This partially obscured a series of erotic wall-paintings – the feature for which these baths are best known (see Chapter IV for discussion). The baths may have been privately-owned.

The Central Baths

These baths (IX.4) were under construction in AD 79, but the work was far from completion. The walls of the bath buildings had been erected, but not plastered, and the furnace for the hypocaust was unfinished. Preparation had been made for mosaic pavements and marble revetment on the walls, but work had not started, and the drains in various rooms had not been fitted with pipes and filters. The ground had been excavated for a large swimming pool, but this had not yet been installed. Although the baths took up an entire insula, there was only one bath suite, so either the baths were intended for the use of

A 19th-century painting (left) by Giuseppe Abbate of the stucco in the apodyterium of the Stabian Baths gives an idea of what the elaborate decoration found in many baths would have looked like. The photo (far left) shows some of the same decoration in its current decayed condition.

(Below) An imitation cave with waterfall, at the end of the cold swimming pool of the Suburban Baths. It is decorated with a mosaic panel depicting Mars.

men only, or men and women would have bathed at different times of the day. The bath complex was surrounded on two sides by a series of one-room shops, none of which were connected to the baths.

Pompeii's baths served many purposes. Citizens paid a small entrance fee in order to clean themselves, to meet their friends, to discuss politics and to conduct business. As with other types of public building, the provision of baths was a means of fulfilling the magisterial obligation to the people and in return receiving their goodwill and political support. But baths were also a fundamental part of everyday life and played an important part in Pompeian life after the foundation of the Roman colony.

The majority of Pompeii's public buildings and entertainments were constructed by its public magistrates as part of their civic duty and in return for high public office and prestige. Such benefactions were popular with the people, and important because they provided an outlet for social and political aspects of life. It was at the theatre or amphitheatre that the populace could protest or make their opinions known en masse, whereas the baths were where business could be transacted and politics discussed. All of these establishments were ideal places for politicians to call attention to their beneficence and gain political support from a grateful public. It is clear that public building and the provision of amenities and entertainment served many interrelated functions in the Roman town. There was rarely any centralized policy or plan relating to this, which means that the evidence reflects a genuine enthusiasm for public life.

VI
HOUSES AND SOCIETY

There was a luxury of sentiment in being alone in Pompeii – of having, as it were, an entire city to one's self in the broad day, that had a peculiar charm to me. I dived into cellars, I ascended dilapidated staircases, I pried into ladies' boudoirs, nay, even into their bed-chambers, stood before family altars, criticised the cook's department – in fine, explored with unblushing effrontery the domestic secrets of every household, rich or poor, plebeian or patrician, which attracted me, without a human voice to break the spell.

'A Day at Pompeii.' *Harper's New Monthly Magazine,*
November, 1855

In the houses of Pompeii we have a tantalizing glimpse of the activities that took place in the home and of the beliefs and values that structured everyday life. The Roman house was a complex environment. It was a home, protected by its own household deities. But at the same time it could be a place of work and business, and an environment that communicated messages to outsiders about its inhabitants. We can study the structure, decoration and contents of the houses, but it is more difficult to reconstruct the composition of the individual household, its domestic organization and the relationship between the different activities that took place within the house. Despite this, some of the best surviving examples of Roman houses from the entire Roman empire have been found at Pompeii and Herculaneum, and these towns have dominated scholarly discussion of Roman private life.

View of the elegant atrium and tablinum of the House of Marcus Lucretius Fronto (V.4.a), famous for its well-preserved Third Style wall-paintings. This relatively small house was restored immediately after its excavation in 1899–1900 to preserve its beautiful decoration.

The Ideal Roman House

WRITING IN THE AGE OF AUGUSTUS, THE ROMAN ARCHItect Vitruvius described variations of an 'atrium' house. Modern scholars have used his account to reconstruct the 'ideal' Roman house. This consisted of a narrow entrance corridor (fauces) leading into a central courtyard (atrium) around which were arranged the other rooms of the house. There was an open room (tablinum) at the far end of the atrium, opposite the fauces, and one or more open rooms (alae) off the atrium. Other rooms (cubicula and triclinia) were also located off the atrium. The atrium was roofed, but had an opening (compluvium) through which rain could enter. The rain was collected in a central basin (impluvium) and channelled into a cistern beneath the atrium floor. Based on other ancient literary sources, scholars have traditionally assigned particular functions to the various room-types identified by Vitruvius. Thus, cubicula were bedrooms, triclinia were dining-rooms, alae were where the funeral masks of important family ancestors were displayed, the tablinum was where documents would be stored. It is generally accepted that during the 2nd century BC this ideal plan was altered to include a colonnaded garden (peristyle). Gradually, the more elaborately decorated and important cubicula and triclinia of the house came to be located around the peristyle and the atrium became less important.

The Pompeian house

The atrium house has traditionally been considered the oldest form of housing in Italy, and a large number – approximately 40 per cent – of Pompeii's houses follow this form. But there is also great variety in the housing, particularly in the smallest houses that simply did not have the space for a central atrium or any need for its associated reception and dining rooms. Another element that until recently has been overlooked is the evidence for upper floors in houses, which may represent rented apartments.

Recent archaeological evidence from Rome itself and other Italian towns such as Cosa and Fregellae has begun to suggest that the atrium house may not have been the original 'Italic' form of housing. Stratigraphic excavations at Pompeii in recent years have also demonstrated that the houses of Regions I and II were originally laid out in equal strips sometime in the 2nd century BC. Four types of simple house have been identified in these strips, all of which had central courtyards without any roof. In later periods, many of these houses were amalgamated into larger (sometimes 'atrium') properties, or demolished to make way for large gardens and cultivated plots. Thus it now seems likely that there were many different forms of housing in Italy, but the one thing that these different types of house often have in common is an emphasis on a central space or courtyard.

Reconstructed section through the House of the Tragic Poet (VI.8.3), showing the standard linear progression from the fauces through the atrium, tablinum and into the peristyle garden. The household shrine at the rear of the garden was visible from the front door.

Compluvium

Impluvium

Atrium

Fauces

The House of the Surgeon (VI.1.10)

Based on its opus quadratum facade and opus africanum internal walls, and its First Style wall-painting, the House of the Surgeon has often been identified as the oldest house in Pompeii, dating back to the 4th century BC. In fact, stratigraphic excavations have revealed that the impluvium was only added to the house in the 2nd century BC. In plan, it respects the Vitruvian ideal, with fauces, atrium and associated rooms, and tablinum. To the rear is a small garden. The name of the house derives from the discovery of a collection of bronze and iron surgeon's tools found during excavations in 1771. Unfortunately, the house was stripped of its finds by the excavators and today only two of the 17 or so surgical instruments found can be identified in the Naples Museum.

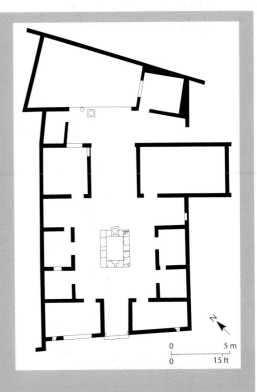

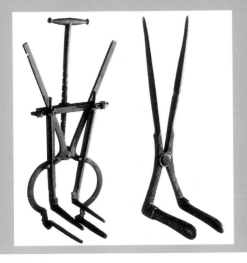

Plan of the House of the Surgeon and two of the surgical instruments found in the house that give it its modern name.

Tablinum

Lararium

Peristyle

The Role of the House in Roman Society

THE ATRIUM HOUSE MAY BE THE DOMINANT TYPE OF housing at Pompeii, but not all of Pompeii's atrium houses conform to the Vitruvian ideal. The exact plan of a house would have depended on the space available, the resources and social status of its inhabitants and the wider role it played in their lives.

According to the ancient architect, Vitruvius, the Roman house had to be 'appropriate' to its owner.

When we have arranged our plan with a view to aspect, we must go on to consider how, in private buildings, the rooms belonging to the family, and how those which are shared with visitors, should be planned. For into the private rooms no one can come uninvited, such as the bedrooms, dining-rooms, baths and other apartments which have similar purposes. The common rooms are those into which, though uninvited, persons of the people can come by such as vestibules, courtyards, peristyles and apartments of similar uses. Therefore magnificent vestibules and alcoves and halls are not necessary to persons of a common fortune, because they pay their respects by visiting among others, and are not visited by others. But those who depend upon country produce must have stalls for cattle and shops in the forecourt, and, within the main building, cellars, barns, stores and other apartments which are for the storage of produce rather than for an elegant effect. Again, the houses of bankers and farmers of the revenue should be more spacious and imposing and safe from burglars. Advocates and professors of rhetoric should be

housed with distinction, and in sufficient space to accommodate their audiences. For persons of high rank who hold office and magistracies, and whose duty it is to serve the state, we must provide princely vestibules, lofty halls and very spacious peristyles, plantations and broad avenues finished in a majestic manner; further, libraries and basilicas arranged in a similar fashion with the magnificence of public structures, because, in such palaces, public deliberations and private trials and judgements are often transacted.

Therefore if buildings are planned with a view to the status of the client, as was set forth in the first book under the head of decor, we shall escape censure. For our rules will be convenient and exact in every respect. Moreover, we shall take account of these matters, not only when we build in town, but in the country; except that, in town, the halls adjoin the entrance, in the country the peristyles of mansions built town-fashion come first, then the atria surrounded by paved colonnades overlooking the palaestra and the promenades.

Vitruvius *On Architecture* VI.5.1–3

The wealthy elite needed large houses in which to conduct their political and business dealings, and for reception and entertainment purposes; the ordinary masses did not. There was a connection between the number of visitors to a house, its size and the political success of its owner. For this reason, visitors were wanted. But they had to be visible in order to highlight the status of the house's owner. This might explain why the atrium house was so open in plan. From the entrance of an atrium house, it would have been possible to see through the atrium all the way to the peristyle, and thus to see the number of visitors to the house or even to identify who these visitors were. Some houses, such as the House of Menander (I.10.4), even had masonry benches outside the front door, presumably for the use of those waiting to enter the house.

But the house was not simply open to any passerby; access to it could be easily controlled. The narrow entrance corridor allowed a glimpse of the house beyond, but could be guarded by a porter or closed off with a door. Once inside the house, there was also a difference between public and private areas. The atrium was accessible to all, but only the most important visitors might receive an invitation into the more private family rooms. In his *Consolation to Marcia* (10.1), Seneca talks of 'spacious atria and vestibules packed with a throng of unadmitted clients'. These people are in the house without having access to any private area. From the literary sources we know that houses had wooden screens, doors, curtains and blinds. Remnants of these were sometimes found during the excavation of Pompeii's houses, although the vast majority of such items, made of organic materials, have perished. Any of these could have been used to close off particular parts of the house, to obscure the view of passers-by or to prevent unauthorized access, and there is one surviving example of a wooden screen at Herculaneum (in a house dubbed by the excavators the 'House of the Wooden Partition') that was used to separate the tablinum from the atrium and that demonstrates that this did indeed happen. In addition, the plan of the house may have been 'open', but access may well have been restricted to particular times of the day or to particular events. Certainly there were rules governing access to the house. Perhaps this explains the mosaics of guard-dogs that have been found in

the entrances of several Pompeian houses, such as the House of the Tragic Poet (VI.8.5) and the House of Paquius Proculus (I.7.1).

The ancient literary sources document a surge in interest in houses from the end of the 2nd century BC. This can be directly related to the profits of empire. The Roman elite suddenly had huge disposable incomes, and this wealth gradually filtered down into other sections of society. Wealthy Romans spent massive amounts of money on building bigger and more luxurious houses with more amenities such as private bath suites and separate

(Below) Mosaic of a guard-dog, from the fauces of the House of Paquius Proculus (I.7.1). Several similar mosaics have been found in Pompeian houses, a reminder to guests that they were entering a protected environment. Sometimes the words Cave Canem – *Beware of the dog – were added to the mosaic.*

service quarters, and on other indicators of wealth such as marble columns, special room types, water-features, furniture and fixtures, elaborate wall-paintings and mosaics. Some ancient authors such as Pliny the Elder condemned this activity as a waste of money and a sign of the decline of Roman morality and culture. Whether or not this was the case, as a social phenomenon such expenditure on housing reflects the increasing competitiveness of Roman society and politics. Houses became more and more elaborate as individual Romans attempted to highlight their personal power and status within the community as a whole.

The House of the Chaste Lovers

The House of the Chaste Lovers (IX.12.6) is the most recent house – or rather complex of five different properties – to have been excavated at Pompeii. Begun in 1987, the excavation is still in progress.

The house gets its modern name from a series of wall-paintings depicting banqueting couples found in one of the excavated rooms. This room is actually connected to a bakery, and has been interpreted by the excavator as a restaurant. The bakery appears to have been in course of reconstruction in AD 79. There were heaps of lime in different rooms and the millstones had been dismantled. There are visible repairs to the brickwork of the baker's oven. Some of the wall decoration had also been renewed. The

wall-paintings of one of the walls in the 'restaurant' were fresh, and there was a practice sketch of a sac-rificial scene on the west wall of the garden that then had been painted in a niche on the same wall. The skeletons of five mules were found in an adjoining stable, along with the remains of a wooden manger containing hay.

Behind the bakery was a peristyle garden and sur-rounding rooms, part of a separate house, now known as the House of the Painters at Work, that has not been fully excavated. The entrance to this house has not yet been uncovered. Following the techniques pioneered by Jashemski, the excavation of the garden revealed a formal garden lain out with a path, trellis and pergola, and trees and raised beds of roses and ferns. A fountain statue of a child and dolphin was uncovered between the columns of the portico to the north – this was not attached to a fountain and the excavators believe that its location in the portico was temporary. To the north of the peristyle were rooms decorated in Fourth Style wall-paintings, although these paintings had not been finished and were missing their central panels. A large room to the east of the peristyle was also in course of redecora-tion. Interestingly, pigments with pestles and mortar, lime plaster and decorators' tools (such as bronze compasses and rules) were found in this room, and the central panel of the north wall revealed a sketch of the scene that was about to be painted.

couches were inscriptions painted in white letters that asked guests not to behave in excess:

Water cleanses the feet, and after they have been bathed a slave will dry them; a cloth covers the bed, take care and don't soil our linen.

Keep your lustful gaze and languid eyes averted from another man's wife; your mouth should be decent.

Avoid conflicts and put off hateful quarrels, if you can; otherwise go to your own home. (*CIL* IV 7698a–c)

The triclinium of the House of the Moralist (II.4.2–3). It has permanent masonry couches and central table, suggesting that the room was used only for dining. For this photograph, the excavators added a selection of table vessels including a wine crater (large bowl) and jugs.

161

Mosaics

THE FASHION FOR MOSAICS REACHED ITALY FROM THE Greek world in the 1st century BC, and many of the finest and best-known examples are from Pompeii, where they are found mainly in the largest atrium houses, in combination with first-rate wall-paintings. The earliest mosaics have simple geometric designs and have been described as carpets, arranged at the centre of a room. Later, some house-owners added an inset ('emblema') to the centre of the general design of their mosaics. This would have been made in a workshop with specially shaped irregular tesserae in a technique known as *opus vermiculatum* ('wormlike style', because the tessarae are very small); a customer would choose his emblemata, which would then be made, transported to his house and inserted into the mosaic floor. A particularly fine example, of pygmies on the Nile, can be seen in the House of Menander (I.10.4).

Mosaic in opus vermiculatum of pygmies on the Nile, from the House of Menander. This beautiful multicoloured mosaic was the centrepiece of a small room off the peristyle of the house.

Styles of mosaic changed over the years, reflecting changes in styles of wall-painting, and emblemata had gone out of fashion by the end of the 1st century BC. *Opus sectile* (floors composed of cut marble segments in a variety of colours) became more popular, and was the most common form of mosaic at Pompeii in AD 79. But regardless of changes in fashion, mosaics were expensive and only the wealthiest could afford them. Thus the number of mosaics in the House of the Faun demonstrates the importance of its inhabitants from the 1st century BC onwards.

The House of the Faun

Originally excavated in 1830–32, the House of the Faun (VI.12.2) was stripped of its elaborate mosaics by the excavators, abandoned to the elements, and finally damaged in the Allied bombing of 1943. What can be seen today only hints at the grandeur of the house, which occupies an entire insula and, at approximately 3,000 sq. m (32,000 sq. ft), is the largest house in Pompeii.

There is some evidence for earlier occupation on the site (pottery dating to the 6th century BC, and the remains of a house of the 3rd century BC), but in its current shape the house was built in the early 2nd century BC and reconstructed later in the same century. The main entrance is on the Via della Fortuna. There is a mosaic of coloured limestone tesserae on the threshold to the house exclaiming 'HAVE' (*CIL* X 872 a) or 'welcome' in Latin. The fauces then lead into the largest atrium in Pompeii, 16 m (52 ft) in length, adorned by a bronze fountain statue of a faun set up in the impluvium. The visual axis from the fauces passes through the atrium, tablinum and first peristyle, culminating in the exedra where the most famous of Pompeian mosaics was discovered: the Alexander mosaic.

The Alexander mosaic is one of the most important finds from Pompeii. It depicts one of Alexander's victorious battles with the King of Persia, Darius III, during the conquest of Asia. The mosaic adorned the floor of an exedra that opened onto the peristyle of the house. Alexander is seen to the left, on horseback at the head of his cavalry; Darius stands on a chariot to the right. Around them, their soldiers are engaged in combat. The mosaic measures slightly less than 20 sq. m (215 sq. ft), and is a work of epic proportions in fine opus vermiculatum. A precise replica of the mosaic has recently been finished, using a total of approximately 1 million tesserae. It must have taken years to complete, and, given its size and complexity, it is likely that the work took place inside the house rather than in a workshop. It is thought that the Alexander mosaic may have been a copy of a painting made of the battle shortly after it was fought. Pliny the Elder (*Natural*

The famous Alexander mosaic from the House of the Faun (VI.12.2), excavated in 1830–32 and removed to the Naples Museum. A replica was recently commissioned by the Soprintendenza; this has now been placed in the house itself.

History 35, 110) actually mentions a famous painting of a battle between Alexander and Darius by Philoxenos of Eretria. It has been suggested that the mosaic was commissioned to celebrate the role of an ancestor of the owner of the house in the battle itself. Whether or not this could be the case, the mosaic formed the visual focus and highlight of the house, and sets it apart from all other Pompeian houses. From the time of its construction in the 2nd century BC until AD 79, this was one of the wealthiest and most striking houses in Pompeii.

The articulation and decoration of the rest of the house underline its importance. The main part of the house was extensively decorated in First Style stucco and wall-painting, much of it imitating marble revetment. This decoration was already about 200 years old in AD 79, but its quality and preservation was such that one scholar has suggested that the house had been preserved as a kind of museum to the past influence and power of an important Pompeian family. The pavements and mosaics from the house are also particularly fine and some of the most famous from Pompeii. They include scenes of marine fauna, Nile fauna, ducks on the Nile, Bacchus riding a tiger, doves, a satyr and nymph, and a cat killing a duck.

This is also one of the rare houses in Pompeii to have separate service quarters. These lie around a small atrium immediately to the east of the main atrium, and consist of a kitchen with oven and domestic shrine, a bath with hypocaust and latrine, and many small rooms. There was an upper floor over the entire area. The service quarters had been reconstructed in the final years before the eruption and were mostly decorated in a simple Third Style wall-painting. A long corridor to the east of the first peristyle separated the service quarters from the main areas of the house, but also allowed easy access to it.

The owners of this house are unknown. One theory suggests that, as the most palatial house in Pompeii, it became the property of Publius Cornelius Sulla, the leader of the Roman colony in 80 BC. It has also been suggested, on the basis of an

Mosaics from the House of the Faun (VI.12.2).

(Opposite) The mosaic of Bacchus riding a tiger with a lion's head was located in one of the triclinia of the house. Bacchus is portrayed as a winged child, drinking from a large cup. The border of the mosaic is made up of tragic masks amidst festoons of fruit and leaves.

(Left) In this mosaic from one of the alae (open rooms off the atrium), a cat seizes a quail. Beneath them, two ducks are seated in the midst of a still-life of fish, seafood and birds.

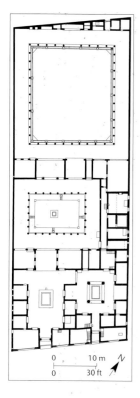

honorific base with an Oscan inscription of the aedile Satrius found in the tablinum, that it belonged to the Satrii, an old Campanian family.

Several skeletons were found in the atrium of the service quarters, one of a woman adorned with two heavy gold bracelets in the form of serpents, earrings and rings (one ring inscribed with the name 'Cassia'). Around 100 silver coins, 15 bronze coins and 2 gold coins were also found in this part of the house. Drawings published in 1854 illustrate some of the other artifacts found in this house, and there has been recent success in identifying a number of these in the storerooms of the Naples Museum, such as ornamental bronze plaques and studs that would have been attached to wooden furniture, marble furniture supports, a bronze brazier and water-heater, some bronze and glass vessels, a few lamps, and also some more unusual items such as a flute and a 'sistrum' (ritual rattle used in the worship of Isis). In general, however, the vast majority of the finds from the House of the Faun cannot be identified today.

Plan of the House of the Faun – the largest house in Pompeii – and a view from the fauces of its stately atrium through to its grand peristyle. A bronze statue of a faun, which stood in the impluvium, gives the house its modern name. The original faun can be seen in the Naples Museum.

(Above) Mosaics are found only in the largest and most impressive houses of Pompeii, and were a clear symbol of wealth and status. The atrium of the House of Paquius Proculus (I.7.1) was decorated with a stunning mosaic carpet divided into panels; at the centre of each panel is the figure of a bird. The mosaic band around the impluvium is decorated with marine fauna. Such an elaborate mosaic in an atrium is highly unusual. Surprisingly, the atrium does not have side rooms (alae); instead the main living quarters of the house were the rooms around the large peristyle.

(Right) Mosaic of a boxer standing on a podium, now in the Naples Museum. His hands are wrapped in bandages and strapped with leather cords.

Wall-Painting

WALL-PAINTING IS A VERY PROMINENT PART OF THE surviving archaeological record of Pompeii, and can be seen in houses and public buildings of all shapes and sizes. The walls of Roman houses were decorated to a much greater extent than we are accustomed to today, and wall-painting appears to have become an important method of expressing wealth, status and social aspirations. As such it was closely connected to the issue of traditional Roman morality. Pliny the Elder, for example, praised the wisdom of Rome's ancestors, 'for they did not decorate walls, merely for the owners of property, or houses, which would remain in one place and which could not be saved from a fire' (*Natural History* 35.37).

The Romans believed that before the Punic Wars (3rd–2nd centuries BC) the walls of their houses were not even plastered and that their ancestors had no need for luxury. Whether or not this was true, by the 2nd century BC wall decoration was becoming fashionable. The most famous passage about the development of wall-painting was written by the Augustan architect, Vitruvius at the end of the 1st century BC. Vitruvius documented the changing fashions in wall-painting and used these changes to comment on the moral decline of his age. On the basis of Vitruvius' description, the German historian August Mau identified four styles of wall-painting at the end of the 19th century, which he attributed to different chronological periods (see box overleaf).

Over the last 100 years, scholars have refined Mau's chronology, and added transitional phases between the four styles, but most would still accept its broad outline. Along with the chronology of building materials and techniques, the four styles have become one of the major means of dating the construction of and developments within particular houses and buildings.

Mau's chronology is a useful tool, a means to conceptualize changing fashions, but there are problems with trying to apply it strictly to Pompeian decoration. Vitruvius' passage was based on fashions in Rome, not Pompeii, so to what extent should it be applied to a small provincial town like Pompeii? Vitruvius' tone is also moralizing. He approves of the paintings of his ancestors and strongly criticizes what he thinks is the 'unrealistic' style of his contemporaries: 'Yet when people view these falsehoods, they approve rather than condemn, failing to consider whether any of them can really occur or not.' Vitruvius is not an unbiased observer of the changing fashions.

It is clear, too, that sometimes the different styles overlap. Some houses are painted in a single style, but there are examples of houses that contain all four styles of painting (a good example is the aptly named House of the Four Styles (I.8.17)). Different rooms may have been painted in different chronological periods, but there is also the issue of personal taste. Rooms may have been deliberately decorated in different styles to provide variety. Some home-owners may not have wanted the latest style, which would explain the First Style decoration of the House of the Faun and the Second Style decoration of the Villa of the Mysteries. First and Second Style wall-paintings certainly had connotations of grandeur and wealth, but they may simply reflect a preference (like Vitruvius' own) for more traditional styles.

Regardless of the problems with Mau's four styles of wall-painting, it is clear that for two centuries there was extraordinary innovation in wall-painting and the use of elaborate decoration spread through all sections of Roman society. This phenomenon has been described as emulation – the lower classes copy their betters, causing the upper classes to innovate and experiment and to waste even more money in order to maintain their social distance and highlight their superior social status. Wall-painting can be seen as a means of defining one's place in society.

(Below) Wall-painting of the poet Menander, from an exedra in the peristyle of the House of Menander. The poet wears an ivy-wreath and sits on a throne holding an open scroll. His name was written both on a label beneath the throne and on the scroll, and three comic masks were painted on the adjacent wall. There was also a bearded portrait on the wall facing Menander with adjacent tragic masks, probably of the tragic poet Euripides. Unfortunately, only the incised guidelines of this second portrait remain.

The House of Menander

Another particularly prominent house is the House of Menander (I.10.4), located to the south of the Via dell' Abbondanza and excavated by Amedeo Maiuri from 1926 to 1932. It occupies about 55 per cent of its insula, but probably owned many of the neighbouring properties. From the fauces, there was a view through the atrium and tablinum to a large peristyle. The wall-paintings of the house are predominantly Fourth Style, many of them probably dating to the period after the earthquake of AD 63. Although there are some nicely decorated rooms around the atrium, the grandest rooms are located around the peristyle. These included a vast banquet hall, 11.5 x 7.5 m (38 x 25 ft) in size, which is one of the largest reception rooms to have been found in Pompeii, capable of holding large numbers of visitors to the house, and underlining the social importance of its owner. Wall-paintings of Menander and Euripides were found in large niches in the south wall of the peristyle, directly opposite the fauces, along with comic and tragic theatrical masks. Maiuri suggested that a room next to these was a library. The house also had a set of private baths, consisting of laconicum, apodyterium, tepidarium and caldarium, heated by a hypocaust, and elaborately decorated. Much of the bath suite was out of use in the period immediately before the eruption in AD 79, although the caldarium had been repaired and redecorated. There was evidence throughout the house of on-going building work and repairs.

The house was large enough to have extensive and separate service quarters. These are found in two parts of the house. On the east side of the house

The four styles of Pompeian wall-painting

In 1882 the German art historian August Mau identified four styles of wall-painting at Pompeii which he attributed to four distinct chronological periods. His styles were based on a passage written by the Roman architect, Vitruvius, which describes how styles of wall-painting developed (Vitruvius, *On Architecture* VII.5.1–4).

Example of First Style wall-painting, from the House of Sallust (VI.2.4).

First Style

'Incrustation Style', dated by Mau to 150–90 BC.

Passage of Vitruvius on which identification of the style is based

Vitruvius VII.5.1: 'In other apartments for use in spring, autumn or summer, and also in atria and cloisters, the ancients used definite methods of painting definite objects. For by painting an image is made of what is, or of what may be; for example, men, buildings, ships, and other objects; of these definite and circumscribed bodies, imitations are taken and fashioned in their likeness. Hence the ancients who first used polished stucco, began by imitating the variety and arrangement of marble inlay; then the varied distribution of festoons, ferns, coloured strips.'

Description of the style

First Style wall-painting imitates the coloured marble blocks of temple architecture. Plaster was moulded and painted to resemble marble. Moulded details might also include pediments, capitals and doorframes.

Famous examples

House of the Faun (VI.12.2), House of Sallust (VI.2.4).

Example of Third Style wall-painting, from the 'red room' of the Villa of Agrippa Postumus at Boscotrecase.

Third Style

'Ornate Style', dated by Mau to 25 BC – AD 40.

Passage of Vitruvius on which identification of the style is based

Vitruvius VII.5.3: 'But these which were imitations based upon realty are now disdained by the improper taste of the present. On the stucco are monsters rather than definite representations taken from definite things. Instead of columns there rise up stalks; instead of gables, striped panels with curled leaves and volutes. Candelabra uphold pictured shrines and above the summits of these, clusters of thin stalks rise from their roots in tendrils with little figures seated upon them at random. Again, slender stalks with heads of men and of animals attached to half the body.'

Description of the style

Mau considered the Third Style to have developed out of the Second Style during the late Augustan period. Perspective is lost and the walls become flat surfaces with unrealistic architectural details. Walls are divided into panels by ornate but refined and unrealistic columns that form a kind of shrine around a central painting, many of which are mythological scenes.

Famous examples

House of Marcus Lucretius Fronto (V.4.a), House of Fabius Rufus (VII. Ins. Occ. 16–19), House of the Ceii (I.6.15), Villa of Agrippa Postumus at Boscotrecase.

Second Style

'Architectural Style,' dated by Mau to 90–25 BC.

Passage of Vitruvius on which identification of the style is based

Vitruvius VII.5.2: 'Then they proceeded to imitate the contours of buildings, the outstanding projections of columns and gables; in open spaces, like exedrae, they designed scenery on a large scale in tragic, comic, or satyric style; in covered promenades, because of the length of the walls, they used for ornament the varieties of landscape gardening, finding subjects in the characteristics of particular places; for they paint harbours, headlands, shores, rivers, springs, straits, temples, groves, hills, cattle, shepherds. In places, some have also the anatomy of statues, the images of the gods, or the representations of legends; further, the battles of Troy and the wanderings of Ulysses over the countryside with other subjects in like manner from Nature.'

Description of the style

Mau believed that the Second Style could be related to the foundation of the Roman colony at Pompeii. Second Style is an elaboration of First Style, with an emphasis on architectural reality but without the moulded plasterwork of the earlier style. Columns, ledges, doors, were painted as realistically as possible and in proper perspective. Receding views were created through columns to scenes with a mixture of reality and illusion.

Famous examples

Villa of the Mysteries, House of the Labyrinth (VI.11.10), and Villa A at Oplontis. The famous paintings in the Metropolitan Museum in New York also belong to this style, and originated from the Villa of Publius Fannius Synistor at Boscoreale.

Fourth Style

'Intricate Style', dated by Mau to AD 40 onwards.

Passage of Vitruvius on which identification of the style is based

Vitruvius was not alive to witness this style.

Description of the style

Although Vitruvius only commented on three styles of wall-painting, Mau identified a Fourth Style (although he did not describe it in as much detail as the first three styles). Fourth Style is basically a combination of the two styles that went before it. Architectural details are neither as solid as in Second Style nor as flimsy as in Third Style. Scenes are painted within panels that are located usually within a broader architectural framework. Ornamental motifs, such as garlands and grotesques, are more elaborate than previously, and there are more decorative figures, either floating free in panels or perched on architectural features.

Example of Fourth Style wall-painting, from the House of the Vettii (VI.15.1).

Famous examples

House of the Vettii (VI.15.1), House of Menander (I.10.4), House of Loreius Tiburtinus (II.2.2), House of the Painters at Work (IX.12). Some 80 per cent of the walls of Pompeii's houses are decorated in this style.

is a long corridor with many small rooms, with a stable at one end (found to contain a wagon, many amphorae and a selection of agricultural tools at the time of the eruption) and a small atrium and surrounding rooms at the other. Maiuri thought that this small atrium was part of the quarters of the steward of the house, and identified him as Quintus Poppaeus Eros on the basis of a signet-ring found next to a skeleton in one of the rooms here. It has been estimated that 30 people could have lived in this part of the house. The second service area lies to the west of the peristyle, and consists of a kitchen, latrine, service rooms and a small cultivated garden, with access to cellars beneath the bath building. It was in these cellars that a large collection of 118 silver vessels was discovered, mostly in a wooden chest bound with bronze. In the top of the chest were jewelry and gold and silver coins (13 aurei and 33 denarii, with a value of 1,432 sesterces); beneath them the silver vessels were wrapped in cloth and neatly stacked. The handles and feet of the vessels had been removed and stored separated. There were plates and trays for eating, spoons and ladles for serving, and cups, bowls and jugs for drinking, some of which were paired – two, for example, had Dionysiac scenes, and another two depicted the labours of Hercules. Many of the vessels had similar decoration on theirs handles and rims, allowing Maiuri to identify two separate 'services' within the hoard.

Who lived in the houses of Pompeii?

The names of Pompeii's houses today are modern inventions, created by the excavators on the basis of programmata on their facades, objects or decoration found inside them, or important visitors during the excavations. The name of the House of the Centenary (IX.8.6) commemorates the year of its excavation – 1879, 1,800 years after the eruption of Vesuvius that destroyed it. The House of the Lyre-Player (I.4.25) was named after a bronze statue of Apollo playing the lyre found in its peristyle, and the House of the Faun is named for the bronze Faun that adorned its impluvium in the atrium.

Other houses have been named for the people who are thought to have lived in them, based on electoral programmata, graffiti or signet-rings. For example,

A 19th-century engraving of keys, locks, stamps and signet-rings found during the early excavations. Such finds have frequently been used to identify the owners or residents of particular houses.

the House of Sallust (VI.2.4) gets its name from an electoral programmata on its facade that calls for the election of Gaius Sallustius. But it is not clear to what extent this sort of evidence can really be used to identify the inhabitants of houses, and often there is contradictory evidence to consider. The House of Loreius Tiburtinus (II.2.2) is so-called because programmata on its facade name 'Loreius' and 'Tiburtinus' (see p.131), but these names are not linked in the programmata and appear to refer to different people. In addition, the bronze signet-ring of a 'Octavius Quartio' was found inside the house, leading some scholars to think that he was its owner (the house is often referred to as the House of Octavius Quartio).

In other cases, the names in programmata may indeed relate to the inhabitants of a house. In a programma on the facade of house I.9.12, an 'Amarantus' calls for the election of Quintus Postumius Proculus as aedile; the house was named the 'House of Amarantus' as a result. During excavations in this house in the 1990s, an amphora was discovered that had the name 'SEX POMPEII AMARANTI' written on it in black ink, leading to the conclusion that Amarantus was indeed the likely occupant of this property. A combination of programmata and two signet-rings (one of Aulus Vettius Conviva, known also from the archive of Lucius Caecilius Jucundus (see p.220), the other of Aulus Vettius Restitutus) probably makes the House of the Vettii an accurate identification. Less clear is the case of the House of the Moralist (III.4.2-3), named for inscriptions found in its summer triclinium (see above). Five programmata on the external facade give the name Marcus Epidius Hymenaeus, and inside the house were found six amphorae addressed to this man. However, the signet-ring of Gaius Arrius Crescens was also found inside the house, along with another amphorae addressed to Titus Arrius Polites.

The names of the inhabitants of the vast majority of Pompeii's houses are unknown. Houses could accommodate large, extended families: the male head of the family, his wife and children, but also other relatives, freedmen and slaves, and possibly even lodgers. The more important the head of the family, the greater the number of dependants likely to be living with him.

It is unclear why these valuable silver objects should have been stored in a cellar. Maiuri's explanation was the building work that had been underway in the house at the time of the eruption. He thought that the owners of the house had moved out temporarily, leaving the house in the hands of the steward, and locking his valuables out of sight. Strangely, though, the key to the chest had been left in its lock. It has since been suggested that the treasure had been put in the cellar as an emergency measure, perhaps in response to the eruption itself.

The House of the Faun and the House of Menander are two of the largest and most palatial houses at Pompeii; there are only a few other houses that can compete with them in terms of scale and decoration, such as the House of the Centenary (IX.8.6), the House of the Lyre-Player (I.4.25), and the House of Paquius Proculus (I.7.1). These must have been the

homes of Pompeii's very wealthiest families, although, of course, we can only guess at the names of their inhabitants.

There are many substantial houses in Pompeii that must have belonged to the rest of Pompeii's social and economic elite. These are mostly atrium houses, with peristyles, and are extensively decorated. Some also have service quarters. Some, such as the House of the Vettii (VI.15.1) are particularly grand, even if not on the same scale as the House of the Faun.

The Sack of Troy, part of a 'Trojan cycle' in an alae off the atrium of the House of Menander. The Trojan king Priam (centre) watches as Helen (left) is seized by her estranged husband Menelaus. Cassandra (right) clings to the Palladium, the wooden effigy of the goddess Athena; the Greek warrior Ajax tries to drag her away from it, but she clings on tightly.

A silver skyphos (cup), part of the Menander hoard, decorated with pastoral scenes including an oarsman and a shepherd with a ram. The Greek name 'Apelles' – the artisan who created the cup – was stamped on the bottom of the cup, which had been repaired in antiquity.

The House of the Vettii

The House of the Vettii (VI.15.1) was excavated from 1894 to 1895, and was the first house to be fully restored by the excavators. It is particularly famous for its Fourth Style wall-paintings, many with mythological scenes and figures, and the statuary found in its peristyle. This was one of the few large houses not to have been disturbed by salvagers and treasure-hunters before its formal excavation.

In AD 79 the house had been newly redecorated and repaired, probably because of damage suffered in the seismic activity from AD 63. High-quality materials had been used in this work, an indication of the wealth and resources of its owners who are thought to have been the two affluent freedmen, the Vettii. The house was actually formed of two smaller houses that had been combined some time during the 1st century BC. The atrium was found to contain two iron-clad chests on masonry bases. It led directly into the peristyle (there is no tablinum), which was the visual focus of the house and could be seen from the front door. Particularly famous wall-paintings from this house include the punishment of Dirce, Daedalus and the wooden bull, Ariadne abandoned by Theseus, Hercules strangling the serpent, and Pentheus torn apart by the Baccantes. A large triclinium off the peristyle had nine famous friezes of cupids: 1) engaged in archery; 2) picking flowers and making garlands; 3) making perfumes; 4) racing chariots; 5) working metal; 6) baking bread;

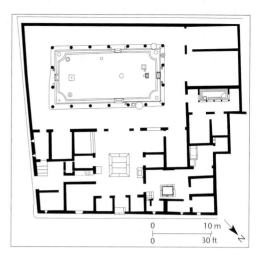

7) harvesting and treading grapes; 8) celebrating a festival; and 9) buying and selling wine.

The house also had two service quarters. One had service rooms and a stairway to the upper floor. Harnesses were found in one of the rooms, so there may have been a stable in this part of the house. On the other side of the peristyle, the second service area consisted of a small atrium, kitchen and small room with erotic paintings. The atrium had a stairway to an upper floor, and a large lararium. Here the genius of the family was depicted as a man in a toga, head veiled, carrying a libation dish and incense box. He is flanked by the household Lares dressed in tunics with drinking horns and wine buckets.

Wall-painting of the star-crossed lovers, Pyramus and Thisbe, from the biclinium at the end of the upper euripus (canal) of the House of Loreius Tiburtinus (II.2.2). On finding the body of her lover, Thisbe stabs herself through the heart with his sword. This wall-painting was paired with another of Narcissus.

Two canals (euripi) intersect the large garden of the house of Loreius Tiburtinus. The longer euripus extended the entire length of the garden and was spanned by bridges, fountains and pergolas and adorned with numerous statuettes.

The House of Loreius Tiburtinus

This house (II.2.2) was excavated from 1916 to 1921, and occupies almost an entire insula. The impluvium in the atrium had a fountain jet and was framed with flower-boxes. There are no rooms off the atrium; instead the main part of the house is located to the south of the atrium. Here a small peristyle took the place of the traditional tablinum and elaborately decorated cubicula and triclinia were located around it. In one room the history of Troy is depicted: an upper register portrays Hercules in combat with Laomedon, the king of Troy, while a lower register illustrates scenes from the Trojan War. In another room, there is a wall-painting of a priest of Isis, dressed in white with a shaven head.

The name 'Amulius Faventinus Tiburs' is written beneath this portrait.

To the south of this complex of rooms are two euripi. The upper euripus ran from west to east and was adorned with many garden statues and culminated in a garden biclinium decorated with paintings of Narcissus and Pyramus and Thisbe, one of which had been signed by the painter ('Lucius pinxit'). The lower euripus ran the length of the large garden from north to south, intersected by two small shrines with fountains. The garden was planted with acanthus and fruit trees.

The extent of wall decoration

By the 1st century AD, elaborate wall-painting had spread through all sections of Roman society. Wall-painting was only one way of displaying wealth and status, but it is the most prominently visible one today. There are many smaller atrium houses where the extent and quality of decoration suggests that their inhabitants sought to impress their peers and imitate their betters. The House of the Ceii (I.6.15) covers 300 sq. m (3,200 sq. ft), and has good-quality Third Style wall-painting throughout. The

walls of its small peristyle were adorned with garden paintings depicting Nile scenes (pygmies fighting hippopotami and crocodiles, amphorae being transported on ships, sacred buildings on the banks of a river). Similarly, the smaller House of the Priest Amandus (I.7.7), 230 sq. m (2,500 sq. m) in size, has mythological wall-paintings depicting the fall of Icarus, the rescue of Andromeda, Hercules in the garden of Hesperides and the seduction of Helen by Paris. The paintings of the house belong to both the Third and Fourth Styles. The triclinium, for example, was painted in Third Style and had an emblema of coloured marble at the centre of the room, marking the place of the table around which the three triclinium beds would have been placed.

The majority of Pompeii's citizens lived in small houses, often with a central space if not an atrium, and with decoration in a few rooms but not through the entire house. The plan of these houses was frequently irregular, since they fit in and around larger houses. The House of Fabius Amandus (I.7.3), for example, is a small atrium house of *c.* 125 sq. m (*c.* 1,350 sq. ft) off the Via dell' Abbondanza. It was too small to have a proper garden or peristyle but had a light-well at the rear garden paintings, to give the illusion of a garden to those looking through the front door. The house had been painted in Fourth Style, and one room even had a mosaic panel. It is hard to imagine large numbers of clients being received into this house, but its occupants were still concerned to give a good impression and to follow the latest fashions. A similar example (slightly bigger at *c.* 170 sq. m (*c.* 1,800 sq. ft)) is the House of the Venus in Bikini (I.11.6), which was also decorated in the Fourth Style and displayed a marble statue of Venus on a base behind the impluvium of the atrium, which was visible from the entrance (see p.195). But many houses of a similar size have little decoration and appear to have combined living spaces with workshops and shops. I.8.13, for example, consists of a courtyard with eight rooms to its rear and no decoration at all. I.9.10 has a central space with simply plastered surrounding rooms and a small garden to the rear. The smallest and plainest accommodations were small rooms above shops or workshops, apartments of mostly unknown plan above houses, and tiny houses with little or no decoration. Many people must have lived where they worked.

Household Artifacts

THE ARCHITECTURE AND DECORATION OF POMPEII'S houses have been the traditional focus of scholarship. It is only in recent years that the objects found inside the houses have begun to be studied systematically. This work is surprisingly difficult. Much depends on the period in which the excavations of a particular house took place. Compare the House of the Faun and the House of Menander, excavated from 1830–32 and 1928–32 respectively. Although there has been some recent success in identifying some of the artifacts removed from the House of the Faun to Naples Museum, the vast majority were not properly recorded or even preserved. In contrast, the House of Menander has detailed excavation reports, and its domestic contents can (mostly) be reconstructed.

The artifacts often give a very different picture from that generated by the architecture and decoration of a house. The House of the Fruit Orchard (I.9.5), for example, has beautiful wall-paintings in several rooms and a small but pretty peristyle garden. In AD 79 this garden and its portico were being used to store wine amphorae. This is not an exceptional example; there are many houses and rooms where the types and distribution of artifacts seem surprising to the modern viewer, such as everyday pots and pans found in elaborately decorated rooms. But it is important to consider issues such as time of the day and season. Amphorae may have been stacked in the peristyle of the House of the Fruit Orchard because it was the season for making wine, but they may not have been stored there all year round. Similarly, a cubiculum could be

Domestic artifacts in the House of Ceres

A collection of terra sigillata vessels and an elegant marble fountain-head in the shape of a dolphin, from the House of Ceres (I.9.13).

The name of this house (I.9.13) derives from the terracotta bust of the goddess Ceres that was discovered in the atrium during its excavation in 1951. A large number of artifacts along with evidence for wooden furniture was discovered here. The excavators succeeded in making plaster-casts of the front-door, and a number of cupboards, beds and tables. One small bedroom, for example, had once contained a wooden cupboard, bed, table and shelf.

It appears that, as well as being used to receive guests, the atrium was a utility space. Ashes and traces of carbonized material – probably relating to cooking – were found on a long masonry structure along one wall (which obscured the Second Style wall-painting), along with several upside-down amphorae-points, used to support cooking pots. The remains of a cupboard were found next to this bank, inside which were a few cooking pots and also some ceramic table vessels and a bronze bucket (to draw water for cooking?). Four more upside-down amphorae-points were discovered on an iron brazier in the portico before the garden, again with a residue of carbonized ash.

A fairly large collection of tools was uncovered, including an axe, a clamp, two hammers, a hatchet, two hooks, and a spade, and there was also evidence for wool-working – five spindles for spinning and a group of fifteen ceramic loom-weights and a lead loom-weight (it is very unusual at Pompeii to find a group of loom-weights together like this).

There were a large number of table vessels (plates, bowls and jugs). Many were made of terra sigillata (red-gloss ceramic), mostly of Italian origin but a few had been imported from further afield. Some had been stored together in a wooden chest, but others were found in many different rooms. There was also a wide range of storage vessels: more than 20 amphorae and table-amphorae and a selection of small jars that may have been used to store food. In contrast, objects which can be described as personal belongings were rarer. There were a couple of buckles and buttons, two gold earrings, and some beads that would have been part of a necklace. However, there were eleven glass perfume-bottles, a pair of tweezers, two probes (used either for medical or cosmetic purposes) and a shell that might have been used to mix cosmetics. There was also a die and 16 complete lamps.

The House of Ceres was fairly scruffy in AD 79. A group of four marble dolphins, actually fountain-jets, were found in the tablinum, but there was no basin or fountain in the house to which they could be attached. The wall-paintings – mostly Second Style – were in poor condition and had been patched in places, and there is other evidence for repairs to plasterwork and to the impluvium in the atrium. There was some evidence for building activity in the house (a small stack of roof tiles), possibly suggesting that structural changes or further repairs may have been intended. In general, however, the artifacts found in this house tend to suggest that its inhabitants were not particularly prosperous.

a bedroom at night, but may have been used to receive guests during the day. Storage is another factor to take into account, since objects may not have been stored where they were used.

The range of artifacts within a single house can be very diverse. There is usually evidence for normal domestic activities, such as cooking, eating, personal hygiene, plus lamps and objects such as dice and jewelry, but also widespread evidence for work and craft activities, even in the biggest houses, which means that these houses were not just designed for entertaining or impressing guests. Many different activities could take place within a single house. The largest houses had differentiation of space (such as distinct service quarters in the House of the Faun, the House of Menander and the House of the Vettii), but the vast majority did not. Atria, for example, might have been used to receive guests in the morning and for work in the afternoon.

The patera (flat bowl with cylindrical handle), iron and bronze brazier and bronze ewer with silver detailing were all found in the House of Menander (I.10.4). At the time of its excavation, the brazier still contained ashes. The bronze tripod was found in the Praedia of Julia Felix (II.4.2) in the 18th century, and consigned by the excavators to the 'Secret Cabinet' of 'erotic' images and objects that the general public were not allowed to view. In fact, the offending satyrs were intended to avert evil.

(Above) A 19th-century engraving of artifacts found in the House of the Faun (VI.12.2), including candelabra, marble table supports, bronze jugs, a brazier, an iron tripod, an amphora and bronze door handles. The vast majority of artifacts from this house can no longer be identified today amongst the thousands of objects stored at the Naples Museum.

Gardens

(Opposite) The garden of the House of Marcus Lucretius Fronto (IX.3.5/24), which was in plain view from the entrance of the house, was once the setting for a large number of marble statuettes and herms, including four double-headed herms, two cupids riding dolphins, a satyr inspecting the foot of a bearded Pan, and several other satyrs. Around the pool, into which a statue of Silenus poured water from a wine-skin, were numerous statuettes of animals (duck, ibises, hares, a deer and a cow), some of which were fountain-heads that spouted water into the pool.

(Right) The garden of the House of the Vettii (VI.15.1) is famous for its symmetrically laid out formal garden, which incorporated marble basins, fountains and statuettes. Originally left in situ by the excavators, the bronze cupids holding ducks are now replicas; the other marble statuettes – including Bacchus, Paris, satyrs and cupids – have been removed.

THE MANY GARDENS OF POMPEII HAD NEVER BEEN systematically studied before the work of Wilhelmina Jashemski in the 1960s and 1970s. She made plaster casts of root-cavities to identify plants, examined soil contours to reveal planting beds and irrigation channels, and analyzed floral and faunal remains. Thanks to her exhaustive research of the excavation reports and wall-paintings, and her surveys and excavations in the gardens themselves, the significance of gardens in both everyday life and the economy of Pompeii has become apparent. Jashemski estimated that gardens and cultivated areas within the walls made up almost one-fifth of the total area of Pompeii, and documented an astonishing diversity in purpose and planting of these areas. Her success in part depended on the period in which the gardens she studied had originally been excavated. Those which had been excavated before the 20th century often had left no physical remains to study other

than records of garden wall-paintings or sometimes the paintings themselves. However, the more recent excavation of other areas, Regions I and II in particular, meant that some of her garden reconstructions are extremely detailed and accurate. Even the smallest houses had garden areas, and many also had garden wall-paintings. But there was also a great deal of evidence for cultivation within the town walls, particularly viticulture but also vegetable patches and orchards. The impression that we are left with is one of an intensive use of garden space for both pleasure and profit, both elements often found in the same garden.

181

(Right and opposite) Garden wall-paintings from the House of the Golden Bracelet (VI.17.42). The lush vegetation and depictions of garden ornaments served as a back-drop for a real formal garden and out-door triclinium, helping to create a beautiful dining area.

(Below) One section of the extensive garden painting in the peristyle of the House of Venus in a Shell (II.3.3), featuring an ornamental basin or bird bath – a common feature both in garden paintings and actual formal gardens – and overlooked by a theatrical mask. A domestic shrine, in the form of a niche in the wall decorated with painted vegetation, has been incorporated into this imaginary garden.

The formal garden

The small garden of the House of the Golden Bracelet, also known as the House of the Wedding of Alexander (VI.17.42), was the first formal garden to have been excavated scientifically. The house was built over the town walls in the 1st century BC and is terraced on three levels. The garden is located on the lowest level. Jashemski's work revealed a rectangular

planted area with slightly raised beds, possibly evidence of a formal hedge. At the centre of the rectangle was an oval flower-bed. A vaulted garden room decorated with wall-paintings of lush vegetation opened to the north of the garden, and next to this was an exedra, also adorned by garden paintings. An outdoor triclinium was located in the exedra, along with a marble fountain and an apsed mosaic fountain. There was a pool with 28 fountain jets in front of the triclinium. Here the garden served to complement the dining area; the overriding impression is one of luxury and comfort, reinforced by the extensive use of water features. These dated from the construction of the aqueduct during the Augustan period, which allowed water to be piped into some of the larger and wealthier houses of the town. Gardens throughout the town flourished from this period because there was no longer any need to choose plants that could survive without a lot of water (such as trees). The range of plants that could be grown successfully increased dramatically, which must have had an enormous impact on the colour and texture of gardens. Add to this the possibility of introducing water features such as pools and fountains to a garden and it is fair to say that the Augustan period saw a revolution in the gardens of Pompeii.

Gardens 183

(Right) Garden painting from the House of Venus in a Shell (II.3.3). This painting is the visual focus of the house, meant to be seen from a distance, dominating the rear wall of the peristyle. Venus reclines in a shell that is pulled along by a dolphin, helped by two cupids. (Below) A view of the peristyle, which has been restored in recent years.

Formal gardens are often complemented by formal garden wall-paintings. A good example can be found in the House of the Venus in a Shell (II.3.3) where a painting of Venus reclining in a shell amongst lush vegetation serves as a backdrop to formally planted beds. From the entrance to the house, one can see right through the house and garden to this painting, and as a result the house seems much bigger than it actually is.

The informal garden

The House of Julius Polybius (IX.12.1–3) was mainly excavated from 1966 to 1978, although its facade on the Via dell' Abbondanza had been uncovered in 1913. The house occupies about three-quarters of an entire insula and owes its unorthodox shape to the fact that it is actually two houses that were later amalgamated into one. One of these original houses became the service quarters of the main house. The main part of the house has an unusual covered courtyard, decorated in First Style, before the atrium. Most of the living-rooms of the house were decorated in Third Style wall-paintings. Like its neighbour, the House of the Chaste Lovers, the House of Julius Polybius was being restored in AD 79 and building materials were found, such as a heap of yellow pozzolana (used to make mortar) and a group of broken amphorae (piled in the north-west corner of the covered courtyard) that would probably have been crushed for use in an *opus signinum* pavement. The decoration of the triclinium was unfinished, but the remains of the wooden triclinium couches and many bronze table vessels were found on the floor here, along with a bronze statue of Apollo, used as a lamp-holder. These objects may have been stored here while other parts of the house were being restored.

The garden is small and enclosed on three sides by a portico. Plaster casts were made of a series of wooden chests that were located along the east wall of the portico of the peristyle. Unlike the House of the Golden Bracelet, this house had not been supplied with piped water from the aqueduct, but relied on a large cistern under the eastern side of the portico. The planting of the garden suited the limited availability of water. Excavations uncovered the root-cavities of five large trees and also some smaller trees and shrubs. The cavities of stakes revealed that these had been used to support the branches of what were clearly fruit and/or nut trees. The fragments of four-holed planting pots were found in the root cavities of some of the smaller trees. It appears that these had originally been planted in the pots and then espaliered onto the western wall of the garden. A further interesting discovery were the marks left at the centre of the garden by a long and narrow ladder, a type still in use in the region today and designed specifically to fit into the branches of fruit trees. This garden seems quite crowded and shady, but would have produced a fairly large crop of fruit and nuts for the inhabitants of the house.

The kitchen garden

The House of Pansa (VI.6.1) occupies an entire insula block, and is one of the two houses in Pompeii where there is definite evidence for rental accommodation (see Chapter VIII for discussion). The house has a large atrium with associated rooms, and a peristyle garden with a portico and pool. To the rear of the peristyle a colonnade looks out over a further large garden, which takes up approximately one-third of the entire area of the insula. Excavations revealed that this area had been laid out into separate and regular plots, about 2.5 m (8 ft) wide and divided by irrigation channels. Unlike the peristyle, this was not an ornamental garden but a kitchen allotment.

Although the largest example to date of a kitchen garden at Pompeii, this is not the only example. For example, a very small vegetable garden was found in the House of the Ephebe (I.7.11), located to one side of a garden triclinium. Here we have a nice example of food being produced and consumed in the same small area. Such kitchen gardens were perhaps a throwback to an earlier period of Pompeii's history, when all houses would have had vegetable patches, rather than the norm in AD 79. Excavations in the garden of the House of the Faun (VI.12.2) revealed that a kitchen garden had once formed part of this large and impressive residence. However, it had been destroyed to make way for a formal peristyle garden at some point during the 2nd century BC. This was a period in which vast sums of money were being spent on houses, and clearly the peristyle garden was more prestigious in form and appearance than the working kitchen garden.

The houses of Pompeii were much more than the shells that can be seen today, but a fair degree of imagination is necessary for the visitor to appreciate their complexity. It is difficult to visualize the day-to-day activities that took place because the houses have been stripped of their contents by their excavators. Ironically, it is this evidence that would shed the most light on what is was like to live in a Roman house at one particular moment in time. However, the variety of living conditions is clear: there are the large and luxurious houses of the wealthy elite, the smaller and nicely decorated homes of those with social aspirations, and the rooms and apartments of the poorest inhabitants of the town. The ancient literary sources also reveal the political, social and religious significance of the Roman house, and the remains of wall paintings illustrate the importance many placed on keeping up with changing fashions. This was a dynamic environment, and at Pompeii we gain a valuable insight into the significance placed upon the house in Roman society.

Amphorae piled in the northwest corner of the covered courtyard of the House of Julius Polybius (IX.12.1–3). Building work may have been underway in this house at the time of the eruption of Vesuvius in AD 79.

VII
GODS, TEMPLES AND CULTS

Sextus Pompeius Ruma, freedman of Sextus, willingly fulfilled his vow to Neptune.

Found outside the walls of Pompeii (*CIL* X 8157)

The purpose of traditional Roman religion was to appease the gods with sacrifices, prayers and dedications. There were gods and goddesses for all aspects of life, some more powerful than others but all capable of bringing disaster or misfortune to an individual, his or her family and community. A man (or town) might favour one or two particular gods, but all had to be honoured. This can be seen at Pompeii where there is widespread evidence for the worship of the official gods of the Roman state and the town's divine protectors, and approved 'foreign' cults such as that of Isis. The importance of these gods is evident from the temples that cluster around the area of the Forum and near the Large Theatre, but their role in the everyday life and economy of the town is also illustrated by paintings on street facades and shop fronts, by statuettes in gardens, and by inscriptions and graffiti. There were more personal options, too. Each family had its own tutelary deities that it honoured in the home, and there is some evidence for the presence of 'mystery' cults in Pompeii who attracted their followers with the promise of life after death. The gods and goddesses of Pompeii had major roles to play in the daily lives of the inhabitants of the town, and their influence can be seen throughout the town.

Detail of a miniature wall-painting from the triclinium of the House the Vettii (VI.15.1), part of a much larger decorative scheme including the famous 'working cupids'. A priestess, holding a double-headed sacrificial axe, is about to sacrifice a bull to Diana/Artemis, who wears hunting garb. Apollo, carrying his lyre, plays music to accompany the rite.

Pre-Roman Gods and Temples

MOST OF POMPEII'S TEMPLES DATE TO AFTER THE 2ND century BC. However, there are two temples that can be dated back to the 6th century BC on the basis of archaeological evidence. These are the Doric Temple and the Temple of Apollo, both of which appear to relate to the initial foundation of the settlement (see Chapter III). There may also have been a temple to Mephitis, the Samnite goddess of love, from the 3rd century BC. A temple to Bacchus in the suburbs of the town was also built before the Roman period.

The Doric Temple

The so-called Doric Temple had a particularly prominent location, overlooking the River Sarno, and would have been visible to travellers approaching the town from the river or the sea. On the basis of the decoration on architectural terracottas that probably came from the temple roof, and an incomplete Oscan inscription painted on a wall at the junction of the street leading to the temple from the Via dell' Abbondanza, it has been suggested that the temple may have been jointly dedicated to Hercules and Minerva. Hercules was the honoured mythical founder of various settlements in the region, Herculaneum being the best example. Minerva is thought to have been a goddess of Etruscan origin (Menrva or Menerva) who later became equated with Athena, the Greek goddess of wisdom and war. The temple was built in the 6th century BC according to a peripteral (Greek) design, although with an unusual number of columns. In the 2nd century BC, its *cella* (the chamber in the middle where the cult statue(s) would have been housed) appears to have received new roof tiles, but the outer parts of the temple may have been in ruins. It has been argued that the temple went out of use after the foundation of the Roman colony in 80 BC and that by AD 79 only its platform and several broken columns remained, a deliberate and striking contrast to the new temples built by the Roman colonists. An exedra built on the west side of the Triangular Forum actually encroaches onto the temple platform, supporting this theory. However, it is also possible that the impression of ruin may simply be due to the treasure-hunting of excavators in the 18th and 19th centuries.

The Temple of Bacchus at Sant' Abbondio

The only other evidence for religious activity that predates the period of Roman dominance from the 2nd century BC is the Temple of Bacchus. This was not located inside the town, but a short distance from its walls in the neighbourhood now known as Sant' Abbondio. It may be that it was thought more appropriate that the rituals connected with the worship of Bacchus take place outside the town proper, although this is only speculation. For Bacchus was the god of fertility and wine and closely connected in southern Italy with the local god Liber, the liberator of inhibitions. His cult was associated with drunkenness and promiscuity. The popularity of the cult at Pompeii is attested by the frequent discovery of symbols or statues of Bacchus.

The temple at Sant' Abbondio is traditionally Doric in form. Its pediment is decorated with Dionysiac scenes – Dionysus with grapes and a wine cup, a panther, and a female figure (Ariadne?). To either side of an altar two triclinium couches with circular tables were set, presumably for feasting relating to the cult activities. The triclinia and tables were added to the temple in the Roman period, but the temple itself was established by Samnite magistrates from Pompeii, possibly in the 3rd century BC.

An inscription on the front and back of the altar identifies these magistrates:

> Maras Atinius, son of Maras, aedile, at his own expense. (Poccetti 1979, 107)

A mosaic inscription on the ramp leading into temple reads:

> Ovius Epidius, son of Ovius, and Trebius Mettius, son of Trebius, aediles. (Poccetti 1979, 108)

The temple was still in use at the time of the eruption in AD 79.

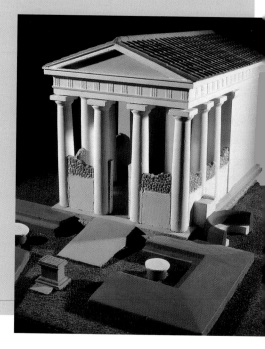

Model of the Temple of Bacchus at Sant' Abbondio. Two triclinium couches lie immediately in front of the temple, to either side of an altar. A ramp leads between them to the temple.

The Temple of Apollo

The Temple of Apollo – or rather a sacred area on its site, next to the Forum – has been dated to the 6th century BC by stratigraphic excavations. It is not clear that in its initial phase it was dedicated to Apollo – excavations in the 1980s to install electricity cables to offices on the site cut across the temple precinct and discovered only terracotta votives relating to a female deity. It has been suggested that the temple was actually dedicated to Ceres, with Apollo among the associated deities worshipped there. As with the Doric Temple, this temple was altered many times over the centuries. Its precinct was paved in large stone blocks during the 4th century BC, by which time there was a large temple on a high podium. It received its definitive form during the 2nd century BC when the temple cella was reduced in size, the precinct curtailed by the construction of the Basilica to the south, and a two-tiered tuff portico was built around its margins. A new pavement was laid in the cella, and an inscription found on the threshold of the room demonstrates that the temple was dedicated to Apollo by this period:

> Ovius Cam[panius, son of?], quaestor, by decree of the assembly, with the money of Apollo […] issued a contract and approved it. (Vetter (1953) no. 18)

An inscription records that a new travertine and limestone altar crowned with marble was set up at public expense in front of the temple in the years immediately after the foundation of the colony (*CIL* X 800), demonstrating the importance of Apollo to the Romans. In the Augustan age, the duumvirs Marcus Holconius Rufus and Gnaeus Egnatius Postumus, made structural changes to the precinct of the temple (*CIL* X 787), and later duumvirs, Lucius Sepunius Sandilianus and Marcus Herennius Epidianus, donated a sundial (*CIL* X 802). The temple has both Greek features (the Corinthian colonnade surrounding the small cella) and Italic features (the high dias and central flight of stairs). In AD 79 the temple contained bronze statues of Apollo and Diana, both as archers, and a herm of Mercury. There may have been two fountains. Drawings made of the temple at the time of its excavation reveal that it had been decorated with a rich stucco.

There is no physical evidence for the worship of gods other than Apollo, Hercules and Minerva before the 4th century BC, although it has been suggested that Dionysus (or Bacchus) and Venus were also important deities in the region around Pompeii, given the extensive evidence for their popularity in later periods. There are many examples of statuettes of Hercules, Dionysus and Venus in the small domestic shrines of Pompeii's houses, attesting to their role as protectors and patrons in the community. Recent excavations

have revealed what may be a temple relating to the Samnite period (4th century BC) beneath the much later Roman Temple of Venus. Initial reports have indicated the discovery of a pre-Roman temple wall, some clay offerings to Mephitis, and a basin and terracotta pipes that may indicate the presence of a ritual bath. This temple was demolished at an unknown date, and the Temple of Venus was built on the site after the establishment of the Roman colony in 80 BC. It is not clear if this Samnite temple was destroyed deliberately to make way for the Temple of Venus.

(Above) The bronze statue of Apollo from the Temple of Apollo, in front of a portico of Ionic columns.

(Right) Bronze statuette of Bacchus; now in a private collection, its exact find-spot at Pompeii is unknown.

Pre-Roman Temples and Gods 189

Deities worshipped at Pompeii as part of town-sponsored or accepted cults

Deity	Attributes	Associated temples at Pompeii	Date of construction of temples
Aesculapius	God of healing and patron of doctors.	Temple of Aesculapius?	2nd century BC (if this temple is indeed dedicated to Aesculapius).
Apollo	Greek god of colonists, archery, medicine, prophecy and poetry, among other things.	Temple of Apollo.	6th century BC.
Ceres	Nature goddess and patron of married women.	Location of temple unknown; possibly the Temple of Apollo.	Unknown.
Diana	Goddess of procreation and the hunt, and patroness of women.	Unknown.	Unknown.
Dionysus/ Bacchus	God of fertility, reproduction, and seasonal death and rebirth. In southern Italy he was associated with the local deity Liber (liberator of inhibitions).	The Temple of Dionysus/ Bacchus at Sant' Abbondio.	3rd century BC?
Hercules	Patron of entrepreneurs. The mythical founder of Herculaneum.	The Doric Temple?	6th century BC.
Isis	Associated with the idea of eternal life and resurrection. Goddess of safety and patron of sailors.	Temple of Isis.	2nd century BC.
Juno	Goddess of defence and childbirth, patroness of the Roman state and women.	Capitolium.	Temple of Jupiter transformed into a Capitolium in 1st century BC.
Jupiter	Patron deity of the Roman state.	The Temple of Jupiter in the Forum (Capitolium) and the Temple of Jupiter Meilichios (the location of which is uncertain).	Temple of Jupiter: 2nd century BC; transformed into a Capitolium in 1st century BC. Location of the Temple of Jupiter Meilichios is disputed; that traditionally ascribed was built in the 2nd century BC.
Mars	God of war; as the legendary father of Romulus, Mars was also a tutelary diety of the Romans.	Unknown.	Unknown.
Mercury	God of merchants and journeys.	Unknown.	Unknown.
Minerva	Goddess of war, wisdom, medicine and craft and trade, and patroness of the Roman state.	The Doric Temple?; Capitolium.	6th century BC.
Neptune	God of the sea, patron of seafarers.	Probably located outside the town walls, near modern Bottaro.	Unknown.
Venus	Goddess of love and nature.	Temple of Venus.	1st century BC. There may have been an earlier temple to Mephitis, the Samnite goddess of Love, on the same spot from the 4th century BC.

Garden painting from the House of Venus in a Shell (II.3.3) of a marble statue of Mars standing on a podium.

Selected additional evidence for worship at Pompeii

Identification of temple based on the discovery of a statue of Aesculapius in the so-called 'Temple of Jupiter Meilichios'.

Wall-paintings on shop facades (IX.8.1 and IX.11.1) on the Via dell' Abbondanza. Statues of Apollo in several Pompeian houses.

Inscriptions attest to the presence of priestesses of Ceres.

Bronze statue of Diana as an archer in the Temple of Apollo. Wall-paintings on shop facades (IX.8.1 and IX.11.1) on the Via dell' Abbondanza. Statuette from the House of the Moralist (III.4.2–3).

The famous wall-painting of Dionysus and Vesuvius from the lararium of the House of the Centenary (IX.8.6). Statue in the Temple of Isis of Bacchus as Osiris. Small bust in niche at IX.8.1.

Statuettes, for example, in the Garden of Hercules (II.8.6), and in houses I.10.7 and IX.3.2. Paintings in lararium shrines, such as those in the House of the Silver Wedding (V.2.i), the house at VII.4.26 and the garden of V.2.h. Wall-painting on the facade of IX.11.1 on the Via dell' Abbondanza.

Statuettes found in household lararia; wall-paintings with Egyptian motifs or figures (for example, an Egyptian priest in the House of Loreius Tiburtinus (II.2.2).

Wall-painting on the facade of IX.11.1 on the Via dell' Abbondanza. Terracotta cult statue in the Temple of Jupiter Meilichios. Occasionally found in household lararia, e.g. the House of the Gilded Cupids (VI.16.7).

Dedicatory inscriptions found in the Temple of Jupiter and elsewhere in the town. Wall-paintings on shop facades (IX.8.1 and IX.11.1) on the Via dell' Abbondanza. Statuette in lararium of House of Gilded Cupids (VI.16.7).

Represented in wall-paintings in private houses, such as the House of Marcus Lurectius Fronto (V.4.a) and the House of Venus in a Shell (II.3.3).

Cult of Mercury and Maia well attested in inscriptions. Herm in Temple of Apollo. Wall-paintings on many shop facades and house entrances, and occasionally in lararium (such as in the House of the Cryptoporticus, I.6.2).

Marble inscription found on Via dell' Abbondanza. Wall-painting on the facade of IX.11.1 on the Via dell' Abbondanza.

An inscription to Neptune was found outside the town walls, towards the sea, and may relate to a temple.

Images (wall-paintings, marble and bronze statuettes) of Venus have been found all over Pompeii. For example, marble statuettes were found in houses I.2.6, I.2.17, I.11.12, VII.12.23, and VII.3.6. Wall-paintings on shop facades (IX.8.1 and IX.11.1) on the Via dell' Abbondanza. Venus is invoked in numerous graffiti.

Public Religion and Temples in the Roman Period

FROM THE 2ND CENTURY BC, THE ROMANS DOMINATED Campania both politically and culturally. Although Pompeii maintained its independence as an allied town, it was subject to wide-ranging Roman influences. In the sphere of religious activity, Roman gods began to dominate. Indeed, the vast majority of the evidence at Pompeii relates to the Roman period. Temples were the most prominent buildings in the town and became a forceful means of emphasizing new political situations, in the 2nd century BC, after 80 BC when Pompeii formally became a Roman colony, and from the Augustan period when public religion came to include divinities associated with the spirits of the emperors, dead or alive. These public cults – and their associated major temples – emphasized the dominance of Roman gods and signalled allegiance to Rome. They had little to do with personal religious feeling, but are better described as 'civic' or 'state' cults.

Bust of Jupiter found during excavations of the Temple of Jupiter in the 18th century.

The Temple of Jupiter

Jupiter was the supreme god of the Roman state, the god of light and sky and the protector of the state and its laws. Each new year at Rome began with prayers and sacrifices to Jupiter Optimus Maximus (Jupiter Best and Greatest). His temple, shared with Juno and Minerva (collectively they are known as the Capitoline triad), was the centre of political life at Rome, where records of treaties and alliances were preserved. As the Romans extended their empire, temples to Jupiter or to the Capitoline triad became common in provincial towns. At Pompeii, a temple to Jupiter was first built, probably at public expense, in the period 150–120 BC at the northern end of the Forum. Stratigraphic excavations demonstrate that this new temple stood on virgin ground and did not replace any earlier building. Such a prominent position was surely no accident, but a deliberate reference to the power of Rome's most important patron. After the establishment of the Roman colony in 80 BC, the temple was extensively refurbished and transformed into a Capitolium, with mosaic floors and Second Style wall-painting. The temple consisted of three chambers (cellae) on a high podium that could only be accessed by means of steps at the front of the podium. The chambers were dedicated to Jupiter, Juno and Minerva. During the excavations of the 18th century, a colossal marble head of Jupiter was found in the temple, although no other cult statues were discovered. Instead, a semi-colossal foot, a colossal mask and various fragments of statues were found amongst the ruins of its cella, leading at least one scholar to believe that the temple had fallen out of use in AD 79. Others, however, have speculated that the strange nature of the finds here may well be due to the extensive robbing of the site that took place in the centuries after the eruption (see Chapter IX for a fuller discussion).

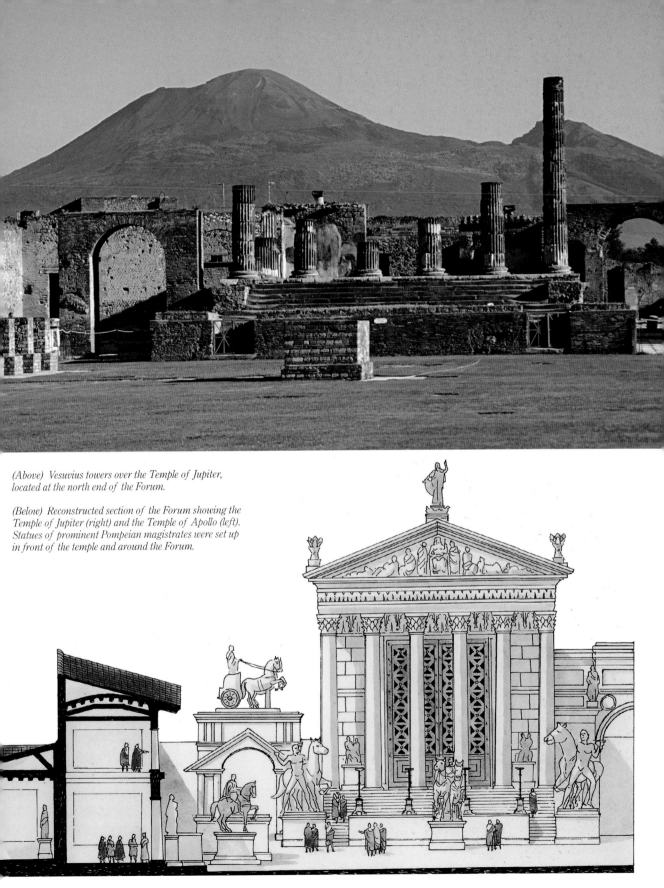

*(Above) Vesuvius towers over the Temple of Jupiter,
located at the north end of the Forum.*

*(Below) Reconstructed section of the Forum showing the
Temple of Jupiter (right) and the Temple of Apollo (left).
Statues of prominent Pompeian magistrates were set up
in front of the temple and around the Forum.*

The Temple of Jupiter Meilichios

Another temple built in the 2nd century BC was the so-called Temple of Jupiter Meilichios (Jupiter 'sweet as honey'). This is a very small temple, close to the Large Theatre, and its identification was based upon an Oscan inscription regulating road construction:

> M. Suttius, son of M., and Numerius Pontius, son of M., aediles, marked out this road as far as the lower Stabian road. The road is marked out over 100 feet. The same magistrates marked out the Pompeian road over 30 feet as far as the Temple of Meilichios. They officially established from scratch these roads and the road of Jupiter and the (?) road by order of the Pompeian chief magistrate. The same aediles approved the work. (Vetter (1953) no. 8)

Unfortunately, this inscription was found by the Stabian Gate, not near the temple in question, and it is possible that it refers to a suburban sanctuary rather than a temple within the town walls. Two terracotta cult statues were found inside the temple during excavations in the 18th century: an unidentified female deity that may represent Juno and a statue originally identified as Jupiter Meilichios but that is now thought to represent Aesculapius, the Greek god of medicine and healing. A bust of Athena was also found with these two statues. On the basis of these finds, the temple has also been identified as a temple to Aesculapius.

The Temple of Venus

Venus, the goddess of love and nature, was the favourite goddess of Sulla, the Roman general who put down the rebellion of Rome's allies in 89 BC and conquered Pompeii. The Roman colony at Pompeii was founded in 80 BC by Sulla's nephew, and Venus became the town's new tutelary goddess. It is thought that the large temple to the rear of the Basilica was dedicated to her, based on the discovery of the fragmentary remains of a marble votive statue of Venus. This temple was constructed over the remains of an earlier temple, thought to have been dedicated to the Samnite goddess of love, Mephitis, so this might be an appropriate place to establish the cult of Venus. This second temple was rebuilt on a monumental scale after 80 BC and was in the course of a second major reconstruction at the time of the eruption in AD 79. The temple stood on a huge artificial platform, surrounded by a double colonnade, open towards the River Sarno and clearly visible to anyone approaching by sea.

Some time before AD 63, the Temple of Venus was rebuilt in marble. It was damaged in the earthquake of that year and appears to have been in course of restoration at the time of the eruption in AD 79.

The location of two more temples is uncertain. The first is the Temple of Ceres, an ancient Italian nature goddess and patron of married women, which is known to have existed because inscriptions document priestesses of the cult of Ceres. She may originally have been worshipped in the Temple of Apollo, or her temple may lie in part of the town that has yet to be excavated. The other 'missing' temple is the Temple of Neptune, which is thought to have existed from the time that Pompeii became a port. The existence of this temple is based primarily on an inscription dedicated to Neptune that was found close to the sea at modern Bottaro (see quotation on p.186); more recently votive offerings were uncovered in the same area, lending support to the theory that a temple or sanctuary was located here.

(Above) This terracotta statue of Aesculapius, originally identified as Jupiter Meilichios, was found inside the temple in the 18th century, along with another of a female deity, probably Juno.

(Below) Sir William Gell's 1930 reconstruction of the small Temple of Jupiter Meilichios, with its ornate altar before the temple precinct.

Wall-painting of Dionysiac cult objects (unprovenanced from Pompeii): on the steps are arranged a pair of cymbals, a spray of bay, a tambourine, a wicker basket containing a drinking cup and a drinking horn draped with a panther skin, a thyrsus (ritual staff tipped with a pine cone) and another drinking cup. In front of the steps a panther and snake fight.

Pompeian Venus

More statuettes and wall-paintings of Venus have been found in the houses and streets of Pompeii than any other deity. It is not always clear if these images related to cult activity or were simply decorative features, but they demonstrate the popular status of Venus as patroness of the town.

Images of Venus are generally of two types: 'matronly' public representations and nude or semi-nude private statues or paintings. For example, a wall-painting on the facade of the so-called 'lanarii coactiliari' (felters') workshop (IX.7.5–7) on the Via dell' Abbondanza depicts her as 'Pompeian Venus', crowned in flowing robes, standing in a chariot drawn by four elephants (see p.209). To the left is a figure of Fortune and to the right a depiction of the genius of the colony. In contrast, marble statuettes, many of them originally painted, show her as 'Venus Anadyomene' (naked, emerging from the sea). An example is that found in the House of Venus in Bikini (I.11.6), which was set up on a base behind the impluvium of the house and clearly visible from the street. Interestingly, the fauces of this house was decorated with female portraits painted in medallions. A graffito scratched in the plaster here exclaimed 'Come in, Lovers!' There is also a very large garden-painting of a semi-naked Venus in the House of Venus in a Shell (II.3.3), also partially visible from the entrance to the house (see p.184). Statuettes of Venus were also commonly found in household shrines, relating to private, domestic cults, and it has been noted that statuettes of Venus are often larger than those of other deities found in household shrines.

Venus was often evoked in graffiti, inscriptions and programmata, in her roles both as patroness of Pompeii and patroness of lovers:

> I call on you to elect that fine man Numerius Barcha to the office of duumvir. May the rites of Pompeian Venus be propitious for you. (*CIL* IV 26)

> Methe, slave of Cominia, from Atella, loves Chrestus. May Pompeian Venus be in each of their hearts and may they always live harmoniously. (*CIL* IV 2457)

The famous statue of 'Venus in Bikini'. Venus adjusts her sandal as she leans on a statue of Priapus, watched by Eros at her feet. Her bikini, sandals and jewelry are gilded and there are traces of red paint on her lips.

The Imperial Cult

(Opposite) Hypothetical reconstruction of the Temple of Augustan Fortune dating to the 19th century, by G. De Simone and D. Capri.

FROM THE TIME OF ALEXANDER THE GREAT (4TH century BC), it was common for mortal kings and rulers in the Greek East to be considered divine. Traditionally it has been thought that such an idea was unacceptable to the Romans until much later, and that, while alive, the emperor could only be worshipped in association with other gods such as 'Fortune' or 'Roma'. Recent research has challenged this belief, however, and points to the epigraphic evidence of private divine cults throughout Italy. State cults to the emperor may have been unacceptable, but there seem to have been many privately-funded temples, altars and sacrifices dedicated to the living emperor from the age of Augustus onwards. In addition, statues of living members of the imperial family were also set up in public sanctuaries and other prominent spots; from the later 1st century BC, this became a way of honouring living members of the imperial family. The imperial cult swiftly became one of the most important cults in provincial towns. It allowed citizens to express their loyalty to Rome and to the emperor, but it also provided them with opportunities to advance socially and politically, and generated a sense of belonging to the wider empire. Wealthy citizens could dedicate buildings and entertainments to the emperor to demonstrate both their allegiance to Rome and highlight their own beneficence and status within the community.

Pompeii is often thought to be an excellent example of the importance of the imperial cult in a provincial community. Traditionally, three imperial cult buildings have been identified in or near to the Forum, at least two of which constructed by private individuals.

The Temple of Augustan Fortune

At the beginning of the 1st century AD, a Temple of Augustan Fortune was built directly opposite the Forum Baths and just to the north of the Forum by Marcus Tullius, a duumvir who was later honoured with a tomb outside the Stabian Gate and paid for at public expense. A dedicatory inscription records his benefaction:

> Marcus Tullius, son of Marcus, duumvir for lawsuits three times, quinquennial duumvir, augur, elected military tribune by the people, built the Temple of Augustan Fortune on his own land and at his own expense. (*CIL* X 820)

This temple had elaborate Corinthian columns with white marble capitals, and its marble-faced podium jutted out into the street. A cult statue of Fortuna Augusta was placed on the raised platform at the

Two statues were found in the Temple of Augustan Fortune in the early 1800s; this drawing of one of them – probably a relative of Marcus Tullius – is by the 19th-century artist Giuseppe Abbate.

rear of the temple; niches on the side-walls of the temple are thought to have held four statues of the members of Tullius' family. An inscription identifies one as a statue of Marcus Tullius himself, but there are no inscriptions to securely identify the other statues. A statue of Augustus was also set up in the temple. There may have been some confusion over what land belonged to the temple and what was still owned by Marcus Tullius, a problem solved by a small tufa marker on the south side of the temple:

> Private land of Marcus Tullius, son of Marcus. (*CIL* X 821)

The cult itself appears to have been managed by freedmen with *ministri* (slave attendants), but regulated by the duumvirs. Statue bases found inside the temple were set up by ministri and name some of these attendants, for example:

> Agathermus, slave of Vettius; Suavis, slave of Caesia Prima; Pothus, slave of Numitor; Anteros, slave of Lucutulanus, first attendants of Augustan Fortune, by order of Marcus Staius Rufus and Gnaeus Melissaeus, duumvirs for judicial proceedings, in the consulship of Publius Silius and Lucius Volusius Saturninus. (*CIL* X 824)

The Temple of Vespasian

The identification of this temple is disputed. Traditionally it has been associated with the emperor Vespasian, who died and was deified shortly before the eruption in AD 79. But it is now thought that the temple was constructed much earlier in the 1st century AD, possibly in the Augustan period. It may have been paid for by the public priestess, Mamia (see p.115). A fragmentary marble inscription was found near the Forum, but not inside the temple, that records a dedication by Mamia to the genius ('divine spirit') of someone or something:

> Mamia, daughter of Publius, public priestess, built this to the genius [...] on her own land at private expense. (*CIL* X 816)

The inscription is commonly thought to refer to the genius of Augustus (hence the building is sometimes called the 'Temple of the Genius of Augustus'), although recently it has been suggested that the 'genius of the colony' or 'genius of Pompeii' is more likely since cults of town genii are known from other towns, especially in Campania. However, it cannot be said with certainty that this inscription belonged to this building.

Despite this, there is good evidence to suggest that this was an imperial cult building. The temple is located within and to the rear of a high walled enclosure. In front of it stood a solid marble altar, decorated in relief. The relief on the front of the altar depicted a scene of the sacrifice of a bull to the emperor (probably Augustus); imperial emblems – the oak wreath and laurels decreed to Augustus by the Roman Senate in 27 BC – can be seen in the relief on the back of the altar. On its sides were sacrificial instruments such as the incense box and wine-jug.

The Sanctuary of the Public Lares

The purpose of this building is unknown, and its identification is disputed. Traditionally it has been thought to be the focus of worship of the public Lares, the guardian spirits of the town, but a more recent comparison with other towns in Roman Italy suggested that it was intended to display statues of members of the imperial family (thus it is now often referred to as the 'Imperial Cult Building'). However, no statues or inscriptions were found in this building, so there is no definitive proof that it was connected to the imperial cult.

The building consists of a large, unroofed square courtyard, open to the Forum, with recesses on three sides that have lots of niches for statues. The floor was paved with coloured marble slabs forming a regular pattern. At the centre of the courtyard was an altar, although this no longer survives today. Maiuri identified this altar as the one depicted in the famous earthquake reliefs found in the House of Caecilius Jucundus (see p.220). At the rear of the courtyard was a podium where the German historian August Mau proposed that a statue of the genius of Augustus stood in the midst of statues of the public Lares. The building has been dated to the 1st century AD.

It has been claimed that other buildings in the Forum were used to honour the imperial family, although not necessarily as locations of cult activity. For example, the porch in the Eumachia Building was dedicated to Augustan Concord and Piety and statues of members of the imperial family may have been displayed in niches inside it. Similarly, it has been suggested that statues of the imperial family were set up in the Macellum, but the evidence is slim. In the 1820s a statue fragment – an arm holding a globe – was discovered here (but is now lost), leading some to think that it belonged to a statue of the emperor. But otherwise only two complete statues were found, both (a woman and a youth) thought to be of local notables rather than members of the imperial family.

It is clear that emperor worship took place in Pompeii. There was at least one temple, in the Forum, associated with the imperial cult, and we know of many priests of Augustus from epigraphic evidence. But the surviving evidence fails to support the idea that the imperial cult and its activities dominated the Forum.

Marble altar at the centre of the 'Temple of Vespasian'. The relief depicts a priest with covered head before an altar, and a bull led to sacrifice.

Public Participation in Religion

The Neighbourhood Lares

Over 30 shrines are located at street corners or important crossroads in Pompeii. They appear to have marked the different districts of the town and were dedicated to the guardian gods (Lares compitales) of each district. They probably served also as a focal point for the different neighbourhoods. Participation in these district cults may have been an important way for freedmen to enhance their social status among their fellow inhabitants, since they make up the majority of the annually appointed *magistri* (officials or presidents) who maintained the district shrines and organized cult activities and festivals. One such festival was the *Compitalia*, in origin a rural festival celebrated between 17 December and 5 January each year to mark the end of the agricultural year.

Pompeii's neighbourhood shrines vary in size and decoration, presumably depending on available space and generosity of local donors. Some are merely paintings, others quite large masonry aedicules. Some of the shrines appear to have had painted inscriptions that listed the magistri of a particular year. For example:

When Gaius Julius Caesar was Dictator for the second time and Marcus Antonius was Master of the Horse [i.e. 47 BC], the magistri of the neighbourhood and of the crossroads were:

Marcus Blattius, son of Marcus
Marcus Cerrinius, son of Marcus
Marcus Sepullius […]
[…]
Quintus Pra[…]
Gaius Corne[lius]
[…]
Publius Ro[…]ius, slave of […]
Salvius E[…]ro, slave of Marcus. (CIL IV 60)

This painted inscription was over a hundred years old at the time of the eruption in AD 79, so it is not surprising that it is fragmentary and hard to read. The stone that it was on had also been reused so the inscription was not immediately visible upon excavation, and the altar itself had not survived. But other street shrines were well maintained, and a few have inscriptions that refer to the '*magistri Augusti*', as they became known later on. Usually they take the form of a masonry altar, although a few are more elaborate. A wall-painting is commonly associated with the shrine, for example a depiction of the Lares, a snake (representing the *genius locus* – the divine spirit of the location) and magistri with ministri carrying out cult activities. A good example is the shrine found at the corner of Insula I.9 (between I.9 and I.11). Behind the small altar was a painting of the Lares and a serpent. The remains of the final sacrifice were found in situ on the altar.

A neighbourhood shrine was uncovered outside IX.11.1 during the excavations of the Via dell' Abbondanza (see also p.208). The shrine is painted on two levels: the upper level depicts the 12 'Di Consentes' (the town's protective deities); the lower level depicts a genius flanked by Lares. To the right is a masonry altar, above which is a painting of a serpent and, above that, the magistri of the neighbourhood.

The Lares

The origin of the Lares is unclear, but they were probably gods of farmland or particular areas of land, later introduced into the household as guardian spirits. They are also associated with the spirits of the dead. Eventually they became guardians of crossroads, protectors of roads and travellers, and ultimately guardians of the state in general. They are found in three roles at Pompeii.

Public Lares. Possibly worshipped in the Sanctuary of the Public Lares in the Forum.

Lares compitales. Worshipped at neighbourhood shrines located at the intersection of four streets. This cult came to be associated with the imperial cult.

Domestic Lares. Worshipped at the family hearth on the Kalends, Nones and Ides of each month, and before any notable family event or feast. The hearth would be decorated with garlands, and offerings made of first fruits. It was the duty of the male head of the family (the 'paterfamilias') to maintain the household shrine or 'lararium', but the cult involved the entire family, including slaves.

Priests and priestesses

The priests of Pompeii's most important cults were mostly men from Pompeii's governing class – the wealthy and freeborn social elite, to whom holding a priesthood was a means of displaying high social status. Women, too, could be priestesses in the cults of certain goddesses. The women known to have held priesthoods also came from prominent families.

In contrast to the older and traditional cults, participation in the imperial cult was not restricted to the aristocratic elite of a town, but gave an outlet to the social and political ambitions of wealthy freedmen who were otherwise barred from political office. We know from inscriptions that Augustales were appointed by the town council. Wealth was a necessary prerequisite of office because fulfilling the priestly obligations could be very expensive, but holding this priesthood was a high honour and gave freedmen public recognition that they gladly recorded on their tombs (see Chapter IV). It is not clear where in Pompeii the activities related to this cult took place, since, unlike at Herculaneum, the cult building has not been identified. This may lie in the unexcavated part of the town, but it has also been suggested, on the basis of its architectural similarities with the so-called 'basilica' at Herculaneum, that the Eumachia Building could have hosted meetings of the Augustales (see p. 129 for further discussion).

The imperial cult appears gradually to have become connected to pre-existing cults, particularly the cult to Mercury and Maia and to the neighbourhood cults to the public Lares. They were run by freedmen under the authority of the town council. All appear to have had magistri and ministri, probably freedmen and slaves respectively.

The cult of Mercury and Maia

Mercury was the god of journeys, commercial success and abundance, and patron of merchants. Maia was his mother, and was associated with the growth of living things. Little is known about the purpose and organization of this cult, but a series of plaques relating to its activities has been discovered that name some of those involved in its administration. For example:

> Gratus, slave of Arrius; Messius Arrius Inventus; Memor, slave of Istacidius, attendants of Augustus, Mercury and Maia, by decree of the town councillors, by order of [...]. (*CIL* X 888)

Images of Mercury are common at Pompeii, particularly at shop entrances, and sometimes in association with other deities, such as Hercules. He is usually depicted carrying the caduceus (herald's staff with two entwined serpents), and wearing a winged hat and sandals.

Dedications

Dedications within the temples, such as altars and statues, could be made both by town magistrates and by private individuals, male and female, freeborn or freed. One inscription in the Temple of Isis records:

> Numerius Popidius Ampliatus, the father, at his own expense (*CIL* X 847)

It refers to the fact that the temple itself had been rebuilt by his son. An inscription beneath the statue of Isis in the temple colonnade recorded that:

> Lucius Caecilius Phoebus set this up in the place given by decree of the town council. (*CIL* X 849)

Both Numerius Popidius Ampliatus and Lucius Caecilius Phoebus were freedmen of prominent Pompeians.

An ox is led to the slaughter during the festival at which Jason – by the wine-table – is recognised by the usurper, Pelias, who is standing on steps overlooking the scene. Pelias will later send Jason to steal the Golden Fleece. Mythological wall-painting from the House of Jason (IX.5.18).

Mystery Religions and 'Foreign' Cults

(Right) One of two 'magic vases' that were found in the House of the Magic Rites (II.1.12) along with two votive hands of Sabazius. This large terracotta vase was decorated with crude representations of objects such as musical instruments, a lizard, a bunch of grapes, a tortoise and a snake. These vases must relate somehow to the ritual activities connected to Sabazius that took place in the house, but their exact function is unknown.

MYSTERY RELIGIONS – INTRODUCED TO ITALY FROM THE East – are those that offered adherents a more personal form of religion, often related to the promise of an afterlife. Such religions were frequently treated with suspicion by the Roman establishment, although some foreign mystery cults, such as those related to Cybele and Mithras, were tolerated by the authorities in Roman Italy.

Several foreign or mystery cults appear to have been present at Pompeii, although it is difficult to know whether the evidence for them represents their growing popularity or simply the presence of a few of their adherents in the town. A good example is a statue of Lakshmi, the Hindu goddess of fertility, beauty and wealth, found in House of the Four Styles (I.8.17). Lakshmi was the wife of Vishnu, and her cult appears to have originated in Nabatea (modern Jordan). In this statue, she is represented as Indus Aphrodite, but it is not clear if this is an ornament or a cult object. Worship of Lakshmi may have arrived in Italy by means of commercial links to the east, possibly via the port of Puteoli, to the north of Naples, but its precise point of entry is unknown.

There is slightly more evidence at Pompeii for the worship of another Near Eastern deity, Sabazius. Sabazius was known in Greece from the 5th century BC and was often equated with Zeus or Dionysus. From descriptions in the literary sources, we know

(Right) Ivory statuette of Lakshmi, found in the House of the Four Styles (I.8.17).

(Far right) Bronze statuette of Sabazius, from I.13.9. Sabazius wears a tall fruit basket as a hat, and from it overflow grapes, figs, plums, ears of wheat and a loaf of bread – all symbols of fertility. This figure was originally mounted on a wooden pole.

that rituals took place at night; a priest would hit worshippers with a snake and wash them with mud and bran to symbolize death. Then there would be chanting to bring about spiritual reunion with Sabazius. A humble shrine to this nature god was discovered in the garden of the house at II.1.12. At the entrance to the house were crude paintings of Venus, Mercury, Bacchus and Priapus. A simple masonry altar was located at the far end of a large peristyle. Behind it was a shuttered room that has been interpreted as a 'sacellum' or shrine. At its entrance was a drawing of a naked priest doing some kind of ritual dance and holding a tambourine, and another drawing of an Egyptian ibis. To either side of the shrine were storerooms which contained cult objects, including two bronze talismanic hands. The fingers of these hands are positioned in gestures of benediction, and the figure of Sabazius sits in their palms. Sacred serpents entwine the hands. It is possible that this house was a cult-centre for the worship of Sabazius in Pompeii. A similar bronze votive to Sabazius was found in Herculaneum.

There is some evidence that may point to the presence of Jews and Christians in Pompeii and Herculaneum. Jewish names such as Mary and Martha have been found inscribed on walls, and there are a few examples of Semitic inscriptions on amphorae, which may indicate the presence of Jewish traders. It is unclear, however, whether this evidence relates simply to individual traders or permanent inhabitants (either free or slave), or whether it can be used as evidence for a small Jewish community at Pompeii. Given the limited scale of the evidence, a community of Jews seems very unlikely. Similarly, while it is plausible that a few Christians were among the inhabitants of Pompeii and Herculaneum – the New Testament, for example, claims that there were Christians in nearby Puteoli – the evidence for a Christian community is inconclusive. A faded and incomplete inscription was discovered in the House of the Christian Inscription (VII.11.11) that clearly uses the word 'Christian'. At Herculaneum, a stucco panel with the impression of a cross was discovered in a room on the upper floor of the House of the Bicentenary. This has been controversially interpreted as a private Christian shrine, although in fact it was a cupboard support. But such examples are extremely rare and reflect the fact that, in the 1st century AD, Christian worship was only just beginning to spread.

(Above) One of two votive hands found in a shrine in the house at II.1.12. Sabazius sits in the centre of the palm with his arms raised in benediction. Around the hand are a snake, a caduceus (staff), a knife, a scale and a woman with child (one of Sabazius' roles was protector of childbirth). Similar hands have been found in Herculaneum.

A mosaic signed by the artist Dioskourides of Samos found in the Villa of Cicero, outside the Herculaneum Gate, and now in Naples Museum. There have been different interpretations of the subject-matter: it has been suggested that all three women are witches, that two women are consulting a witch, or that it is a scene from a Greek comedy. Another mosaic in the same villa was also signed by this artist.

(Above) The nine overlapping scenes of the mysteries megalographia are painted across three walls of a room, possibly in sequential order. The reclining figure of Dionysus at the centre of the central grouping of figures is the visual focus of the room.

Villa of the Mysteries: the Mysteries fresco

The Villa of the Mysteries was first discovered in 1909. Only a small part of the villa was excavated at this time, including the famous 'Mysteries' frieze. The remainder of the villa was excavated by Amedeo Maiuri from 1929 to 1930, and is discussed in Chapter VIII.

The Mysteries frieze covers three walls of a room that faced towards the sea. It is a megalographia (a depiction of life-size figures) painted on an architectural background, thought to date to the middle of the 1st century BC. The panels of the fresco appear to show a series of consecutive events, although their interpretation is much debated.

Most commonly, the fresco is thought to illustrate initiation into a secret cult, either of Dionysus, god of wine and mystic ecstasy, whose cult was particularly attractive to women, or of a secret woman's cult. The initiand to the cult would be subjected to trials, suffer, undergo purification and be initiated into the mysteries. The scenes are also thought to depict the initiand at successive stages in the transition from girlhood to matronhood. There are different scenes in the fresco, probably intended to hint at the mystery but not reveal what it was. These scenes overlap and are not separate, and it is not clear whether they are meant to portray successive events or events occurring simultaneously. Nor

is it clear exactly where the scenes are meant to start and finish, but they can be divided into three groupings: firstly, scenes of preparation – women are involved in ritual readings and the preparation of a meal; secondly, scenes of Dionysus and the immortal realm – a woman runs in fright, either from the mysteries divined by Silenus, from the sight of the god (the central scene) or from the scenes that follow, the ritual revelation of the phallus and the flagellation of a young initiand; and thirdly, the adorning of the bride, observed by a seated matron.

It is interesting that women feature so prominently in this fresco, and for this reason the room has been interpreted as part of the apartments of the 'materfamilias' (mother of the family) of the house. It has been suggested, too, that the materfamilias was a priestess of a mystery cult whose rituals took place in the room. While there is no evidence at all to support either of these theories, the fact that the room is not easily accessible from the main parts of the villa means that entry to it could have been strictly controlled. The implication is that use of the room was restricted to particular family members or to certain formal events or occasions. It may have been used as a dining-room or as a meeting-place, or it may have had several different functions. Ultimately, its purpose remains a mystery.

(Below, from left to right)
A woman pulls a veil from a box held by a servant, while another servant pours water over her right hand. Silenus plays a lyre while another figure plays the pipes and a woman suckles a kid.
A woman throws up her right arm in surprise or terror and her cloak billows behind her.
A naked woman – about to be whipped – seeks comfort in the lap of another while a dancing woman holds cymbals above her head.

(Below) Marble statue of Isis from her temple. The statue was originally painted – traces of red were found on her eyebrows and eyes and there was gilding on her hair and on the hem of her tunic.
(Below right) A reconstruction of the temple and its rites, by Jean Louis Desprez (1781–86).

The Temple of Isis

Egyptian cults were introduced into Italy as a whole during the late 2nd century BC. Isis had resurrected her husband Osiris from the dead, and her followers believed that she would give them eternal life after death too. It is possible that Isis originally represented real, deified, Egyptian queens, but by the Roman period she was associated with the idea of resurrection, was seen as a Mother Goddess and had also become the patron of sailors. If the literary sources are to be believed, many Romans, including the emperor Augustus, were deeply suspicious of the cult of Isis, because it was thought to threaten traditional Roman values. Despite this, it appears to have been one of the most established and popular religious cults at Pompeii. Little is known about the cult since its ceremonies and initiations rituals were secret. However, it is known that ceremonies were performed twice a day, at sunrise and at 2 pm, and there were elaborate festivals and processions during the year. Rites were conducted by male priests, but unlike the majority of Roman cults, women could hold positions within the cult and participate in ceremonies.

Private shrines to Isis may have existed in a few Pompeian houses. In the House of Loreius Tiburtinus (II.2.2), for example, one room has a painting of a priest of Isis, dressed in white with a shaven head. Beneath this painting is written 'Amulius Faventinus Tiburs', thought to be the priest's name. Images and statuettes of Isis have been found in more than 20 houses, such as one in the garden of the House of the Moralist (III.4.2–3). In Herculaneum, a famous wall-painting depicts a temple of Isis: a high priest stands at the entrance to the temple and looks down on the ceremony beneath him, which is supervised by priests with shaven heads. One priest tends the sacred fire and another behind him leads the faithful (gathered in two ranks) in worship. In the foreground of the painting can be seen two ibises, sacred to Isis, and to the right is a flautist.

But the most important evidence for the cult of Isis at Pompeii is the temple that was discovered in 1765. This is the best preserved of all the temple sanctuaries at Pompeii. Ash and small pieces of burnt bone were found on its main altar, and the burnt remains of figs, pine-kernels, nuts and dates were found in two holes in the courtyard. There were large numbers of artifacts throughout the complex, including coins and everyday vessels. A skeleton was also found beneath the collapsed columns of the portico. Unsurprisingly, reports of its excavation gripped the imagination of people throughout Europe in the 18th and 19th century, fuelling a fashion for all things Egyptian. The following is a description of the temple by the poet Shelley:

> The temple of Isis is more perfect. It is surrounded by a portico of fluted columns, and in the area around it are two altars, and many ceppi for statues; and a little chapel of white stucco, as hard as stone, of the most exquisite proportion; its panels are adorned with figures in bas-relief, slightly indicated, but of a workmanship the most delicate and perfect

This famous wall-painting of priests of Isis performing a religious ceremony was found in Herculaneum.

that can be conceived. They are Egyptian subjects, executed by a Greek artist, who has harmonized all the unnatural extravagances of the original conception into the Supernatural loveliness of his country's genius. They scarcely touch the ground with their feet, and their wind-uplifted robes seem in the place of wings. The temple in the midst, raised on a high platform, and approached by steps, was decorated with exquisite paintings, some of which we saw in the museum at Portici. It is small, of the same materials as the chapel, with a pavement of mosaic, and fluted Ionic columns of white stucco, so white that it dazzles you to look at it.

> A description of Pompeii in 1818 from the
> *Letters of Percy Bysshe Shelley.*

Because of such interest, the excavations were fairly well reported, although the wall-paintings and other objects of value were still removed to the Royal Museum at Portici. However, many of the earliest visitors to the temple made drawings of the paintings before their removal and, in recent years, there has been great success in reconstructing the original find-spots of these paintings and objects so that we have a fairly good idea of what the temple looked like in AD 79.

The Temple of Isis consists of a large porticoed courtyard within which were altars dedicated to Anubis and Harpocrates, an enclosure with a basin for the water used in purification rites, and the temple itself with its cella on a raised dias. There is

a large open room to the rear of the temple building, called the 'Ekklesiasterion'. Few of the objects found within the temple had actually come from Egypt. However, there was a tablet inscribed with hieroglyphs, found with two statues of faience, one dating to the Ptolemaic period, the other to the 7th century BC. The table had been placed on a pillar next to the steps leading up to the temple podium. The temple was decorated with a large number of elaborate Fourth Style wall-paintings and rich stucco work, mostly depicting Egyptian scenes or deities, such as Isis, Osiris, Harpocrates, Bes, or landscapes with ibis, crocodiles and pygmies.

There is some archaeological evidence for an earlier temple, on the site of the later Temple of Isis, but in AD 79 the Temple of Isis was newly rebuilt.

(Below) Bronze cymbals, commonly played during religious rites, and a bronze sistrum, associated with the cult of Isis, which was rattled during ceremonies and processions. Many other examples of these have been found in Pompeii and Herculaneum.

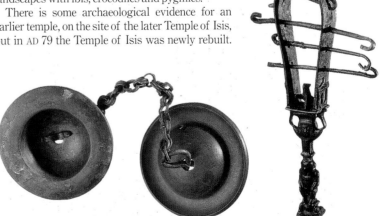

An inscription over the entrance to the temple records this:

> Numerius Popidius Celsinus, son of Numerius when the temple of Isis had collapsed in the earthquake he restored it from the ground up at his own expense. The town council, in return for his generosity, although he was only six years old, adlected him into their order without (the customary) fee. (*CIL* X 846)

It would appear that Numerius Ampliatus, the father of this six-year-old boy, was a freedman and thus ineligible for high political office himself. However, his act of generosity in rebuilding the temple gained him a voice on the town council through his son. Ampliatus also dedicated a statue of Osiris-Bacchus, which was located prominently on the rear wall of the temple. The Popidii family appear to have been important patrons of the cult. Other freedmen donated also statues to the temple.

It is often thought that in the period after the devastating earthquake of AD 63 the cult of Isis was more popular than many of the more traditional Roman cults, possibly because, unlike the more traditional Roman deities, Isis offered the possibility of life after death. It is impossible to know if this was really the case, but it is striking that the town council should allow a boy of six to join its ranks as a reward for rebuilding the temple. The temple appears to have been one of the first public buildings to be repaired fully after the earthquake of AD 63, and the only temple that had been completely restored by the time of the eruption in AD 79. This means that the cult must have had the support of many members of the town's elite. It is possible that the popularity of the cult amongst the people of Pompeii made it politically important. Certainly members of the cult of Isis were interested in politics since several painted electoral programmata were found on the external walls of the temple:

> All the followers of Isis call for Gnaeus Helvius Sabinus as aedile. (*CIL* IV 787)

> His client Popidius Natalis and all the followers of Isis call for Cuspius Pansa as aedile. (*CIL* IV 1011)

The Temple of Isis in its present condition. Originally it had been decorated in Fourth Style wall-paintings of Egyptian scenes and figures and elaborate stuccowork. The wall-paintings were removed shortly after its excavation and the temple itself was left to the elements.

CICERO WROTE THIS SHORTLY AFTER HIS OWN HOME HAD been destroyed by one of his political enemies; nevertheless it reveals the central role of domestic ritual and rite and the importance of each family's household gods. Each family had its own personal domestic guardians, with specific roles, which were individual to the family.

The Lares were the protectors of the family. They are usually depicted in wall-paintings and statuettes as youths dressed in short tunics, either standing or in motion, and holding ritual objects, such as the patera (bowl) or rhyton (drinking horn), or symbols of prosperity such as the cornucopia.

The Penates were also guardians of the family, and specifically of the store-rooms of the house. They were associated with Vesta, the goddess of the hearth. The Penates could be separated out into individual deities favoured by the family, sometimes including major gods or goddesses, such as the statuette of Fortune, the goddess of luck, found in the lararium of the House of Fortune (IX.7.20).

The genius ('divine spirit') was the protector of the family line of the male head of the family (the 'paterfamilias'), in whom it was thought to reside. The genius was worshipped on the birthday of the paterfamilias. Eventually, the genius also came to be associated with Augustus, and by decree of the Senate in Rome a libation to the genius of Augustus had to be poured at all formal dinners. The genius is depicted in wall-paintings either as a man dressed in a toga in the act of a libation or sacrifice, or as a serpent.

Most houses at Pompeii have some form of lararium or domestic shrine. This can be an elaborate aedicule, a simple niche in a wall, or a painting on a wall. Houses without permanent shrines may well have had makeshift arrangements with small portable altars. The more elaborate shrines are commonly found in atria and other public areas of the house, where they would be seen by many people, and are often found to contain statuettes of the household deities in silver, bronze or even ivory. In contrast, many simpler lararia, sometimes consisting of simple paintings on a wall, have been found near to kitchens or other service areas of the house. It has been suggested that they were connected to the preparation and serving of food to the family. Traditional offerings to the household gods included fruit, eggs and pinecones, all symbols of prosperity and fertility. A portion of each meal would be set aside and thrown on the flames of the hearth, and important family events usually involved a prayer to the Lares and Penates. Sometimes dedications have been found on household

What is more sacred, what is more inviolably hedged about by every kind of sanctity, than the house of every individual citizen? Within its circle are his altars, his hearths, his household gods, his religion, his observances, his ritual; it is a sanctuary so holy in the eyes of all, that it were sacrilege to tear an owner therefrom.

Cicero, *De Domo Sua* XLI.109

(Left above) Bronze statuette of a Lar, holding the ritual rhyton (drinking horn) aloft and the patera (dish) extended. Such statuettes are commonly found in the lararia of Pompeii and Herculaneum.

(Left below) The lararium in the atrium of the House of Menander (I.10.4), a particularly grand aedicule shrine. Many of Pompeii's shrines are much simpler.

shrines, such as in the House of Julius Polybius (IX.13.1–3):

> Publius Cornelius Felix and Vitalis, slave of Cuspius, made a vow here to the household gods for the safety, return and victory of Gaius Iulius Philippus. (*AE*, 1985, 285)

A marble tablet fixed to the altar of the lararium in the House of Epidius Rufus (IX.1.20) read:

> To the genius of our Marcus and to the Lares.
> The two Diadumeni, freedmen (set this up). (*CIL* X 861)

It is fairly common to find statuettes or wall-paintings of other deities in household shrines, such as Hercules, Venus, Bacchus and Isis. It appears that there was a great deal of personal choice about worship, which makes household religion quite different from the formally organized state cults. A lararium found in a villa in Pompeii's hinterland (in modern Scafati) contained silver statuettes of a nude Venus, Isis and the genius as a serpent – all deities of good fortune. The House of the Gilded Cupids (VI.16.7) contained two aedicule lararia on opposite sides of its peristyle. One contained statuettes of the Jupiter, Juno and Minerva as the Capitoline triad, and Mercury and the Lares. The other, painted, lararium depicted Isis flanked by Harpocrates and Anubis to one side and Osiris to the other, and objects related to the cult of Isis such as the sistrum (rattle), revealing how both traditional and mystery gods could be venerated together.

The role of gods in everyday life

The gods permeated all levels of Pompeian society. Images of gods and goddesses were common on the streets of Pompeii, and are seen particularly well on the Via dell' Abbondanza. Hercules and Minerva overlook the entrance to the house at IX.11.7, Mercury the house at IX.12.1. The bar at II.4.1 was protected by a nude Hercules and Mercury. The fauces of the house at I.9.1 bore two separate scenes on either side of the entrance. One depicted Hercules, Mercury and possibly Bacchus; the other Minerva, Juno and probably Venus. These are all representations of private cults, illustrating how the inhabitants of Pompeii favoured particular deities.

Images of the gods also jostle for position among the programmata and shop signs found on the street. A series of paintings of gods were found at the entrance to the shop at IX.8.1. Above the shop entrance were portraits of Apollo-Sol, Jupiter, Mercury and Diana. To either side of the entrance were Pompeian Venus and Cybele, the mother-goddess, on a throne in a procession with priests of her cult. A small niche here also contained a bust of Dionysus. The facade of the house at IX.11.1 consisted of a large painted aedicule with painted sacred scenes on two levels (see illustration on p.198). The upper level depicted the 12 'Di Consentes', the town's protective deities. From left to right, there were painted statues of Jupiter, Juno, Mars, Minerva, Hercules, Venus, Mercury, Proserpina, Vulcan, Ceres, Apollo and Diana. Venus and Mercury stand at the centre, emphasizing their particular importance. The lower level depicts a genius, possibly of Augustus, with a lar to either side. Immediately to the right of these paintings there was a masonry altar upon which were discovered the ashes of the final sacrifice to have been made upon it. Above the altar was a painting of the magistri of the neighbourhood, with their names written above them – Concessus, Victor, Asclepiades and Cosstas, and below was a painting of the serpent. A similar depiction of the 12 protective deities was also found on the facade of an insula in Region VIII.

There are inscriptions and graffiti that reveal some of the ways in which the gods were evoked on a daily basis.

> He who scorns life easily despises god. (*CIL* IV 5370)

The lararium in the House of Julius Polybius (IX.13.1–3). A snake is entwined around the domestic shrine, at which the paterfamilias is sacrificing. The Lares look on. Snakes are commonly painted on lararia and represent the genius ('divine spirit') of the paterfamilias.

Philocalus willingly discharged his vow to the god who had earned it. *(CIL IV 882)*

Watch out, you'll make Jupiter angry if you show disrespect by crapping here. *(CIL IV 7716)*

Before the Roman period, it appears that the most important deities were Dionysus (Liber), Venus (Mephitis) and Hercules. The popularity of these gods seems to have continued into the Roman period since their images are commonly found across the town. Roman gods – particularly Jupiter, Juno and Minerva – may have taken over in the public sphere from the 2nd century BC onwards, but the personal preference of many Pompeians may have remained with their original local deities. Yet context is important, and the importance and role of particular gods varied accordingly. Jupiter was honoured as the supreme god of the Roman state, but is rarely found in any more private context. Images of Mercury are most commonly found in shops, underlining his role as patron of merchants. It is also interesting that five of the gods worshipped at Pompeii during the

Roman period – Neptune, Mercury, Isis, Minerva and Hercules – were patron deities of aspects of travel, trade or the sea. This may well reflect the importance of commerce and Pompeii's port in the town's economy. Many of Pompeii's state cults had political as well as religious importance. Some deities, such as Jupiter and Venus, served as a focus of public, or communal, worship, and can be seen as a means of bringing the people of Pompeii together. The neighbourhood Lares served the same function on a smaller scale. Worship of Jupiter emphasized loyalty to Rome. A banquet at the Temple of Bacchus could reinforce links between members of the elite. The imperial cult allowed freedmen to have status in the wider community. With the exception of a few inscriptions and graffiti, it is impossible to know the religious beliefs of individual Pompeians, but it is clear that a wide range of deities were worshipped as a matter of daily course and that Pompeii's gods had important roles in the political, social and economic lives of her inhabitants.

VIII
ECONOMIC LIFE IN A ROMAN TOWN

All hail, profit.

Mosaic inscription at the entrance
to the house at VII.1.46 (*CIL* X 874)

A short walk along the Via dell' Abbondanza serves to highlight the liveliness of Pompeii's economy. Houses are fronted by shops and interspersed with workshops and bars. Street signs, posters and graffiti identify the various types of commercial activity and name some of the people involved in them. Here and there amphorae rest in corners for the collection of urine, used in the laundering of clothes. The Amphitheatre lies at the end of the street, and at times would have been surrounded by temporary stalls serving refreshments to spectators or selling other local goods. As one of the main thoroughfares to the Forum, the Via dell' Abbondanza was a hub of commercial activity, and the way in which it was excavated and recorded has preserved an image of its busy everyday life. Economic activities were not restricted to main roads, however, but were located all over the town, with little evidence that they were restricted to particular areas, like modern shopping centres or industrial estates. Indeed, the economy of Pompeii was complex and pervasive, encompassing agriculture as well as craft and trade, and people of all social classes were involved in it.

The Via dell' Abbondanza, stretching from the Forum all the way to the Sarno Gate. This was the busiest thoroughfare of the town, crowded with shops, workshops, bars and houses.

Rural Territory and Agriculture

BESIDES THE TOWN ITSELF, POMPEII ADMINISTERED A large chunk of its surrounding countryside, including the flat valley of the River Sarno and the slopes of Mount Vesuvius. The fertility of this land, due to the volcanic soil, was famed in antiquity.

Knowledge of a town's hinterland is normally gained by archaeological field survey (the study of rural settlement through examination of surface remains and detritus of buried sites). Unfortunately this technique is not possible in the area around Pompeii because the ancient remains have been buried too deeply by successive eruptions of Vesuvius. This means that our knowledge of farms or 'villas' in this area is mostly derived from accidental finds by modern farmers, or during intensive construction work. So far, over 140 villas have been discovered in the countryside around Pompeii, but we know relatively little about them. Mostly they appear to have been unspectacular buildings, the homes of farmers, and lacked beautiful wall-paintings and mosaics. Thus they were never accorded much interest and many were destroyed after rather desultory excavation and documentation. A few of the villas were larger, with nicely decorated living quarters and even bath suites, but these too were demolished after their wall-paintings were re-moved. There are only a few that can be studied in any detail today. Here are a few examples:

Many villas have been discovered in Pompeii's hinterland, but the majority have not been preserved. This perspective view shows the locations of those known in the area directly around Pompeii – others are known further along the coast towards Herculaneum, and it is likely that there are still more which have not yet been discovered.

The Villa Pisanella at Boscoreale

This villa (also known as Villa 13) was excavated between 1876 and 1899 by private landowners, and is famous for the discovery of a collection of 109 items of silver plate that was spirited off to the Louvre without the knowledge of the Italian authorities (see pp.58–9). Some of the silver pieces had the name 'Caecilia' stamped on them, leading to speculation that they were owned by the daughter of Lucius Caecilius Jucundus, the famous Pompeian banker (see p.220), and that the villa itself was his property. The villa no longer exists today, but there is a detailed description of it dating from 1897. It consisted of two separate but inter-linked parts – living quarters arranged around a courtyard, including a bath suite with mosaics, with an extensive upper floor; and a working farm. There was a single, wide entrance into the villa, leading straight into the courtyard. Wagon-ruts on the threshold of this door reveal that carts were driven through the courtyard and directly into the *torcularium* (room for pressing grapes). The pressed grape juice was then fermented in a *cella vinaria*, a courtyard of sunken terracotta *dolia* (large jars). At least 72 dolia were used to ferment wine in this courtyard; twelve more appear to have held olive oil or grain. There was also an olive press and another cluster of dolia for olive oil (it has been suggested that these dolia held the best-quality olive oil from the first pressing and that the dolia in the cella vinaria contained the oil from later pressings). Finally there was a threshing floor, a stable and separate service quarters. On the basis of the capacity of the dolia in the cella vinaria, it has been estimated that the villa cultivated at least 25 hectares (62 acres) of its surrounding countryside, and that it could produce approximately 90,000 litres (24,000 gallons) of wine each year.

The Villa Regina

The excavation of the Villa Regina near Boscoreale is one of the most important excavations to have taken place in the territory of Pompeii because it was the first villa here to have been excavated and published to modern standards. The villa was discovered during construction work, and

Herculaneum

Pompeii

Nuceria

Bay of Naples

Stabiae

N

0   5 km

0   3 miles

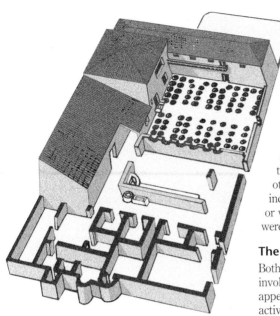

press. At the centre of the courtyard were 18 sunken dolia, which could have held a maximum of 10,000 litres (2,650 gallons) of fermenting wine. From this figure it has been estimated that the inhabitants of the villa cultivated a vineyard of 1–2 hectares (2.5–5 acres) in size. The patterns of planting in the area immediately surrounding the villa were also analyzed and revealed an unexpected density of planting. Although viticulture was clearly the most important activity here, a range of other trees were grown amongst the vines, including olive, almond, fig, apricot, and cherry or walnut. In total, more than 80 species of plant were grown in the grounds of the villa.

The archaeology of wine

Both the Pisanella Villa and the Villa Regina were involved in fairly intensive wine production, and it appears that viticulture was an important local activity. In 1932 John Day concluded that at least 26 of the 39 villas that had been discovered by that date had evidence of wine production. Given how many villas have been discovered since then, it is likely that more wine was produced in the hinterland of Pompeii than could possibly have been consumed by local people. Pompeii itself did not

(Left) Reconstruction of the Villa Pisanella at Boscoreale, a large country villa combining a working farm with luxurious accommodation. The villa itself no longer survives.

excavated between 1978 and 1980. It is made up of ten rooms loosely arranged around a courtyard. Three rooms had simple wall-paintings and presumably were the living quarters of the villa. There was also a threshing-floor, hay-store and a wine-

(Below) The Villa Regina at Boscoreale was one of many small farms in Pompeii's hinterland, and was significantly smaller than the Villa Pisanella. It was extensively restored during excavation in 1978–80.

(Right) Detail of a dolium (large jar), used for fermenting wine, stamped with the name 'A Apulei Hilarionis' ('of A. Apuleius Hilarion').

have a reputation for producing wine that was fine or desirable, and Pliny the Elder even claimed that it gave a headache that lasted until noon the next day. But wines of differing qualities, some perhaps for local consumption and some for export, must have been produced in the region. Indeed, some wines from the region had good reputations, such as the Falernian from northern Campania. The names of several types of wine grown on the slopes of Vesuvius and the surrounding plain are recorded in ancient sources. 'Horconian' has been connected speculatively with the prominent Holconian family of Pompeii (members of which were responsible for refurbishing the Large Theatre). The name 'Vesuvinum' has been found on wine amphorae in both Pompeii and in Carthage. 'Pompeianum' and 'Surrentinum' (from Sorrento, to the south of Pompeii) were both known at Rome. Pompeian wine amphorae have also been found in Ostia (Italy), Ampurias (Spain), Alesia (Gaul), Vindonissa and Augst (Switzerland), Trier (Germany), and even in Stanmore, Middlesex (Britain).

The evidence of amphorae demonstrates that wine from Pompeii and its hinterland was found all over the Mediterranean and beyond, and sometimes even reveals the names of those involved in its export. Amphorae from the Antheor shipwreck of *c.* 80 BC, off the coast of southern France between Cannes and S.

Raphael, were stamped with 'M. C. Lassi', a very rare name which can probably be connected to the Lassius family known from both Pompeii and Sorrento. At Carthage more than 40 amphorae were found in a dump dating from *c.* 43 to 25 BC with the stamp of L. Eumachius, probably the father of the famous Pompeian priestess Eumachia. In the same dump there were six other examples of amphorae stamped with known Pompeian names. It would appear that some of Pompeii's leading citizens were involved in the production and export of local wine.

Although the Bay of Naples was renowned for its holiday villas, the remains of most of the villas discovered so far demonstrate that they were real

(Below) The courtyard of sunken dolia in the Villa Regina, estimated to have had a maximum capacity of 10,000 litres (2,600 gallons). The grape-must trodden or pressed in the torcularium was strained and then fermented in these dolia. According to ancient writers, the fermentation period might be anything from nine days to several months, or – in the case of particular vintages – for many years.

working farms and not merely country retreats (although a few combined working areas with luxurious living quarters). The yields of these villas would have varied according to their size and the extent of land they farmed. All would have been self-sufficient, but many would also have produced a surplus that could be sold in the markets of Pompeii or other nearby towns. However, it is clear that Pompeii did not simply rely on these villas for its food since there is widespread evidence of agricultural production in its suburbs and in the town itself.

The villas at modern Terzigno

Three villas (Villas 1, 2 and 6) were excavated about 6 km (3.5 miles) to the north of Pompeii, in an area that probably lay within the town's rural territory. It is thought that all three villas were located near to the road that ran from Pompeii to Nola in antiquity. Excavation of the villas identified wine presses and cellars, revealing that these too were involved in wine production. This appears to have been one of the principal uses of land in many of the small villas in the region.

Suburban villa: The Villa of the Mysteries

The best example of a suburban villa is the Villa of the Mysteries, which was first discovered by private landowners in 1909. The excavations uncovered only a very small part of the villa, but included the famous 'Mysteries' frescos (discussed on pp.202–3). Very little is known about these initial excavations. There is only a very brief published note, which focuses on the wall-paintings to the exclusion of any other finds. The majority of the villa was excavated by Amedeo Maiuri from 1929 to 1930. His elaborate publication of the excavations still forms our main source of knowledge about the villa even today.

While the Villa of the Mysteries is best known for its frescos, it was also a working farm, and was located outside the Herculaneum Gate of Pompeii and within easy walking distance of the town. Maiuri dated the original construction of the villa to the 2nd century BC, but believed it had been remodelled twice, once around 60 BC and again in the mid-1st century AD. Its luxurious living quarters, made up of a series of both large and small rooms elaborately decorated in Second Style wall-painting, and a small bath suite, faced the coast and presumably had views across the sea.

The working part of the villa was located around the peristyle and consisted of an extensive kitchen area, a large group of rooms to the rear of the villa and a torcularium (wine press) to one side of the peristyle. In the centre of the peristyle itself is a small cellar, possibly for the storage of wine. The territory immediately around the villa has not been excavated, so the extent of the land farmed by the villa is unknown.

(Above) Modern reconstruction of one of two wooden wine-presses found in the torcularium of the Villa of the Mysteries. After its first treading, the remaining grape-must was crushed by the press.

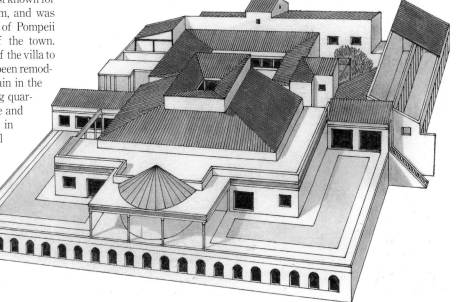

(Right) Hypothetical reconstruction of the Villa of the Mysteries. The living quarters of this suburban villa overlooked the sea; the working farm, located around the peristyle, faced nearby Pompeii.

Agriculture Within the Town Walls

FROM THE 1960S ONWARDS, WILHELMINA JASHEMSKI'S ground-breaking study and excavation of gardens and open spaces within Pompeii revealed the existence of food-producing areas such as commercial market gardens, orchards, vineyards, and even kitchen gardens, and led to the revelation that almost 10 per cent of the excavated town was turned over to cultivation. The scale of this cultivation varied considerably. There was a fairly large kitchen garden in the House of Pansa (VI.6.1), for example; in contrast, a very small vegetable garden was found next to an elaborate garden triclinium in the House of the Ephebe (I.7.11). Other cultivated plots were clearly commercial in nature:

The House of the Ship Europa

The garden of this house (I.15.3) is very large and Jashemski's examination of the soil contours and root cavities revealed that it was almost entirely cultivated. Much of the lower garden was covered in vines. These appear to have been young plants since there was no evidence for supporting stakes. But there were also two carefully laid-out vegetable gardens, and 31 irregularly spaced trees. These were probably fruit and nut trees since numerous remains of carbonized fruit and nuts (such as almond and fig) were found. Vegetables may also have been cultivated in amongst the vines, but the root cavities that these leave would have been too small to survive. The range and extent of cultivation in this garden reveals that it must have been a commercial market garden since its yield was surely too great just for the inhabitants of the two adjoining houses. The produce may have been sold on the premises or in the local markets that took place every week. The excavations also uncovered animal bones (dog, pig, sheep, chicken and possibly goat), most probably the remains of domestic animals, but some possibly related to meals consumed in the house.

The vineyard at II.5

Insula II.5 was traditionally known as the 'Cattle Market' because 50 animal bones, split for their marrow, had been found here when the area was first excavated in 1755. Jashemski's excavations from 1966 to 1970 uncovered 2,014 vine-root cavities and an equal number of stake cavities. The vines were planted almost exactly 4 Roman feet apart and trained onto a trellis with a rectangular frame. The vineyard was divided into four sections by two intersecting paths. Evidence for posts was found along the paths, probably indicating that they were arboured. There was a total of 58 trees planted along the paths, at the edges of the vineyard and at intervals throughout it. Vegetables may have been grown under the vines since carbonized broad beans were also found. Not only were vines cultivated here, but wine was fermented too. There was a wine-press and ten sunken dolia with an estimated capacity of 1,250 litres (275 gallons) each (the equivalent of 40 wine-amphorae). The wine could also be consumed on the premises: there were two outdoor triclinia located at the entrances to the vineyard. Given the proximity of the vineyard to the Amphitheatre it is likely that it served refreshments to the spectators of games.

Smaller vineyards

There is also much evidence for the cultivation of wine in the town on a slightly smaller scale. A good example is the Inn of Euxinus (I.11.10-11), also close to the Amphitheatre. Here 32 vines were planted in irregular rows and two large sunken dolia were used to ferment wine (*c.* 450 litres or 100 gallons

Plan of the house and garden of the House of the Ship Europa (I.15.3). Excavations in the garden revealed that it had been extensively cultivated with vines, vegetables and fruit and nut trees.

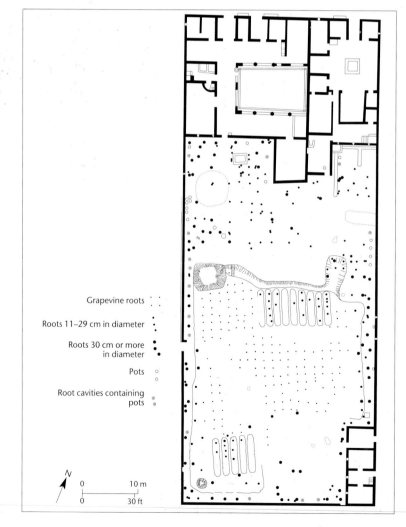

Grapevine roots

Roots 11–29 cm in diameter

Roots 30 cm or more in diameter

Pots

Root cavities containing pots

N

0   10 m

0   30 ft

each). There was a serving counter and a large open area where customers could stroll about. Yet it appears that either the inn could not produce enough of its own wine to satisfy demand, or it sought to give its customers a choice. A number of wine-amphorae were found on the premises with the following label:

> To the innkeeper Euxinus, at Pompeii near the Amphitheatre. (*AE*, 1967, 86d)

Evidently Euxinus was buying in wine to supplement that which he produced in his own vineyard. A painted sign, of a phoenix and two peacocks, was discovered outside this inn with the following declaration to customers:

> The phoenix is happy, and you will be too. (*CIL* IV 9850)

The premises of another wine-seller, a simple and plainly decorated house (IX.9.6-7) located near the Nola Gate, were also identified by Jashemski on the basis of the large number of amphorae found in the house and its attached shop. Most were stored inside the house: there were only five in the shop itself. A room off the garden held 29 empty amphorae that had been stacked upside-down. In total, there were 114 amphorae, 60 of which were labelled. Some had more than one label, and had been used more than once. A few had contained foodstuffs other than

wine. Four may have held meal or flour, another four contained olives, and seven were fish-sauce vessels. However, the remaining amphorae had contained wine – mostly local, but a few had held wine from northern Campania (Falernian) and Surrentum. There was also a single dolium, with a capacity of 450 litres (100 gallons), and Jashemski suggested that the garden of this house had been planted with vines. Another wine-shop may be located in the House of the Fruit Orchard (I.9.5). The garden here was too small to have been planted with vines, but more than 117 wine-amphorae were found stacked upright (thus presumably full) in the portico of the peristyle and in other rooms of the house (only three were found in the attached shop). In both cases, the premises would have been interpreted as normal houses if large numbers of amphorae had not been found within them. A similar situation was discovered in another house in Insula I.9. The House of Amarantus (I.9.11/12) consists of two connected houses, a traditional 'atrium' house (I.9.12) and a bar with a large peristyle behind it (I.9.11). Stacks of amphorae were found in both houses, particularly in the atrium of house 12 and in the garden attached to the bar of house 11 (see pp.78–9). Over 30 of the amphorae in the atrium were Cretan; they were all upright (i.e. full) and it has been suggested that they had recently been imported as a single consignment

This vineyard in Insula II.5 was replanted in recent years. There are many vineyards and cultivated gardens in Regions I and II.

from Crete. The amphorae in the garden area had mostly been stacked upside down (i.e. empty), and consisted of both local Campanian (Dressel 2–4), and Aegean and Cretan types. The bar itself was under repair in AD 79, so could not have been used in a traditional way to serve food and drinks. In addition, there was no attempt to grow vines in the House of Amarantus. It would appear that the proprietors were engaged only in the wholesale import and sale of wine.

Other types of cultivation

The cultivation of vines was clearly important both within the walls of the town and in the countryside surrounding it. There is also evidence of other types of cultivation on a commercial scale occurring inside the town walls. Two flower-gardens have been identified (I.21.2 and II.8.6) on the basis of rows of small root-cavities separated by irrigation channels, along with the fragmentary remains of perfume vessels. The flowers from these gardens could have been used to make garlands (common, for example, in religious ceremonies) or perfumed oils. There is also evidence of a large orchard in the garden attached to Insula I.22. Only half of this very large garden was excavated, but approximately 150 root-cavities were discovered, the majority of which had been made by small trees. It was possible to identify filberts and fig (or olive) trees from the structure of some of the roots, but Jashemski was forced to speculate about the other tree varieties that had been cultivated here. Drawing on discussion of fruit-trees in ancient literary sources, she suggested that possible varieties were peach, apple, pear, apricot and various types of nut. Interestingly, several electoral posters were set up by 'pomarii' (fruit-sellers) at Pompeii. The shop at I.8.1 has also been identified as a fruit-shop, although this is based on a poster written on its facade rather than any direct evidence for the sale of fruit taking place there.

These are only a few examples of the evidence for cultivation within Pompeii's walls, but they highlight the importance of agriculture and particularly viticulture in the daily lives of many of the town's inhabitants. Pompeii certainly lived off its hinterland, but it also exploited the resources within its walls. Some farmers may simply have produced enough for their own needs, but others produced a surplus that could be sold in local markets or perhaps exported further afield. An interesting illustration of this can be found in a lararium (domestic shrine) painting from a house in Region I (the House of the Sarno Lararium, I.14.6–7). This painting appears to depict onions being loaded onto boats on the Sarno. Our problem is to understand the scale of this surplus production and thus its general significance for the local economy. It is likely that the majority of any surplus was sold in local markets (possibly creating an incentive to grow a surplus), but some products were deliberately grown for export – such as certain types of wine.

Painted lararium from the House of the Sarno Lararium (I.14.6–7). Inside the lararium niche is a depiction of the genius. Beneath the niche, the god of the river (left) overlooks a harbour scene. Donkeys or mules carry goods to and from barges; the cargo may be onions or other local produce.

Craft and Commerce at Pompeii

THERE ARE MANY TRADES AND TRANSACTIONS THAT have left no visible traces at Pompeii, but they are known from many inscriptions and graffiti found across the town, and from another archive of wax tablets that was found in the House of Caecilius Jucundus (see box overleaf). The box overleaf lists the trades and occupations known from epigraphic sources.

Unfortunately, unless these activities required specific equipment, such as the ovens and grinding-stones of a bakery, or the vats and sinks of a fullery, all of which required a considerable investment of money, it can be difficult to locate them in the archaeological record. Craft activities – spinning, making clothes, small-scale metal-working – could take place inside houses rather than specialized workshops. A good example is a very small house in Region I (I.9.9) which is unremarkable from the point of view of architecture and decoration, but which at the time of excavation was found to contain hundreds of small paint-pots and colour pigments, along with various implements used in painting. Evidently this was a painter's (or paint-maker's) workshop. Other crafts could have taken place in almost any of the 900 or so shops or craftshops that have been identified at Pompeii to date.

Often the only evidence used to identify a premise as the location of a particular type of shop or workshop is a particular wall-painting or graffito. Such identifications are often tenuous. For example, the following graffito found in the small house at

VI.11.13 refers to laundering of clothes and may relate to textile-working:

> 12 days before the Kalends of May [20 April]
> (I gave to be washed) a cloak; on the Nones of May
> [7 May] a headband; 8 days before the Ides of May
> [8 May] two tunics. (*CIL* IV 1393)

A shop near the Forum (VII.1) may have been run by a retired soldier. A graffito (*CIL* IV 1711) identifying Marcus Nonius Campanus as a soldier of the ninth praetorian cohort was found next to another (*CIL* IV 1712) that refers to particular tools, such as a chisel. The actual trade that took place here is unknown, however. On the basis of a rough painting depicting potters at work discovered in house I.8.10, it has been suggested that this was a pottery; however, there is no other evidence from this house to suggest that this was the case. Another pottery may have existed in one of the shops outside the Herculaneum Gate. Unfortunately this workshop was originally excavated in the 18th century, when few records were kept, and it was left to deteriorate

Marble relief showing a coppersmith's workshop, probably a shop-sign (its provenance is now unknown). The smith is seen weighing something on scales, holding something with tongs while another man prepares to strike it with a hammer, and seated at a workbench engraving the finished product. On the shelves above him are finished buckets, plates and bowls.

The archive of Lucius Caecilius Jucundus

Bronze bust of a Lucius Caecilius Jucundus (possibly the father of the famous banker) set up by his freedman Felix in the atrium of the House of Caecilius Jucundus. A wax tablet from the archive, blackened but still partially legible.

One of the most important sources of information about the economic life of Pompeii is the archive of Lucius Caecilius Jucundus. Excavations in V.1.26 (now known as the House of Caecilius Jucundus) in 1875 uncovered 154 partially legible documents written on wooden tablets that were originally covered in wax and stored in a wooden box in the upper storey of the house. The tablets date from AD 15 to 62. The majority were written after AD 52 and record Jucundus' financial dealings. However, the tablets are not a complete record of his affairs during that time and it is not clear why this should be the case. In addition, many of the tablets are damaged, which means that they can be hard to read and that the information recorded on them is sometimes fragmentary.

The tablets relate to two different types of business activity. In the majority (137), Jucundus carried out transactions on behalf of other people and charged a commission for his services. Mostly his activities relate to auction sales and consist of witnessed 'receipts' from a seller. For example, Jucundus auctioned a slave, Nymphius, on behalf of Lucius Iunius Aquila for 1,567 sesterces and this sum was paid to Aquila after Jucundus had deducted his commission. Another receipt documents an auction of linen belonging to an Alexandrian trader called Ptolemy. The preservation of the receipts varies, but they tend to give the names of Jucundus or his representative and the seller, the date, the marks of witnesses and the sum paid.

A further 16 tablets record agreements between Jucundus and the town authorities. For example, Jucundus paid 2,675 sesterces each year for the right to collect a tax that is thought to have been levied by the town council for the use of publically owned pasture).

Jucundus was involved in a wide range of business activities, many of which are otherwise invisible in the archaeological record of Pompeii. Thanks to his archive, we have information about auctions and the sorts of things that were sold at them, of tax farming (contracting the right to collect taxes on behalf of the town), of the sort of property (such as fulleries and market stalls) owned by the town and rented out to private individuals. The receipts also reveal the presence of foreigners in the town. Such details remind us of the complexity of the economy of the ancient town and of the myriad transactions and activities that will never be fully revealed.

The Lucius Caecilius Jucundus archive supplements our knowledge of the economy of Pompeii, but it also provides information about its society. For example, it is likely that witnesses of receipts were listed in hierarchical order, with the most important men at the top of the list. In some cases names appear to have been erased and rewritten in a different order. Women were not usually allowed to act as witnesses, and although they clearly engaged in business with Jucundus, none of them signed their own names on the receipts. This may mean that they were illiterate, but more likely it reflects the fact that men were required to act as their legal representatives.

Selected transactions from the Lucius Caecilius Jucundus archive

CIL no.	Date	Document
IV 3340.1	May AD 15	Receipt for sale of a mule at auction by Caecilius Felix.
IV 3340.5	May AD 54	Receipt for sale at auction of boxwood belonging to Gaius Iulius Onesimus.
IV 3340.6	May AD 54	Receipt for auction of goods from the estate of Nasennius Nigidius Vaccula.
IV 3340.7	May – June AD 54	Receipt for sale at auction of slave of Lucius Iunius Aquila.
IV 3340.10	January AD 55	Receipt for 38,079 sesterces from auction for Marcus Lucretius Lerus.
IV 3340.22	November AD 56	Receipt for proceeds from auction for Histria Ichimas.
IV 3340.23	November AD 56	Receipt for sale of fixtures and fittings at auction by Umbricia Antiochis.
IV 3340.24	December AD 56	Receipt for sale of slave by Umbricia Antiochis.
IV 3340.25	December AD 56	Receipt for goods auctioned for Umbricia Ianuaria.
IV 3340.40	December AD 57	Receipt for auction of goods by Tullia Lampyris.

in the elements. It is now in a ruinous condition and it is impossible to see whether there was ever a furnace for firing pots here. Indeed, there is only one workshop (I.20.2–3) that can be securely identified as a pottery, specializing in the production of lamps, since it has an appropriate furnace within which were found lamp moulds. Lamps may have been sold in a nearby house at I.9.8: large numbers were discovered, along with lamp moulds. But there was no furnace here, and no other signs of craft activity, so the lamps were not made on the premises.

The House of Pinarius Cerialis

The entrance to this small house (III.4.b) is located on a side-street just off the Via dell' Abbondanza. It was excavated between 1917 and 1918. Three painted posters and two graffiti found on the facade of this house record the name 'Pinarius Cerialis'. There is no atrium in the house; instead it consists of a series of rooms around a peristyle garden, some of which are nicely decorated with Fourth Style wall-painting. The remains of a wooden chest were found in one of these rooms; it contained 140 precious stones, such as amethysts and agates, and glass-paste beads of different shapes and sizes. Of these, 29 had been worked (23 intaglio, 6 cameo), but 79 were either rough or only partially cut. It is not clear whether this was an actual gem-cutter's workshop or whether Pinarius Cerialis (if he indeed owned the property) was merely a merchant selling gems of different quality and finish. On the one hand, several tools relating to gem-cutting were discovered in the house; on the other, many of the gems were scratched and showed signs of having been used previously (for example in rings) which might support the idea that this was a merchant's house rather than a workshop.

Despite the problem of finding tangible archaeological evidence for many crafts and trades in Pompeii, it is clear that there was a remarkable diversity in the range of economic activities that took place. It appears that the majority of this activity was on a fairly small scale. For example, study of terracotta lamps found in Pompeii has revealed that many were of the same types being produced in the town's only lamp workshop (I.20.2–3), and, although there are examples of lamps that were imported from outside Pompeii, it is likely that this shop supplied much of the local demand.

What we see, therefore, is a large degree of specialization in the manufacture of products, organized on a fairly small scale and probably serving just the town and its immediate vicinity. However, there has been considerable speculation about the extent and importance of a few particular trades and crafts.

Occupations attested at Pompeii in inscriptions, graffiti and wax tablets

Baker	Engraver	Miller	Scorer
Banker	Farmer	Money-lender	Scribe
Barber	Felt-worker	Mule-driver	Soothsayer
Bath-attendant	Fisherman	Ointment seller	Spinner
Builder	Fruit-seller	Onion-sellers	Surveyor
Carpenter	Fuller	Outfitter	Tanner
Carriage-driver	Furnace-stoker	Painter	Theatre official
Chicken-keeper	Gem-cutter	Pastry-cook	Waggoner
Clapper-beater	Goldsmith	Pig-breeder	Weaver
Cloak-seller	Grape-picker	Porter	Wine-seller
Cobbler	Guard	Priest's attendant	Wool-worker
Cushion-seller	Herdsman	Prostitute	
Doorman	Innkeeper	Rag-and-bone man	
Dyer	Lupin-seller	Sauce-makers	

This wall-painting from the small house at VII.3.30 (and now in the Naples Museum) has been interpreted both as a shop selling bread (the painting would therefore be a type of shop-sign) or as a representing the distribution of free bread, possibly by a magistrate or even by a private citizen. Carbonized loaves similar to those depicted here have been found during the excavations, some still in the ovens where they were being baked.

(Opposite above)
Wall-paintings from the
workshop of Veranius
Hypsaeus (VI.8.20–22) show
the different stages of fulling.
Here (left) the cloth is carded
and (right) displayed to the
customer. The workshop itself
was large, and included
troughs for soaking the cloth
and large bronze basins in
which it was trodden, all
located around a peristyle.

Reconstruction of the Fullery
of Stephanus (I.6.7) showing
the different working areas
used in the processing of
cloth, including multiple
basins for soaking, washing
and treading the cloth.

Wool production and processing

The scale of textile production at Pompeii is disputed. Some scholars have claimed that it was a major activity, arguing that the number of fulleries (wool or cloth-washing establishments where newly woven material could be finished or old material could be washed) and dye-shops far exceeded local demand and should be interpreted as evidence of an important export trade. The physical remains of these premises are fairly easy to identify since they required fixed facilities – vats and tanks for washing, soaking and rinsing, or cauldrons for heating water, all of which imply an initial large investment to get the business off the ground. Of the fulleries identified, four are large – the Fullery of Stephanus (I.6.7), the Fullery of Lucius Veranius Hypsaeus (VI.8.20–22), the Fullery of Vesonius Primus (VI.14.21–22) and a Fullery at VI.16.3–4. There are also several examples of smaller establishments. Perhaps the most famous is the Fullery of Stephanus (I.6.7), which is a good example of the facilities found in a typical fullery. Here there was a clothes press, a large balcony from which to hang cloth and clothes, one large basin for washing clothes, five small foot-basins for treading the cloth (human or animal urine was used since there was no soap to break down grease and dirt) and three large, interconnecting basins for rinsing it. There was also a balcony overlooking the atrium area from which finished cloth could have been hung to dry. Near the

entrance a skeleton was found with gold, silver and bronze coins to the value of 1,089 sesterces, which may represent the takings of the fullery.

Six dye-shops (e.g. at IX.3.1–2, IX.7.2 and VII.2.11) have also been identified on the basis of soaking vats and cauldrons needed in the dyeing process. There is some suggestion that felt-making may also have taken place in the town, although the evidence for this is disputed. A felt-making establishment would require work-surfaces for the kneading of wool and a small furnace. Two premises have been identified on the basis of electoral programmata (painted posters) and signs on their facades (IX.7.1 and IX.7.5/7), but the shops themselves have not actually been excavated. It has been claimed that two further establishments with furnaces (I.12.4 and IX.3.16) also belonged to felt-makers, but there is no other supporting evidence and the function of the furnaces is unclear.

Wool-sellers and fullers also appear fairly prominently in programmata and inscriptions (for example, in the Eumachia Building, which has been interpreted controversially as the headquarters of the fullers' guild), encouraging speculation that theirs was a particularly important industry at Pompeii.

Such interpretations are controversial and much discussed. The problem is to understand the scale of production. Were all fulleries and dye-shops used to

wash and prepare new wool? If so, it is possible that the scale of activity was large enough to justify claims of a large export industry. But how many of these fulleries and dye-shops were used for simple laundering or re-dyeing of old clothes, thus fulfilling a purely local need? These establishments may have been engaged in both types of activity, but it is impossible to be sure exactly how they were used, and thus impossible to know whether wool production and processing was an important export trade at Pompeii or not.

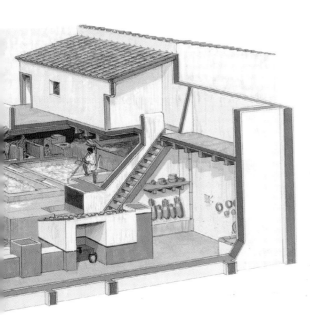

(Right) The atrium of the Fullery of Stephanus. The traditional impluvium has been transformed into a large basin for washing cloth. In the background, (modern) wooden stairs lead to the upper floor where cloth was hung to dry.

Fish sauce

Fish sauce or 'garum' (also known as *liquamen*, *allec* and *muria*) became popular throughout the Roman empire from the Augustan period onwards. It could be made from different types of fish that were left to ferment for approximately one to three months. It was then used to flavour meat, vegetables, fish or fruit, and also as a medicine. Pliny the Elder claimed both that garum could be very expensive and that the garum of Pompeii was famous. The hundreds of labelled garum containers of a distinctive shape, known as *urcei*, found at Pompeii demonstrate its popularity in the town. The labels reveal that some garum had been

Pompeii's harbour

The exact location of Pompeii's harbour is unknown, the task of finding it made difficult by the dramatic changes to the coastline and the course of the River Sarno caused by the eruption of Vesuvius in AD 79. This plan illustrates some of the hypothetical reconstructions of the coastline that have been suggested.

According to the Greek geographer, Strabo, Pompeii served as a port for the inland cities of Nuceria and Nola. This means that it was a centre for both imports and exports. The wall-painting found in the lararium of the House of the Sarno Lararium (I.14.6–7) appears to illustrate port activities. The local river god, Sarno, overlooks the scene.

Unfortunately, the location of Pompeii's harbour is unknown today. The many eruptions of Vesuvius since AD 79 have caused dramatic changes to the coastline and there has been considerable subsidence to the land. In recent years a series of *c.* 70 bore-holes were drilled around the town in an attempt to reconstruct the coastal environment of ancient Pompeii. The results suggest that in AD 79 the coast lay approximately 1 km (*c.* 3,000 ft) further inland than today, and that the River Sarno was about 1 km to the southwest of the town. However, the actual course of the Sarno in antiquity is unknown, although it appears that it meandered much more than it does today. On the far side of the Sarno from Pompeii there was an extensive area of marshes with bogs and ponds. It has been commonly thought that Pompeii itself was located on an old coastal ridge formed from a prehistoric lava flow; beneath it was a beach ridge, now known as the Bottaro-Pioppaino ridge, which stretched all the way to the Sarno. More recently, it has been claimed that Pompeii was located, not on a ridge, but at the edge of an extinct prehistoric volcanic crater – that is, next to a large natural coastal harbour.

If Pompeii was indeed located on a beach ridge, it is likely that the harbour was in one of the Sarno's meanders, probably in the vicinity of Murecine, near the Stabian Gate. This would make it a river port, rather than a sea port, which would have implications for the scale of possible commercial activity and the size of boats or ships that could use the port. However, if there was a large natural coastal harbour, Pompeii's port – probably located outside the Marine Gate – must face the sea. This would have been much more accessible to large ships and therefore much more important in the local economy. The problem is that there is evidence to support both of these proposed locations for the port.

Near Murecine, the remains of houses and possibly workshops have been found, including the buildings where the Sulpicii Archive was discovered. Just to the north of the Marine Gate there are a series of 'ring-stones', traditionally interpreted as mooring-blocks for ships, although this has been disputed recently because the ring-stones are too high above the level of the sea. Warehouses relating to port activities have been identified beneath the Temple of Venus, immediately to the south of the Marine Gate. It has been claimed that these are the only warehouses in Pompeii – or in any of the other places suggested as harbour locations – large enough for the storage of imported products.

This evidence has been interpreted in several different ways. One theory relates the ring-stones near the Marine Gate to Republican 'navalia' (a port for military vessels). Military ships were much larger than their commercial equivalents and were usually beached out of the water on ramps. It is suggested that the navalia went out of use before the 1st century AD. The commercial port instead was located beneath the Temple of Venus, near to the warehouses found there. This same reconstruction notes the complete lack of archaeological finds in the area to the north of Murecine and Pompeii and hypothesizes a large natural lagoon between Pompeii and the coast, supporting the idea that Pompeii was located at the edge of an extinct volcanic crater. A temple to Neptune (the precise location of which is unknown, see Chapter VII) may have been located near the coast at modern Bottaro, overlooking the lagoon.

Another theory suggests that Pompeii had two fully integrated ports, one on the coast beneath the Temple of Venus and the other on a meander of the Sarno in the vicinity of Murecine.

Both theories underline the importance that Pompeii's port played in the economy of Campania as a whole, on the possible scale of imports and exports, and on the urban development and history of the town.

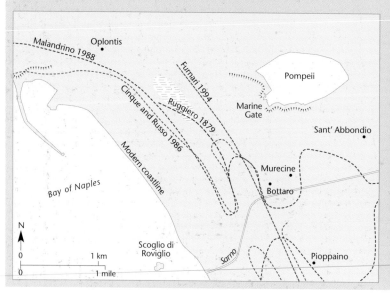

imported from Spain, but the majority of the garum was produced locally. It must have been an important local product, and *salsamentarii* (sauce-makers) are attested at Pompeii by an electoral notice found on the external wall of a house in Region II (II.7.10). Oscan inscriptions, dating to before 80 BC, also identify the Herculaneum Gate as the 'Salt Gate'. However, as yet no production site has been identified. From comparative evidence in North Africa and Spain, where 'salteries' have been discovered outside towns and by the sea, it seems likely that at Pompeii too the fish were fermented in facilities outside the town, near the coast where salt water was readily available. Some form of garum processing did take place in the town, however, in a house in Region I (I.12.8). This was a simple house with no shop-front or retail counter, but the peristyle garden appears to have been used as a work area. There were no salting vats, but five sunken dolia, originally intended for the fermentation of wine, were found to contain desiccated fish-sauce remains and anchovy bones. There were no urcei, but there was a large number of reused wine-amphorae, many of them empty and stored upside-down at the time of the eruption. At the time of excavation, in 1961, Amedeo Maiuri

Famous mosaic from the triclinium of the House of the Faun (VI.12) depicting a fight between a lobster and an octopus, surrounded by a variety of other sea creatures, such as moray, red mullet, scorpion fish, sea perch, eel and bream.

claimed that these vessels still smelt of fish when excavated from the eruption lapilli. It is not entirely clear which stages of garum production took place in this house. Much of the working space of the peristyle garden was actually taken up by trees in AD 79. The working conditions must have been shady and pleasant but the scale of production, with limited space and only five dolia, must have been small. It has been suggested that this was a place where ready-made garum was brought to be processed further, by the addition of herbs, spices or even wine. It could then be sold wholesale to shops in large amphorae and decanted into the usual urcei in those shops.

The name of one man who sold garum in the last 20 years of Pompeii's existence is well known. Aulus Umbricius Scaurus owned at least six workshops (none of them located) producing garum, and run by members of his household. Approximately 30 per cent of all labels found on garum containers in Campania carry his name or that of his extended family. Examples found in Pompeii itself include:

The best liquamen of A. Umbricius Scaurus. (*CIL* IV 5711)

Scaurus' flower of garum made from mackerel, from the workshop of Scaurus, by Martial, imperial freedman. (*CIL* IV 9406)

A. Umbricius Scaurus' garum made of mackerel, from the workshop of Scaurus. (*CIL* IV 2574)

Scaurus appears to have played a dominant role in the production and sale of garum in Campania, and he also exported his goods. His name has been found on urcei in southern France. Indeed, Scaurus was so proud of his business that he celebrated it inside his own house. A mosaic in the secondary atrium of the house in Region VII (VII.16 Ins. Occ. 12–15) depicts four urcei that are labelled with his name and their fish-sauce contents:

a) Scaurus' flower of garum made from mackerel
b) Flower of liquamen
c) The best liquamen from the workshop of Scaurus
d) Scaurus' flower of garum made from mackerel, from the workshop of Scaurus. (*AE*, 1992, 278 a–d)

Craft and commerce in the Roman economy

One of the wax tablets found in 1959 in Murecine belonging to the Sulpicii archive and relating to their business activities at the major Campanian port of Puteoli. It records that Gaius Novius Eunus deposited grains and legumes in the public granaries of Puteoli as surety for a loan received from Hesychus, slave of Euenus Primianus.

Trade and 'industry' were nowhere near as important in antiquity as they are in the post-industrial revolution modern world. Ancient cities were not major centres of 'industry' in the sense that we use that word. The evidence suggests that the majority of production took place on a small scale, often by individual craftsmen. There were only a few 'industries' that were organized on a larger scale into what we might recognize as factories, a good example being the production of Arretine pottery in northern Italy. In addition, upper-class Romans disdained (at least in public) many forms of business. Indeed, Roman senators were actually forbidden by law from owning ships that were used for profit. This, however, was the ideal rather than the practice. Many upper-class Romans got round this problem by acting through agents, such as their slaves or freedmen. This is the situation that we find in the Sulpicii archive.

The Sulpicii archive
The wax tablets of the Sulpicii archive were found in 1959 at Murecine, about 600 m (2,000 ft) from Pompeii's Stabian Gate, during the construction of a highway. The building where the tablets were found was only partially excavated. The tablets document transactions relating to business affairs in Puteoli, Campania's largest port, and until the construction of the harbour at Ostia the most important port in Italy. It is not clear why these documents should have been found near Pompeii, or what the function of the building in which they were discovered was. So far, 170 texts have been published. They range in date from AD 26 to 61, and relate to the business activities of the Sulpicii, all of whom were freedmen or freeborn sons of freedmen. The precise nature of their business activities is debated. It is possible that they merely undertook to look after important documents for clients, but they may have been moneylenders or professional bankers, too. Some 87 of the Sulpicii tablets are business documents – for example, contracts of sale, loan and lease, IOUs and accounts. Other tablets refer to judicial matters. The tablets reveal involvement in trade by individuals at the highest levels of the Roman elite, although this trade was always carried out second hand, through slaves or freedmen, like the Sulpicii. The archive is important for many reasons, not least because it sheds light on the world of investment and money-lending; but it also gives a clear picture of business transactions that were important in the local economy (such as the rental of a public granary which was used to store wheat from Alexandria) but that could never be identified in the archaeological record.

The Umbricii were not one of Pompeii's old landowning families, and are only attested at Pompeii from the early 1st century BC. However, they quickly became prominent at Pompeii. Aulus Umbricius Scaurus himself appears to have concentrated solely on his business affairs, but his son of the same name is known to have been more politically active. The epitaph from the family's tomb was discovered outside the Herculaneum Gate in 1813 (which tomb it actually belonged to is a matter of dispute):

> For A. Umbricius Scaurus, son of Aulus, of the Menenian tribe, duumvir with judicial power, the decurions decreed the place for his monument and 2,000 sesterces towards the cost of his funeral and an equestrian statue to be placed in the Forum. Scaurus, the father, to his son. (*CIL* X 1024)

It appears from this inscription that Scaurus' son held high political office at Pompeii and was prominent enough to have been honoured with an equestrian statue in the Forum. His success in entering Pompeii's political elite must have been due to his father's wealth.

Export of goods from Pompeii

Garum was not the only product exported from Pompeii. Wine has already been discussed, and we have seen that amphorae from Pompeii have been found as far afield as Middlesex in the United Kingdom. We know from the literary sources that Campania, and particularly the town of Capua, was famous for its bronze vessels, so it is possible that bronzes were also worked in, and exported from, Pompeii. An interesting relief was found in Pompeii that depicts metal-workers (see p.219), although its find-spot was not recorded. But although the location of several metal-working premises have been suggested within the town, only one – a workshop outside the Vesuvius Gate – can be identified securely from the discovery of hammers and anvils, and the extent of its activities are unknown. Similarly, there is little evidence for the production of pottery beyond the lamp workshop (I.20.2–3), where lamp-molds, finished lamps and two furnaces were uncovered, and a possible pottery outside the Herculaneum Gate.

In general, therefore, there is no clear picture of the scale or importance of exported goods from Pompeii. It would appear that only particular items – garum and wine – were exported and that the majority of goods made in the town were produced on a small-scale and intended for local distribution.

Import of goods to Pompeii

There is more evidence of goods imported into Pompeii, both on a regional basis and long distance. For example, red-slipped 'terra sigillata' vessels (table vessels) from the Puteoli area have been found at Pompeii, along with baking pans and various cookwares and coarsewares of Campanian production. There is also sigillata from further afield – examples of vessels have been found that were manufactured in northern Italy, southern Gaul and Cyprus. One particularly important discovery was a chest containing 90 carefully packed and unused South Gaulish bowls and 37 unused earthenware lamps in a house in Region VIII (VIII.5.9) in 1881. These items are thought to represent a consignment recently received in Pompeii from a wholesaler of such wares. Amphorae containing wine were imported from Kos, Crete, Rhodes and the Aegean, Turkey, Sicily, Palestine and central Italy; others containing olive oil came from Libya and Spain. Garum was also imported from Spain.

The majority of the goods known to have been imported from further afield can be classed as 'luxury' items. Wine, oil, garum and tablewares were all produced locally, but inhabitants of Pompeii chose to buy them from further afield. Thus they must have had a particular status, perhaps as a sign of wealth and disposable income. As with export goods, it would seem that imports were restricted to particular types of item.

Mosaic of a garum urceus, from the House of Umbricius Scaurus (VII. Ins. Occ. 12–15). The inscription reads LIQUA(MEN) FLOS ('flower of liquamen').

This terra sigillata bowl with geometric decoration was made in South Gaul and imported into Pompeii. Its base was stamped with the (illegible) mark of the manufacturer. Many different types and shapes of terra sigillata vessel have been found in Pompeii.

Shops and Markets

THE MAIN THOROUGHFARES OF POMPEII WERE CROWDED with shops. These mostly had one or two rooms, with a wide entrance onto the street, and sometimes with a mezzanine floor. Many were connected to the house that lay behind them, which means that the shop was run by the house-owner (or at least by his representatives). In cases such as these, goods sold in the shop may sometimes have been stored in the house – as in the examples of wine-sellers that were discussed earlier in this chapter. Some house-owners even advertised their commercial interests. The mosaic in the House of Umbricius Scaurus is probably the best example, but others are found across the town. A mosaic at the entrances to house VI.14.39 proclaimed 'Profit is my joy' (*CIL* X 875); another of uncertain provenance declared 'Make profit' (*CIL* X 876).

In general, as with workshops, it can be very difficult to establish what was being sold in shops because of the lack of physical evidence left behind. Some may have been small workshops, such as the shop at I.9.1, which contained a collection of different types of knife and may possibly have been a cutler's premises. But for most shops this type of evidence is lacking. We do not know what was being sold or if it related to craft activities taking place in the shop or adjoining house. Occasionally it is possible to identify a shop from wall-paintings, either inside the shop or on its facade, entrance mosaics, terracotta or stone plaques with relief sculpture, graffiti or more rarely from professionally painted signs. Particularly well-known examples include the tuff relief of a mason's tools (an inscribed name identifies the mason as 'Diogenes') from the Vicolo del Gallo and the terracotta relief of a carpenter's tools found on the Via Stabiana. Another marble relief, depicting activities in a workshop, may also be the shop-sign of a Pompeian coppersmith, but its find-spot was not recorded.

Although difficult to envisage today, there were also shops in the Forum, for example, inside and outside the Macellum, the meat and fish market. On the opposite side of the Forum there may also have been a cereal and pulse market. But not all vendors required permanent locations to sell their wares. Some may have travelled from town to town. Other evidence appears to represent occasional sales:

Eupemus [is selling] manure from the farm and a wheel. (*CIL* IV 1754; found on a wall near the Marine Gate)

There is also plenty of evidence for temporary stalls. The wall-paintings from the atrium of the Praedia of Julia Felix (II.4.2) reveal such stalls in the Forum. The scenes depict mules and a cart carrying merchandise; a man displaying shoes; cloth merchants showing their wares to two women; a man beating a metal vessel with a hammer; a man selling bread; and a fruit and vegetable stall. It is not clear whether these scenes relate to everyday activities in the Forum or to the regular markets that are known to have taken place from graffiti that have been discovered. This is the most famous example, found on the facade of III.4.1 (Shop of the Potter Zosimus):

Day	Markets
Saturn's day	Pompeii
Sun's day	Nuceria
Moon's day	Atella ~~Cumae~~
Mars' day	Nola
Mercury's day	Cumae
Jupiter's day	Puteoli
Venus' day	Roma
	Capua *(CIL* IV 886)

Fresh produce, the surplus from the villas and farms of the region or the market gardens within the town walls, was probably sold on occasions like these. The famous wall-painting from the House of Actius Anicetus (I.3.23) depicting the riot in the Amphitheatre in AD 59 also depicts temporary stalls, presumably set up to sell refreshments to spectators of the games (see Chapter V).

We have some idea of the cost of food at Pompeii from various graffiti found in private houses and in the Large Palaestra. Two graffiti were found in a small room in a house in Region VII (VII.2.30), which give a list of what appear to be household expenses. One of them reads (the amounts are probably in *asses*):

Firewood	(no amount given)
[unclear]	4
Bread	6
Cabbage	2
Beetroot	1
Mustard	1
Mint	1
Salt	1 *(CIL* IV 4888)

Roman prices tended to fluctuate according to local conditions, so it is not easy to relate the value of ancient coins to modern values.

In the 1st century AD, the basic Roman denominations were:

the gold *aureus*, worth 25 *denarii*
the silver *denarius*, worth 4 *sestertii*
the bronze *sestertius*, worth 4 copper *asses*

One of four identical statuettes found amongst the remains of a wooden chest in the House of the Ephebe (I.7.10–12), thought to represent placentarii *(itinerant pie-sellers). Made of gilded bronze and silver, the statuettes were probably used to serve food at banquets.*

The coins found at Pompeii are particularly interesting because they were mostly in circulation in AD 79 (at other sites, recovered coins are usually those that have been hoarded or lost). It is common to find gold and silver coins with the bodies of those killed in the eruption – such as the 47 silver coins, with 22 bronze coins, found in the remains of a cloth bag with the body of a woman (of whom a cast was made), and the 13 silver denarii and one bronze sesterces found with a skeleton outside the Vesuvius Gate in 1910. But, thousands of poor quality copper coins have also been found at Pompeii, mostly very worn from circulation, in all sorts of locations. One particularly interesting find was a collection of 1,600 coins, totalling 585 sesterces, found in a dolium embedded in a counter in the Inn of Lucius Vetutius Placidus (I.8.8). There were a few coins dating to the reigns of Claudius, Tiberius, Nero and Galba, but the majority were Vespasianic (that is, fairly new) coins and in good condition. It is thought that this collection represents more than just the day's takings in the bar, since it has been estimated, on the basis of the graffiti cited above, that a small family might spend approximately six or seven sesterces a day on food and provisions, and that an average annual income might have been 2,500 sesterces.

A 19th-century reconstruction of the Amphitheatre, illustrating the mass of people who would have frequented the area on spectacle days and the temporary street stalls set up to serve them with refreshments or to sell other goods.

Pompeii prices

A long list of foodstuffs and their prices (mostly in asses) were found scratched in uneven columns on the wall of an atrium in house IX.7.24–5 (*CIL* IV 5380):

7 days before the Ides, cheese I
  bread VIII
  oil III
  wine III
6 days before the Ides
  bread VIII
  olive V
  onion V
  cooking pot I
  bread for slaves II
  wine II
5 days before the Ides, bread VIII
  bread for slave IV
  porridge III
4 days before the Ides, wine I denarius
  bread VIII, wine II, cheese II
3 days before the Ides
  [?]
  bread II
  female (?) VIII
  wheat I denarius
  beef (?) I, dates I
  incense I, cheese I
  small sausage I
    soft cheese IV
    oil VII

For Servatus
[?]
oil I denarius, VIII
bread IV, cheese IV

leek I, for a small plate I
[?]

2 days before the Ides, bread II
  bread for slaves II

1 day before the Ides, bread for slaves II
  plain bread II
  leek II

On the Ides, plain bread II
  oil V
  porridge III
  whitebait II

These coins were fused together by the heat of the eruption in AD 79.

Bars and Inns

MANY DIFFERENT KINDS OF BAR AND INN HAVE BEEN identified at Pompeii. Various terms are used to label these establishments, based on descriptions found in Latin literature. A *popina* was a bar that served food and drink, associated in the literary sources with drunkenness, fighting and prostitution (the term 'thermopolium' – from the Greek for 'selling hot things – is often applied by archaeologists to this type of shop); a *caupona* was an inn that did not serve hot food; a *hospitium* was a guest house; and a *stabulum* was an inn or tavern for travellers and their animals. It is difficult to know whether it is really appropriate to use these terms to describe the bars and inns of Pompeii, and it can be a futile exercise trying to distinguish between the different types. It is probably enough to say that bars and inns have been found all over the town, particularly on main streets and near the gates.

(Below) The shop attached to the House of Neptune and Amphitrite at Herculaneum. The way in which Herculaneum was buried meant that parts of a wooden mezzanine floor were preserved in this shop (seen here amidst modern reconstruction), on which amphorae were stacked. Mezzanine floors would have been used in many of Pompeii's shops, too.

Bars can typically be identified from their masonry counters. These counters usually held embedded dolia. It was once thought that these dolia were used to serve hot meals and drinks. However, it has been pointed out that there would have been no way to clean out these vessels after use. Indeed, in Herculaneum, the carbonized remains of nuts were found in a dolium in the bar attached to the House of Neptune and Amphitrite. It seems likely that other dried foodstuffs, such as grains, dried fruits and vegetables would have commonly been stored in shop dolia. Food could also be suspended from hooks above the counter (as seen in a wall-painting in VI.10.1). It may well be that some of these 'bars' actually functioned as grocery shops. However, in some establishments there is plenty of

evidence that drinking and eating were primary activities, as seen in the following inscription (found to the left of the entrance of the bar at VII.2.45):

Hedone says: drinks cost an *as* here, but you get a better drink if you spend two. If you hand over four *asses*, you can drink Falernian wine. (*CIL* IV 1679)

There is evidence that some bars had wooden racks, attached to walls or suspended from ceilings, which were stacked with amphorae. The Bar of Asellina (IX.11.12) on the Via dell' Abbondanza, and that of Salvius (VI.14.35–36), near the Vesuvius Gate, are good examples of bars where drink was served.

The Bar of Asellina was excavated in 1911. It has a masonry counter with four terracotta dolia and a built-in hearth. A wooden staircase at the rear of the shop led to rooms above. Objects discovered in the bar included jugs in the shape of a rooster and a fox, wine-amphorae, and a bronze cauldron. There was also a bronze lamp with five bells. A series of electoral posters on the facade of the shop give the names Zmyrina, Aegle, Maria and Asellina, sometimes thought to have been waitresses who worked in the bar. A graffito on the right-hand side of the entrance depicted a male figure with the head of an animal and a huge phallus in his hand.

The Bar of Salvius could be entered either from the main street or a side street. In the front room, there was a typical masonry counter with two embedded dolia. There was also a back room and a kitchen, and an upper floor reached by means of a

The Bar of Lucius Vetutius Placidus (I.8.9), with its elaborate lararium (shrine) at the end of the counter. When it was excavated in 1939, one of the embedded dolia in the counter was found to contain over 1,600 coins to the value of 585 sesterces. Normally, however, they were probably used to store dried foodstuffs.

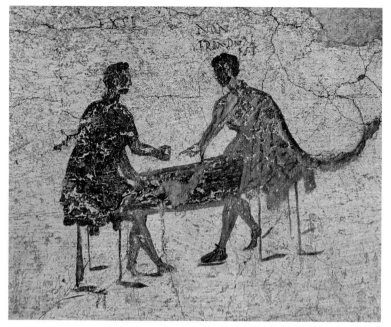

wooden staircase. The bar is famous for the painted panels found in the front room. These were set in white panels above a red dado on the north wall, and consist of:

> A scene of drinkers: a man calls to a barmaid, 'Over here'; another man on the right says, 'No, it's mine'. The barmaid says, 'Whoever wants it should take it. Oceanus, come here and drink';
>
> A scene of gambling: a man says, 'I've got it'; another man on the right says, 'It's two, not three';
>
> A scene of conflict (damaged): the men fight and the innkeeper tells them to leave);
>
> A scene of a man and woman kissing: the man says, 'I don't want to do it with Myrtale'.

Some inns are relatively easy to identify, since they accommodated animals as well as people. An example of what may have been an inn can be found at I.1.6-9 (known as the Inn of Hermes) near the Stabian Gate. Here, an entrance wide enough to admit a cart led into a broad passageway ending in a large courtyard. Stairs led to a series of rooms on the upper floor. Another similar building, with a wide entrance into a central courtyard with rooms around it, was found near the Forum, at VII.12.35. What is particularly interesting about this property is the collection of graffiti found on its walls that may well have been written by those who stayed there. Examples include:

(Above) One of four painted panels from the backroom of the Bar of Salvius, depicting two men gambling. The drinking, gambling, fighting and kissing scenes reveal the kinds of activity that went on at such establishments. Dice are found commonly in the excavations, not just in bars but in houses, too, demonstrating the popularity of gaming.

(Right) Excavation photograph from 1911 of the Bar of Asellina (IX.11.2). Large numbers of amphorae and other objects were found here. The inn was later extensively restored by the excavators.

Gaius Valerius Venustus, soldier of the first
praetorian cohort. (*CIL* IV 2145)

Marcus Clodius Primio was here. (*CIL* IV 2147)

Vibius Restitutus slept here alone and longed for
his woman Urbana. (*CIL* IV 2146)

But lodging-places for people without animals may
have existed in almost any type of building – above
a shop, in the back room or a bar, or even in a house.
Occasionally a graffito or inscription helps us to
identify an inn in this way, but such examples are
rare. One painted inscription was found on the east
side of the Vico del Lupanar and reads:

Rental accommodation here: dining-room with three
couches. (*CIL* IV 807)

Some graffiti were presumably written by discon-
tented guests rather than by the innkeepers
themselves:

We pissed in the bed, I admit, and we're bad guests,
but if you ask why, it was because there was no
chamber-pot. (CIL IV 4957, found in VIII.7.6)

I hope you get punished for your lies, innkeeper;
you sell water and you drink the pure wine yourself.
(*CIL* IV 3948, found in I.2.24)

Rental property

It is possible that many properties in Pompeii were
rented out on long-term leases, rather than simply
to travellers or visitors to the town. There are, for
example, plenty of examples of upper-storey rooms
and apartments that were reached by external stairways, unrelated to the house or shop beneath, which
may represent rental accommodation. However,
there are only two definite examples of this phenomenon, confirmed by the evidence of painted
inscriptions. One is the Praedia of Julia Felix (II.4.2;
see Chapter IV); the other the Insula Arriana
Polliana (VI.6), which includes the famous House of
Pansa. The poster on this insula reads:

For rent in the Insula Arriana Polliana, now the
property of Gnaeus Alleius Nigidius Maius, from
1 July this year: shops with mezzanine floors,
equestrian apartments, and a house [or houses].
Prospective renters contact Primus, slave of
Gnaeus Alleius Nigidius Maius. (*CIL* IV 138)

Gnaeus Alleius Nigidius Maius was the quinquennial duumvir, acclaimed 'leader of the colony'
and 'chief of games' (see Chapter V), and it is interesting that such a prominent Pompeian should
derive some of his income from renting out property. In all likelihood many upper-class Pompeians
engaged in this practice, although, like Gnaeus
Alleius Nigidius Maius, they probably used slaves
or freedmen as intermediaries. Urban real estate is
likely to have been an important source of income
for the elite, one of the ways in which they were
able to fund the construction of public buildings or

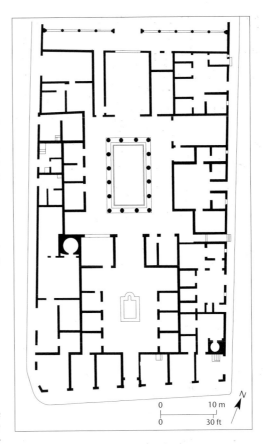

*Plan of the Insula Arriana
Polliana (VI.6), illustrating the
different rental apartments in
the insula. Three self-
contained apartments with
their own street entrances are
visible on the eastern side of
the Insula, while shops and a
bakery line the southern and
western sides (to the north is
a garden). This is one of only
two securely known examples
of rented accommodation at
Pompeii, but it is likely that
many rented apartments were
located above shops or houses.*

```
0          10 m
0          30 ft
```

put on spectacles in the Amphitheatre – the type of
beneficence that helped them to gain and maintain
political office.

What was the economy of Pompeii like? We have
seen extensive evidence of cultivation and of the
many different crafts, shops, bars and inns. Econom-
ically, Pompeii must have been very busy. But it is
often difficult to establish the scale and importance
of this activity from the surviving archaeological
evidence. Agriculture and cultivation must have
played an extremely important part in Pompeii's
economy, both within its walls and in its hinterland.
Ultimately this activity must have been the most
important factor in the local economy. Many
wealthy families with landed estates were probably
largely self-sufficient, and surplus produce could
have been sold at local markets. At some villas, the
scale of cultivation was such that exports – the best
example is wine – were possible, but the majority of
villas appear to have been fairly small. The extensive and varied evidence of craft and trade indicates
a busy economy within Pompeii. But it was mostly
on a small scale, and probably served local needs primarily. Particular luxury objects were imported or
exported, but in general local products appear to
have dominated in the market-place. The impression
we have is of a lively economy, but one centred on
local produce and production.

IX
THE LAST YEARS OF POMPEII

…and the densely settled town of Pompeii was mostly ruined by an earthquake.

Tacitus, *Annals* 15.22

In AD 79 Pompeii was already an ancient town. It had suffered war, conquest and political upheaval, and it had prospered from the stability brought by Roman control. Although the ruins that can be seen today provide glimpses of this long and complex history, as a whole they reflect the condition of the town and the lives of its inhabitants in the final few years of Pompeii's existence. These were years of turmoil rather than prosperity, and the remains of the houses, shops and public buildings all illustrate the difficulties faced by those living in the town. This situation dated from a single, dramatic event: in AD 63, a massive earthquake had devastated Pompeii and the surrounding region. This was probably an unsuccessful attempt by Vesuvius to force open a vent, and a clear sign that the volcano was awakening once more. The 16 years from this earthquake in AD 63 to the eruption of Vesuvius in AD 79 were marked by disruption as the inhabitants of the town attempted to rebuild their lives, and endured further seismic activity.

The centre-piece of the pavement of the summer triclinium in I.5.2, this mosaic is an allegory of death. Death (the skull) is suspended from the plumb-line of a builder's level above a butterfly (symbolizing the spirit) balanced on a wheel (Fortune), together representing the fragility of life. The arms of the level are perfectly balanced by the symbols of poverty and wealth: to the right, the beggar's sack and staff; to the left, the royal sceptre and purple. The message is clear: death cancels out the differences between the rich and the poor, the powerful and the weak.

The Impact of the Earthquake of AD 63

THE SERIOUSNESS OF THE EARTHQUAKE OF AD 63 WAS such that it is mentioned by two contemporary literary writers, briefly by the historian Tacitus (see p.234) and in much greater detail by the philosopher and playwright Seneca. Indeed, Seneca's description of the damage and its consequences has been fundamental to the discussion of living conditions in the last years of Pompeii's life and gives a vivid picture of the disruption and chaos caused by the earthquake. The damage was not uniform: Pompeii and Herculaneum suffered to a much greater extent than many of the other settlements in the region, and there was also damage in the countryside, to villas and even to livestock. Seneca claimed that some people abandoned the area in the aftermath of the earthquake, presumably because of the extent of the devastation to their property and fear of further tremors. He himself was puzzled by the fact that the earthquake lasted for several days – a further indication of its severity.

The earthquake is documented in inscriptions and reliefs found at Pompeii and Herculaneum. In Pompeii, an inscription records that the Temple of Isis was restored and enlarged at private expense after an earthquake. The most vivid depiction of the event is found in two marble reliefs found in the atrium of the house of the banker Lucius Caecilius Jucundus (V.1.26) in Pompeii that had once adorned the lararium. One relief depicts the northern end of the Forum. The Temple of Jupiter totters precariously. On either side of the steps to the temple platform there is an equestrian statue. To the left of the temple can be seen a monumental arch and to the right an altar. The second relief shows the collapse of the Vesuvius Gate – two mules and a cart narrowly avoid being crushed. The Castellum Aquae can be seen next to the gate. Archaeological evidence supports the picture given by these reliefs: the Temple of Jupiter, the Vesuvius Gate and the Castellum Aquae were indeed all damaged severely. An inscription from Herculaneum (*CIL* X 1406) also records that the Emperor Vespasian restored the Temple of the Mater Deum (Mother of the Gods) in AD 76.

It is not clear whether the earthquake that damaged this temple was that of AD 63, or a later one since over the past 20 years it has become apparent that Campania was hit by more than one earthquake during the period from AD 63 to AD 79. Comparative studies in other regions with active volcanoes and analyses of later eruptions of Vesuvius have shown that seismic activity is common in the years and months before a major 'explosive' eruption. For example, the eruption of Vesuvius in 1631 was preceded by at least six months of frequent seismic activity. We have a glimpse of this continuing volcanic activity in our literary sources in the run-up to the eruption of AD 79: in AD 64, an earthquake hit Naples while the Emperor Nero was performing on stage (according to the imperial biographer Suetonius, he ignored it and continued with his performance). There is ample archaeological evidence of further seismic activity after AD 63, too. New evidence from recent excavations in Region I of Pompeii suggests that there were at least another two serious earthquakes in the period AD 63 to 79, the last of which probably took place only months before the eruption of AD 79. In addition, it is likely that the town experienced fairly frequent small-scale tremors in the 17 years before the eruption of Vesuvius. This extended period of seismic activity, from AD 63 to 79, had a significant impact on Pompeii, to its public buildings and also to its private houses.

Seneca's description of the earthquake

'Lucilius, my good friend, I have just heard that Pompeii, the famous town in Campania, has been laid low by an earthquake which also disturbed all the adjacent districts. The town is in a pleasant bay, back a ways from the open sea, and bounded by the shores of Surrentum and Stabiae on one side and the shores of Herculaneum on the other; the shores meet there. In fact, it occurred in days of winter, a season which our ancestors used to claim was free from such disaster. This earthquake was on the Nones of February, in the consulship of Regulus and Verginius. It caused great destruction in Campania, which had never been safe from this danger but had never been damaged and time and again had got off with a fright. Also, part of the town of Herculaneum is in ruins and even the structures which are left standing are shaky. The colony of Nuceria escaped destruction but still has much to complain about. Naples also lost many private dwellings but no public buildings and was only mildly grazed by the great disaster; but some villas collapsed, others here and there shook without damage. To these calamities others were added: they say that a flock of hundreds of sheep was killed, statues were cracked, and some people were deranged and afterwards wandered about unable to help themselves.

'...Accordingly, let us have great courage in the face of that disaster, which can neither be averted nor foreseen. Let us stop listening to those who have renounced Campania and who have emigrated after this catastrophe and say they will never visit that district again.

'...Yet why has an earthquake lasted for several days? For Campania did not cease its continuous trembling; the earthquake became milder but still caused great damage because it shook things already shaken, and since they were scarcely standing, and were ready to fall, they did not need to be pushed but only to be shaken.'

Seneca, *Natural Questions*
6.1.1–2, 6.1.10, 6.31.1

These marble reliefs depicting the earthquake of AD 63 adorned the lararium in the atrium of the House of Caecilius Jucundus (VI.1.26). In one, the Temple of Jupiter in the Forum is shaken, in the other the Vesuvius Gate collapses. Replicas can now be seen in the house itself; one of the originals was stolen, the other removed to storage.

What we have is an extremely varied picture of earthquake damage in the period after AD 63. It is important to note that not all buildings were damaged to the same extent, so not all needed the same degree of restoration or repair. Nevertheless, the period from the earthquake of AD 63 to the eruption of AD 79 saw extensive building and restoration work at Pompeii and Herculaneum, and many of these projects had not been completed by AD 79. For example, the lower rows of seating and parts of the stage building in Pompeii's Large Theatre had been repaired but the top of the cavea (seating area) had not been restored. This can be explained by several different factors. The on-going seismic activity undoubtedly caused some disruption to building work. There are cases (that we shall look at below) where repairs had to be made to buildings that had already been restored, and a few examples of restoration work that appears to have been abandoned before AD 79. In addition, there would have been a high demand for both building materials and workmen – it is unlikely that Pompeii was able to meet the demand for these from its own resources and inhabitants. The cost of repairs should also be taken into account. For private individuals, repairs may have had to wait until the resources and money to pay for them could be found. Even the town council, with its control over public finances, would have had to prioritize and choose which buildings, or which parts of buildings to restore first. Repairs were taking place across the town, but by AD 79 they had been completed in only a few of the major public buildings.

Earthquake damage in the Forum

The varied speed and extent of the restoration work can be seen particularly well in the Forum, and it is here, too, that much of the debate about the impact of the earthquake on the state of the town in its final years has focused. In the past, it has often been concluded that the Forum was so badly damaged by the earthquake of AD 63 that it could not have been functioning properly in AD 79.

For example, a strange collection of artifacts was discovered in the cella (chamber housing the cult statues) of the Temple of Jupiter, including a semi-colossal foot, a headless colossal marble bust, a colossal mask and various fragments of other statues. The German scholar, August Mau, claimed that the temple must have been used as the workshop of marble workers engaged in carrying out restorations in the Forum. The temple itself had been only partially repaired and was still without a roof in AD 79. It has also been pointed out that no complete statues, either standing or equestrian, were found during the excavations in the Forum, which has been interpreted as another sign that the Forum stood in ruins and was not in use. However, a recent study of the Forum challenged this view and claimed instead that a large and elaborate programme of restoration was taking place, possibly with the aid of imperial funding from Rome. This interpretation claims that the ruinous condition of the Forum can be explained by two factors. First, tremors during the eruption of AD 79 (not in the earthquake of AD 63) could have caused damage to buildings. Indeed, the excavators recorded the discovery of the skeleton of a man who had been trapped when a column from the Temple of Jupiter fell on him. Secondly, the activities of salvagers after the eruption (and in the intervening years before the official rediscovery of the town) could explain the lack of statues in the Forum. Here a contrast is drawn with Herculaneum where salvaging was rendered impossible by the depth to which the town was buried in the eruption and where statues were found in all major public areas. In addition, the fragments of statues and marble found in the

Earthquake damage and repair in public buildings

Public building	Extent of earthquake damage	Evidence of repairs and restoration	Completed by AD 79?
Forum (VII.8)	The triumphal arches, Forum portico and pavement were all damaged.	Several new statue bases had been built at the south end of the square. Pavement and colonnade only partly finished in AD 79. East side of Forum repaired to a large degree.	No
Temple of Jupiter (Capitolium) (VII.8.1)	The roof collapsed and the marble pavement was damaged; the cella was in ruins.	Little evidence of restoration; there was still no roof over the cella.	No
Comitium (VIII.3.1/31/33)	The building was made structurally weak; entrances to it were damaged.	Six of the entrances into the building were closed off; a new podium was constructed and the walls and pavement were refurbished with marble.	No
Municipal Buildings (VIII.2.10–6)	The facades of all three buildings were damaged.	Earthquake damage repaired with brickwork and buildings extended by c. 1.5 m (5 ft); in two of the three buildings the marble revetments of the walls had not yet been replaced.	No
Eumachia Building (VII.9.1/67)	Extensive damage to all perimeter and internal walls, and to the internal portico.	The entire facade was restored, the perimeter walls were rebuilt, door-jambs were repaired, extensive repairs to interior. The building had been lavishly redecorated with plaster, stucco (with marble dust) and marble veneer.	Yes
Temple of Vespasian/ Genius of the Emperor (VII.9.2)	Extensive damage to perimeter walls and altar.	The sanctuary was rebuilt and was in process of being redecorated in AD 79. The altar had been restored.	Yes
Basilica (VIII.1.1)	The roof probably collapsed.	It is not clear whether any restoration work had taken place by AD 79.	No
Macellum (VII.9.7–8/19/52)	Severe damage to perimeter walls, internal colonnade and shops.	Extensive renovations, including reconstruction of perimeter walls, facade and shops, and re-erection of inner colonnade. The building had been extensively redecorated with plaster, stucco and marble, including elaborate Fourth Style wall-paintings.	Yes
Temple of Apollo (VII.7.32)	Damage to colonnade and cella.	Repairs to colonnade, cella, and north wall of enclosure. Six of the nine entrances onto the Forum in the east enclosure wall were closed off.	No
Temple of Augustan Fortune (VII.4.1)	Entire building damaged.	Only the cella had been repaired, and its external walls had been redecorated with marble revetments.	No
Temple of Venus (VIII.1.3)	Presumably heavily damaged, but specific damage masked by later reconstruction and enlargement of the Temple.	Temple complex enlarged to the south, by means of a new terrace that encroached onto the southwest corner of the Villa Imperiale. Only part of podium constructed; stockpiles of cut stone and marble.	No
Temple of Isis (VIII.7.28)	Extensive damage throughout the temple.	Restoration and enlargement at private expense by a six-year-old boy; new portico and complete redecoration in Fourth Style.	Yes
Stabian Baths (VII.1.8)	Damage to entrances to the baths, the Palaestra, and to the vaulted roofs of the tepidarium and calidarium.	Entrances repaired after AD 63 but some later walled up after further tremors; the vaulted roofs of tepidarium and caldarium in disrepair and there was evidence of scaffolding in the Palaestra. However, in general, the repairs were almost complete, and much of the bath complex had been redecorated in Fourth Style painting and stuccowork.	No
Forum Baths (VII.5)	Only light damage.	Fully repaired. Stucco redecoration. The only public baths open in AD 79.	Yes
Suburban Baths	Badly damaged.	Evidence that restoration work had been damaged by later seismic activity and repaired again; the baths were being redecorated in AD 79.	No
Large Theatre (VIII.7.20)	Damage to cavea and scaenae frons.	Lower rows of seats and some of scaenae frons repaired, but top of cavea not finished.	No
Amphitheatre (II.6)	Damage to cavea and internal corridors.	Top part of cavea rebuilt; reinforcements to internal corridors; parapet frescos renewed.	Yes
Large Palaestra (II.7)	Walls and columns damaged.	Walls and colonnade repaired with brickwork. Some columns squared off by use of lead nuggets, not all had been re-covered with stucco. Water-pipes in swimming-pool not yet connected up to water supply.	No
Castellum Aquae and the water supply	Castellum Aquae heavily damaged and water supply disrupted across the town.	The walls of the Castellum Aquae had been mostly shored up. It is not clear if it was fully functional in AD 79. The pavements along Via dell' Abbondanza and in other parts of the town were open trenches in AD AD 79 because the water pipes were being replaced.	No

Temple of Jupiter and other locations can possibly be related to the process of excavation. Many such fragments were discovered and recorded during the excavations, and the excavators needed to find somewhere to store them. Some were taken to the Naples Museum, but others may have been stacked on site out of the way of the excavations.

The condition of the Forum in AD 79, and thus the functioning of public affairs, remains controversial but most scholars now accept that repairs here were taking place slowly. It appears that most of the buildings on the east side of the Forum had been largely repaired, including the Macellum and the Eumachia Building (the last probably at private expense). There is also some suggestion that the facades of these buildings were deliberately being linked to present a more pleasing aspect. One building – known to us as the Sanctuary of the Public Lares – may have been built from scratch (there is no consensus on this issue). In addition, repairs are evident in the 'Municipal Buildings' to the south of the Forum, with several new statue bases in front of them, in the Comitium and in the Basilica. In contrast, the west side of the Forum and the Temple of Apollo were still being restored in AD 79, and repairs had not been completed to the Forum's pavement and portico.

The restoration of other public buildings

Two public buildings had been completely restored by AD 79, the Amphitheatre and the Temple of Isis, both of which had partly collapsed in AD 63.

As we have previously seen, the Temple of Isis was restored and enlarged at private expense by a freedman in the name of his six-year old son. The restoration of the Amphitheatre was perhaps paid for, at least partly, by members of a prominent Pompeian family. Gaius Cuspius Pansa and his son of the same name may have been acting in accordance with the *Lex Petronia*, an obscure law that gave local magistrates special powers in emergencies (the elder Cuspius Pansa may have been appointed prefect to oversee repairs in the town). The top part of the cavea was rebuilt and brick-faced concrete reinforcements were made to its internal passages. It appears that the elaborate fresco decoration of the parapet walls may have been renewed. The names of the Cuspii Pansae appear in stone inscriptions beneath two niches at the end of the main entrance corridor to the Amphitheatre.

Gaius Cuspius Pansa, son of Gaius, the father, duumvir four times and quinquennial duumvir, prefect for legal judgments, by decree of the decurions under the provision of the Petronian Law. (*CIL* X 858)

Gaius Cuspius Pansa, son of Gaius, the son, pontifex, duumvir with judicial powers. (*CIL* X 859)

It is not clear whether these niches contained statues of these benefactors or, given the remains of iron grilles in front of them, whether they displayed valuable objects donated by these men.

The damage caused by the earthquake of AD 63 created an opportunity for changes to be made to some of Pompeii's public buildings. This can be seen in the Forum where the reconstruction allowed for the redesign of the overall appearance of the space, and in the Temple of Venus which was being completely replaced by a much grander temple. Only part of the temple podium had been completed by AD 79, but the excavators uncovered

The external facade of the Eumachia Building where the Via dell' Abbondanza meets the Forum. The brickwork of the facade had been repaired before AD 79, presumably due to damage caused by the earthquake of AD 63, or later seismic activity.

stockpiles of cut stone and marble. A completely new set of baths (the Central Baths, IX.4.5/18) were being constructed over the area of an entire insula. Presumably the houses that had originally occupied this insula had suffered extensive earthquake damage and were demolished to make room for the new baths. The opportunity was being taken to provide Pompeii with a modern bath facility, using new technology developed in Rome to improve wall-heating. Similarly, on the basis of similarities to new architectural ideas in the *Domus Aurea* (Nero's Golden House) in Rome, it has been controversially suggested that the Sanctuary of the Public Lares was built after AD 63. The function of other public buildings was transformed. The best example is the portico of the Large Theatre, which was converted into a gladiatorial barracks and training-ground.

Restoration in private houses

The variable picture of damage and restoration can also be seen in the houses of Pompeii. Particularly good examples of restoration work can be seen in the most recently excavated houses, the House of the Chaste Lovers (IX.12.6) and the House of the Painters at Work (IX.12). In the first, some of the wall-paintings of the triclinium had been recently redone, but one was still damaged. A thick pile of lime on the floor suggests that repairs were about to be made to this. In the second house, one can see unfinished wall-paintings alongside bronze compasses, mortars and pestles and other tools, and amphorae full of lime. In other houses the repairs had been completed. There is a difference in the type and extent of restoration work, however. Some houses, such as the House of the Vettii (VI.15.1), had been completely rebuilt and redecorated; others were simply patched up. There

Pompeii's water supply

At Pompeii, as elsewhere, drinking water had traditionally been supplied by wells or from rainwater collected in cisterns, although there is now some suggestion that from the Samnite period the town may have been connected to an aqueduct. This was certainly the case from the Augustan period (*c.* 27 BC),

when a system of aqueducts was constructed in Campania; the Serino branch of this system gave Pompeii a reliable supply of water. The water flowed first into a new Castellum Aquae just inside the Vesuvius Gate. It was then piped to public baths, houses and street fountains in different parts of the town. Secondary water-towers, often located at street-corners, close to public fountains, served to regulate the flow of water by reducing its pressure.

The regular supply of water had a huge impact on Pompeii. This is seen particularly in the largest houses of Pompeii, whose owners could afford to pay for the installation of a piped water supply. Smaller houses continued to make use of cisterns. At least 91, but probably more, of these houses were connected by pipes to the main water supply. In these houses, ornamental fountains, pools and other water features became common. Some houses were even provided with private baths from this period. Examples include the House of Menander (I.10.4), the House of Paquius Proculus (I.7.1) and the House of the Vestals (VI.1.6–8, 24–26). In the last case, the new water supply appears to have led to a dramatic and expensive restructuring of the house, with a new and deliberate focus on prominent water-features. Interestingly, water was never piped directly into the kitchens, toilets or service-areas of these houses. Instead, water for basic domestic uses was still provided by cisterns.

The earthquake of AD 63 and the subsequent seismic activity of Pompeii's last years had a dramatic effect on the use of water in the town. The supply of piped water was seriously disrupted. The Castellum Aquae was damaged, and in general it appears that water-pipes across the town needed to be replaced. In the first instance, these may have been patched up in order to re-establish a supply of water to different parts of the town. Public fountains were prioritized, and the supply to private houses was entirely stopped. Later, however, a major overhaul of the water supply system appears to have been undertaken and the pipes leading from the Castellum Aquae were being are even examples of houses where there are no immediately evident signs of earthquake damage, but where extensive structural changes took place anyway – such as the House of the Vestals (VI.1.6–8, 24–26) which appears to have been radically remodelled and redecorated in reaction to the disruption of Pompeii's water supply. Some buildings were restored, then later underwent more repairs. A good example is the House of Menander (I.10.4), where fragments of the new, post-AD 63 wall-decoration of the peristyle were discovered in the debris used to fill abandoned cellars beneath the house's private baths, probably due to damage caused by seismic activity after AD 63 and after the initial repairs. Other examples include the House of Paquius Proculus (I.7.1), the House of the Chaste Lovers (IX.12), the House of the Ship Europa (I.15.3), the House of the Gilded Cupids (VI.16.7) and the House of Fabius Rufus (VII. Ins. Occ.

16–19). In other houses, the repairs appear to have been abandoned. In the House of Amarantus (I.9.12), for example, large quantities of building materials (such as mortar, blocks of limestone, wall-plaster) were found. However, before AD 79, soil had accumulated over some of the wall-plaster and wine-amphorae had been stacked over much of the building debris. In the House of the Coloured Capitals (VII.4.31/51) extensive restoration to both walls and wall decoration had taken place after AD 63. However, at some point the new marble veneer of the atrium and tablinum was systematically removed, and the use of the atrium and surrounding rooms appears to have been abandoned. In contrast, the rooms around the peristyle retained their lavish decoration, which suggests that habitation was now focused on this part of the house. These developments have been attributed to seismic activity after AD 63.

replaced. This is seen particularly well along large parts of pavement along the south side of the Via dell' Abbondanza which consisted of open trenches in AD 79. The swimming-pool of the Large Palaestra had not yet been connected up to the town's water supply. Many houses, such as the House of Menander and the House of the Vestals, that had previously had a supply of piped water had ripped up their pipes and transformed their running water features into standing ones, sometimes with considerable architectural changes, and presumably at great expense. It has also been estimated that around one-third of all private baths in Pompeii's houses, such as in the House of the Cryptoporticus (I.6.2) and the House of the Silver Wedding (V.2.c), went out of use after AD 63.

(Above right) A bronze fountain mouth in the form of a lion's head, possibly from Herculaneum, and a bronze tap, one of many found in Pompeii.

(Right) The Castellum Aquae just inside the Vesuvius Gate. Water from the Serino aqueduct was piped via the Castellum Aquae to the public baths, fountains and houses of Pompeii.

(Opposite) Water-towers and public fountains are usually located at crossroads within the town. The tower and fountain in this photograph are located near the Stabian Baths.

Life in Pompeii
AD 63–79

NO ONE CAN DENY THAT THE YEARS AFTER AD 63 WERE ones of disruption to normal patterns of living. There must have been chaos: blocked streets, a damaged water-supply, difficulties in food provision, a need for emergency accommodation and so on. This means that there would have been a long period of disruption and chaos in the town. But although much archaeological evidence can be brought forward to demonstrate the extent of damage caused by seismic activity and the widespread repairs and restorations which followed, there is little agreement about the socio-economic impact of the disruption. The question is whether the disruption caused and the responses to it can be interpreted as evidence of a permanent social and economic decline. How did a major earthquake and regular seismic activity affect the lives of the people of Pompeii?

One particular theory has dominated the debate about living conditions in Pompeii's final years. Amedeo Maiuri, one of the major excavators of Pompeii and Herculaneum, claimed that during the 1st century BC a social revolution was taking place in Pompeii, and that this revolution was accelerated after the earthquake of AD 63. The wealthy upper classes were slowly being replaced by a lower, commercial, class. Maiuri thought that the larger houses of the noble classes were those most damaged in the earthquake, with the result that they were unable to find all the necessary funds to rebuild their properties and so were forced to sell parts of them. The lowered prices of property and land meant that merchants and artisans profited from the disaster, and were able to open new shops and workshops. Maiuri also claimed that existing shops and professional establishments were restored to working order more quickly than public buildings and houses, since there was a general need to earn money to finance repairs throughout the town.

This would mean that the social composition of the population of Pompeii changed in its last years of life. The rich abandoned the town, the nouveaux riches began to dominate socially and politically, and the need for skilled labour to carry out restorations led to an influx of workers from outside the region. For example, Maiuri claimed that the freedmen Aulus Vettius Restitutus and Aulus Vettius Conviva acquired the House of the Vettii after AD 63. They were wealthy enough to be able to rebuild and redecorate the house completely in the period

from AD 63 to 79. He also thought that the Villa of the Mysteries was taken over by a Greek freedman called Lucius Istacidus Zosimus, whose bronze seal was found there (although Zosimus has also been interpreted as the agent of the Istacidii, a fairly prominent Pompeian family). In his description of the villa, Maiuri claimed that after AD 63 it 'fell into rougher hands, was despoiled of all its best furniture, and the rooms (poorly redecorated) were put to the most humble uses'. Others have suggested that the swift restoration of the Amphitheatre and the Temple of Isis represent the different 'values' of Pompeii's dominant new elite, with a new emphasis on blood-sports and 'foreign' cults. This is hard to accept, however, given the long tradition of games in Campania and the fact that the cult of Isis was introduced to Pompeii in the 2nd century BC.

Maiuri's theories have been echoed frequently, despite the fact that they were also criticised from the moment of their publication. First, his work is based on anecdotal rather than statistical evidence: there is no discussion of the various degrees to which different buildings had been restored by AD 79, and the emphasis of his study was on public buildings, which, although ideologically and politically important, cannot be used as evidence of a *social* revolution. In addition, there is no evidence to suggest that Pompeii's wealthy elite were uninvolved in the commercial development of the town, or that the break-up of their houses related to their sale to merchants and craftsmen. There is also no need to assume that the emergence

Titus Suedius Clemens and land reclamation at Pompeii

Four identical stone inscriptions were found outside four of Pompeii's gates – the Nuceria, Herculaneum, Marina and Vesuvius Gates – and others probably existed outside the remaining gates of the town, too. The inscriptions read:

> On the authority of Caesar Vespasian Augustus, Titus Suedius Clemens, tribune, restored the public lands of the Pompeian state that had been taken over by private individuals, having investigated the cases and carried out (appropriate) surveys. (*CIL* IV 1018)

It appears that public land had been taken without permission into private hands and Titus Suedius Clemens was sent by the Emperor Vespasian to investigate this abuse and restore the land to public ownership. The consequences of Suedius' judgment can be identified in the archaeological record. For example, a number of tombs just to the of a new 'commercial' class – if this occurred – meant that the elite were supplanted or driven out. Indeed, we have no way of knowing whether certain groups of inhabitants did actually abandon the site, because we have no clear idea of the social make-up of the town before AD 63. This means that it is impossible to make comparisons between the two periods. In addition, comparative evidence from earthquakes in Catania (1693), Lisbon (1755) and Messina (1783) has been used to argue that it is unlikely that the earthquake stimulated economic activity, or that property prices were lowered. Houses may have been broken up, not for financial gain, but to cope with an accommodation crisis following the earthquake. In fact, the evidence for such division of houses is complex. There is wide-scale evidence for the construction of new, upper-storey apartments. This can be seen in the House of Menander, where the doorways to the west of the atrium and the ceilings of all the rooms behind them were lowered to accommodate a new upper apartment with its own separate entrance from the street. But it has also been estimated that only 20 of the 600 or more shops of Pompeii were demonstrably built after AD 63. This leads us to the most important point: the lack of extensive stratigraphic excavation at Pompeii means that it is usually impossible to compare the situation after AD 63 with the situation before that date. Without such excavation, we have no way of knowing exactly when a house was broken up or a shop installed, and there is no reason to believe that this only occurred after AD 63.

There is no consistent pattern of disruption and abandonment in Pompeii's last years. Houses and public buildings were affected to different extents and thus the experiences of individuals and families must have varied considerably. People must have reacted differently. Some may have finally understood the threat that Vesuvius posed and, as Seneca claimed, left the region and abandoned their property. Others, like the millions living in Vesuvius' shadow today, may have ignored or denied this threat. Some of the wealthiest inhabitants probably moved temporarily to properties in other areas to minimize disruption to their lives, while repairs were completed by their slaves and dependants. Those without such resources would have had nowhere else to go and simply got on with rebuilding their lives as best as they could. This is seen in the scale of repairs and restorations that were going on in the years between the first earthquake of AD 63 and the eruption of AD 79. There is some evidence of abandonment, but new buildings using new architectural ideas were also constructed in this period. The situation was complex – some people suffered greatly, others may have profited. But clearly large sums of money were being spent on the restoration and rejuvenation of Pompeii in its final years, and this is hard to reconcile with the idea of a town in decline.

It was, however, a town on the verge of destruction. In AD 79 the violent eruption of Vesuvius buried Pompeii, preserving for posterity a glimpse of the daily struggles and joys of its inhabitants.

east of the Nuceria Gate were destroyed at about this time, and presumably had been constructed on the public land. The so-called Villa Imperiale, located outside the Marine Gate, was also abandoned sometime between the years AD 69 and 79, despite having been widely renovated after AD 63. Again, this was probably due to Suedius' land reclamation, particularly since the Villa Imperiale made way for the construction of a large warehouse and for terraces related to the enlargement of the Temple of Venus.

The Suedius inscriptions have frequently been interpreted as evidence of opportunism and social disorder after the earthquake of AD 63. More recently, they have been related to the wider context of events in Italy. After the civil wars of AD 68–69, the Emperor Vespasian was concerned to correct such abuses across the empire in an attempt to improve its finances. Pompeii was not the only town where land was reclaimed. However, the presence of Suedius in Pompeii in its final years and the reclamation of public land suggest that Rome took an interest in the rejuvenation of the town after the devastation caused by the earthquake of AD 63.

The stone inscription outside the Nuceria Gate that records the judgment of Titus Suedius Clemens. The inscription was located in a prominent position where passers-by could not fail to see it.

Visiting Pompeii

How to get there

Unless you travel with an organized group, it is best to travel by train. From Naples, there are three options: the easiest for the day-tripper is to take the Circumvesuviana line to Sorrento (or to Naples if coming from Sorrento), which stops at 'Pompei Scavi – Villa dei Misteri'; access to the site is then through the Porta Marina (Marine Gate, directly opposite the station) or the Piazza Esedra. Two other train lines run through modern Pompeii, the Circumvesuviana line to Poggiomarino, which stops at 'Pompei Santuario' and the Ferrovia dello Stato train to Salerno, which stops at 'Pompei'. From both these stations it is necessary to walk through the modern town to reach the entrance to the excavations at the Piazza Anfiteatro.

Opening times

The excavations open at 8.30 am. From November to March, they close at 5 pm (last admission is 3.30 pm), and from April to October, they close at 7.30 pm (last admission at 6 pm). The site is closed on 1 January, 1 May and 25 December only. Pompeii is extremely busy during the summer months, and very hot and dusty; it is often more pleasant to visit outside the summer season.

Admission

At the time of writing, a daily ticket to the site costs €11.00 (concessionary tickets are available). There is also a three-day ticket allowing access to Pompeii, Herculaneum, Oplontis, Stabiae and Boscoreale which costs €20.00.

Other useful information

At the Porta Marina entrance there is an information point which offers free maps of the town and suggested itineraries for visitors, and a bookshop. Audio-guides in various languages can be hired at both the Porta Marina and Piazza Anfiteatro entrances, and there are also left-luggage facilities at both.

There is a restaurant on site in the Forum Baths, to the north of the Forum. It provides drinks, snacks and meals, and also has a gift shop. It can, however, get very busy, and there is nowhere else inside the excavations to buy drinks or food – so it is a good idea to bring a bottle of water with you, at the very least.

Visitors are often surprised by the size of Pompeii, and walking its streets with their cobbled pavements can be very tiring. It is sensible to wear flat shoes and to plan your itinerary in advance. Those wishing to see as much as possible should expect to visit over more than one day.

Due to the conservation problems posed by the site, parts of it are closed to visitors, and others are only open intermittently. It is sometimes possible to book to see particular houses and buildings normally closed to the public (at no extra cost), but this depends on current conservation work. Tickets, if available, must be booked online with Arethusa (http://www.arethusa.net). Frustratingly, this website is in Italian only.

Highlights

Around the Nuceria Gate: visit the street of tombs outside the walls and then enter through the gate to see some of the large gardens and cultivated areas of Regions I and II, such as the Garden of the Fugitives and the House of the Ship Europa (I.15.3).

From the Amphitheatre to the Holconius crossroads: after visiting the Amphitheatre and Large Palaestra, walk along the Via dell' Abbondanza to see its bars and shops, such as the Fullery of Stephanus (I.6.7) and the Bar of Asellina (IX.11.12). Some beautiful and interesting houses had their main entrances onto this important thoroughfare. Particularly worthy of a visit are the Houses of Venus in a Shell (II.3.3), Loreius Tiburtinus (II.2.2), Julius Polybius (IX.13.1–3), and the Lyre-Player (I.4.5/25). A brief detour to the south will also take you to the House of Menander (I.10.4) and the House of the Ceii (I.6.15).

From the Holconius crossroads to the Vesuvius Gate: note the Houses of Caecilius Jucundus (V.1.26), Marcus Lucretius, the Gilded Cupids (VI.16.7) and the Large Altar (VI.16.15–17) on your way to the Castellum Aquae and the tombs outside the gate.

The theatre quarter: from the Stabian Baths, turn south to visit the Large Theatre and theatre portico, the Covered Theatre, the Temple of Isis and the Triangular Forum and Doric Temple. Further along the Via dell' Abbondanza towards the Forum, enter the 'Vicolo Storto' and visit the Lupanar.

Around the Marine Gate and Forum: visit the Suburban Baths then enter the Marine Gate, passing the Temples of Venus and Apollo into the Forum. Apart from the major buildings here, note the 'mensa ponderaria' (table of weights and measures) and the ancient granary (Forum Holitorium) now used to store large objects found in the excavations. To the north of the Forum, visit the Forum Baths.

From the Forum to the Herculaneum Gate: some of the most famous Pompeian houses are in this part of the town: the Houses of the Faun (VI.12.2), the Vettii (VI.15.1), Pansa (VI.6.1), Sallust (VI.2.4), the Small Fountain (VI.8.23), the Tragic Poet (VI.8.3–5), the Surgeon (VI.1.9–10), Meleager (VI.9.2) and the Dioscuri (VI.9.6). Visit the street of tombs outside the gate and continue on to the Villa of the Mysteries.

Other sites in the region

Herculaneum: opening times and ticket prices are the same as for Pompeii. From Naples, take any Circumvesuviana train – they all stop at 'Ercolano', then walk straight down to the entrance of the excavations (5 minutes). Many of the houses and buildings are closed for restoration, but it sometimes possible to book visits to the Villa of the Papyri (through Arethusa – see above). Things to see (if they are open to the public) include the Houses of the Stags (IV.21), the Relief of Telephus (I.2), the Wooden Partition (III.11), the Mosaic Atrium (IV.–2), Neptune and Amphitrite, and the Samnite House (V.1), and also the Suburban Baths and the Hall of the Augustales (VI.21/24).

Boscoreale, Stabiae and Oplontis: opening times are also the same as for Pompeii. A single ticket costing €5.50 is valid for all three sites. Arriving at Oplontis is fairly straightforward – the Circumvesuviana trains all stop at 'Torre Annunziata' and Villa A is a two-minute walk from the stations. Visiting Boscoreale and Stabiae is more challenging (and easier with a car). The Antiquarium and Villa Regina of Boscoreale can be found at Via Settetermini 15, loc. Villaregina, in modern Boscoreale. By train, take the Circumvesuviana line to Poggiomarino and get off at 'Boscotrecase'. Then take a bus to 'Villa Regina'. The villas of Stabiae are above the modern town of Castellamare di Stabia, on Via Passeggiata Archeologica. Take the Circumvesuviana line to 'Via Nocera'; then take a bus to the villas (Red bus no.1).

Naples Museum (Museo Nazionale Archeologico di Napoli): home to extensive and spectacular collections of ancient art, sculpture and artifacts. Pride of place goes, of course, to the galleries of antiquities from Pompeii and Herculaneum, which include wall-paintings and mosaics (including a room devoted to the House of the Faun), sculpture from the Villa of the Papyri, gladiatorial armour, collections of silver plate and jewelry, frescos from the Temple of Isis, and the infamous 'Secret Cabinet'. No visit to Pompeii and Herculaneum is complete without a trip to this wonderful museum.

The museum is located at Piazza Museo 19 (80135 Napoli). Various buses from the main train station (Piazza Garibaldi) pass the museum; the nearest underground stops are Piazza Cavour and Museo. It is open daily (except Tuesdays) 9 am – 8 pm. The museum is shut on 1 January, 1 May and 25 December. Tickets cost €8.

Further Reading

For an exhaustive list of everything published up to 1998 about Pompeii, Herculaneum and the other places destroyed by Vesuvius in AD 79, see Garcia y Garcia, L., *Nova bibliotheca pompeiana: 250 anni di bibliografia archeologica: catalogo dei libri e degli scritti riguardanti la storia, l'arte e gli scavi di Pompei, Ercolano, Stabia ed Oplonti con numerose referenze per l'eruzione vesuviana del 79 d.C., i papiri ercolanesi, le raccolte del Museo Nazionale di Napoli e per i libri dei viaggiatori in Campania.* (Rome: Bardi, 1998).

Major publications of the excavations of Pompeii and Herculaneum in the 18th and 19th centuries (arranged in order of publication)

Le antichità di Ercolano esposte. 8 vols. (1757–92).

Winkelmann, J. J., *Sendschreiben von den Herculanischen Entdeckungen,* (1762), and *Nachrichten von den neuesten Herculanischen Entdeckungen,* (1764).

Hamilton, Hon. Sir William, *An Account of the Discoveries at Pompeii, Communicated to the Society of Antiquaries of London.* (London, 1777).

Mazois, François, *Les Ruines de Pompéi dessinées et mesurées pendant les années MDCCCIX, MDCCCX, MDCCCXI publiée à Paris en MDCCCXII, Première et secondième parties.* 2 vols (Paris, 1813–24).

Gell, Sir William F.R.S.F.S.A. and John P. Gandy, *Pompeiana: The Topography, Edifices, and Ornaments of Pompeii.* 2 vols (London, 1817–19).

Gell, Sir William F.R.S.F.S.A., *Pompeiana: The Topography, Edifices, and Ornaments of Pompeii, the result of excavations since 1832.* (London, 1832).

Wilkins, Henry, *Suite de vues pittoresques des Ruines de Pompéi et un précis historique de la ville: Avec un plan des fouilles qui ont été faites jusqu'en Février 1819 et un description des objets les plus intéressant.* (Rome, 1819).

Hüber, J. W., *Vues pittoresques des ruines le plus remarquables de l'ancienne ville de Pompéi: Dessinées et gravées à l'acqua tinta par J. W. Hüber, peintre.* (Zurich, 1824).

Zahn, W., *Die schönsten Ornamente und merkwürdigsten Gemälde aus Pompeji, Herkulanum und Stabiae, nebst einigen Grundrissen und Ansichten: Mit deutschem und französichem Text.* 3 vols (Berlin, 1827–59).

Rossini, Luigi, *Le antichità di Pompei delineate su le scoperte fatte sino a tutto l' anno 1830 ed incise dall' architetto Luigi Rossini, Ravennate e dal medesimo brevemente illustrate.* (Rome, 1830).

de Cesare, Francesco, *Le più belle ruine di Pompei descritte e misurate, e disegnate da Francesco De Cesare professore di architettura civile, socio corrispondente della Reale Accademia di Belle Arti di Napoli ec. Colle notizie de' scavi da che ebbero principio sino al 1835.* (Naples, 1835).

Roux, M., *Chois de peintures de Pompéi la plupart de sujet historique, lithographiées en couleur par M. Roux, et publiées avec l' explication archéologique de chaque peinture et une Introduction sur l' histoire de la peinture chez les Grecs et chez le Romains par ./ Raoul-Rochette.* 7 vols (Paris, 1844–53).

Niccolini, Fausto and Felice, *Le case e monumenti di Pompei.* 4 vols (Naples, 1854–96).

Breton, Ernest, *Pompeia décrite et desinée par Ernest Breton de la Société Impériale des Antiquaires de France, etc., Suivie d'une notice sur Herculaneum.* (Paris, 1855).

Sasso, C. N., *Il Vesuvio, Ercolano e Pompei.* (Naples, 1857).

Roux Ainé, H. and M. L. Barre, *Herculanum et Pompéi recueil general des peintures, bronzes, mosaïques, etc. découverts jusqu'à ce jour, et reproduits d'après 'Le antichità di Ercolano,' 'Il Museo Borbonic' et tous les ouvrages analogues augmentés de sujets inédits graves au trait sur cuivre par H. Roux Ainé et accompanés d'un Text explicatif par M. L. Barré.* 7 vols (Paris, 1861–62).

Mau, August, *Geschichte der decorativen Wandmalerei in Pompeji* (Berlin, 1882).

Overbeck, Johannes, *Pompeji in seinen Gebäuden: Alterhümern und Kunstwerken dargestellt von Johannes Overbeck vierte im Vereine mit August Mau durchgearbeitete und vermehrte Auflage.* (Leipzig, 1884).

General sources, discussions, catalogues and works of reference

Bassaldare, I. (ed.), *Pitture e Mosaici di Pompei.* Vols 1 and 2 (Rome: Istituto della Enciclopedia Italiana, 1990).

Beard, M., *Pompeii: the life of a Roman town.* (London: Profile Books, 2008).

Borriello, M. *et al.*, *Pompei: Abitare sotto il Vesuvio.* (Ferrara: Ferrara arte, 1996).

Bon, S. E. and R. Jones (eds.), *Sequence and Space in Pompeii.* (Oxford: Oxbow Books, 1997).

Bragantini, I., M. de Vos, F. Parise Badoni and V. Sampaolo (eds.), *Pitture e Pavimenti di Pompei.* (Rome: Ministero per i beni culturali e ambientali, Istituto centrale per il catalogo e la documentazione, 1981–1992).

Ciarallo, A. and E. De Carolis, *Homo Faber. Natura, scienza e tecnica nell' antica Pompei.* (Milan: Electa, 1999).

Conticello De Spagnolis, M. and E. De Carolis, *Le Lucerne di bronzo di Ercolano e Pompei.* (Rome: L'Erma di Bretschneider, 1988).

Cooley, A., *Pompeii.* (London: Duckworth, 2002).

—— and Cooley, M., *Pompeii. A sourcebook.* (London: Routledge, 2004).

D'Ambrosio, A. and M. Borriello, *Le terrecotte figurate di Pompei.* (Rome: L'Erma di Bretschneider, 1990).

De Caro, S., *Il Museo archeologico nazionale di Napoli.* (Naples: Electa Napoli, 1994).

de la Bedoyere, G., *Cities of Roman Italy: Pompeii, Herculaneum and Ostia.* (London: Bristol Classical Press, 2010).

de Vos, A. and M. de Vos, *Pompei, Ercolano, Stabiae.* (Rome: G. Laterza, 1982).

Dobbins, J. and P. Foss, *The World of Pompeii.* (London/New York: Routledge, 2007).

Guzzo, P. G. (ed.), *Pompei: scienza e società: 250 anniversario degli scavi di Pompei.* Convegno internazionale, Napoli, 25–27 novembre 1998 / a cura di Pier Giovanni Guzzo. (Milan: Electa, 2001).

—— and M. Guidobaldi (eds.), *Nuove ricerche archeologiche a Pompei ed Ercolano: atti del convegno internazionale, Roma, 28–30 Novembre 2002.* (Naples: Electa, 2005).

Jashemski, W. F. and F. G. Meyer (eds.), *The Natural History of Pompeii* (Cambridge University Press, 2002).

Keppie, L., *Romans on the Bay of Naples: an archaeological guide.* (Stroud: The History Press, 2009).

La Rocca, E., M. de Vos and A. de Vos, *Pompei.* (Milan: Mondadori, 2nd ed. 1994).

Laurence, R., *Roman Pompeii: space and society.* (London: Routledge 1994).

—— and Newsome, D. (eds.), *Rome, Ostia, Pompeii: movement and space.* Oxford University Press, 2011.

Ling, R., *Pompeii: history, life and afterlife.* (Stroud: Tempus, 2005).

Maiuri, A. (ed.), *Pompeiana: Raccolta di studi per il secondo centenario degli scavi di Pompei.* (Naples: Gaetano Macchiaroli Editore, 1950).

Pirozzi, M. E. A., *Herculaneum. The Excavations, Local History and Surroundings.* (Rome: Bardi, 2000).

Poehler, E., M. Flohr and K. Cole, (eds.), *Pompeii: art, industry, and infrastructure.* (Oxford; Oakville, CT: Oxbow Books, 2011).

Pompei: L' informatica al servizio di una città antica. (Rome: L'Erma di Bretschneider, 1988).

Pompei 1748–1980: i tempi della documentazione. (Rome: Multigrafica Editrice, 1981).

Ranieri Panetta, M. (ed.), *Pompeii. The History, Life and Art of the Buried City* (Vercelli: White Star, 2004).

Rediscovering Pompeii. Ministero per I Beni Culturali e Ambientali & Soprintendenza Archeologica di Pompei (Rome, L'Erma di Bretschneider, 1990).

Senatore, F. (ed.), *Pompei, il Sarno e la Penisola Sorrentina: atti del primo ciclo di Conferenze di geologia, storia e archeologia.* Pompei, Istituto "B. Longo", aprile–giugno 1997 (Pompei: Rufus, 1998).

Senatore, F., *Pompei, il Vesuvio e la Penisola sorrentina: atti del secondo ciclo di conferenze di geologia, storia e archeologia, Pompei, Istituto B. Longo, ottobre 1997 – febbraio 1998.* (Rome: Bardi, 1999).

—— *Pompei, Capri e la Penisola Sorrentina: atti del quinto Ciclo di conferenze di geologia, storia, e archeologia, Pompei, Anacapri, Scafati, Castellammare di Stabia, ottobre 2002 – aprile 2003.* (Capri: Oebalus, 2004).

Tassinari, S., *Il vasellame bronzeo di Pompei.* 2 vols. (Rome: L'Erma di Bretschneider, 1993).

Ward-Perkins, J. B. & A. Claridge, *Pompeii AD 79.* (Bristol: Imperial Tobacco, 1976).

Zevi, F., *Pompei 79. Raccolta di studi per il decimonono centenario dell' eruzione Vesuviana.* (Naples: G. Macchiaroli, 1979).

Chapter I

Barker, E. R., 'Past excavations at Herculaneum'. *The Classical Review* 22.1 (1908), 2–5.

Budetta, T. and M. Pagano, *Ercolano: legni e piccoli bronzi. Testimonianze dell' arredo e delle suppellettini della casa romana.* (Naples: Soprintendenza Archeologica di Pompei, 1988).

Ciarallo, A. and E. De Carolis, 'La data dell'eruzione'. *Rivista di Studi Pompeiani* 9 (1998), 63–73.

De Carolis, E., 'Lo scavo dei fornici 7 ed 8 sulla marina di Ercolano'. In *Rivista di Studi Pompeiani*, VI (1993–94), 167–86.

—— *Vesuvius, AD 79.* (Los Angeles: Getty Publications, 2003).

De Vivo, B. *et al.* (eds.), *Mount Vesuvius: special issue. Journal of Volcanology and Geothermal Research* 58 (1993), 1–381.

Descoeudres, J-P., 'Did some Pompeians return to their city after the eruption of Mt. Vesuvius in AD 79? Observations in the House of the Coloured Capitals'. In L. Franchi dell' Orto (ed.), *Ercolano 1738–1988. 250 anni di ricerca archeologica* (Rome: L'Erma di Bretschneider, 1993), 165–78.

Franchi dell' Orto, L., *Ercolano 1738–1988. 250 anni di ricerca archeologica.* Atti del Convegno Internazionale Ravello-Ercolano-Napoli-Pompei 30 ottobre – 5 novembre 1988. (Rome: L'Erma di Bretschneider, 1993).

Gigante, M., *Philodemus in Italy: the books from Herculaneum.* (Ann Arbor: University of Michigan Press, 1995).

Guzzo, P. G., *Tales from an eruption: Pompeii, Herculaneum, Oplontis.* Guide to the exhibition. (Milan: Electa, 2003).

—— and Peroni, R., *Archeologia e vulcanologia in Campania: atti del convegno, Pompei, 21 dicembre 1996.* (Naples: Arte tipografica, 1998).

Lazer, E., *Resurrecting Pompeii.* London: Routledge, 2009.

—— 'Victims of the cataclysm'. In J. Dobbins and P. Foss (eds.), *The World of Pompeii.* (London: Routledge, 2007), 607–19.

Pagano, M., 'Metodologia dei restauri borbonici a Pompei ed Ercolano'. In *Rivista di Studi Pompeiani V* (1991–92), 169–91.

Pappalardo, U., 'L' eruzione pliniana del Vesuvio del 79 d.C.: Ercolano'. In C. Albore-Livadie (ed.), *Volcanology and Archaeology* (1990),

197–215.

Scarth, A. *Vesuvius: a biography.* (Princeton: Princeton University Press, 2009).

Sigurdsson, H. *et al.*, 'The eruption of Vesuvius in AD 79.' *American Journal of Archaeology* 86 (1982), 39–51.

Sigurdsson, H., 'Mount Vesuvius before the disaster'. In W. F. Jashemski and F. G. Meyer (eds.), *The Natural History of Pompeii* (Cambridge: Cambridge University Press, 2002), 29–36.

—— and Carey, S., 'The eruption of Vesuvius in AD 79'. In W. F. Jashemski and F. G. Meyer (eds.), *The Natural History of Pompeii* (Cambridge: Cambridge University Press, 2002), 37–64.

—— 'The environmental and geomorphological context of the volcano'. In J. Dobbins and P. Foss (eds.), *The World of Pompeii.* (London: Routledge, 2007), 43–62.

Stefani, G., 'La vera data dell' eruzione'. *Archeo* 260 (2006), 10–13.

Varone, A. and A. Marturano, 'L'eruzione vesuviana del 24 agosto del 79 d.C. attraverso le letture di Plinio il Giovane e le nuove evidenze archaeologiche'. *Rivista di Studi Pompeiani* 8 (1997), 57–72.

Zevi, F., 'Gli Scavi di Ercolano'. In *Civiltà del '700 a Napoli*, II. (Naples, 1980), 58–68.

Chapter II

Baratte, F., *Le Trésor D' Orfèverie Romaine de Boscoreales.* (Paris: Editions de la Réunion des Musées Nationaux, 1986).

Bowersock, G., 'The rediscovery of Herculaneum and Pompeii'. *The American Scholar* 47 (1978), 461–70.

Castiglione Morelli, V., *A Giuseppe Fiorelli nel primo centenario della morte.* (Naples: Arte Tipografica, 1999).

D'Ambrosio, A. (ed.), *Pompeii: gli scavi dal 1748 al 1860.* (Milan: Electa/Pompeii: Soprintendenza Archeologica di Pompei, 2002).

De Carolis, E., 'Gli sviluppo dell' archeologie pompeiana: 1748–1900'. In *Fotografia a Pompei nell' 800 dalle collezioni del Museo Alinari.* Soprintendenza Archeologica di Pompei. (Florence, 1990), 11–20.

de Franciscis, A. *et al.*, *Amedeo Maiuri nel centenario della nascita. Memorie dell' istituto Italiano per gli studi filosofici.* (Naples: Bibliopolis, 1990).

Descoeudres, J-P., 'History and historical sources'. In J. Dobbins and P. Foss (eds.), *The World of Pompeii.* London: Routledge, 2007, 9–27.

Dwyer, E., 'From fragments to icons: stages in the making and exhibiting of the casts of Pompeian Victims, 1863–88. *Interpreting Ceramics 8* (2005), (available online: http://www.interpretingceramics.com/issue00 8/articles/06.htm).

—— *Pompeii's Living Statues.* (Ann Arbor: University of Michigan Press, 2010).

Il Tesoro di Boscoreale. Gli argento del Louvre e il corredo domestico della 'Pisanella'. Pompeii, Casina dell' Aquila, 20th agosto – 30 settembre 1988. Soprintendenza Archeologica di Pompei. (Milan: Franco Maria Ricci, 1988).

Falkner, E., 'Report on a house at Pompeii, excavated under personal superintendence in 1847'. In *Museum of Classical Antiquities. Essays on ancient art.* (London, 1852), 2–89.

Fiorelli, G., *Pompeianarum Antiquitatum Historia* I – II. (Naples, 1860–64).

—— *Relazione sugli Scavi di Pompei dal 1861 al 1872.* (Naples, 1873).

—— *Descrizione di Pompei.* (Naples: Tipografia Italiana, 1875).

Foss, P., 'Rediscovery and resurrection'. In J. Dobbins and P. Foss (eds.), *The World of Pompeii.* London: Routledge, 2007, 28–42.

Garcia y Garcia, L., *Danni di Guerra a Pompei. Una dolorosa vicenda quasi dimenticata.* Studi della Soprintendenza Archeologica di Pompei, 15 (Rome: L'Erma di Bretschneider, 2006).

Grant, M., 'Bourbon patronage and foreign involvement at Pompeii and Herculaneum'. In E. Chaney and N. Ritchie (eds.), *Oxford, China and Italy. Writings in honour of Sir Harold Acton on his Eightieth Birthday.* (London: Thames and Hudson, 1984), 161–68.

Hales, S. and J. Paul., *Pompeii in the Public Imagination from its Rediscovery to Today.* (Oxford: Oxford University Press, 2011).

Harris, J., *Pompeii Awakened: a story of rediscovery.* London: I.B. Taurus, 2007

Laidlaw, A., 'Mining the early published sources: problems and pitfalls'. In J. Dobbins and P. Foss (eds.), *The World of Pompeii.* London: Routledge, 2007, 620–36.

Lazer, E., *Resurrecting Pompeii.* London: Routledge, 2009.

Longobardi, G., *Pompei sostenibile.* (Rome: L'Erma di Bretschneider, 2002).

Maiuri, A., 'Gli Scavi di Pompei dal 1879 al 1948'. In *Pompeiana. Raccolta di Studi per il secondo centenario degli scavi di Pompei.* (Naples: Gaetano Macchiaroli Editore, 1950), 9–40.

Oettel, A., *Fundkontexte römischer Vesuvvillen im Gebiet um Pompeji: die Grabungen von 1894 bis 1908.* (Mainz: Verlag Philipp von Zabern, 1996).

Pace, S., *Herculaneum and European Culture between the Eighteenth and Nineteenth Centuries* (Rome: Bardi, 2000).

Paderni, C., 'Extracts of two letters from Sign. Camillo Paderni at Rome, to Mr. Allan Ramsey, Painter, in Covent-Garden, concerning some ancient statues, pictures and other curiosities, found in a subterraneous town, lately discovered near Naples…' *Philosophical Transactions (1683–1775)* vol. 41 (1739–1741), 484–89.

Pagano, M., *I diari di scavo di Pompei, Ercolano e Stabia di Francesco e Pietro La Vega (1764–1810): raccolta e studio di documenti* inediti. (Rome: L'Erma di Bretschneider, 1997).

—— *I primi anni degli scavi di Ercolano, Pompei e Stabiae: raccolta e studio di documenti e disegni inediti.* (Rome: L'Erma di Bretschneider, 2005).

Pappalardo, U., *La descrizione di Pompei per Giuseppe Fiorelli (1875): con una cronistoria per immagini e la lettera alla Guardia Nazionale del distretto di Castellammare di Stabia.* (Naples: Massa Editore, 2001).

Parslow, C., *Rediscovering antiquity Karl Weber and the excavation of Herculaneum, Pompeii, and Stabiae.* (Cambridge: Cambridge University Press, 1995).

Pasqui, A., 'La Villa Pompeiana della Pisanella presso Boscoreale'. In *Monumenti Antichi dell' Accademia dei Lincei* 7 (1897), 398–554.

Pompeii as source and inspiration: reflections in 18th and 19th century art. (Ann Arbor: University of Michigan Press, 1977).

Ramage, N. H., 'Sir William Hamilton as collector, exporter and dealer: the acquisition and dispersal of his collections'. *American Journal of Archaeology* 94.3 (July 1990) 469–80.

—— 'Goods, graves and scholars: 18th century archaeologists in Britain and Italy'. *American Journal of Archaeology* 96.4 (Oct. 1992) 653–61.

Robotti, C., *Immagini di Ercolano e Pompei: disegni, rilievi, vedute dei secoli XVIII e XIX.* (Naples: Ferraro, 1987).

Sider, D., 'The special case of Herculaneum'. In Roger S. Bagnall (ed.), *The Oxford Handbook of Papyrology* (Oxford: OUP, 2009), 303–19.

Spinazzola, V., *Pompei alla luce degli scavi nuovi di via dell' Abbondanza (anni 1910–23).* 3 vols (Rome, 1953).

Strazzullo, F., *Alcubierre-Weber-Paderni: un difficile tandem nello scavo di Ercolano-Pompei-Stabia.* (Naples: Accademia di archeologia, lettere e belle arti, 1999).

Zarmakoupi, M., *The Villa of the Papyri at Herculaneum: archaeology, reception, and digital reconstruction.* Berlin: De Gruyter, 2010.

Zevi, F., 'La Storia degli Scavi e della documentazione'. In *Pompei 1748–1980. I tempi della documentazione* (Rome: Multigrafica Editrice, 1981), 11–21.

Chapter III

Antonini, R., 'Iscrizioni osche pompeiane'. *Studi Etrusci* 45 (1977), 317–40.

Arthur, P., 'Problems of the urbanization of Pompeii'. *Antiquaries Journal* 66 (1986) 29–44.

Berry, J. (ed.), *Unpeeling Pompeii: studies in Region I of Pompeii.* (Milan: Electa, 1998).

Bonghi Jovino, M. (ed.), *Ricerche a Pompei: l'insula 5 della Regio VI dalle origini al 79 d.C* (Rome: L'Erma di Bretschneider, 1984).

Bon, S. E., R. Jones, B. Kurchin and D. Robinson, 'The context of the House of the Surgeon: investigations in Insula VI.1 at Pompeii'. In Bon and Jones, *Sequence and Space at Pompeii* (Oxford: Oxbow Books, 1997), 32–49.

Carafa, P., 'What was Pompeii before 200 BC? Excavations in the House of Joseph II, in the Triangular Forum and in the House of the Wedding of Hercules'. In S.E. Bonn and R. Jones (eds.), *Sequence and Space in Pompeii* (Oxford: Oxbow, 1997).

—— 'The investigations of the University of Rome 'La Sapienza' in Regions VII and VIII: the ancient history of Pompeii'. In T. McGinn *et al.*, *Pompeian Brothels, Pompeii's Ancient History, Mirrors and Mysteries, Art and Nature at Oplontis, and the Herculaneum Basilica* (Portsmouth, R.I.: Journal of Roman Archaeology Suppl. 47, 2002), 47–61.

—— 'Recent work on early Pompeii'. In J. Dobbins and P. Foss (eds.), *The World of Pompeii.* (London: Routledge, 2007), 63–72.

Chiaramonte Treré, C., *Nuovi contributi sulle fortificazioni pompeiane.* (Milan: Cisalpino-Goliardica, 1986).

Conticello de' Spagnolis, M., *Pompei e la valle del Sarno in epoca preromana: la cultura delle tombe a Fossa.* (Rome: L'Erma di Bretschneider, 2001).

Cooley, A., 'The survival of Oscan in Roman Pompeii'. In A. E. Cooley (ed.), *Becoming Roman, Writing Latin? Literacy and epigraphy in the Roman West* (Portsmouth, R.I: Journal of Roman Archaeology Suppl. 48, 2002), 77–86.

D'Alessio, M. T., *Materiali votivi dal Foro Triangolare di Pompei.* (Rome: G. Bretschneider, 2001).

De Caro, S., 'Nuove indagini sulle forticazione di Pompei'. *Annali dell'Instituto Orientale di Napoli* (1985), 75–114.

—— *Saggi nell'area del tempio di Apollo a Pompei: scavi stratigrafici di A. Maiuri nel 1931–32 e 1942–43.* (Naples: Istituto universitario orientale, Dipartimento di studi del mondo classico e del Mediterraneo antico, 1986).

—— 'La città sannitica urbanistica e architettura'. In F. Zevi (ed.), *Pompei I* (Naples: Banco di Napoli, 1991), 23–46.

—— 'The first sanctuaries'. In J. Dobbins and P. Foss (eds.), *The World of Pompeii.* (London: Routledge, 2007), 73–81.

Ellis, S. J. R. (ed.), *The Making of Pompeii: studies in the history and urban development of an ancient town.* (Portsmouth, R.I.: JRA Suppl. 85, 2011)

Eschebach, H., *Die städtebauliche Entwicklung des antiken Pompeji.* (Mitteilungen des Deutschen Archäologischen Instituts, Römische Abteilung Erganzungsheft 17, 1970).

—— and Eschebach, L. *Gebäudeverzeichnis und Stadtplan der antiken Stadt Pompeji.* (Cologne: Böhlau, 1993).

—— *Pompeji, vom 7. Jahrhundert v. Chr. bis 79 n. Chr.* (Cologne: Böhlau, 1995).

Fulford, M. and A. Wallace-Hadrill, 'The House of Amarantus at Pompeii (I.9.11–12): an interim report on survey and excavations in 1995–96'. *Rivista di studi pompeiani* 7 (1995–96), 77–113.

—— 'Unpeeling Pompeii'. *Antiquity* 72 (1998), 128–45.

—— 'Towards a history of pre-Roman Pompeii: Excavations beneath the House of Amarantus (I.9.11–12), 1995–98.' *Papers of the British School at Rome* 67: 37–144.

Geertman, H., 'The urban development of the pre-Roman city'. In J. Dobbins and P. Foss (eds.), *The World of Pompeii.* (London: Routledge, 2007), 82–98.

Guzzo, P. G., 'City and country: an introduction'. In J. Dobbins and P. Foss (eds.), *The World of Pompeii.* (London: Routledge, 2007), 3–8.

Hoffman, A., 'L'Architectura Privata'. In F. Zevi (ed.), *Pompei 79. Raccolta di studi per il decimonono centenario dell' eruzione Vesuviana* (Naples: G. Macchiaroli, 1979), 105–118.

Jones, R. and D. Robinson, 'The making of an elite house: the House of the Vestals at Pompeii'. *Journal of Roman Archaeology* 17 (2004), 107–30.

—— 'Water, wealth, and social status at Pompeii : the House of the Vestals in the first century'. *American Journal of Archaeology* 109 (2005), 695–710.

—— 'Intensification, heterogeneity and power in the development of Insula VI.1'. In J. Dobbins and P. Foss (eds.) *The World of Pompeii* (London/New York: Routledge, 2007), 389–406

—— 'The economic development of the Commercial Triangle (VI.1.14–18, 20–21)'. In Guzzo, P. and Guidobaldi, M. (eds.), *Nuove ricerche archeologiche a Pompei ed Ercolano: atti del convegno internazionale, Roma, 28–30 Novembre 2002* (Naples: Electa, 2005), 270–7.

—— 'The structural development of the House of the Vestals (VI.6–8, 24–26)'. In P. Guzzo and M. Guidobaldi (eds.), *Nuove ricerche archeologiche a Pompei ed Ercolano: atti del convegno internazionale, Roma, 28–30 Novembre 2002.* (Naples: Electa, 2005), 257–69.

Ling. R., *The Insula of the Menander at Pompeii.* (Oxford: Clarendon Press, 1997).

Maiuri, A., *Alla ricerca di Pompei preromana.* (Naples: Società editrice napoletana, 1973).

Nappo, S. C., 'Urban transformation at Pompeii in the late third and early second centuries BC'. In R. Laurence and A. Wallace-Hadrill (eds.), *Domestic space in the Roman world* (Portsmouth, R.I.: JRA Suppl. 22, 1997), 91–120.

Pirson, F. and J-A. Dickmann, 'Die Casa dei Postumii VIII 4, 4.49 und ihre Insula'. *Fünfter Vorbericht, Mitteilungen des Deutschen Archäologischen Instituts, Römische Abteilung* 109 (2002), 235–308.

Richardson, L. Jr., *Pompeii: An architectural history* (Baltimore: Johns Hopkins University Press, 1988).

Wallace-Hadrill, A., 'The development of the Campanian house'. In J. Dobbins and P. Foss (eds.), *The World of Pompeii*. (London: Routledge, 2007), 279–91.

Ward-Perkins, J. P., 'Note di topografia e urbanistica di Pompei'. In F. Zevi (ed.), *Pompei 79. Raccolta di studi per il decimonono centenario dell' eruzione Vesuviana*: (Naples: G. Macchiaroli, 1979), 25–44.

Westfall, C., 'Urban planning, roads, streets and neighbourhoods'. In J. Dobbins and P. Foss (eds.), *The World of Pompeii*. (London: Routledge, 2007), 129–39.

Zanker, P., *Pompeii: public and private life*. (Cambridge, Mass: Harvard University Press, 1998).

Chapter IV

Benefiel, R. R., 'Dialogues of ancient graffiti in the house of Maius Castricius in Pompeii'. *American Journal of Archaeology* 114 (2010), 59–101.

Bernstein, F. S., 'Pompeian women'. In J. Dobbins and P. Foss (eds.), *The World of Pompeii*. (London: Routledge, 2007), 526–37.

Camodeca, G., 'Per una riedizione delle tabulae Herculanenses, I'. In *Cronache Ercolanesi*, 23 (1993), 109–19.

Cormack, S., 'The tombs at Pompeii'. In J. Dobbins and P. Foss (eds.), *The World of Pompeii*. (London: Routledge, 2007), 585–606.

D'Ambrosio, A. and S. De Caro, *Un impegno per Pompei: fotopiano e documentazione della necropoli di Porta Nocera*. (Milan, TOTAL, Touring club italiano, 1983).

D'Ambrosio, A., 'Scavi e scoperte nel suburbio di Pompei'. *Rivista di Studi Pompeiani* IX (1998), 197–9.

De Caro, S., 'Scavi nell' area fuori Porta Nola a Pompei'. *Cronache Pompeiane* 5 (1979), 61–101.

—— *Museo archeologico nazionale di Napoli. Il Gabinetto segreto del museo archeologico nazionale di Napoli: guida alla collezione* (Milan: Electa, 2000).

DeFelice, J. F., *Roman hospitality: the professional women of Pompeii*. (Warren Center, Penn: Shangri-La Publications, 2001).

De Franciscis, A., 'Sepolcro di M. Obellius Firmus'. *Cronache Pompeiani* 2 (1976), 246–8.

De'Spagnolis Conticello, M., 'Sul rinvenimento della villa e del monumento funerario dei Lucretii Valentes'. *Rivista di Studi Pompeiani* VI (1993–1994): 147–66.

Emmerson, A. L. C., 'Evidence for Junian Latins in the tombs of Pompeii?' *Journal of Roman Archaeology* 24 (2011), 161–90.

George, M., 'The lives of slaves'. In J. Dobbins and P. Foss (eds.), *The World of Pompeii*. (London: Routledge, 2007), 538–49.

Giordano, C. and A. Casale, 'Iscrizioni pompeiane inedite scoperte tra gli anni 1954–1978'. *Atti della Accademia Pontaniana* n.s. (1991), 273–378.

Giordano, C., *The Jews in Pompeii, Herculaneum, Stabiae and in the cities of Campania Felix* (3rd ed., Rome: Bardi, 2001).

Guadagno, G., 'Herculanensium Augustalium aedes'. In *Cronache Ercolanesi* 13 (1983), 159–73.

Jacobelli, L., *Le pitture erotiche delle Terme Suburbane di Pompei*. (Rome: L'Erma di Bretschneider, 1995).

Jongman, W., 'M. Obellius M. f. Firmus, Pompeian duovir'. *Talenta* 10–11 (1978–1979), 62–5.

Kockel, V., *Die Grabbauten vor den Herkulaner Tor in Pompeji*. (Mainz am Rhein: P.v. Zabern, 1983).

—— 'Im Tode gleich? Die Sullanischen Kolonisten und ihr kulturelles Gewicht in Pompeji am Beispeil der Nekropolen'. In H. Von Hesberg and P. Zanker (eds.), *Römische Gräberstrassen: Selbstdarstellung, Status, Standard* (Munich: Bayerischen Akademie der Wissenschaften, 1987), 183–96.

Lazer, E., 'Pompeii AD 79: a population in flux?' In S. E. Bonn and R. Jones *Sequence and Space in Pompeii* (Oxford: Oxbow Books, 1997), 102–20.

Maulucci, F., *Pompei: i graffiti figurati*. (Foggia: Bastogi, 1993).

—— *Pompei: I graffiti d'amore*. (Foggia: Bastogi, 1995)

McGinn, T. A., 'Pompeian brothels and social history'. In T. McGinn *et al.*, *Pompeian Brothels, Pompeii's Ancient History, Mirrors and Mysteries, Art and Nature at Oplontis, and the Herculaneum Basilica* (Portsmouth, R.I.: Journal of Roman Archaeology Suppl. 47, 2002), 7–46.

Mols, S. T. A. M. and E. M. Moorman, 'Ex parvo crevit. Proposta per una lettura iconografia della Tomba di Vestorius Priscus fuori Porta Vesuvio a Pompei'. *Rivista di Studi Pompeiani* 6 (1993–1994), 15–52.

Najbjerg, T., 'A reconstruction and reconsideration of the so-called Basilica in Herculaneum'. In T. McGinn *et al.*, *Pompeian Brothels, Pompeii's Ancient History, Mirrors and Mysteries, Art and Nature at Oplontis, and the Herculaneum Basilica* (Portsmouth, R.I.: Journal of Roman Archaeology Suppl. 47, 2002), 122–165.

Nappo, S. C., 'Fregio dipinto dal 'praedium' di Giulia Felice con rappresentazione dal foro di Pompei'. *Rivista di Studi Pompeiani* 3 (1989), 79–96.

Pompei oltre la vita. Nuove testimonianze dale necropolis. (Naples: Soprintendenza Archeologica di Pompei, 1998).

Robinson, D., 'The social texture of Pompeii'. In S.E. Bonn and R. Jones, *Sequence and Space in Pompeii* (Oxford: Oxbow Books, 1997), 135–44.

Wallace-Hadrill, A. F., 'Public honour and private shame: the urban texture of Pompeii?' In T. Cornell and K. Lomas (eds.), *Urban Society in Roman Italy* (London: UCL Press, 1995), 39–62.

Varone, A., *Eroticism in Pompeii*. (Rome: L'Erma di Bretschneider, 2000).

—— *Erotica pompeiana: love inscriptions on the walls of Pompeii*. (Rome: L'Erma di Bretschneider, 2002).

Chapter V

Bernstein, F. S., 'Pompeian women and the Programmata'. In R. Curtis (ed.), *Studia Pompeiana et classica in honor of Wilhelmina F. Jashemski* (vol. I, New Rochelle, N.Y: A. D. Caratzas, 1988), 1–18.

Castrén, P., *Ordo populusque Pompeianus. Polity and society in Roman Pompeii*. Acta Instituti Romani Finlandiae 8 (Rome: Bardi, 1975).

Chiavia, C., *Programmata: manifesti elettorali nella colonia romana di Pompei*. (Turin: S. Zamorani, 2002).

D'Arms, J. H., 'Pompeii and Rome in the Augustan age and beyond: the eminence of the Gens Holconia'. In R. Curtis (ed.), *Studia Pompeiana et classica in honor of Wilhelmina F. Jashemski* (New Rochelle, N.Y: A. D. Caratzas, 1988), 51–73.

Dessau, H., 'C. Quinctius Valgus, der Erbauer des Amphitheaters zu Pompeji. *Hermes* 18 (1883), 620–2.

Dobbins, J., 'The Forum and its dependencies'. In J. Dobbins and P. Foss (eds.), *The World of Pompeii*. (London: Routledge, 2007), 150–83

Franklin, J. L., 'Notes on Pompeian prosopography: programmatum scriptores'. *Cronache Pompeiane* 4 (1978), 54–74.

—— *Pompeii: the electoral programmata, campaigns and politics, AD 71–79*. (Papers and Monographs of the American Academy in Rome 28, 1980).

—— 'Pantomimists at Pompeii: Actius Anicetus and his troop'. *American Journal of Philology* 108 (1987), 95–107.

—— 'Cn. Alleius Maius and the amphitheatre: *munera* and a distinguished career at ancient Pompeii'. *Historia* 96 (1987), 434–47.

—— *Pompeis difficile est: studies in the political life of imperial Pompeii*. (Ann Arbor: University of Michigan Press, 2001).

—— 'Epigraphy and society'. In J. Dobbins and P. Foss (eds.), *The World of Pompeii*. (London: Routledge, 2007), 518–25.

Gradel, I., 'Mamia's dedication: emperor and genius. The imperial cult in Italy and the Genius coloniae at Pompeii'. *Analecta Romana Instituti Danici* 20 (1992), 43–58.

Hartnett, J., 'Si quis hic sederit: streetside benches and urban society in Pompeii'. *American Journal of Archaeology* 112 (2008), 91–119.

Jacobelli, L., *Gladiators at Pompeii*. (Los Angeles: J. Paul Getty Museum, 2003).

Koloski-Ostrow, A., 'The city baths of Pompeii and Herculaneum'. In J. Dobbins and P. Foss (eds.), *The World of Pompeii*. (London: Routledge, 2007), 224–256.

Ling, R., 'Development of Pompeii's public landscape in the Roman period'. In J. Dobbins and P. Foss (eds.), *The World of Pompeii*. (London: Routledge, 2007), 119–128.

Moeller, W. O., 'The riot of AD 59 at Pompeii'. *Historia* 19 (1970), 84–95.

—— 'The date and dedication of the building of Eumachia'. *Cronache Pompeiane* 1 (1975), 232–6.

Mouritsen, H., *Elections, magistrates and municipal élite. Studies in Pompeian epigraphy*. Analecta Romana Instituti Danici Supplementum 15 (Rome: L'Erma di Bretschneider, 1988).

Ohr, K., *Die Basilika in Pompeji*. (Berlin, New York: W. de Gruyter, 1991).

Pagano, M., 'Il teatro di Ercolano'. In *Cronache Ercolanesi* 23 (1993), 121–56).

Parslow, C., 'Entertainment at Pompeii'. In J. Dobbins and P. Foss (eds.), *The World of Pompeii*. (London: Routledge, 2007), 212–23.

Sabbatini Tumolesi, P., *Gladiatorum paria: annunci di spettacoli gladiatorii a Pompeii*. (Rome: Edizioni di storia e letteratura, 1980).

Savunen, L., 'Women and elections in Pompeii'. In R. Hawley and B. Levick (eds.), *Women in antiquity, new assessments* (London: Routledge, 1995), 194–206.

Small, A., 'The shrine of the imperial family in the Macellum at Pompeii'. In A. Small (ed.), *Subject and ruler: the cult of the ruling power in classical antiquity* (Journal of Roman Archaeology Suppl. 17, 1996), 115–41.

Van Buren, A. W., 'Gnaeus Alleius Nigidius Maius of Pompeii'. *American Journal of Philology* 68.4 (1947), 382–93.

Wallace-Hadrill, A., 'The monumental centre of Herculaneum: in search of the identities of the public buildings'. *Journal of Roman Archaeology* 24 (2011), 121–60.

Wallat, K., 'Der mamorfries am Eingangsportal des Gebäudes der Eumachia (VII.9.1) in Pompeji und sein ursprünglicher Anbringungsort'. *Archäologische Anzeiger* (1995), 345–73.

—— *Die Ostseite des Forums von Pompeji*. (Frankfurt am Main: Peter Lang, 1997).

Zevi, F., 'Personaggi della Pompei sillana'. *Papers of the British School at Rome* 63 (1995), 1–24.

Chapter VI

Allison, P., *Pompeian households: an analysis of the material culture*. (Los Angeles: Cotsen Institute of Archaeology at University of California, Los Angeles, 2004).

—— *The Insula of the Menander at Pompeii. Vol. 3, The finds, a contextual study*. (Oxford: Clarendon Press, 2006).

—— and Sear, F., *Casa della Caccia antica: (VII 4, 48)*. (Munich: Hirmer, 2002).

Annecchino, M. *et al.*, *L' Instrumentum Domesticum di Ercolano e Pompeii nella prima età imperiale*. (Rome: L'erma di Bretschneider, 1977).

Berry, J., 'Household artifacts: towards a reinterpretation of Roman domestic space'. In R. Laurence and A. Wallace-Hadrill (eds.), *Domestic space in the Roman world* Portsmouth, R.I: Journal of Roman Archaeology, Suppl, 22, 1996), 183–95.

—— 'Instrumentum Domesticum: a case study'. In J. Dobbins and P. Foss (eds.), *The World of Pompeii*. (London: Routledge, 2007), 292–301.

Clarke, J. R., *The Houses of Roman Italy* (Berkeley: University of California Press, 1991).

—— 'Domestic decoration: mosaics and stucco'. In J. Dobbins and P. Foss (eds.), *The World of Pompeii*. (London: Routledge, 2007), 323–35.

De Caro, S., *I mosaici: La casa del fauno*. (Naples, Electa, 2001).

Dickmann, J.-A., *Domus frequentata: anspruchsvolles Wohnen im pompejanischen Stadthaus*. (Munich: Verlag Dr. Friedrich Pfeil, 1999).

—— 'Residences in Herculaneum'. In J. Dobbins and P. Foss (eds.), *The World of Pompeii*. (London: Routledge, 2007), 421–34.

Dwyer, E. J., *Pompeian Domestic Sculpture: A Study of Five Pompeian Houses and Their Contents*. (Rome: Giorgio Bretschneider, 1982).

Ehrhardt, W., *Casa dell' Orso (VII.2.44–46)*. Munich: Hirmer Verlag, 1988.

—— *Casa di Paquius Proculus (I 7.1.20)*. (Munich: Hirmer Verlag, 1998).

Fröhlich, T., *Casa della fontana piccola: (VI 8.23.24)*. (Munich: Hirmer Verlag, 1996).

Gazda, E. (ed.), *Roman art in the private sphere. New perspectives on the architecture and decor of the domus, villa, and insula*. (Ann Arbor: University of Michigan Press, 1991).

Grahame, M., *Reading space: social interaction and identity in the houses of Roman Pompeii: a syntactical approach to the analysis and interpretation of built space*. (Oxford: Archaeopress, 2000).

Jashemski, W., *The gardens of Pompeii, Herculaneum and the villas destroyed by Vesuvius*. Vol I (New York: Caratzas Brothers, 1979).

—— *The gardens of Pompeii, Herculaneum and the villas destroyed by Vesuvius*. Vol II (New York: Caratzas Brothers, 1993).

—— 'Gardens'. In J. Dobbins and P. Foss (eds.), *The World of Pompeii*. (London: Routledge, 2007), 487–98.

Jones, R. and D. Robinson, 'Intensification, heterogeneity and power in the development of insula VI.1'. In J. Dobbins and P. Foss (eds.), *The World of Pompeii*. (London: Routledge, 2007), 389–406.

Laurence, R. and A. Wallace-Hadrill (eds.), *Domestic space in the Roman world* (Portsmouth, R.I: Journal of Roman Archaeology, Suppl, 22, 1996).

Ling, R., *Roman painting* (Cambridge: Cambridge University Press, 1991).

—— *The Insula of the Menander at Pompeii. Volume 1, The Structures*. (Clarendon Press Oxford, 1997).

—— and L. Ling, *The Insula of the Menander at Pompeii. Volume 2, The Decorations*. (Oxford: Clarendon Press, 2005).

Maiuri, A., *Pompei: I nuovi scavi e la Villa dei Misteri*. (Rome: Istituto Poligrafico dello Stato, 1931).

—— *La Casa del Menandro e il suo tesoro di argenteria*. 2 vols (Rome: La Libreria dello Stato, 1933).

Michel, D., *Casa dei Cei (I 6, 15)*. (Munich: Hirmer Verlag, 1990).

Mols, S., *Wooden furniture in Herculaneum: form, technique and function*. (Amsterdam: Gieben, 1999).

Nappo, S., 'The houses of Regions I and II'. In J. Dobbins and P. Foss (eds.), *The World of Pompeii*. (London: Routledge, 2007), 347–72.

Painter, K., *The Insula of the Menander at Pompeii. Vol. 4, The silver treasure*. (Oxford: Clarendon Press, 2001).

Pessando, F., *Domus: edilizia privata e società pompeiana fra III e I secolo a.C*. (Rome: L'Erma di Bretschneider, 1997).

—— *Pompei: la pittura*. (Florence: Giunti, 2003).

Peterse, K., 'Select residences in Regions V and IX: early anonymous domestic architecture'. In J. Dobbins and P. Foss (eds.), *The World of Pompeii*. (London: Routledge, 2007), 373–89.

Seiler, F., *Casa degli Amorini dorati (VI 16, 7.38)*. (Munich: Hirmer, 1992).

Stemmer, K., *Casa dell'Ara massima (VI 16, 15–17)*. (Munich: Hirmer, 1992).

Sogliano, A., 'La Casa dei Vettii in Pompei'. *Monumenti Antichi dell' Accademia dei Lincei* 8 (1898), 233–388.

Staub Gierow, M., *Casa della Parete nera (VII 4, 58–60) und Casa delle Forme di creta (VII 4, 61–63)*. (Munich: Hirmer, 2000).

—— *Casa del Granduca (VII, 4, 56) und Casa dei Capitelli figurati (VII, 4, 57)*. (Munich: Hirmer Verlag, 1994).

Strocka, V. M., *Casa del Principe di Napoli (VI, 15, 7.8)*. (Tübingen: Ernst Wasmuth, 1984).

—— *Casa del Labirinto (VI 11, 8–10)*. (Munich: Hirmer Verlag, 1991).

Strocka, V., 'Domestic decoration and the "Four Styles"'. In J. Dobbins and P. Foss (eds.), *The World of Pompeii*. (London: Routledge, 2007), 302–22.

Tybout, R., 'Rooms with a view: residences built on terraces along the edge of Pompeii (Regions VI, VII and VIII)'. In J. Dobbins and P. Foss (eds.), *The World of Pompeii*. (London: Routledge, 2007), 407–20.

Wallace-Hadrill, A., *Houses and society in Pompeii and Herculaneum*. (Princeton:

Princeton University Press, 1994).

Chapter VII

Alla ricerca di Iside: analisi, studi e restauri dell'Iseo pompeiano nel Museo di Napoli. Soprintendenza archeologica per le province di Napoli e Caserta. (Rome: ARTI, 1992).

Boyce, G. K., *Corpus of the Lararia of Pompeii.* Memoirs of the American Academy in Rome, 14 (Rome: American Academy in Rome, 1937).

D'Ambrosio, A. and M. Borriello, *Arule e bruciaprofumi fittili da Pompei.* (Naples: Electa Napoli, 2001).

Coralini, A., *Hercules domesticus: immagini di Ercole nelle case della regione vesuviana : 1. secolo a.C.–79. d.C.* (Naples: Electa Napoli, 2001).

De Caro, S., *Alla ricerca di Iside: Analisi, studi e restauri dell' Iseo pompeiano nel Museo di Napoli.* (Rome: Arti, 1992).

De Carolis, E., *Dei ed eroi nella pittura pompeiana.* (Rome: L'Erma di Bretschneider, 2000).

De Waele, J. A. K. E., *Il tempio dorico del foro triangolare di Pompei.* (Rome: L'Erma di Bretschneider, 2001).

Dobbins, J. J., 'The altar in the sanctuary of the Genius of Augustus in the Forum at Pompeii'. *Mitteilungen des deutsches archaeologischen Institute Rom* 99 (1992), 251–63.

—— 'The imperial cult building in the forum at Pompeii'. In A. Small (ed.), *Subject and ruler: the cult of the ruling power in classical antiquity* (Portsmouth, R.I.: Journal of Roman Archaeology Suppl. 17, 1996), 99–114.

Elia, O. and Pugliese Carratelli, G., 'Il santuario dionisiaco di Pompei'. *Parola del Passato* 34 (1979), 442–81.

Fishwick, D., 'The inscription of Mamia again: the cult of the *Genius Augusti* and the temple of the imperial cult on the *Forum* of Pompeii'. *Epigraphica* 57 (1995), 17–38.

Foss, P,. 'Watchful *Lares.* Roman household organization and the rituals of cooking and eating'. In R. Laurence and A. Wallace-Hadrill (eds.), *Domestic Space in the Roman World: Pompeii and beyond* (Portsmouth, R.I. Journal of Roman Archaeology Suppl. 22, 1997), 196–218.

Fröhlich, T., *Lararien und Fassadenbildter in den Vesuvstädten: Untersuchungen zur 'volkstümlichen' pompejanischen Malerei.* (Mainz: Zabern, 1991).

Gazda, E. K. (ed.), *The Villa of the Mysteries in Pompeii: ancient ritual, modern muse.* (Ann Arbor: University of Michigan Museum of Art, Kelsey Museum of Archaeology, 2000).

Maiuri, A., 'Pompei: Santuario Dionisiaco in località S. Abbondio'. *Fasti Archeologici* 2 (1947), 197, no. 1656.

Orr, D. G., 'Roman domestic religion: the evidence of the household shrines'. *Aufstieg und Niedergang der römischen Welt* II.16.2 (Berlin, 1978) 1557–91.

Potts, C. R., 'The Art of Piety and Profit at Pompeii: a new interpretation of the painted shop façade at ix.7.1–2'. *Greece and Rome* 56.1 (April 2009), 55–70.

Tran Tam Tinh, V., *Essai sur le culte d'Isis à Pompéi.* (Paris: E. de Boccard, 1964).

—— *Le culte des divinités orientales en Campanie en dehors de Pompéi, de Stabies et d'Herculanum.* (Leiden: E. J. Brill, 1972).

Chapter VIII

Andreau, J., 'Remarques sur la société pompéienne (à la propos des tablettes de L. Caecilius Jucundus)'. *Dialoghi di Archeologia* 7 (2–3) (1973), 213–54.

—— *Les affaires de Monsieur Jucundus.* (Rome: Ecole francais de Rome, 1974).

—— *Banking and Business in the Roman World.* (Cambridge: Cambridge University Press, 1999).

Angelone, R., *L' officina coactiliaria di M. Vecilio Verecondo a Pompei.* (Naples: L'Arte Tipografica, 1986)

Atkinson, D., 'A Hoard of Samian Ware from Pompeii'. *Journal of Roman Studies* 4 (1914), 27–64.

Avvisati, C., *Pompei: mestieri e botteghe 2000 fa.* (Rome: Bardi, 2003).

Carrington, R. C., 'Studies in the Campanian "Villae Rusticae"'. *Journal of Roman Studies* 21 (1931), 110–30.

—— Some Ancient Italian Country Houses. *Antiquity* 8 (1934), 261–80.

Curtis, R. I., 'The garum shop of Pompeii'. *Cronache Pompeiane* 5 (1979), 5–23.

—— 'A personalized floor mosaic from Pompeii'. *American Journal of Archaeology* 88 (1984), 557–66.

—— 'A. Umbricius Scaurus of Pompeii'. In R. I. Curtis (ed.), *Studia Pompeiana et classica in honor of Wilhelmina F. Jashemski* (vol. I, New Rochelle, N.Y 1988), 19–50.

D'Arms, J., 'Ville rustiche e ville di 'otium''. In Zevi, F. (ed.) *Pompei 79. Raccolta di studi per il decimonono centenario dell' eruzione Vesuviana.* (Naples: G. Macchiaroli, 1979), 65–86.

Day, J., 'Agriculture in the life of Pompeii.' *Yale Classical Studies* 3 (1932), 165–208.

De Caro, S., *La Villa Rustica in Località Villa Regina a Boscoreale.* (Rome: Giorgio Bretschneider, 1994).

DeFelice, J., 'Inns and taverns'. In J. Dobbins and P. Foss (eds.), *The World of Pompeii.* (London: Routledge, 2007), 474–86.

Gassner, V., *Die Kaufläden in Pompeji.* (Vienna, 1986).

Guzzo, P. G., 'City and country: an introduction'. In J. Dobbins and P. Foss (eds.), *The World of Pompeii.* (London: Routledge, 2007), 3–8.

Homo faber: studies on nature, technology and science at the time of Pompeii. (Rome: L'Erma di Bretschneider, 2002).

Jashemski, W., 'The caupona of Euxinus at Pompeii'. *Archaeology* 20 (1967), 36–44.

Jongman, W., *The economy and society of Pompeii.* (Amsterdam: Gieben, 1988).

—— 'The loss of innocence: Pompeian economy and society between past and present'. In J. Dobbins and P. Foss (eds.), *The World of Pompeii.* (London: Routledge, 2007), 499–517.

La Torre, G., 'Gli impianti commerciali ed artigianali nel tessuto urbano di Pompei'. In *Pompei: L' informatica al servizio di una città antica.* (Rome: L'Erma di Bretschneider, 1988), 74–102.

MacMahon, A., 'The *taberna* counters of Pompeii and Herculaneum'. In A. Mac Mahon and J. Price (eds.), *Roman Working Lives and Urban Living* (Oxford: Oxbow, 2005), 70–87.

Mattusch, C. C., *Pompeii and the Roman Villa: art and culture around the Bay of Naples.* (Washington: National Gallery of Art, 2008).

Mayeske, B.-J., 'A Pompeian bakery on the Via dell'Abbondanza'. In R. Curtis (ed.), *Studia Pompeiana et classica in honor of Wilhelmina F. Jashemski* (vol. I, New Rochelle, N.Y 1988), 149–66.

—— 'Bakers, bakeshops, and bread: a social and economic study'. In *Pompeii and the Vesuvian landscape* (Washington D.C. 1979), 39–57.

Moeller, W .O., 'The felt shops of Pompeii'. *American Journal of Archaeology* 75.2 (April 1971) 188–9.

—— *The wool trade of ancient Pompeii.* (Leiden: Brill, 1976)

Moorman, E., 'Villas surrounding Pompeii and Herculaneum'. In J. Dobbins and P. Foss (eds.), *The World of Pompeii.* (London: Routledge, 2007), 435–54.

Packer, J., 'Inns at Pompeii: a short survey'. *Cronache Pompeiane* 4 (1978), 5–53.

Panuti, U., 'Pinarius Cerialis, gemmarius pompeianus'. In *Bollettino d' Arte* 60 (1975), 178–90.

Peña, J. T. and M. McCallum, 'The production and distribution of pottery at Pompeii: a review of the evidence, 1. Production'. *American Journal of Archaeology* (2009) 57–79.

—— 'The production and distribution of pottery at Pompeii. A review of the evidence, 2. The material basis for production and distribution'. *American Journal of Archaeology* 113 (2009), 165–201.

Pirson, F., 'Rented accommodation at Pompeii: the evidence of the *Insula Arriana Polliana* VI.6'. In R. Laurence and A. Wallace-Hadrill (eds.), *Domestic Space in the Roman World: Pompeii and beyond.* (Portsmouth, R.I.: Journal of Roman Archaeology Suppl. 22, 1997), 165–81.

—— *Mietwohnungen in Pompeji und Herkulaneum: Untersuchungen zur Architektur, zum Wohnen und zur Sozial- und Wirtschaftsgeschichte der Vesuvstädte.* (Munich: F. Pfeil, 1999).

Pirson, F., 'Shops and industries'. In J. Dobbins and P. Foss (eds.), *The World of Pompeii.* (London: Routledge, 2007), 457–73.

Robinson, D., 'Re-thinking the social organization of trade and industry in first century AD Pompeii'. In A. Mac Mahon and J. Price (eds.), *Roman Working Lives and Urban Living* (Oxford: Oxbow, 2005), 88–105.

Scarano Ussani, V., *Moregine: suburbio 'portuale' di Pompei*. (Naples, Loffredo, 2005).

Tchernia, A., 'Il vino: produzione e commercio'. In F. Zevi (ed.), *Pompei 79. Raccolta di studi per il decimonono centenario dell' eruzione Vesuviana*. (Naples: G. Macchiaroli, 1979), 87–96.

Chapter IX

Adam, J-P,. *Dégradation et restauration de l' architecture pompéienne*. (Paris: CNRS, 1980)

—— 'Conséquences du séisme de l' an 62 à Pompéi'. In B. Helly and A. Pollino (eds.), *Tremblements de terre, histoire et archéologie. IVémes Rencontres internationales d' archéologie et d' histoire d' Antibes, 2, 3, 4, novembre 1983* (Valbonne, 1984)

——'Observations techniques sur les suites du sèisme de 62 à Pompéi'. In C. Albore Livadie (ed.), *Tremblements de terre, éruptions volcaniques et vie des hommes dans la Campanie antique*: 67–87. (Naples: Bibliothèque de l' Institut français de Naples, ser. II.7, 1986).

—— 'Osservazioni tecniche sugli effetti del terremoto di Pompei del 62 d.C'. In E. Guidoboni (ed.), *I terremoti prima del Mille in Italia e nell' area Mediterranea*: 460–74. (Bologna: ING-SGA, 1989)

Andreau, J., 'Histoire des séismes et histoire economique: le tremblement de terre di Pompei (62 ap. J.-C.)'. *Annales E.S.C.* 28 (1973), 369–95.

—— 'Il terremoto del 62'. In F. Zevi (ed.), *Pompei 79. Raccolta di studi per il decimonono centenario dell' eruzione Vesuviana.* (Naples: G. Macchiaroli, 1979), 40–4.

Allison, P., 'On-going seismic activity and its effects on the living conditions in Pompeii in the last decades'. In T. Fröhlich and L. Jacobelli (eds.), *Archäologie und Seismologie. La regione vesuviana dal 62 al 79 D.C. Problemi archeologici e sismologici.* (Munich: Biering and Brinkmann, 1995), 183–90.

Berry, J., 'Conditions of life in Pompeii in AD 79'. *Papers of the British School at Rome* 65 (1997), 103–25.

Dobbins, J. J., 'Problems of chronology, decoration, and urban design in the forum at Pompeii'. *American Journal of Archaeology* 98.4 (1994), 629–94.

Faviccio, C., *I danni del terremoto del 62 d.C. a Pompei nella regio VIII: metodo di ricerca, scoperte.* (Naples: Libreria l'ateneo di G. Pironti, 1996).

Fröhlich, T. and Jacobelli, L. (eds.), *Archäologie und Seismologie. La regione vesuviana dal 62 al 79 D.C. Problemi archeologici e sismologici.* (Munich: Biering and Brinkmann, 1995).

Hine, H., 'The date of the Campanian earthquake: AD 62 or AD 63, or both?' *L'Antiquité Classique* (1984), 266–9.

Lepore, E., 'Orientamenti per la storia sociale di Pompei'. In A. Maiuri (ed.), *Pompeiana. Racolta di studi per il secondo centenario degli scavi di Pompei* (Naples: Gaetano Macchiaroli Editore, 1950), 144–66.

Maiuri, A., *L' Ultima Fase Edilizia di Pompei, edizione anastatica dell'edizione del 1942.* (Rome: Bardi, 2002).

Nappo. S., 'Evidenze di danni strutturali, restauri e rifacimenti nelle Insulae gravitanti su Via Nocera a Pompei'. In T. Fröhlich and L. Jacobelli (eds.), *Archäologie und Seismologie. La regione vesuviana dal 62 al 79 D.C. Problemi archeologici e sismologici* (Munich: Biering and Brinkmann, 1995), 49–51.

Nappo, S. C., 'L'impianto idrico a Pompei nel 79 d.C.: Nuovi dati'. In *Cura Aquarum in Campania* (*Babesch*, Suppl. 4, Leiden 1996) 37–45.

Widemann, F., (1990) 'Implications économiques des désastres volcaniques. Le court et le long terme dans le cas de Pompéi'. In C. A. Livadie et F. Widemann (eds.), *Volcanology and Archaeology. Volcanologie et archéologie. Actes des Ateliers Européens de Ravello, 19–27 novembre 1987 et 30–31 mars 1989* (Strasbourg: PACT 25, 1990), 217–231.

Acknowledgments

I would like to thank Pietro Giovanni Guzzo and Antonio D'Ambrosio for allowing me to undertake research at Pompeii, and the staff of the Soprintendenza di Pompei for all their help over the years. This book would have been impossible without the help and support of many friends and colleagues. Andrew Wallace-Hadrill suggested that I write the book in the first place, and I am grateful for his helpful comments on the text. I am also indebted to Melvin and Alison Cooley for their meticulous reading of early versions of the text. Damian Robinson and Rick Jones generously provided me with then unpublished material about their work at Pompeii, and supplied plans and photos of their excavations. Paolo Carafa and Maria Teresa D'Alessio also provided plans and photos, and good-humouredly put up with repeated requests for images at higher resolution or in different format. I would also like to thank James Andrews, Birgit Bergmann, Christian Biggi, Sarah Court, Byron Harries, Laurentino Garcia y Garcia and Felice Senatore for help with sourcing material and images for the book. James Andrews also did a fine job of drawing some of the plans for the book at very short notice.

I would like to thank Colin Ridler, Ben Plumridge, Sally Nicholls, Rowena Alsey, Celia Falconer and Melissa Danny at Thames & Hudson for their tireless work on this book and for all the help and support they have given to me.

The time I have spent at Pompeii has been made very special by a particular group of friends: Francesco Amato, Stanislao Borriello, Raffaele Cassese, Giovanni Longobardi, Nicola Longobardi, Salvatore Vitiello and Elio Vozza. Their friendship and support have meant everything to me. I was also befriended by Felice Senatore, Paolo Carafa, Maria Teresa D'Alessio and Filippo Avellino almost as soon as I started working at Pompeii, and I would like to thank them for the many happy days and evenings spent in their company that have made being in Pompeii so much fun.

Finally, and most importantly, I am grateful to my husband, Nigel Pollard, for his comments, help with translations, proof-reading, and unfailing support and encouragement. The book is, of course, dedicated to him and to our daughters, Maria and Livia.

Sources of Illustrations

a: above, b: below, c: centre, l: left, r: right

Akg-images 16, 39, 49, 120–121
Akg-images/Peter Connolly 222–223
Akg-images/Nimatallah 139
M.T. D'Alessio 67
Archivi Alinari 64–65, 83, 115, 126a, 134a, 148, 189b, 192
James Andrews © Thames & Hudson Ltd., London 8–9, 15a, 41, 61b, 66, 100–101 (after Berti F. Weber), 157ar, 166al, 174a, 216 (after W. Jashemski), 224, 233
The Art Archive/Archaeological Museum, Naples/Dagli Orti (A) 1, 30a, 70br, 112al, 195
The Art Archive/Bibliothèque des Arts Décoratifs, Paris/Dagli Orti (A) 47, 56a
Breton, Ernest, *Pompeia décrite et desinée par Ernest Breton de la Société Impériale des Antiquaires de France, etc., Suivie d'une notice sur Herculaneum.* (Paris, 1855) 22
Visual Resources Center, Bryn Mawr College, Pennsylvania 74, 93, 128b, 155a
Giovanni Caselli 10–11, 12, 19, 30b, 50, 51b, 55ar, 111a, 114r, 126–127, 130b, 147a, 149a, 150, 153b, 156-157, 159b, 169b, 170b, 171a, 174b, 192–193, 202–203, 205a, 207b, 212, 215b, 230–231
Vittorio Celantano, British School at Rome 68–69
© CORBIS 48a
© Bettmann/CORBIS 29
© Mimmo Jodice/CORBIS 32, 33, 112–113, 138, 166b, 215a, 230b, 234–235
© David Lees/CORBIS 162–163
© Richard T. Nowitz/CORBIS 214a
© Roger Ressmeyer/CORBIS 18
© Reproduced by permission of the State Hermitage Museum, St. Petersburg, Russia/CORBIS 48br

© Sean Sexton Collection/CORBIS 24
Gell, Sir William, *Pompeiana: The Topography, Edifices, and Ornaments of Pompeii.* (London, 1832) 1835 158, 194, 204br
Getty Images/The Bridgeman Art Library 52
Getty Images/The Image Bank/Moritz Steiger 217
Getty Images/Lonely Planet Images/Martin Moos 189a
Getty Images/National Geographic/O. Louis Mazzatenta 7, 28, 36
© 2006 The J. Paul Getty Trust 43a
Hamilton, Hon. Sir William, *An Account of the Discoveries at Pompeii, Communicated to the Society of Antiquaries of London.* (London, 1777) 71a
Sophie Hay and Anthony Sibthorpe, British School at Rome 178
Jones, O., *The Grammar of Ornament.* (London, 1856) 48br
Imperial War Museum, London 61a
Giovanni Lattanzi 2, 27a, 31b, 45, 53, 56b, 62, 63a, 68, 86–87, 89, 95, 103, 106, 109, 113a, 114a, 119, 124–125, 128a, 129, 130cr, 132b, 134b, 141, 144, 152, 154–155, 161a, 162, 166–167, 168, 169a, 171b, 173a, 175, 176, 177, 180–181, 181a, 182b, 184, 185, 193a, 197b, 208, 210–211, 218, 221
© Schmuel Magal, www.sitesandphotos.com 75, 81, 85, 97b, 98, 99a, 104, 107, 110a, 110–111, 131, 132a, 136–137, 146, 147b, 159a, 182a, 182–183, 186–187, 190–191, 199, 209, 213, 214b, 223, 232a, 240, 241b
Biblioteca Nazionale, Naples 44a
Museo Archeologico Nazionale, Naples 4, 42a, 43b, 72, 73, 90, 92, 99b, 105, 108, 113c, 117, 118, 125cr, 134, 136, 140, 142, 145, 155b, 157c, 160, 164, 165, 173b, 179c, 179b, 188, 195b, 200, 201, 204l, 205b, 207a, 219, 220, 225, 226, 228, 229a, 232c, 241c
Metropolitan Museum of Art, New York, Rogers

Fund, 1903 (03.14.13) 59
Niccolini, Fausto and Felice, *Le case e monumenti di Pompei.* 4 vols (Naples, 1854–96) 55al, 80, 116, 123, 125a, 130cl, 143, 149b, 153ar, 167b, 172, 179a, 196, 197a, 229b
Sally Nicholls 170a
Ben Plumridge 15b, 33a, 44b, 63b, 69b, 96, 125br, 153al, 206, 239, 243
Soprintendenza Archeologica di Pompei 31r, 34–35, 54, 57, 60, 79a, 113b, 151br, 161b, 198, 227, 232b, 237
Princeton University Art Museum, Museum purchase, gift of Franklin H. Kissner y1969–89. Photo: Bruce M. White © 2000 Trustees of Princeton University 21
Private Collection 46
Private Collection, Naples 36b, 38
Photo RMN – Les frères Chuzeville 58a
Photo RMN – Hervé Lewandowski 58b
Sasso, C.N., *Il Vesuvio, Ercolano e Pompei.* (Naples, 1857) 51a
Photo Scala, Florence – courtesy of the Ministero Beni e Att. Culturali 42b, 43b, 70bl, 88, 91
Photo Scala, Florence/Fotografica Foglia – courtesy of the Ministero Beni e Att. Culturali 40, 55b, 195a
State Hermitage Museum, St. Petersburg 23
Jennifer Stephens/Anglo-American Project Pompeii 82, 84
Drazen Tomic © Thames & Hudson Ltd., London 6, 15a, 27b, 76, 212
Courtesy University of Reading and British School at Rome 79b
U.S. Geological Survey 26
Österreichisches Nationalbibliothek, Vienna 37
Walker Art Gallery, National Museums of Liverpool 97a
Werner Forman Archives 13
Photo Ole Woldby, by courtesy of the Trustees of Sir John Soane's Museum, London 71b

Sources of Quotations

The quotations used in this book are taken from the following sources:

Joanne Berry and Nigel Pollard 96, 100–101, 102–103, 105, 106, 109, 111, 114–115, 117, 118, 119, 124, 131 (except *CIL* IV 7539), 132, 133, 137, 138, 139, 140, 141, 142, 144, 145, 146 (except Vetter), 147, 152, 160, 161, 186, 195, 196, 198, 199, 206, 208, 209, 210, 217, 219, 226, 227, 228, 229, 231, 232, 233, 238, 242
Sir Edward Bulwer Lytton 120 (*The Last Days of Pompeii* (1834))
Melvin and Alison Cooley 18, 66, 146 (box), 188, 189, 194, 220–221
Charles Dickens 86 (*Pictures from Italy, 1844–45* (1946))
Edward Falkener 31 ('Report on a house at Pompeii excavated under personal

superintendence in 1847'. In *The Museum of Classical Antiquities. Essays on Ancient Art, March 1852* (London, 1860))
James Franklin 131 (*CIL* IV 7539)
Johann Wolfgang von Goethe 34 (*Italian Journey/Italienische Reise, 13 March 1787* (1816/7 in German, trans. Joanne Berry))
Harper's New Monthly Magazine 154 ('A day at Pompeii', LXVI (November, 1855), Vol. XI)
Norman Lewis 16 (*Naples '44: An Intelligence Officer in the Italian Labyrinth* (London, 1978))
Loeb Classical Library 30 (Dio Cassius, *Roman History* (66.21–23), trans. Ernest Carey, 1968), 158, 170–171 (Vitruvius, *On Architecture*, Vol II (VI.5.1–3), trans. F. Granger, 1934), 168 (Pliny the Elder, *Natural History* (35.37), trans. H. Rackham, 1952), 206 (Cicero, *De Domo Sua* (XLI.109), trans. N. H. Watts, 1923), 236 (Seneca, *Natural Questions* (6.1.1–2, 6.1.10, 6.31.1), trans T. H. Corcoran, 1972)

Nigel Pollard 20–24 (Pliny, *Ep.* 6.16, 6.20), 234 (Tacitus, *Ann.* 15.22)
Percy Bysshe Shelley 204–205 ('A description of Pompeii in 1818 (Letter XVI)'. In *Essays, Letters from Abroad, Translations and Fragments*, Vol. II (1840) edited by Mary Shelley)
The Times 54 ('An eye-witness account of the early plastercasts' (17 June, 1893)), 60 ('Bomb damage to Pompeii' (9 November, 1943))
Mark Twain 1, 64 (*Innocents Abroad* (1869)).
Horace Walpole 38 ('Letter to Richard West, Esq., 14 June 1740'. In W. S. Lewis, G. L. Lam and C. H. Bennett (eds.), *Horace Walpole's correspondence with Thomas Gray, Richard West and Thomas Ashton* (New Haven, 1948)).
Johann Joachim Winckelmann 46 (*Sendschreiben von den herculanischen Entdeckungen* (Rome, 1762))

Index